Praise for *Bev*

"*Beverly Hills Noir* is that perfect blend: wildly entertaining, fascinating, and informative. What a fun ride. I highly recommend it! Enjoy!"

MARCIA CLARK, attorney, former prosecutor and
author of bestselling fiction and nonfiction

"Scott Huver is the ultimate tour guide in ritzy, smoky old Hollywood and 90210. You don't need a time machine; you just need this delicious, scandalous collection of stories."

CAROLINE KEPNES, *New York Times* Bestselling author of *You*

"*Beverly Hill Noir* is not just a crime story, it's a ghost story—the dark past of a glamorous city, refusing to be forgotten. Scott Huver tells every sinister story with a vivid, hard-boiled honesty that brings it all back to life. *Beverly Hills Noir* is proof that money doesn't buy happiness. Sometimes, it costs you everything."

ANTHONY BREZNICAN, Senior Hollywood Correspondent, *Vanity Fair*

"Exacting, entertaining, and enlightening, *Beverly Hills Noir* presents detailed accounts of legendary mysteries and scandals that are so outrageous they've got to be true. Scott Huver captures the tone and cadence of the movie genre that gives his book its title, and he's capable of achieving a level of suspense on par with the last ten minutes of *Sorry, Wrong Number*. He approaches his subjects with a documentarian's attention to research and a historian's devotion to facts, sculpting into high relief the tinsel and tarnish of the rich, the beautiful and the frequently immoral."

JEREMY HELLIGAR, Executive Editor, *PEOPLE* Magazine

"Scott Huver chronicles true crime in such detail that it's hard to believe you were not in the room as some of most notorious criminals wreaked havoc on the world's most expensive zip code. Each chapter of *Beverly Hills Noir* is its own crime thriller told in vivid technicolor."

MARC MALKIN, Senior Editor, Culture & Events, *Variety*

"For anyone interested in show business, crime, celebrity, history, or any combination thereof, Scott Huver's book is cause for excitement. The veteran reporter chronicles—with remarkable detail and insight—some of the most shocking 90210-area misdeeds of the past century, from the murder of one of the city's wealthiest denizens, to the shooting of a top agent in his groin, to a movie star with kleptomaniac tendencies. Buckle up for a wild ride!"

Scott Feinberg, Executive Editor of Awards, *The Hollywood Reporter*

"Scott Huver is hands down one of the finest reporters on the beat. Nuanced in his reporting and engaging in his storytelling, *Beverly Hills Noir* is the book you absolutely need in your collection. It's rich, detailed, and shines a light on the true crime that has captivated the world's most well-known zip code."

Kelley L. Carter, Sr. Entertainment Reporter ESPN's Andscape

"Scott Huver is one of my favorite writers. He's done it again by writing a delicious story with a flawless atmosphere that really captures the history of my hometown of Beverly Hills. I especially enjoy the mention of historic places and real street names! It's Vintage Los Angeles personified!"

Alison Martino, Spectrum News 1 newscaster; founder, Vintage Los Angeles

BEVERLY HILLS
HILLS
Noir

CRIME, SIN, & SCANDAL IN 90210

SCOTT HUVER

Post Hill
PRESS

A POST HILL PRESS BOOK
ISBN: 978-1-63758-885-7
ISBN (eBook): 978-1-63758-886-4

Cover design by Conroy Accord
Cover concept by Scott Huver

All people, locations, events, and situations are portrayed to the best of the author's memory. While all of the events described are true, many names and identifying details have been changed to protect the privacy of the people involved.

Post Hill Press
New York • Nashville
posthillpress.com

Published in the United States of America
1 2 3 4 5 6 7 8 9 10

Dedicated to the loving memory of my stepfather Dan Cline, who introduced me to the absorbing world of TV police potboilers like *Hill Street Blues*. To my mother, Nancy Cline, whose love of a good crime thriller or courtroom drama, fact or fiction, remains infectious (your hero Perry Mason made it in the book, Mom), and who let me skip school on my sixteenth birthday to see *Beverly Hills Cop* in the theater, setting the stage for things to come.

To my wife, Cynthia Huver, for her endless reservoir of unconditional support and encouragement, including the kick in the pants to turn this pandemic project into a reality—not to mention for resisting the urge to turn tail when first laying eyes on my library overflowing with "books about murder or pin-up girls." And to our faithful dog Nimoy, who spent countless hours on the sofa as I wrote, wondering, I'm sure, what could possibly be more fascinating than him.

"*I live here because you can live a normal life just like they do in Topeka.*"
—Groucho Marx

"*In many respects, Beverly Hills is a place where the unique is commonplace, and the bizarre is routine.*"
—Walter Winchell

"*This is the cleanest and nicest police car I've ever been in in my life. This thing's nicer than my apartment.*"
—Eddie Murphy as Axel Foley in *Beverly Hills Cop*

"*In Beverly Hills, the faster you climb, the harder you fall.*"
—Brandi Glanville

TABLE OF CONTENTS

INTRODUCTION

"How many people who came to the Brown Derby today dreamed they'd be having lunch in the Beverly Hills pokey?"

—**Alfred Hitchcock**

I t was September, 24, 1956, in Beverly Hills, California, and Alfred Hitchcock was in custody at the police station, fingerprinted, photographed, and accused of having gotten away with murder.

On a mid-day Monday, a collection of journalists had assembled at the Brown Derby restaurant—not the iconic, hat-shaped original eatery several miles east, nor the ritzier, higher-profile locale at Hollywood and Vine, world-famous for its all-star array of diners, walls overloaded with classy celebrity caricatures and flashbulbs popping outside. Launched in 1931, the Beverly Hills Brown Derby was the chain's third outpost, anchoring the intersection of Wilshire Boulevard and Rodeo Drive—a decade before the dawn of that street's high-fashion heyday, but still plenty swank—across the street from the world-class Beverly Wilshire Hotel. While upholding the elegant aesthetic and elite cuisine standards of its seen-and-be-seen Hollywood sister site, the Beverly Hills berth offered a more informal experience, where wealthy and famous locals could take a step back from the spotlight and enjoy a relaxed meal alongside their neighbors—especially on Thursday evenings, known locally as "the maid's night off."

From its earliest days, that's what defined Beverly Hills: glitzy, luxurious, and sometimes over-the-top, but also offering a cozy small-town ambiance. Even in the middle of the day, the city's casually starry cachet was on display as the newshounds spied Betty Grable, the plucky actress and pinup queen whose shapely gams adorned every military barracks during the Second World War, dabbing at her salad plate in the main dining room.

But on this day, reporters had been summoned to lunch by an equally distinctive silhouette: Alfred Hitchcock, who'd earned his title as The Master of Suspense several times over. In the previous four years, he'd delivered an astonishing succession of ingeniously inventive, gloriously cinematic thrillers—*Strangers on a Train, Dial 'M' for Murder, Rear Window, To Catch a Thief, The Trouble with Harry*, and *The Man Who Knew Too Much*—which would keep audiences on the edges of their seats for generations to come.

The British-born director, then fifty-seven, had also planted his flag in the newly emerging medium of television a year prior with the successful launch of his anthology series *Alfred Hitchcock Presents*, which aired Sunday nights on CBS and featured cleverly plotted standalone stories in Hitchcock's pitch-black style—mysteries, dramas and thrillers marked by an unexpected twist. Along with occasionally directing episodes, he lent his familiar, portly profile to the show's logo and hosted morbidly amusing wraparound segments, making him inarguably the most widely famous and recognizable film director of his day. "Hitch," as he was known to friends and colleagues, had invited the press to celebrate the debut of his series' second season six days hence.

An avid epicurean, Hitchcock spent many a mealtime in Beverly Hills, making the quick drive from his longtime estate on nearby Bel-Air's Bellagio Road to savor the cuisine at a host of local hot spots: he was right at home at Chasen's, Romanoff's and, of course, the Brown Derby. Alongside his frequent collaborator Joan Harrison—who'd contributed to the screenplays of his '40s-era films *Rebecca, Foreign Correspondent, Suspicion*, and *Saboteur*, twice Oscar-nominated for her efforts, and served as a producer of *Alfred Hitchcock Presents*—Hitchcock disarmed the press that day with his formalized, distinctively droll and deadpan demeanor. He opined on various topics: outwitting and outmaneuvering audience members overly fixated on using "moronic logic" to point out plot holes, and the nature of a "McGuffin," the sort of story-motivating but hazily defined plot device—"the thing everybody is after"—he'd later become celebrated for in film studies. The reporters scribbled notes as the efficient waitstaff delivered a steady flow of champagne and cocktails into their free hands.

Suddenly, as the filmmaker was showcasing an example of production art from his series' new season, a voice shouted from the back of the room.

"You're all under arrest!"

Two Beverly Hills police officers strode up to Hitchcock, lifted him bodily from his chair and, as flashbulbs began to explode, strongarmed him through the restaurant's exit. Deposited into an old-fashioned black paddy wagon idling at the curb on Rodeo Drive, he sputtered out mild protests. More policemen flooded in, rounding up all the partygoers, too, herding them into a fleet of squad cars waiting outside. In a sudden rush of shock, bewilderment, and encroaching panic, the guests were whisked a few short blocks away to the Beverly Hills police headquarters, then located at the glorious Spanish Revival-style City Hall building at Santa Monica Boulevard and Crescent Drive, one of the most opulent municipal structures of its day.

Marched into a space bearing the sign "Prisoners' Rooms," they were met with the sight of Hitchcock enduring the booking process, including mugshot and fingerprints, before being locked in a jail cell. "You ain't got nothing on me," grumbled the director haughtily, prompting an officer to shoot back "That's what they all say."

As the guests glanced around, they noticed an array of "Wanted" posters lining the walls—posters that, along with Hitchcock's image, curiously featured photographs of many of the reporters themselves. Clinton H. Anderson—the department's polished but intimidating, hardnosed, and iron-willed Chief of Police who'd risen from beat patrolman to detective to heading the force for the last fourteen years—glowered at Hitchcock. In his famously flinty manner, Anderson told the director he was under arrest for "getting away with murder for years." After a representative of the Bristol-Myers Company, his show's sponsor (which the filmmaker frequently made on-air digs at) appeared to post bail moments later, Hitchcock vowed to be "a little more reverent" going forward. Released from confinement, he took a spot at the head of the room.

"As I was saying…" he resumed, unruffled.

A chorus of relieved laughter rippled through the room as the guests quickly realized that they were unwittingly playing extras in a live enactment of one of Hitchcock's carefully orchestrated signature suspense sequences, capped with a surprise twist. "How many people who came to the Brown Derby today dreamed they'd be having lunch in the Beverly Hills pokey?" Hitchcock asked the crowd, offering his elaborate practical joke as an example of how life was brimming over with the kind of unexpected, suspenseful improbabilities that flavored his art. "Can't use *moronic logic* in a case like this, can you?"

The party then resumed in full swing, with waiters in black-and-white-striped convict garb offering jailhouse cuisine served on a tin plate—wieners, baked beans, and brown bread—followed by the rollout of dessert: a large cake with a hacksaw protruding from the center.

Before the partygoers received a tour of the station and were redeposited at the restaurant in the same vintage paddy wagons rented from Warner Bros studios, the notoriously macabre prankster Hitchcock revealed to the press the inspiration behind his elaborate. He shared a familiar, possibly apocryphal, yarn from his boyhood in England—a bit of self-mythology he'd been repeating and embellishing for ages. "My favorite story is that my father sent me to the local constabulary with a note when I was a tot," he began, spinning the tale of how he arrived at the police station with a missive saying he'd misbehaved. "This is what we do to naughty boys," said the constable, who placed the lad in a cell, where he stayed for about five minutes awash in all-consuming terror.

"My career was determined from there," explained Hitchcock, forever haunted by crippling phobias of authority, imprisonment, and false accusation—fears that informed the common, paranoiac themes that so resonated with moviegoers in his cinematic body of work. His latest, *The Wrong Man*, starring Henry Fonda as a wrongfully accused suspected murderer and due in theaters in two months, was a direct expression of Hitchcock's inner torments. Chief Anderson had agreed to Hitchcock's stunt to help the filmmaker finally conquer his fears (that Anderson, like Hitchcock, also took a certain pleasure in watching people squirm was a bonus).

As the party wound down, Hitchcock felt inspired to offer a reverie on a "wonderful" film he'd dreamed of making for a decade but was thwarted by studio executives as increasingly plausibility-obsessed as any skeptics in the audience. The story began with a dead man at the United Nations, a corpse in a car rolling off a Detroit auto assembly line, and an improbable climax set, as the filmmaker vividly described, "on Mount Rushmore with the villain hiding in the nostril of one of the presidents."

In three years' time, *North by Northwest*, headlined by frequent Hitchcock lead Cary Grant, featured each of those seemingly disparate sequences as another wrongly accused man on the run from both the authorities and mysterious adversaries alike, embroiled in a McGuffin-fueled cat-and-mouse chase across the country. The film would, in visually dynamic form, exhilarate and enthrall lovers of cinema for decades, standing alongside *Vertigo* and *Psycho* among Hitchcock's universally acknowledged masterworks.

Moronic logic be damned.

Aside from the absence of a literal full-blown felony, the Hitchcock anecdote is an ideally metaphoric expression of the stories collected here for *Beverly Hills Noir*. It contains so many of the classic ingredients that, through nearly three decades of exploration, I've found make the most juicy and compelling true crime tales from 90210 unique among all others. And it exemplifies what ties them all together.

Start with fabled Beverly Hills: just six square miles surrounded entirely by the rest of Los Angeles, playground to the wealthy, powerful, talented, and beautiful, international shopping mecca and an 800-thread-count designer sheet bedroom community all at once. World-renowned as a sun-soaked, palm-tree-lined landscape filled with luxurious boutiques, five-star hotels, gourmet restaurants, and opulent estates—even its familiar 90210 zip code is practically a brand—Beverly Hills had been historically populated by some of the most famous names in Hollywood along with tycoons and captains of industry, athletic titans, international jetsetters and, of course, more cosmetic surgeons per capita than any other city of its otherwise modest size. It seems like nothing bad could ever happen there.

But, on occasion, bad things do happen—sometimes very bad things.

There's motive aplenty. The wealth, luxury, power, and beauty boasted by the denizens of the city inspire the kind of envy, avarice, hate, and desire that can fuel a wide-ranging variety of skullduggery from confoundingly clever to staggeringly boneheaded schemes involving burglary, shoplifting, armed robbery, fraud, crimes of passion, an old-fashioned barroom brawl, and a fair share of murder.

In his prank, Hitchcock, his taste for the startlingly implausible overruling "moronic logic," displayed a deep understanding of just how jarring even the suggestion of crime can be for those accustomed to status and privilege suddenly experiencing a harsh real-world plot twist. One moment, you're immersed in your elegant environs; the next, you're at the Beverly Hills jailhouse, uncertain what you did to get there. Or worse, wondering how the police found out what you thought you'd gotten away with. Or worst of all, trying to puzzle out who betrayed you and what they stood to gain.

The recognition that when you have it all, you'll do anything to hold onto it, while others will do anything to take it for themselves. Victim or culprit, the terror and panic of being thrust roughly out of the bubble of comfort and luxury and into a pitch-black nightmare world. The horror of realizing that not only could your fine things and coveted trappings be ripped away, but that something far more precious is at risk: your reputation, your freedom, even your life. All the raw, overwhelming emotions that can accompany crime exposed—guilt, denial, suspicion, paranoia, self-preservation, desperation—magnified by lenses of fame and infamy, amplified by breaking news reports.

That is Beverly Hills Noir.

Scott Huver
Los Angeles, 2024

THERE WILL BE BLOOD

*"The physical facts and the testimony of witnesses do
not jibe. I understand, too, that some people believe the
Doheny family are too influential to tamper with."*

—**Leslie T. White**

L eslie Turner White had never been to the scene of a crime quite like
Greystone Mansion.

He'd been led down a long hallway inside the largest and most sumptuously appointed estate in Beverly Hills, from the cavernous West Hall to
the South Guest Room in the southwest corner of the mansion's ground
story, a masculinely furnished suite doubling as a spare bedroom and study.
It was homier and less ostentatious than the mansion's entry point, though
certainly just as luxurious, but its warmer aspects were disrupted significantly by its two current occupants: a pair of hours-old corpses, blood
pooled around their lifeless forms on the floor.

Throughout his varied career as a Ventura County deputy sheriff, a
police officer in the city of Ventura and an investigator for the Los Angeles
County District Attorney's office, Les White—twenty-five, small-statured,
owlish and bespectacled but with a brash, feisty eagerness to prove himself
in both physical and intellectual combat—had been summoned to many
a site of criminal activity. He'd seen the aftermath of violence, he'd examined and photographed plenty of dead bodies—hell, he'd even been shot
at himself on more than one occasion. And even though he'd only recently
settled in Los Angeles, he was already accustomed to glimpses of outsized
wealth and notoriety.

Prior to his Ventura stint, he'd enjoyed several months of employment at the movie studio owned by two of Beverly Hills's most famous
residents, Mary Pickford and Douglas Fairbanks, watching the superstar
couple shooting their individual films. And just a month earlier, he'd seen

famous celebrities and moneyed socialites filling the courtroom as District Attorney Buron Fitts, White's new boss, successfully prosecuted Fitts's previous boss, disgraced former D.A. Asa Keyes, on bribery charges. Even White's close friend, Ventura attorney Erle Stanley Gardner, was making a national name for himself as a writer of crime and detective stories appearing in pulp magazines.

But nothing could quite prepare him for Greystone Mansion.

Sometime shortly after 2 a.m. on Sunday, February 17, 1929, White had steered his Model T onto the winding, tree-enshrouded entry path at 501 Doheny Road—the side street intersecting Doheny Drive, the central north-south concourse at Beverly Hills's western border, both named for the famous, powerful scion of the staggeringly wealthy family that dwelled within. White approached the front gate that proclaimed the estate's moniker in iron-wrought letters: "GREYSTONE," dubbed in a nod to the prevailing hues of the baronial manor's imposing façade: Indiana limestone, Boise sandstone, Welsh slate roofing, leaded glass windows, and buttressed stone retaining walls armoring its steel-and-concrete skeleton.

Occupying 18.3 acres and completed just a year earlier, Greystone intentionally eclipsed even the most lavish California estates—second only to publishing magnate William Randolph Hearst's outré castle in San Simeon—and to overshadow Beverly Hills itself, where the Dohenys also owned 400 acres surrounding the estate, operating a ranch and getaway home there. The sprawling 67-room, 45,054-square-foot English Gothic/Tudor style mansion sat atop a knoll arcing high above the increasingly gilded community—already elite, even in its infancy, having been established just seventeen years earlier in 1912. The southern exposure offered a breathtaking vista of the Los Angeles Basin and panoramic views spanning all the way from downtown Los Angeles to the Santa Monica Bay, all the way to Catalina on clear days.

But along with the property's expansiveness, White was struck by its hermetically sealed nature. He was confronted at the fortress-like gatehouse by a trio of armed guards determined to hold him at bay until a fourth guard arrived and, ascertaining his identity, waved him to advance up the hill, following a sloping path through meticulously maintained grounds, lush gardens, and elegant fountains to the wide motor court before the main house. Even knowing why he'd been summoned, White was taken aback to find the home surrounded by a cordon of private detectives and additional security guards—not, he noted, police officers. "It would be simpler to crash Buckingham Palace," he wryly observed.

Escorted inside through the glass-and-iron-grillwork front door by "one of those frozen-faced butlers, properly immaculately garbed despite the hour and the tragedy," as he later recalled in his memoir, White descended into the cavernous Grand Entry, a two-level landing down an ornately carved wooden staircase modeled after one in the home of the Earl of Essex, lugging his gear down through sweeping, arches into the West Hall reception area. A checkerboard floor made of black and white Carrera marble, partially obscured by a massive antique carpet, was sparsely adorned with English chairs and candelabras. A cadre of lawmen was already gathered at the scene, hushed tones breaking the gloomy, sepulchral silence that pervaded the property.

"The atmosphere of the mansion made it seem as though there must be some mistake—that this thing could not have happened," recalled White, who'd been roused from the bed he shared with his expectant wife Theresa, pretty enough to have occasionally modeled professionally, with a telephone call tersely indicating what transpired just a few hours prior. He immediately recognized that it would be his "first real taste of really 'big stuff.'"

Murder, specifically, on a most sensational scale. As much as the eerie mood was an effect of the crime itself, it was magnified by the money and power on display.

Amid the officials congregating within Greystone was Charley Blair, Beverly Hills's diminutive, thirty-five-year-old Chief of Police. Born in Scotland and immigrated to Canada, Charles Coutts Blair's previous career as a professional jockey had him racing across the Eastern and Southern United States, until ebbing-and-flowing fortunes eventually led him West in 1910. He found employment as a jack-of-all-trades with the Rodeo Land & Water Company, the group of landowners who in 1912—failing to find oil under the former Mexican ranchero that would become Beverly Hills but instead discovering abundant water—cannily developed it into the now-burgeoning region. In 1916, he was appointed the city's one and only police officer under the city marshal, patrolling the city on a motorcycle (not uncoincidentally, Blair was the only person in town who knew how to ride one). Later, after the city's largely wealthy, often demanding citizenry doubted that the patrolman cruised by each home every hour on the hour as promised, Blair would open the throttle of his four-cylinder Henderson as he passed homes of the louder grousers—until they complained that perhaps they were being given *too much* protection.

By 1919, Blair was appointed as City Marshal, Fire Chief, and City Tax Collector. Despite all that authority, he was a much-liked presence in Beverly Hills, living on Camden Drive along with his wife Pearl and their two children (daughter Virginia was the first child born in the city after its incorporation)—plus the occasional houseguest: the city had no proper jail facility, so arrestees were sometimes lodged overnight at the Blairs, with home-cooked meals from Pearl, until transferred to county authorities. Perhaps owing to his popularity was the fact that when raucous parties thrown by the growing influx of movie folk, often featuring underwear littered across lawns, drew noise complaints, Blair would arrive—now in a sleek black Flint touring car more in keeping with the environs—with a friendly warning to tame the festivities, then stick around for a drink, or three, even after Prohibition became the law of the land.

For his vigilance, Blair became the city's first official Chief of Police in 1927, commanding an expanded, forty-person force, all housed in the new City Hall dedicated two years earlier. For his geniality, he was gifted a diamond-studded replica badge to complement his official one. With the population's ample tax funding, he implemented a then-cutting-edge crime lab complete with fingerprinting analysis, developed efficient patrol and traffic control operations that would serve as models for other communities, and, finally, added that long-absent jail.

Blair's duties were occasionally disrupted by the odd high-dollar burglary or a threat to the safety of one of Beverly Hills's celebrity citizens. There'd been a few too-close-for-comfort incidents of bloodshed in recent years, including a 1923 shootout between a team of Beverly Hills officers and county sheriffs and two robbery/murder suspects a few miles into the rustic hills of the Greystone estate, a battle that left both bandits gravely wounded; and a 1925 incident in which the young wife of the heir to an insurance fortune, alleging she was addled by her mother-in-law's persistent marital meddling, splashed acid in her husband's face before drinking poison (both survived; their union didn't).

But in comparison to the oft-violent landscape of Jazz Age Los Angeles and Hollywood, Beverly Hills remained so largely bucolic and scandal-free that upon his 1926 inauguration as Honorary Mayor, the homespun humorist and film star Will Rogers—whose popular newspaper column datelines from his adopted hometown had contributed to making Beverly

Hills world famous—offered the darkly comic suggestion that the city needed its own headline-grabbing intrigue: "My town of Beverly Hills, what we need is an attractive murder!" Rogers quipped. "Nothing less than this will bring it the notoriety it should have…Please do me the great favor of coming out and shooting somebody some evening." He playfully suggested, "I could pick the victim."

Three years later Rogers's unintentional prophecy had been fulfilled: Beverly Hills now faced its first homicide, and in his folksy parlance, it was a humdinger: *two corpses!* And he would never have imagined that one of the dead men, and very likely both, had shared the same train that brought Rogers home to Beverly Hills just days before his mayoral inauguration.

Upon arriving in the West Hall, White had spied his immediate superior, Captain Lucien C. Wheeler, the voice on the other end of the phone that roused him. Robust, polished, and shrewd at fifty-three, Wheeler had previously served as the chief of the White House Secret Service's presidential guard, responsible for the safety of chief executives including Theodore Roosevelt, William Howard Taft, Woodrow Wilson, and Warren Harding. He subsequently became the Los Angeles bureau chief of the precursor to the modern FBI; few lawmen in the country could boast a depth of experience on par with Wheeler. He was now head of the district attorney's new Bureau of Investigation, a regional detective division patterned after the federal Department of Justice with no political ties to other local law enforcement agencies. Indeed, the Bureau often arrested more corrupt police officers in a week than career criminals. Joining the Bureau the first week in January, White was one of seventy detectives handpicked by the unflappable, always immaculately put-together Wheeler, whom he deeply admired. Even on this occasion, at this ungodly hour.

Nearby stood the district attorney himself, Buron Fitts. Not yet thirty-four but looking older with thinning hair, wide-set ears, and a prominent nose, the Texan earned his law degree at USC, then clerked for the famed criminal defense attorney Earl Rogers (an inspiration for the fictional lawyer Perry Mason, created by White's friend Erle Stanley Gardner). A determined, committed fighter inside *and* outside the courtroom, Fitts served as an infantryman in the Great War: after he'd been burned by mustard gas, shrapnel from an artillery round shattered his right knee at the Battle of Argonne in 1918, leaving Fitts face down on the battlefield in pouring rain, unable to move for hours before he was discovered. Fourteen months later he could walk again.

Fitts spent four years in the county D.A.'s office, rising to chief deputy before being elected lieutenant governor of the State of California in 1927. Within a year he'd resigned to serve as special prosecutor in the bribery case against his ex-boss and former benefactor, bullet-domed Asa "Ace" Keyes. Fitts's victory cemented his reputation as a reform-minded white knight staunchly battling vice and graft. Elected virtually unopposed, largely on his valiant war record and the support of the American Legion and *Los Angeles Times* publisher Harry Chandler, he took over the D.A.'s office in late 1928, cleaning house and installing a trusted array of lawmen (many of them Legionnaires) onto his newly created detective squad. In contrast to his political successes, he experienced a string of accidents—including multiple airplane crashes—and an array of surgeries until his injured leg was finally amputated and replaced with an artificial limb. "It has been a long struggle which has ended in failure," Fitts noted bitterly. The D.A. deeply disliked losing, and he detested criticism even more: detractors considered him thin-skinned and self-pitying, but Les White, a scrappy idealist with a distaste for politics, believed he'd found a kindred pugnacious spirit. "I was for the 'cause' and I loved a fight," White admitted.

White saw the first body in the South Guest Room's entry hallway: face down and spread eagle on the floor. The man was wearing a pinstriped suit with a thick well of blood around his head from the bullet wound that ended his life; bits of brain and skull were smudged on the otherwise pristine ivory walls above him. As he fell to the floor, the rug beneath his feet had slid askew, and he lay slightly upturned with the right arm outstretched and the left pulled closer to the core, still clutching a cigarette that had burned down to a nub and singed a small section of the hand. This man, White was informed, was Theodore Hugh Plunkett, the estate owner's longtime personal secretary and closest confidant who'd overseen many of Greystone's finishing touches and had unfettered access to the property. Hugh Plunkett often spent the night in the very room where his body, a month shy of his thirty-third birthday, now slumped.

White entered the suite's bedroom: less than twelve feet away from Plunkett, at the foot of one of the room's extravagantly plush twin beds, was the lifeless body of the thirty-five-year-old man Greystone had been built for, Edward Laurence Doheny, Jr.—Ned, to those who knew him. Ned lay flat on his back, clad in an ornate dressing gown, green silk night robe, and a pair of expensive slippers. There was a scarlet puddle, no longer pooling, beneath his head from bullet wounds on both sides—the projectile entered just above the left ear, exited through the right temple, and lodged six feet above the floor in the room's southern wall. Dried blood crisscrossed his face, mask-like, in chaotic crimson rivulets. His left arm bent across his midsection; his right splayed out at his side in the direction of a stray, unlit cigarette not far away. A chair lay toppled alongside Doheny's body, seemingly overturned in his fall to the floor; nearby, a glass tumbler, apparently dropped, was tipped over near a small desk that held other glasses and a bottle of Johnnie Walker (Prohibition be damned). On one bed was a telephone directory, open to the "F" pages. The bedclothes were slightly mussed; a pillow had been removed and placed on a chaise across the room. Ned Doheny, White knew, was the only son of the famed oil tycoon hailed as the wealthiest man in Los Angeles, possibly the entire nation. Ned and his young family had lived in the recently completed mansion, built for them by his father, for less than five months.

Before joining law enforcement, White had voraciously consumed Conan Doyle's tales of the brilliant sleuth Sherlock Holmes and sat rapt through films featuring detectives like Boston Blackie. He knew that the minute particulars of the scene would likely tell much of the story, and so he took care to absorb every tiny detail. The tableau had all the earmarks of a murder-suicide. Possessed of an unsentimental ability to view dead bodies clinically as "cold meat," White was surprised, even puzzled, by the sense of unease he felt, but distracted himself with the work at hand. Chief Blair had deferred jurisdiction in the case to the county and the D.A.'s more experienced detectives, so White began taking detailed photographs, packing away potentially evidentiary odds and ends like the glasses and scotch for later study, and fingerprinting both corpses.

Discovering a finely engraved Bisley model .45 caliber Colt revolver under Hugh Plunkett's body, White handled the vintage firearm delicately with a handkerchief so as not to destroy any possible latent prints. Curiously, the well-maintained pistol was still quite warm to the touch, though the fatal shots were reported to have been fired shortly before 11 p.m., three-plus hours earlier. It seemed unlikely that Plunkett's body had somehow kept the gun from cooling.

He finished his photographs, a far, grisly cry from the warm, professional portraiture of engagements, weddings, graduations, and family holidays he'd been shooting as the owner of his own promising Ventura photography studio just months earlier. But even then, he continued to moonlight as a cop and official police photographer, snapping mug shots and even photographing the horrific carnage caused by the 1928 collapse of the St. Francis Dam, which killed hundreds. White's career, however, took an abrupt turn when a sudden case of life-threatening tuberculosis caused a hemorrhaged lung, forcing him to abandon his business literally overnight, as he could no longer spend hours confined in a dark room. Unable to afford to convalesce in Palm Springs's arid climate as his doctors urged, he and his wife headed south to seek treatment and recuperate at his aunt and uncle's Hollywood home, and he soon grew healthy enough to seek out a position among Fitts's investigators.

White packed the collected evidence and returned to the Grand Entry, where his colleagues were interviewing the witnesses. His instincts were already telling him one story, but he was eager to get a clearer sense of who these two men were, and exactly why they were both dead.

Though Ned Doheny and Hugh Plunkett had been near-constant companions for fifteen years, bound together both by their professional relationship and, by all accounts, a deep, abiding friendship, they came from such fundamentally different worlds that it seemed something of a fluke that they'd ever encountered each other at all, let alone become as close as brothers.

Ned was, of course, to the manor born, raised in wealth and privilege. Born in 1893 in Los Angeles, he was the sole surviving child—an eight-year-old sister died of a heart condition a year before Ned's birth—of Edward L. Doheny, Sr., the near-destitute prospector-turned-wildcatter still years away from success, and E.L.'s beautiful but chronically ill first wife, Carrie. Ned's early life had been marred by darkness: his parents' union grew rocky after the loss of their firstborn, compounded by E.L.'s long absences in his tireless pursuit of black gold. Depressed, Carrie drank heavily; seven years later, as E.L.'s fortunes finally began to dramatically escalate, they separated. Distraught by E.L.'s remarriage to a woman nineteen years his junior—just three months after their divorce was finalized—Carrie committed suicide at home in Northern California by ingesting battery acid.

Fortunately for the then seven-year-old Ned, his new stepmother Estelle—a lovely former telephone operator who, according to legend, first captivated E.L. with the sound of her dulcet voice alone—immediately embraced her role as his maternal figure. Ned would act out early on, but

E.L. and Estelle's doting indulgence (when E.L. was home) carried him through the traumatic loss of his mother. Although Ned noticeably lacked his father's formidable iron will and indomitable determination, the pudgy, melancholy child grew into a tall, athletic, and good-looking young man, mathematically inclined and musically gifted, with an appreciably pleasant demeanor and a seeming maturity beyond his years, though he would still shirk performing tasks he deemed unpleasant. After dropping out of Stanford, Ned flourished closer to home at the University of Southern California; he'd remain a steadfast and loyal Trojan for the rest of his days.

An eminently eligible bachelor as his family wealth ballooned, Ned nevertheless was hopelessly smitten with his high school girlfriend Lucy Marceline Smith. Lucy's beauty, shrewd mind, and posh, respectable pedigree—her father was vice president of the Pasadena Rapid Transit District Company and owned auto service stations across Los Angeles—marked her as a choice match immediately embraced by his family as well. The affectionate nickname E.L. gave Lucy, "Sweetheart," would endure well into her adulthood, though he surely recognized that the petite beauty also boasted a steely resolve comparable to his own. Upon entry into the Doheny fold, Lucy, though the youngest in her family, swiftly ascended as its central figure and had no qualms about asserting her controlling dominance. Ned popped the question in a fit of mortal desperation when he was struck by appendicitis, and the couple wed in 1914—two days after E.L. purchased the large parcel of land adjoining his Doheny Ranch property, which in a few years would comprise Greystone's grounds, for nearly $29,000. By then, Ned was being groomed to one day succeed his father, developing an increasingly keen business sense if not E.L.'s notoriously ruthless practicality. The Doheny family's existence was increasingly defined by abundant wealth and luxury, and if Ned had a fancy that rivaled his affection for Lucy, it was for the age's more newfangled indulgence: the automobile. Both passions would bring Hugh Plunkett into his life.

Invited to the Doheny wedding at the Pasadena home of his employer, Lucy's father, William Henry Smith, Hugh likely never imagined he'd ever be welcome among such a swanky high society crowd. Such inclusion seemed contrary to his beginnings, though they were no more humble than the Dohenys. Born in 1896 in Roodhouse, Illinois, he'd migrated west as a child when his parents, Charles and Clara Bell Plunkett, sought brighter opportunities for their children, Hugh and his older brother Charles, Jr., known as "Chick." After relocating to Los Angeles in 1913 and welcoming much younger siblings Robert and Isabell, the tight-knit family slowly began to thrive. When Hugh came of age, he landed regular employment at Smith's service station on Pico Boulevard in downtown Los Angeles, where, as Les White had done, he changed tires and repaired cars. Charismatic and seemingly inexhaustible, Hugh's mechanical acumen was so keen that Smith soon entrusted him with the care of his family's personal automobiles. Thus, Hugh first met Lucy, who in turn introduced him to her fiancé, Ned, who shared Hugh's zeal for the emerging technology, if not his talents under the hood. It's quite likely that Ned may have even worked alongside Hugh for a brief period, as it became a family ritual for subsequent generations of Doheny men to spend a short period of time performing hand-dirtying manual labor at auto shops and filling stations, fueled by once rough-and-tumble wildcatter E.L.'s conviction that honest work forged his pampered heirs into more well-rounded—and manly—men.

Despite their dramatically different backgrounds, Ned and Hugh developed an instant rapport through the common language of car enthusiasts, and Ned hired Hugh to service the Dohenys' growing fleet as well. As a result, he was a warmly welcomed guest at Ned and Lucy's wedding, and shortly thereafter, the couple offered him a position as their personal chauffeur and mechanic; from the outset, he was treated more as a trusted confidant than a paid employee. Following Hugh's wedding that year to Harriett Marian Hall, the bond between the men strengthened so that when both enlisted in the Navy to serve their country on the very same day in 1917, Ned guaranteed that upon the end of the Great War, a job would be waiting for Hugh. Their service, however, radically differed: Ned was promoted in mere weeks to lieutenant, assigned aboard the U.S.S. *Huntington* commanded by Captain John Keeler Robison, who after the war would go on to oversee the naval oil reserves—and become a key figure in the future of the Doheny clan; Ned fulfilled the remainder of his service stateside in the Washington, D.C., office of the Judge Advocate-General. Meanwhile, Hugh served as chief machinist mate in a less comfortable berth aboard a Navy submarine chaser.

Both returned home unharmed and, true to his word, Ned had a position ready for his friend: Hugh was elevated to Ned's personal secretary, an exponential step up in status and responsibility, as Ned became vice president of the Pan American Securities Company, the still-booming family oil business, increasingly positioned to fill his father's shoes. As mogul-in-waiting and charming socialite, Ned's calendar was jam-packed—he sat on various boards, hobnobbed at upper-crust clubs, and steadfastly served USC—as a trustee on the board of regents, the first president of the alumni association, benefactor of a whopping $200,000 endowment and an avid, highly visible fan of Trojan football, attending virtually every home and away game. Meanwhile, his union with Lucy produced five children—Lucy Estelle in 1915 (called "Dickie Dell," due to an infant sibling's inability to properly pronounce her name); Edward L. III, known as Larry, in 1917; William Henry in 1919; Patrick Anson in 1923; and Timothy Hugh (christened in tribute to the Dohenys' dear friend) in 1926. Despite not having children of his own, Hugh managed all Ned's duties with outward aplomb, and the two became ever more inseparable.

Then came Greystone: over the course of two decades, E.L. Doheny had transformed his downtown residence in the gilded Chester Place subdivision into Los Angeles's grandest compound, having purchased every adjoining lot to sell to hand-picked neighbors. Ned and Lucy had a home there as well until E.L., increasingly sentimental in his dotage and dedicated to ensuring his family's status, comfort, and, above all, safety, decided to outdo himself by creating the most extravagantly opulent estate the region had ever seen for Ned's young family, smack in the heart of Beverly Hills, which had emerged as the preferred residence of the region's rich and famous.

Doheny's oilmen cronies, coming up empty on crude, built the lavish Beverly Hills Hotel, situated ideally between downtown and the Pacific, in 1912 as a lure for monied travelers to entice them to purchase property there. After the fledgling city incorporated in 1914, the movie colony, following the lead of privacy-seeking Douglas Fairbanks, flocked there, either seeking to flee association with the scandal-plagued "Hollywoodland" or in search of more fashionable residences than the dimming downtown area as L.A. sprawled westward (during the property boom of the 1920s the population skyrocketed from 700 to 12,000). In 1926, E.L. launched the creation of an eye-popping showplace where Ned and Lucy's young family would reside, both on prominent display and insulated from the world.

Lucy desired the classical English Tudor style prevailing at mansions around the country, despite the glaring incongruity amid the region's abundant Spanish Revival influence, but money bought what money wanted. The Dohenys selected architect Gordon Kaufmann, who designed a smattering of distinguished Beverly Hills-area mansions like banker Ben Meyer's La Collina, which Lucy admired, as well as hallmarks including LaQuinta

Resort & Club, Scripps College, and Westwood Village's Holmby Hall, with Cal-Tech's Athenaeum, Santa Anita Park racetrack, the Los Angeles Times Building, the Hollywood Palladium, and the monumental Hoover Dam among his later triumphs. Kaufmann worked in concert with landscape designer and frequent Lloyd Wright collaborator Paul G. Thiene to craft an estate of unparalleled elegance and opulence—there was, the Dohenys instructed them, no upper limit.

The designers delivered—in spades. The house had been designed with grandeur and glamour foremost, but in smaller-scale dimensions to give it a homier, more livable atmosphere than comparable mansions of the day. There was the expansive Living Room and Minstrel Gallery highlighted by high vaulted ceilings, an eleven-foot baronial stone fireplace, and twin gunmetal steel Georgian chandeliers; a grand Sunroom with black-and-white marble flooring, walls paneled with murals depicting Tuscan backdrops and a marble fountain at the center; a vaulted ceiling Library housing rare first editions, soon a Doheny family signature; an oak-paneled Formal Dining Room highlighted by a black-and-white Italian marble fireplace; a Morning Room with Queen Anne dining set over cork flooring; a Master Bedroom in soft, feminine ivory hues with adjoining his and hers dressing rooms and baths and a massage room, plus similarly sumptuously appointed suites for the children. There were various Sitting Rooms showcasing unique collections, a fur and jewelry vault, a billiard room, a thirty-seat screening room, a two-lane bowling alley, guest rooms, a fifteen-person servants wing, kitchen, sewing rooms, linen rooms, a dedicated gift-wrapping suite, and two staffed switchboards. Secreted throughout the mansion were several hidden passageways, trap doors, and concealed catwalks (for the convenience of workers and the delight of the children) and disguised cachets of alcohol, from secret shelves to a full bar complete with its own bathroom (for the delight of the adults during Prohibition). Outside, multiple ornamental chimney stacks, each with its own unique brick pattern, were a whimsical touch in contrast to the fortress-like exterior. During construction, the mansion's engineers promised that Greystone would be "as permanent as the pyramids."

The terraced hillside grounds were equally lavish, sixteen acres of painstakingly maintained gardens, fountains, brooks, reflecting ponds, an Olympic-sized pool and—Thiene's crowning touch—an eighty-foot waterfall that cascaded into an artificial lake festooned with white lilies, all drawn from the estate's self-contained water system. Winding pathways paved in

Vermont slate weaved past carved stone figures; badminton and tennis courts, a two-bedroom gatehouse, kennels, stables, greenhouse, a small golf course, a fully furnished and livable 2/3-scale children's playhouse, and a working garage staffed with drivers and mechanics to house and service Ned's growing fleet of automobiles. The adjoining ranch also shared a private fire department and security force with the mansion.

Greystone was as much a self-contained, sealed-off principality as it was a home by the time it was completed in 1928. An as-yet-unequaled, almost audacious display of wealth and power, it outshined even Beverly Hills's most opulent estates: automaker E.L. Cord's sprawling property next door; actress Marion Davies' party palace Beverly House on Lexington Drive; screen heartthrob Rudolph Valentino's old-world, cliffside Falcon Lair; John Barrymore's soaring Bella Vista high atop Tower Road; and Douglas Fairbanks's rustic first residence Grayhall and subsequently Pickfair, the world-famous fantasy estate he shared with wife Mary Pickford. A glittery capstone in a well-bejeweled crown, Greystone bested them all, by far the single most expensive residence not just in Beverly Hills but in Southern California, costing even more than Greenacres, silent film comedian Harold Lloyd's jaw-dropping $2 million Benedict Canyon showplace. E.L. Doheny spent between $3 million and $4 million—plus the sleek black Cord automobile given as a bonus to Kaufmann for a job well done. Conversely, Ned and Lucy purchased the property from E.L. for a token ten-dollar payment and moved their family in just before Thanksgiving 1928, grateful for E.L.'s extravagant largess.

As Ned's right-hand man, Hugh assumed responsibility for overseeing Greystone's construction, ensuring that it met every imagined need. Empowered to sign massive checks on Ned's behalf, he managed the legion of workmen and kept the crews on schedule; he assembled a proper staff of nearly 40 to tend to the home and the grounds; he procured the enviable selection of antique and of-the-moment décor and amenities that filled the estate: original letters from George Washington and a framed copy of the Declaration of Independence; the barber chair in Ned's black marble bathroom where he and the boys received regular haircuts; a vault filled with liquor in the basement; the many firearms Ned collected and displayed in his Trophy Room; and a touch of the patriarch with E.L.'s solid silver saddle kept in a place of honor on the circular staircase spiraling between the billiard room and the theater. And there was perhaps Hugh's favorite element: the family motor pool in the neo-Gothic garage, which had its own gas pumps, lifts, and machine shop and housed a 1929 Packard limousine, a Dodge sports sedan, a Ford coupe, a Graham truck, a Lincoln touring car, a Buick, a Zephyr and a pair of rare sixteen-cylinder Cadillacs, two of only twenty of the models ever made.

The garage often housed Hugh's own snazzy vehicle, a dark blue Dodge Sport Cabriolet convertible. He frequently slept over in the first-floor guest room, proving utterly devoted to the entire Doheny family—at the cost of significant friction with his wife, left home alone at their ritzy rental near Macarthur Park brooding over Hugh's near-constant absences and increasing materialism as his compensation escalated. Hugh was living, mixing, mingling, and financially thriving in a world beyond a former mechanic's wildest dreams; as his friendship with Ned deepened, the Dohenys' many varied interests often kept him awake at night. He grew increasingly absent in his own parents' and siblings' lives, though he would particularly dote on his mother whenever he could and, with Ned's aid, enrolled his brother Robert into engineering school at USC.

Hugh's marriage finally crumbled: the couple separated in 1927 and their divorce was finalized a year later, just as the Dohenys settled into their new fiefdom. Citing desertion, which Hugh didn't contest, and indicating a widening spiritual as well as a materialistic gulf between them, Harriett sought solace at Ananda Ashrama, the mysterious 120-acre retreat founded in 1923 by Swami Paramananda in the remote Verdugo Hills above La Crescenta, twenty-five miles from Beverly Hills. With Hugh's financial support, she studied in sequestration as a neophyte in the eclectic, non-sectarian religion—Vedanta-influenced, with twin pillars of meditation and yoga—that most chroniclers of the era openly described as a cult. After the split, Hugh lived at Hollywood's Wilcox Hotel, then settled into an apartment on Cochran Avenue in L.A.'s posh Hancock Park neighborhood, a quick drive to Greystone, which he shared with a roommate, George Riley.

Hugh's personal life now looked as fractured as Ned's appeared idyllic, but, as Les White would learn, both men faced graver concerns that tested even their seemingly unshakeable bond.

Reconvening with his fellow lawmen, White learned the denizens of Greystone were providing a clearer picture of what had transpired, though there were no direct eyewitnesses after the questioning led by the Los Angeles County Sheriffs Department famed Captain William Bright, a former D.A.'s investigator himself and now the commander of the sheriff's Homicide Detail. His squad, formed just six years earlier, was already accustomed to high-profile cases. Buron Fitts and Lucien Wheeler joined in the interviews as the scenario came into focus.

It was around 9:30 p.m. on Saturday, February 16th, when Hugh Plunkett, in pinstripe suit and tie, drove his Cabriolet up to the main gatehouse of Greystone, where he was admitted by night watchman John E. Morris, a veteran employee accustomed to Hugh's constant comings and goings. After parking outside the garage, Hugh ascended a set of stairs to a small storage area to rummage through a closet where he kept fishing equipment and firearms in a gun locker. Proceeding toward the house, Hugh encountered security guard Edward McCarthy and chatted briefly, determining the Dohenys were at home. He admitted himself into the mansion with his own key, as noted by other Greystone employees on the grounds. Inside, he headed to the first-floor West Guest Room and phoned Ned and Lucy. Then, he ascended the grand staircase to the second-floor Master Bedroom where the couple, dressed for bed, were chatting after putting the children asleep in another wing. Ned had expected Hugh; concerned about what was troubling his friend, he greeted him with the usual warmth, though it was apparent to both Ned and Lucy that Hugh was high-strung and agitated. Together Ned and Hugh retreated to the first-floor guest suite where Hugh so often slept over. Readying for bed, Lucy was well aware of the sensitive nature of their discussion but did not expect any dramatic turns.

Ned and Hugh closed the door to the guest suite behind them for privacy while they sipped Johnnie Walker. Their muffled, hour-long conversation grew loud and contentious enough to catch the attention of Lucy's personal maid Kate Walker, butler Alfred Doar—the immaculately garbed, stone-faced servant who later admitted Les White—and Doar's wife Ingrid, nurse to the Doheny children. The exchange grew tense enough that Ned broke it off to place a phone call, then attempted to calm his friend down. Suddenly, shortly before 11 p.m., Lucy heard a loud *thump*—it sounded like someone in the house had overturned a piece of furniture, but she again didn't assume that anything was amiss.

Within a few moments of the thump, Dr. Ernest Clyde Fishbaugh arrived at Greystone, admitted by gatehouse watchmen John Morris, and entered the mansion—he, too, had his own personal key. Graying, mustachioed and bespectacled, the forty-four-year-old medical man cut a distinguished, patrician figure: the Indiana native was educated at Johns Hopkins and served on the staffs of St. Vincent's Hospital and Good Samaritan Hospital, both in tony Westlake near downtown L.A. He ministered to several famous Hollywood movie stars, but for nearly a decade he'd served as one of the Doheny family's personal physicians—he'd even reserved a berth at E.L.'s brand-new Beaux Arts luxury apartment building The Tower, another "no expense spared" property set to open in a few months. Fishbaugh had not only tended to E.L., Ned, and their family, he'd also been treating Hugh for the past two years.

The physician was attending the rollicking stage comedy *Mother's Millions* at the Hollywood Playhouse that night when he was summoned from his seat for an urgent phone call from his maid; Ned had rung for help with Hugh, leaving instructions for the doctor not to call back, as the last switchboard operator had gone home for the evening, but to come to Greystone immediately. Concerned, Fishbaugh had his chauffeur deliver him to the mansion, where he was welcomed by Lucy, calm and in good spirits, still unaware of any trouble brewing. Nothing seemed outwardly abnormal to Fishbaugh as Lucy led him down the long hallway toward the West Guest Room. The anteroom door was slightly ajar, and Hugh suddenly appeared in the frame, looking frantic and unhinged. "'You stay out of here!' he shouted at me," Fishbaugh told investigators the next day. The door slammed shut, either yanked closed by Hugh or by a sudden gust of wind, and Fishbaugh and Lucy were startled by what sounded like a single gunshot.

Entering the anteroom to investigate, Fishbaugh composed himself and directed horror-stricken Lucy to retreat to the Living Room. "I found Hugh Plunkett lying on the floor a few feet inside the door," he reported. "He was shot through the head. He was not breathing." He would also make a curious notation: "Plunkett, to the best of my recollection, was fully clothed." Venturing into the suite—he adamantly declared he'd never treated Ned there at any time before that evening—Fishbaugh found Ned bloodied and splayed on the floor. "He had been shot through the head. He was breathing but unconscious." Watchmen Morris, who'd heard at least one of the shots, raced into the suite as Fishbaugh attempted to revive Ned, but his efforts proved futile.

In Fishbaugh's view, the scenario was as simple as it appeared: though they were, he affirmed, "like brothers," Ned Doheny had been killed by Hugh Plunkett, who then turned his weapon on himself and committed suicide. "I didn't see whether or not he had a gun—I wasn't looking for such a thing, had no reason to," said Fishbaugh, also insisting that he heard only one shot. "If there had been another, even as I arrived, I am sure I would have heard it." Further, he was convinced that when Hugh flung open the door he wasn't intending to escape after apparently slaying Ned. "I hardly think that," the doctor said, "He heard us coming and could have gone the other way." The specifics were hazy, but he recalled first spotting the Colt Bisley on the floor alongside Hugh's body later, after a police officer illuminated it with a flashlight.

But the police had not, in fact, been called for some time. Without disturbing any evidence, so they claimed, Fishbaugh and Morris returned to the Living Room, where a distraught Lucy was only barely holding herself together after the doctor delicately delivered the grim news. The thumping sound she'd dismissed as furniture overturning must have been the gunshot that took Ned's life, they concluded. After much discussion, desperate for help, she called her two brothers: Clark Smith, employed by the firm that built The Tower for the Dohenys; and Warren Smith, a vice president of the family's Petroleum Securities Company, to join her at the mansion. She also called her brother-in-law Anson Lisk, who, with her sister Kate, lived just minutes away on the neighboring Doheny Ranch, managing it and the family's other ranch properties. Lisk, who'd dealt with the Beverly Hills police before, would handle alerting the authorities—but another, even more daunting call had to be given the highest priority.

Near midnight, Edward Lawrence Doheny, Sr., who'd been roused from his sleep in his bedchambers at Chester Place by Lisk's urgent call, arrived at Greystone. Still imposing even through infirmity at age seventy-two, with his tough, rugged mien and shock-white walrus mustache, he nevertheless appeared shaken and frail entering the palatial temple he'd constructed for his sole surviving child, the only thing in his life he held in higher esteem than his own enormous fortune of around $100 million. Lucy's family had hoped to shield the patriarch from the horrific scene in the guest suite for fear of aggravating his weakened health, but the old man insisted that he had to see Ned with his own eyes. Assisted inside by a security guard, E.L. Doheny was silently led to the suite containing Ned's lifeless body. The aged oilman knelt next to his son, stroking Ned's hand gently. At last, an anguished sob.

"My boy."

After what seemed an eternity of stillness, E.L. nearly collapsed but rose to his feet and was led to the Master Bedroom, where Lucy lay stricken with grief and shock. At her bedside, he crumpled to the floor and wept. The servants discreetly closed the door to allow Ned's father and wife to mourn their shared loss, and to ponder how their once-faithful friend Hugh could commit such a stunning betrayal.

It's unclear if the elder Doheny remained in the home or had been quietly whisked back to Chester Place (where the five Doheny children were also sent—much later, it would be revealed that the two eldest, Dickie Dell and Larry, had been hiding in the second-floor landing since Hugh's arrival, listening and trying to make sense of what was happening) by the time two Beverly Hills police officers, Lt. Bill White and Sgt. B.E. McGhee, arrived after midnight. They alerted Chief Blair, who recognized that the situation was far out of his force's element, and summoned D.A. Buron Fitts and his team. Within a half-hour, Bill Bright and the sheriff's homicide squad were also on the scene; Les White arrived by 2 a.m.

"A sufficient lapse of time had passed between the actual shooting and the arrival of the authorities to allow the witnesses to recover their emotional equilibrium," White later observed, noting that the accounts all appeared to be uniquely in lockstep, with little variation in each telling. "The testimony dovetailed with remarkable accuracy." It was all too neatly presented—possibly even rehearsed—to be entirely true, he suspected.

There were a few subtle deviations. Sure, everyone in the mansion, top to bottom, denied that any alcohol had been consumed—such an obvious, knee-jerk deception was *de rigueur* during Prohibition. But at least one maid reported hearing multiple shots in quick succession—"One, two, three!" as she put it—and there was Dr. Fishbaugh's description of seeing the Bisley pistol *next* to Hugh rather than *underneath* him, plus the unusual discovery that the weapon was still warm all those hours later. Other observational clues and those well-honed gut instincts already had White considering alternate theories to the murder-suicide scenario, though, by the wee hours, most of the investigators seemed eager to sign off on it.

"This story did not quite fit the physical facts as I found them, and with a shock I began to suspect that something was wrong," White wrote. "But apparently the other investigators were satisfied with the setup, so I decided to say nothing until I developed some concrete proof."

By then, it was 4 a.m. A local mortician transported the bodies to the morgue. As White made his way out of the mansion, Lucien Wheeler drew him close and whispered in his ear, instructing him to head straight to the morgue and examine the bodies in minute detail. Given that his boss, "whose astuteness I had constant reason to respect," acted clandestinely, White had cause to believe they may be on to something far bigger than it might seem at first glance.

Really big stuff, indeed.

As he drove to the county coroner's office at the recently opened Hall of Justice on Temple Street downtown, White had ample time to consider exactly what might have motivated Hugh Plunkett to so violently end his closest friend's life as well as his own. The initial answer had been provided, in considered clinical opinion, by Dr. Fishbaugh. His diagnosis: after many months of mental deterioration and stress, Hugh had simply gone stark raving mad.

Speaking to the first Beverly Hills police detectives who arrived at Greystone, the physician explained that Hugh had not seemed himself for quite some time, beginning in 1927 when he began suffering from severely abscessed teeth. With each extracted tooth, Hugh would experience what Fishbaugh described as a "severe nervous reaction," one that included spasming muscles and a lack of self-control. But with sedatives he would generally compose himself within a day, managing Ned's daily affairs as normal.

Hugh's bouts of dental torment and unnerving mental fallout continued for many long months, through (and perhaps contributing to) his marital split. The doctor pointed to an even more extreme reaction two months prior, around Christmas 1928: Hugh was afflicted with a painfully swollen abscess over his left eye, a persistent headache, and a fever that further agitated his already intensely frazzled nerves, even after he gradually healed. Increasingly high-strung and subject to twitching spells, "but never irrational," Hugh confided to the doctor that for the previous six months he'd struggled desperately to sleep, just a handful of hours each night, and only with the aid of sedatives like Dial or Veronal, highly narcotic over-the-counter barbiturates frequently taken for insomnia in the Jazz Age. Fishbaugh prescribed bed rest under the watchful eye of a nurse, and there could be no better refuge to escape the stresses of the world than Greystone, thoroughly designed for comfort and ease: Hugh moved in with the Dohenys for three weeks, lodging in the guest suite where his corpse would lie just a few weeks later.

But after his respite at Greystone, Hugh's perpetually anxious, agitated state and sleeplessness quickly resurfaced, and he complained of a powerful ache at the back of his head. In the first weeks of February 1929, Fishbaugh and the Dohenys grew concerned enough to implore Hugh to either take an extended vacation or admit himself into a hospital, but he steadfastly refused. Finally, in Fishbaugh's telling, Hugh's behavior became so erratic—but never violent—that the doctor and his patrons decided an intervention was necessary.

On Saturday, February 16, Fishbaugh met Ned and Lucy at Greystone around 5 p.m. Ned assured the physician that he himself was feeling "splendidly" but added, "Plunkett is the man who needs your attention." When Hugh arrived, they set to their unhappy task: convincing Hugh to commit himself to a sanitarium, or even just a lengthy ocean voyage, for the benefit of his own welfare and safety. "We all urged Plunkett to take a rest," Fishbaugh told the investigators. "He refused. He simply sat there. Almost shaking at times. Hands clenched. Jaws set at times. He said he would come out of it all right. I could see it was no use to push him further and so I left."

But Hugh's terse, stubborn assurances did not sway Ned. "Let him think it over for a while," Ned purportedly told his wife and the doctor. "I will get him later in the evening and I think I can convince him it is the only thing to do." Ned rang Hugh at his Cochran Avenue apartment shortly after and told him that he and Lucy would be stopping by. Hugh canceled his dinner plans with roommate George Riley and awaited the arrival of his friends and employers. Fishbaugh didn't know everything that transpired during the Dohenys' private meeting, but it appeared tense at best. What he did know was that, after Ned and Lucy left the apartment to see a movie—with Hugh declining to join them—around 7 p.m. the doctor received a telephone call from Ned asking him to return to Greystone in case Hugh should turn up there later that night. Because Ned didn't cite any specific reason for concern, and since the doctor had theater tickets to a hot show, Fishbaugh gave Ned instructions to reach him through his messaging service should he need to be summoned on short notice.

The doctor, Lucy, and the servants at Greystone would tell the police that Hugh had phoned from the estate's garage at 9:30 p.m., sounding highly distressed. Answering, Lucy listened to the ruffled secretary's concerns about something that Ned said to him at his apartment that had left him deeply unnerved. "It was only an impulsive remark," Lucy tried to assure him, attempting to dissuade him from coming to the house, but Hugh insisted on seeing Ned.

By 11 p.m., both men would be dead.

"We arrived at the morgue about the same time—the corpses and I," White later wrote sardonically. He set about the business of coaxing some enlightening clarity out of the dead men's bodies. He'd accumulated considerable forensic skills, including an advanced command of fingerprinting techniques, and was on track to becoming an expert-level criminologist. He'd tried on many a role in his young life—timber scaler, firefighter, prizefighter, office worker, service station attendant, land ranger, photographer, private eye, even carnival roustabout—but for the past five years nothing had suited him and his admittedly righteous sense of justice better than the role of lawman. In the spirit of Sherlock Holmes, he had the innate drive and eye for telling detail that made for a keen detective. Developing photos, scouring the scotch bottle and tumblers for latent prints, and carefully studying the cadavers, he was betting on revelation.

The bottle and barware disclosed, to no surprise, that both men had been drinking—White could further prove this with a thorough analysis of the contents of their stomachs. More tellingly, he found powder burns surrounding one of the bullet holes in Ned Doheny's head, strongly indicating that the Colt Bisley was held no further than three inches away from his temple when fired—instantly upending the prevailing theory that a seated Ned was shot from a short distance of a few feet and tumbled from his chair to the floor. Hugh Plunkett's temple had no such burns, making it quite unlikely that he'd put the .45 to his own head and squeezed the trigger.

The murder weapon, which White determined hadn't previously been discharged in some time, proved just as puzzling. Despite firing it several times in rapid succession, he couldn't get it to replicate the same heat he felt when he retrieved it from under Hugh's hours-old corpse. White wondered if someone had actually heated the pistol in an oven or fireplace to give the appearance that it had been recently fired, overdoing their effort. He couldn't lift any fingerprints from the Bisley, despite his best efforts. Experience told White it wasn't unusual to come up empty on readable prints—especially on stored, collectible firearms often kept well-oiled and resistant to prints—but he at least expected to find smudges indicating the steel portion of weapon had been handled. A total absence suggested the gun had been thoroughly wiped clean.

Hugh's telltale cigarette flummoxed White from the start: it was held in his left hand in a manner the detective recognized would have made it impossible for him to throw open and slam close the anteroom door as Fishbaugh described, especially if holding the gun in his right hand—which he had to when he purportedly shot himself, based on the bullet entry point and the fact that in death he still clutched the cigarette as it burned down to singe his flesh.

The ballistic trajectory was similarly confounding. The angle suggested that to fire a bullet, itself quite old, which struck Ned, toppling him from the chair, then lodged high in the wall, Hugh would've had to pull the trigger at waist level, upward at an awkward angle, meaning he had to be kneeling or shooting from the hip—with or without a cigarette in his hand, an unlikely bullseye. Lastly, there was the odd crisscross blood pattern lining Ned's face, which to White only made sense if, after being shot, Ned had fallen face-down on the floor and been turned over.

White's suspicions about the scenario nearly all the other detectives seemed eager to embrace had proven well-founded. Yes, it might have indeed been a murder-suicide, but *who* had pulled the trigger on *whom*? Could it instead have been Ned who shot Hugh and then turned the pistol on himself? Could neither man have been responsible, both murdered by a mysterious third party? The truth seemed more elusive with each new revelation.

As White attempted to wrap his head around his startling discoveries, a veteran deputy sheriff walked into the morgue, perched on a drainage table, and quietly watched White work with intent curiosity. Finally, the deputy asked nonchalantly, "You see anything of interest?"

"Sure," White answered. "I don't believe Plunkett killed Doheny. Something is warped about this case."

"So what?" replied the deputy, a Cheshire cat grin below his drooping mustache.

"What? Why, we've got to get to the bottom..." said White, taken aback by the casual dismissal, but the deputy cut him off with a wag of his head.

"Personally, I think you're right—about the shooting," the deputy said, offering a hint of empathy before continuing coldly. "But there's no 'we' stuff as far as I'm concerned. Old Man Doheny is too big a man for me to monkey with."

The deputy strode off, his last words hanging in the air. His head swimming, White chose to write off the seasoned officer as a corrupt cop, the kind D.A. Fitts was hoping to weed out. But Fitts would see the evidence. Fitts would demand the truth. "We have to get to the bottom…"

Les White knew, as did almost anyone in Los Angeles, even across the country, who'd picked up a newspaper over the last few years, that the lives of the Doheny family were far from free of worry. Their massive wealth could not always insulate them from the consequences of accumulating all that money, and by 1929 both E.L. and Ned had ample reason to be very, very nervous. And if the Dohenys were nervous, Hugh Plunkett—mental and physical maladies notwithstanding—was nervous.

By that time, the phrase "Teapot Dome" was as synonymous with scandal and government corruption as the word "Watergate" would be decades later. It originally referred to a large sandstone rock formation resembling a teapot in Wyoming's Natrona County and later carried over to the neighboring oil field that in 1915 was designated by the U.S. government as a naval petroleum reserve—part of President William Howard Taft's policy ensuring the military would always have an ample fuel supply, and as a hedge against oil industry price gouging during wartime. In 1921, Taft's executive order transferred control of the Teapot Dome oil field from the Navy to the Department of the Interior under Interior Secretary Albert Fall.

The tall, lean Kentuckian Fall was an outsized, often combative personality whose rough-hewn experiences in the Western frontier marked him as a man who could handle himself in just about any situation—and who constantly carried a sidearm as insurance. Widely disliked and distrusted by both his rival Democrats and fellow Republicans, he was nevertheless accomplished in many arenas: he'd been a schoolteacher, an attorney, and an infantry captain in the Spanish-American War, but politics uplifted him: he served New Mexico first as a territory and then as a state as a territorial councilman, judge, associate justice, attorney general, U.S. congressman, and senator. His Senate stint earned him enough allies and political clout to claim a cabinet seat from the President Warren G. Harding's White House in early 1921.

Fall first met young E.L. Doheny, his friend and longtime poker buddy, during the early 1880s in the rowdy and often treacherous frontier mining camps Doheny frequented in his hardscrabble early days, a full decade before he would, at last, discover wells in Los Angeles and Mexico that would make him a multimillionaire. Doheny was just as tough, wily, and single-mindedly determined to realize his ambitions–sometimes to the point of sheer ruthlessness—as Fall, and likeminded in the conviction that the West's natural resources were meant to be claimed and exploited by private enterprise, which in turn would benefit the public.

Their friendship would endure for decades as both muscled their way to the top and Harding, whom Doheny, like many other prominent oilmen, had significantly backed financially, took office. Fall invited Doheny to meet the new president just as American consumption of petroleum, powered by the growing ubiquity of the automobile, was skyrocketing. But Doheny and his fellow oil barons were concerned about a pronounced lack of new crude oil discoveries and a potential product shortage. They vied to gain access to the government's reserves, including the nearly 10,000 acres of Teapot Dome and the even more oil-rich 40,000 acres at Elk Hills in California's Kern County.

Conservationists were aghast when Harding's oil-friendly administration floated the notion of undoing the sacrosanct nature of the reserves. But Fall deftly handled the politics, persuading Secretary of the Navy Edwin Denby to sign off on Harding's executive order that put Fall in charge of contractual bids from private petroleum companies, all under the guise of benefitting national security. What the Navy needed at the ready most of all was fuel oil, not crude; the plan gave the oil barons access to the reserves' underground bounty in exchange—along with a percentage of the crude oil sales—for a large fuel depot in storage tanks to be constructed at the expense of the winning bidder at the increasingly crucial naval base at Pearl Harbor in Hawaii.

Fall shared this and other information with his old crony Doheny, along with enticing gifts—including autographed photos of the president, an invitation to the dedication of the Tomb of the Unknown Soldier, and tickets to the Army-Navy game—that appealed to his vanity and drew their families closer. E.L.'s company effectively prepared the lowest bid for the rights to drill at the plumb Elk Hills reserve, aware that the oil there was estimated to be worth around $100 million over the proposed thirty-year lease period; later, after receiving a stirring, eloquent entreaty about the vital, urgent strategic importance of highly vulnerable Pearl Harbor from Admiral John Keeler Robison—whom E.L. knew as Ned's former commanding officer aboard the USS *Huntington* during the Great War—Doheny also claimed to feel a swell of patriotic duty, despite the high cost of the fuel storage station. He was all in.

To shepherd the sweetheart deal through the government bureaucracy, Fall, the man at the other side of the poker table, asked E.L. to ante up in the form of $100,000. Fall called it a loan; others more pointedly called it a bribe. Eager to seal the deal, E.L. assigned delivery of the "loan" to the person he trusted above all others to handle sensitive, high-priority business dealings with utter discretion and fealty: his son Ned, then twenty-eight, embedded in E.L.'s operations, and, by his father's estimation, due to learn how the real world operated up close.

Sending Ned meant a two-for-one with the unflaggingly loyal Hugh Plunkett. Two days after Thanksgiving 1921, they embarked by train to Ned's townhouse in New York City; Ned withdrew the sum from his personal bank account, wrapped in five $20,000 bundles within a nondescript black leather satchel. Together, they traveled directly to Washington, D.C.'s Wardman Park Hotel, knocking at the door of Albert Fall's seventh-floor suite. After the usual pleasantries, the satchel changed hands; Fall counted the money and handed Ned a signed promissory note guaranteeing the loan. They filled the rest of the day with cocktails and casual conversation before Ned and Hugh returned to Manhattan, while Fall journeyed to his Tres Rios cattle ranch in Three Rivers, New Mexico.

By April 1922, the government awarded the Dohneys' Pan American Company drilling rights to Elk Hills. Simultaneously, Mammoth Oil's Henry Sinclair, E.L.'s chief rival in the petroleum industry, secured similar access to Teapot Dome—though the smaller property, Sinclair had lavished Fall with even greater largess. The under-the-table windfalls from Sinclair and Doheny allowed Fall not only to emerge from the calamitous financial morass he'd fallen into personally, paying off back taxes and a large property debt to revive his once-prosperous ranch—he expanded and significantly upgraded every aspect of the property.

Very soon, the truth of the secret dealings with Doheny and Sinclair bubbled forth like so much crude: as a Senate committee investigation intensified, President Harding first offered full-throated support of his longtime ally Fall, then slowly backed away as the whiff of scandal grew into a stench that prompted Fall to resign. Under pressure and openly fretting over the growing clamor, Harding dropped dead of a stroke while touring the country.

True to its evocative name, Teapot Dome became quite the tempest on a national scale.

Summoned before the Senate committee, E.L. Doheny denied any wrong-doing and insisted that his motives were purely altruistic towards his cash-strapped friend and patriotic towards his country, even as the press breathlessly reported the details of Fall's profligate spending. When Fall's ham-fisted attempt to attribute his loans to another wealthy crony blew up spectacularly, his long friendship with Doheny was among the collateral damage. Furious, Doheny admitted before the Senate that he'd sympathetically given his old comrade the money—"a bagatelle to me...no more than twenty-five or fifty dollars to the ordinary individual," a fair statement given his company's net worth in 1923 was around $175 million. Sending Ned and Hugh as his emissaries was nothing extraordinary either, claimed E.L.: the loan—out of the family's pockets and off the business books—had nothing to do with the Elk Hills lease. But the glare of the spotlight grew increasingly, uncomfortably white-hot, and the public appetite for information about E.L.'s colorful, controversial history, lavish lifestyle, and heretofore-unguessed-at power and influence became insatiable. He was a robber baron to some, a rags-to-riches folk hero to others, and regarded in degrees of awe by all. Nevertheless, he was indicted for bribery and conspiracy by the federal government in 1924, as were Fall and Sinclair—and Ned Doheny.

Ned, facing a very real prospect of prison time, was stunned: in his mind, he'd merely been the courier for the now infamous "little black bag." Subject to scandalous headlines and whispered innuendo, he was even occasionally snubbed in his accustomed place at the hub of the Los Angeles elite. The board of directors of the Methodist Church pressured USC to remove him as a trustee should evidence of criminal culpability emerge, but his well-timed $200,000 endowment bought him goodwill at his alma mater. Advised by his father to live as normally as possible, Ned was nevertheless pensive and traveled extensively, accompanied as ever by Hugh. Lucy was left with the children at Chester Place, weighing her own tenuous position in the society circles she'd inhabited since birth. Conversely, Ned's role as the emissary of E.L.'s "loan" played in the senior Doheny's favor in terms of public perception: a compelling argument emerged that E.L. would never knowingly place his cherished only son in any sort of legal jeopardy—he *must* have believed the monies gifted to Fall were above board.

E.L. made shrewd P.R. moves, cementing close ties with influential newspaper publishers like William Randolph Hearst and sponsoring a glowing biography of Fall (mending fences as they closed ranks to defend themselves against federal prosecutors) but failing to persuade the famed director Cecil B. DeMille to shoot a boosterish film of Doheny's life story. The Irish Catholic oil man also not so subtly appealed to a higher power, funding the construction of the glorious St. Vincent de Paul Church, only the second Catholic parish in Los Angeles, adjacent to Chester Place, earning it the nickname "the Church of Holy Oils" and "Doheny's Fire Escape" (a statue of St. Edward the Confessor at the main altar bore a strong resemblance to E.L.).

But really, his best hope of salvation was to purchase the best defense his considerably deep pockets could buy. He paid $1 million to the brilliant attorney Frank J. Hogan, a commanding orator with a battling spirit akin to Doheny's own. E.L. had lost the lucrative Elk Hills leases during his civil trial (though he magnanimously lived up to his commitment to complete construction on the Pearl Harbor fuel storage facilities). Still, there was far more at stake in his criminal conspiracy trial alongside Fall, which commenced in late 1926. Hogan's thorough, dazzling defense was bolstered by E.L.'s calm, composed, often charming testimony. At one point, grilled about why he'd sent his son to deliver the cash, the aged Doheny—sympathetically nursing an infected right arm in a disarming sling—replied he'd hoped his expected successor would gain key experience from the task: "Even if he had been held up on the way, he would've learned something." Ned, too, came off well during his turn on the stand, and following Hogan's dynamic, emotional summation, a stunning verdict came back: not guilty.

When the Doheny men returned to Los Angeles on the California Limited after E.L.'s acquittal, just in time for Christmas, they were greeted by a jubilant throng of 6,000 dignitaries and well-wishers offering a hero's welcome they exited their private train car "Willow Bank" at Santa Fe railway's Le Grand Station, the precursor to Union Station. Hugh, in all likelihood, attended, either accompanying the Dohenys or among the celebrants. The crowd was so enthusiastic the throng barely acknowledged humorist, movie star and Beverly Hills' honorary mayor-elect Will Rogers as he debarked from the same train, returning home for his inauguration—even though Rogers's own welcome reception included film icons and Beverly Hills locals Tom Mix, Conrad Nagel, and "campaign manager" Douglas Fairbanks, who handed Rogers a cauliflower bouquet and passed out cigars. But the region's wealthiest family had stolen the spotlight.

After E.L. hugged his grandchildren and dozens of women of varying ages planted congratulatory kisses on the old man's cheeks, his eyes welled with tears. "I'm deeply touched at this splendid reception," he said, adding of his acquittal: "I knew that if the matter could properly be presented before a typical American jury, justice would be done." Ned warmly embraced his father, and perhaps to atone for involving Ned in the sordid affair, the elder Doheny would pay loving tribute to his son—still facing his own bribery charges—by building him the most magnificent home imaginable, as extravagant and indulgent as a sultan's palace and as safe and insulated as a military fortress. Plans for Greystone commenced that Christmas.

It seemed at that moment that the storm had been weathered, and the family had returned to the shelter of privilege and power. But the tempest had not calmed yet.

As popular as the elder Doheny appeared upon his return to L.A.—enough that novelist, politician, and social commentator Upton Sinclair would borrow liberally from E.L.'s now-famous backstory to craft a wealthy Doheny-esque oilman in his 1927 novel *Oil!*—there were countless people among the country made furious by his exoneration, believing he'd purchased his freedom with his exorbitant wealth and influence. Not least among the naysayers were federal prosecutors, who were eager to take another stab at conviction.

First, though, Fall and Mammoth Oil's Henry Sinclair faced their days in court. Ned, to his father's consternation, was subpoenaed to testify in Sinclair's 1928 trial, but Hogan argued that with Ned's own trial pending, his Fifth Amendment rights protected him from incriminating himself on the stand. A surprising compromise was struck: the government dropped its case against Ned in exchange for his testimony. Given that the feds refused to drop the bribery trial against E.L., the proposition meant Ned risked giving testimony that could later be used against his father. But Ned was again well-received in court, and Sinclair was acquitted—for a time.

Ned was back on the hook for Fall's bribery trial—and this time, so was Hugh Plunkett. Federal prosecutors pressed to hear *both* men's versions of the delivery of the $100,000 "bagatelle," hoping to convict Fall and strengthen their forthcoming prosecution of E.L. Doheny. The stakes were sky-high: if Fall were acquitted, then logically, E.L.'s case wouldn't even go to trial, and the whole ugly business would finally be behind the family. If convicted, the fallout could be catastrophic. Hugh was said to be thoroughly panicked at the prospect of saying anything that could incriminate his benefactors—or worse, with no immunity deal, himself. The Dohenys had proven to be faithful friends and employers over their years together, but at the end of the day, Hugh was aware that he wasn't blood kin. If the family withdrew its support and considerable resources for any reason, where would that leave him?

The intense stresses in Hugh's life seemed to compound exponentially—shepherding the Dohenys through their Teapot Dome travails, the exhausting completion of Greystone, his protracted marital split, his debilitating physical maladies, his escalating nervous condition, and now impending legal peril. But even if the strain of all that pressure had, in fact, caused Hugh to suffer a mental collapse, the question remained: why would that lead him to murder his dearest friend?

"I don't believe Hugh Plunkett killed Doheny and then committed suicide," Les White told Buron Fitts during a private meeting at the district attorney's home early on February 17, the Sunday morning following the bloodshed at Greystone. It was well after dawn when White concluded his analysis of the evidence, and despite his lack of sleep, he'd telephoned Lucien Wheeler to report his findings. Wheeler directed White to deliver them directly to the feisty D.A.; he'd dragged himself there, fighting growing exhaustion and admittedly crankier and blunter than he might otherwise have been with his boss's boss, especially during their first ever one-on-one exchange. Even in his admiration for Fitts's blend of idealism and practicality, White had noticed that the D.A.'s personality was somewhat malleable, shifting and adapting to whoever was in his presence. He felt genuinely unsure if Fitts would be willing to shine a bright light on the apparently constructed false narrative surrounding Hugh and Ned's deaths.

"At least it could not have happened in the manner described by the witnesses. The physical facts and the testimony of the witnesses do not jibe," White explained. Remembering the sheriff's deputy's warning, he added soberly, "I understand, too, that some people believe the Doheny family is too influential to tamper with."

As hoped, he brought out Fitts's combative brio. "There isn't a man in the United States that's big enough to stop me from conducting a criminal investigation," the D.A. said, dander up, insisting on hearing the details of White's concerns. As he explained the many discrepancies his analyses had revealed, the D.A. took in the impact of the detective's findings.

"But if Plunkett did not kill Doheny, who did?" Fitts asked.

"I can't tell you that at this time," White conceded. "My job is to merely to show you we have not found the truth—as yet."

"We'll damn soon find that out!" the D.A. snapped, promising "a sweeping investigation." White decided the version of Fitts he liked best was the one he encountered here, alone.

After Fitts made a flurry of terse phone calls, White next found himself accompanying the D.A. back to the Hall of Justice, where investigators from Wheeler and Bill Bright's squads escorted in familiar faces from the night before—Dr. Ernest Fishbaugh, Lucy Doheny, her brothers and brother-in-law, the servants, the night watchmen, all surprised to be asked to rehash their stories so soon—as well as Hugh's father Charles and brother Robert. Absent was E.L. Doheny, in seclusion at Chester Place, alternately reported to be either holding up well under the circumstances or in a spiraling state of collapse ("I'd rather not discuss his condition," Fishbaugh told reporters. "There is nothing to say about a man who is suffering as he is suffering").

As Fitts concluded his interview with Dr. Fishbaugh, whose version of events hewed closely but not perfectly to his earlier description, the D.A. asked White if he had any follow-up questions. Sleep-deprived and with little experience interrogating witnesses, White still couldn't resist lobbing a few pointed questions at the physician.

"Doctor, you were at the house at the time the shooting took place and you rushed into the bedroom within a matter of seconds thereafter—is that correct?" the detective asked, receiving an affirmative nod. "Doheny was dead when you arrived?" Another nod. "And the body was not disturbed in any way?"

"It was not disturbed."

"Then, Doctor, as an experienced physician will you kindly explain how blood could run *up* from the ears and cross back and forth over the face of a man who never moved off his back?" replied White in a moment of Holmesian revelation. It had the desired effect: the doctor flinched, caught in White's logical deduction. "He's trapped, and he knows it," White thought.

In a quiet, hesitant voice, Fishbaugh recounted significantly different details than his prior testimony disclosed: after the doctor discovered him, Ned Doheny had remained alive for around twenty minutes. Desperate to save him, Fishbaugh and the night watchman Morris lifted Ned up so the doctor could attempt something—anything—to save him, to no avail. They lowered Ned's body back into a prone position on the floor, which had caused the odd blood patterns on the dead heir's face.

Fitts glowered at the physician for a moment, incensed at his earlier deception, then turned to White. "Any more questions?"

White had made his point, happy to let more seasoned interrogators take the baton from there. And besides, he was overdue for some sleep.

Newspaper headlines blared the news of Ned Doheny's death in massive type across the country the following day, Monday. More precisely, the press collectively announced the murder of Ned Doheny at the hands of Hugh Plunkett, his friend and secretary turned crazed, suicidal killer. Much to Les White's surprise, the prevailing narrative remained murder-suicide, as described in neat, corroborative unison by the denizens of Greystone.

Most reports noted that the district attorney's inquest would be pushing forward, but as Buron Fitts made a formal statement to the press, he seemed—in a marked reversal from his conversation with White twenty-four hours earlier—to have already concluded how and why the slaying occurred, and who was responsible. "This investigation of witnesses is just an additional check on the evidence gathered last night by the investigators at the Doheny home," he said. "So far there has not been a thing developed in the investigation that detracts from the conclusion reached by officers last night that this was a murder and suicide, and Plunkett killed Doheny."

"There is no doubt in my mind that Plunkett was an ill and very nervous man, and that the Doheny family was doing the best they could to put Plunkett in a hospital for his nervous condition," Fitts added, affirming a new detail: that Hugh had at some point agreed to be committed. "He was to go to the hospital today." The newspapers told the story using evocative, charged language like "sudden burst of insanity," "broken mentally," and "madman."

Articles quoted liberally from Fishbaugh's account of Hugh's steady descent toward madness in the last months of his life, and the physician soon offered a massaged, amended version of the tale directly to the press, emphasizing just how quickly Hugh finally, violently snapped—something he never saw coming, he insisted. "He was nervous, very nervous and irritable," the doctor explained. "And he was stubborn, too. But he was rational at all times, as far as I could tell." Not even the Dohenys were privy to the full extent of Hugh's anxieties, he claimed. "He would never say what worried him. He spoke little of his personal affairs. But his nerves were at the trigger's edge." He recounted the ebbs and flows of Hugh's condition, culminating with the Christmastime convalescence at Greystone. "He rallied...[But] recently he became morose and brooding. He would not tell what troubled him, however. He refused all offers to help."

Concerned, Ned and Lucy had yet to give up on convincing their friend, whom they held in such high regard, to seek aid, Fishbaugh explained, leading to Saturday's intervention attempt. "They were trying to get him to drop everything and go to a sanitarium for a rest," he said. "[They] pleaded with him to let up for a while. They warned him and they humored him, but he wouldn't budge." By the time the doctor had been summoned again to the estate, Lucy told him, "Plunkett was incoherent and acting queerly." When Fishbaugh laid eyes on Hugh himself, he claimed to be shocked at the "wild figure" he saw.

The doctor's assertions were supported by Dr. Ellis Jones, another personal physician to E.L. Doheny, who'd consulted on Plunkett's treatment when he suffered from the flu over the holidays. Jones said he, too, prescribed a long rest, but Hugh didn't follow his advice. The Doheny dentist also affirmed the extent of Hugh's oral anguishes. Some of the more thorough press coverage noted the Doheny connection to the Teapot Dome scandal (including some pseudo-sermonizing about the loss of his son being the price of sin exacted on E.L. Doheny), but no article outside of the underground press cited Hugh's link to the exchange of the black bag to Fall or made mention of a possible impending subpoena.

Every aspect of the story unspooling in the media was too much to absorb for Hugh's family, who, even though he'd been increasingly absent from their lives, could scarcely imagine their golden boy acting homicidally, especially toward Ned. "This is all beyond my understanding," his crestfallen father Charles said after taking custody of Hugh's body. "Why, he and young Mr. Doheny were chums...They thought the world of each other." Insanity was truly the only thing that made any sense of it to the elder Plunkett. He'd visited Hugh during his illness and recuperation at Greystone over the holidays, finding him to be cared for and tended to as if he were one of the family—if anything, he thought Hugh had insisted on resuming his duties far too soon after his health breakdown. "I feel that my boy went entirely out of his mind and that he was not in any way responsible for his act—I'm sure he did not know what he was doing."

Hugh's roommate George Riley, who'd seen him shortly before Hugh's meeting with the Dohenys in their apartment, was similarly shellshocked. "He was nervous, but not unusually so," he told the press. "He was a splendid fellow and I know he would not harm anyone intentionally." To Riley, only extreme overwork offered any rationale. "In my opinion, it was his deep devotion to the Doheny interests that made him break under the strain. I've known him to lie awake nights thinking over Doheny affairs."

But the roommates' young Filipino houseman Tony Jaboc told reporters he'd seen a disturbing side of Hugh when he arrived at the apartment that evening, discovering the secretary in a frenzied state, throwing knives at the walls, banging spoons on the tabletops, and demanding that Jaboc summon his landlady. The houseman, fearing for her safety, did not deliver the message. "I became afraid and left," he claimed. Had Jaboc alerted her, the empathetic landlady said, she would've have certainly called a doctor to help her tenant, whatever his ailment.

Hugh's ex-wife Harriett Marion Hall—living under a name conferred on her at the Ananda Ashrama retreat—was reported to be wracked with grief upon learning of his demise; sources within the sect told the *Los Angeles Times* she insisted she'd never seen any evidence of insanity in her former husband, though he was prone to fits of temper that he would later regret. Allowed to pause her metaphysical studies and return to Los Angeles for Hugh's funeral, her status as an abandoned spouse who'd turned to a remote, enigmatic religious sect for solace did little to burnish Hugh's posthumous reputation.

Within a few days, the *Los Angeles Evening Herald*—like all Hearst newspapers at the time, on an aggressively anti-narcotic crusade—reported Dr. Fishbaugh's claims that for about six months prior to the killings, Hugh had been a user of the barbiturates Dial and Veronal in his desperate quest for sleep. Both drugs were under scrutiny. Veronal, in particular, had been shown to be both habit-forming and linked to so many poisonings and suicides that its use had, just two months earlier, become as strictly controlled in Los Angeles as morphine, cocaine, and heroin—addicts of those drugs often substituted Veronal in their absence. The newspaper quoted police drug experts who suggested Veronal caused a loss of muscle control and, more forebodingly, made habitual users more combative and vicious. But Hugh's mother Clara told the *Herald*, "I have never known him to be addicted to the use of stimulants or sedatives of any kind."

Fishbaugh's colleague Dr. E.S. Merrill, head of the psychiatric ward at Los Angeles County General Hospital, came forward claiming he'd been treating Hugh daily for the first nine days in February, after a mutual friend had brought the secretary to his office. Alleging his patient's ailments were tied to "domestic troubles" and confirming an excessive prior use of

Veronal-derived sedatives—which the doctor said had ceased their sedative effect—Merrill said they'd made significant progress in Hugh's treatment: Hugh had been able to sleep up to six hours a night for four days straight and was greatly encouraged, to the point of planning a ten-day trip to Utah's Zion Canyon with an unnamed friend. But the doctor remained concerned that the excessive Veronal use had left Hugh vulnerable to paranoid hallucinations.

"It is my belief that Plunkett may have gotten into a slight argument, over anything, and gone into a frenzy," Merrill told the *Herald*. "He was highly nervous and irritable, but didn't have good brakes to stop himself, once he got upset."

Hugh's autopsy results were immediately made public. Coroner Frank Nance—no stranger to headlines with his inquests into sensational slayings over his eight-year tenure, including those of director William Desmond Taylor, actor Ray Raymond and the infamous "Trunk Murders" committed by Winnie Ruth Judd—and chief autopsy surgeon A.F. Wagner concurred evidence indicated Hugh had placed the vintage Bisley's muzzle against his temple and pulled the trigger. He'd pressed the gun to his head so tightly that powder burns appeared on the *inside* of Hugh's skull, fracturing it four ways on impact and killing him instantly. The contents of both Hugh and Ned's stomachs had been analyzed by the county chemist—a routine process, it was assured. Hugh's contained 16.9 grams of alcohol, a bit more than an average single drink, while Ned's revealed no alcohol. No further autopsy performed on Ned was disclosed, but it was determined that he'd been shot from six feet away. The amount of time Ned had lived after the bullet pierced his brain was reduced, in official statements, from twenty minutes to "a moment."

Around thirty-six hours after the killings and countless screaming headlines later, the District Attorney's office and the Los Angeles County Sheriff's Department marked the inquest officially closed. The deaths of Ned Doheny and Hugh Plunkett were declared "beyond all doubt" to be a homicide and suicide committed by Hugh.

After that, press coverage was as dead as the men Les White found on the floor of Greystone a day earlier. "The newspapers dropped the story as if it burned their fingers," he observed. White recognized, before the reporting screeched to a halt, that the details—largely provided by Doheny relatives, in-laws who happened to be Doheny executives, Doheny-employed servants, physicians on the Doheny payroll, and a houseman likely to soon be looking for work—lined up to provide a sympathetic but ultimately damning portrait of Hugh Plunkett as an increasingly unstable man who'd snapped under the weight of intense personal and professional pressure, chronic illness and drug-induced hysteria, committing a horrific act.

Yes, it all lined up quite neatly. But little of it lined up with the crime scene evidence that White himself had recorded.

The newspapers didn't entirely turn away from the story: there was still the matter of breathlessly reporting how one of the richest families in America lay to its prematurely fallen son to rest, as well as his tragically demented killer. In doing so, as both men's funeral services were conducted within three days of their deaths, other potentially telling details emerged.

Ned's requiem mass was, of course, held at St. Vincent's, the grand and glorious Roman Catholic church his father gifted the community at a cost of $500,000, near E.L.'s Chester Place compound and Ned's alma mater USC, which canceled classes that Tuesday morning so faculty and students could pay last respects to the university's illustrious alumnus, a prince of the city. While an enhanced security detail solemnly patrolled the grounds of Greystone in Beverly Hills, a small legion of motorcycle traffic cops was dispatched downtown to manage the droves who turned out hours early to witness the funeral scene at Figueroa and West Adams. Curious onlookers lined the streets as the church's pews and aisles filled to capacity with invited mourners. Despite the throng, a reverent hush prevailed, the aroma of flowers overflowing on the altar hung in the air, candles flickered, and a tower bell gently tolled. As police created a wedge and held back the crowds, ten burly officers toted Ned's ornate gold casket from the hearse into the sanctuary, where his body lay in state for an hour. Finally, at 11 a.m., the pallbearers made their procession—with District Attorney Buron Fitts, Dr. Ernest Fishbaugh, Dr. Ellis Jones, and attorney Frank Hogan among their ranks. Though Albert Fall's failing health prevented him from making the journey, his wife and daughter attended to represent him.

Delivered by limousine, Ned's widow Lucy entered the procession, head to toe in black and wreathed in heavy mourning veils, accompanied by her mother-in-law Estelle, both softly sobbing. Leaning on the arms of friends for support, the patriarch himself, Edward L. Doheny Sr., appeared next. He was a sad, broken figure shuffling slowly, head bent low, face creased with grief. It was not lost on anyone who laid eyes on the aged tycoon how the once determined, hard-driving man who'd accumulated so much, how visibly bereft he was at the loss of his heir. It offered little solace that E.L. would, from that point on, be regarded with deep public sympathy, seen as having paid the ultimate price for whatever sins he may have committed during his ascent.

The elaborate service was led by Bishop John J. Cantwell of the regional diocese and Father Martin J. O'Malley, St. Vincent's dynamic priest whose work with at-risk youth later inspired Bing Crosby's Father O'Malley character in the film *Going My Way*, conceived and directed by St. Vincent's parishioner Leo McCarey. In his gloomy-to-stirring sermon, O'Malley praised Ned for his "heart of gold" to the very end, dying in a noble attempt to aid his troubled friend—a sentiment commonly echoed in the press.

Following the mass, a smaller band of mourners drove to a private ceremony—ensured so by security guards—at Forest Lawn Memorial Park in Glendale. As devoutly Catholic as his last rites had been, it was a bit of a surprise that Ned would not go to Cavalry Cemetery, the prominent Catholic high society resting place east of downtown. But his casket was instead delivered to the more broadly Christian (yet still segregated) Forest Lawn, interred on the rolling green knoll Sunrise Slope in the Temple of Santa Sabina. The temple featured a 16th-century marble canopy over a sarcophagus distinguished by Venetian mosaics of beaten gold, first constructed at the Santa Sabina Basilica on one of the Seven Hills of Rome and delivered to Los Angeles two years earlier—it was said to have once contained the remains of its namesake Italian saint. Between the exalting sermon and the glorious final resting place, Ned Doheny was as close to canonization as he might get. Weeks later, his father would quietly have the graves of Ned's mother and sister relocated and placed at his side.

One day later, a few hundred mourners assembled to pay respects to Hugh Plunkett with a private funeral service at the White Company Mortuary downtown, awash with flowers sent by the Doheny family in an apparent gesture of grace and goodwill. Carrying the reproached theme further, Ned's brothers-in-law Warren and Clark Smith, and E.L. Doheny's confidential secretary R.M. Sands joined Hugh's roommate George Riley and four others to serve as pallbearers. Harriett Marion Hall, accompanied by two friends, stood slightly apart from the grieving Plunkett family, surrounded by the many friends Hugh accumulated during his lifetime. Rev. Dr. George Davidson, the Episcopal minister from St. John's Church, extolled Hugh's devotion to his duties, even as he acknowledged the shock, and even the enigma, of his end, noting, "I do not think disease, gunshot or accident is the cause of death. They are but the incident…The cause we may not know," he said. "It is difficult for us to understand why. Perhaps we shall never know."

Hugh's casket was transported to his final resting place, which by no small coincidence was also at Forest Lawn's Sunrise Slope, in a modest plot near an olive tree just under fifty paces away from the mausoleum containing Ned Doheny's remains. For seventeen years, one had never been far from the other's side. Now they would be companions for eternity.

It all proved too much to bear for Hugh's twenty-year-old sister Isabell, who swooned immediately after the burial, prompting their brother Robert to also faint. Hugh's loss took a terrible toll on the entire family, including his otherwise stoic father Charles, who suffered a stroke two days after the funeral. Two years later, in 1931, Robert would make a scene storming into a sordid crime-themed sideshow on South Main Street where photos of Ned and Hugh's gruesome death scene—taken by Les White—had somehow found their way out of the D.A.'s files and were on view to the public for a small fee. Robert angrily tore down the displays; exhibitor Leo Gotch and six associates, despite having legal permits and passing a police inspection, were tried for libeling the dead. Arguing that it was simply an attempt at civic moralizing, teaching that crime does not pay, the men were acquitted.

From the outset, the Plunkett family privately refused to believe Hugh murdered Ned and committed suicide, concluding that the Dohenys were covering up the truth in service of some greater purpose known only to them. The Plunketts bore it stoically, brooding and nursing resentment, rebelling in their way: family members later revealed the Dohenys purchased burial plots alongside Hugh's at Forest Lawn for his family. Only Hugh's mother Clara Bell accepted, unable to bear the thought of Hugh facing eternity alone, and was interred alongside him in 1931; Hugh's father and siblings refused to join them.

A month after Ned and Hugh were laid to rest, perhaps in an attempt to escape the pall that had fallen over Greystone, E.L. Doheny took his five grandchildren to a rodeo in Phoenix, Arizona, where he was joined by his old compatriot, Albert Fall. The two men shared fond, dusty memories of horses, cowboys, prospectors, and their days at the poker tables together. Seven months later, without testimony from the two dead young men, Fall was convicted of accepting a bribe in the Teapot Dome scandal, becoming the first former cabinet member to be sentenced to prison, serving nine months and falling into financial ruin. Thus, E.L. was soon back in court for his own bribery trial in 1930. His attorney Frank Hogan, despite failing to exonerate Fall, proved every bit the legal Houdini the press often dubbed him: Hogan risked putting E.L. on the witness stand, and despite the oil baron's pervading depression and ill health, Doheny equated himself admirably, earning the jury's admiration—and sympathies, in a poignant moment when E.L. visibly choked up at the mention of Ned's name. Pushing his gambit further, Hogan took the stand to dramatically recount Ned's prior testimony in the dead man's own words, bringing tears not only to E.L. and Estelle's eyes, but also to many of the courtroom spectators. Ned Doheny, Hogan told the jury, was "speaking to you from the grave" to clear his father's good name. Miraculously, the strategy worked: the jury found E.L. not guilty.

Though he'd escaped prison, the aged oilman—shattered since Ned's death—remained a recluse, caged by increasingly spiraling health and abiding grief. On September 8, 1935, with his wife, daughter-in-law, and grandchildren at his side, Edward Lawrence Doheny, Sr., died at age seventy-nine, having lived twice as long as his son and then some. Following an even grander funeral than Ned's—at St. Vincent's, naturally—he was buried among the region's Catholic elite in the Doheny mausoleum at Cavalry Cemetery. His wife Estelle, who dutifully destroyed his personal papers and records upon his death, joined him there twenty-three years later.

Dr. Ernest Clyde Fishbaugh continued in his role as a respected physician to the social elite of Beverly Hills, Hollywood, and Los Angeles. He attended famous names with medical woes, many of whom carried a whiff of infamy, including silent star Mabel Normand (tuberculosis), Mexican screen siren Dolores Del Rio (near-fatal kidney failure), film comic Harry Langdon (influenza), film noir femme fatale Joan Bennett (broken bones after falling from a horse), stage musical impresario Florenz Ziegfeld (an ultimately fatal case of pleurisy), and the controversial wife of even more controversial theater owner Alexander Pantages while she was in jail and he was on trial (nervous collapse and bronchitis). He also treated but failed to save movie star and "sex goddess" Jean Harlow, who suffered from uremic poisoning and, taking an unexpected turn for the worse, died suddenly at age twenty-six in 1937.

The prosperous doctor's own life was not without scandal: in 1936, his ex-wife took him to court for aggressively re-wooing her but then breaking his promise to remarry, all while he was carrying on with a married society woman. Fishbaugh instead married his mistress; three years after their wedding, despondent over stock market losses and in precarious mental health, she committed suicide by slashing her throat with a razor in the bathroom while he spoke with servants downstairs. His union with his third wife Hortense proved far more stable, and the two were highly popular socialites and party hosts living in Pacific Palisades. He died at ninety in 1975.

In the aftermath of the traumatic double deaths, the Doheny family and servants at Greystone were understandably unnerved when it appeared in late October of 1930 that Greystone might be haunted. For several nights in a row, the staff heard soft "phantom footsteps" in the mansion during the wee hours, but searches turned up nothing and the home's pricey possessions remained securely in their places. Were the restless spirits of the slain men roaming Greystone's halls?

Finally, one night around 2 a.m., security guard William Patch was making rounds in the basement when he heard the eerie sound of footsteps in the darkness. Patch waited in the shadows and, catching a glimpse of a lit match against the basement's blackness, pounced on a phantom figure: Ernest Perplies, a very alive twenty-year-old homeless drifter recently arrived from East Prussia and struggling to find work at the dawn of the Great Depression. He'd scaled Greystone's gate and made a hidden camp on one of the estate's well-forested ridges. Each night, after home's lights has gone out, he slipped past the mansion guards and inside an open basement window, tiptoeing barefoot through the hallways, bypassing tony silverware and priceless antiquities. Instead, he'd help himself to small samplings of the pantry's plentiful food supply that no one would notice missing—just enough to survive. Patch took the youth to the Beverly Hills jail, where Perplies ate his fill of bread and water; later, on Halloween day, the "ghost" received a suspended sentence, was taken in by a sympathetic West Los Angeles couple, and given a job with their limousine service. Greystone's spooky, otherworldly air, especially at night, would give rise to much spectral speculation in the following decades.

For Lucy Smith Doheny, the time came to exorcise her home's lingering ghosts over the months and years to follow. One of the first things she did was legally change the name of her youngest son, Timothy Hugh, so dubbed after her husband's closest friend, now also formally his killer.

That unpleasant reminder erased, the lad became Timothy Michael, the strongest-willed of her brood, with a defiant spirit equal to her own controlling inclinations. Tim's constant challenges to her imposed order would long vex Lucy.

As had ever been her nature, Lucy became the domineering, even iron-fisted, central figure of both the Doheny and Smith clans, her nickname "Sweetheart" uttered with thinly veiled sarcasm. In widowhood, Lucy was the sole mistress of Greystone, her children well-provided for. E.L. shrewdly dodged the government's forthcoming estate tax by dividing and dispersing much of his fortune before he and Ned died, leaving her family with a personal fortune of nearly $15 million. In keeping with Ned's great affection for USC, Lucy added $50,000 to E.L.'s $1 million endowment to build the university's first freestanding library. The Edward Lawrence Doheny, Jr. Memorial Library opened in 1932 as one of the most advanced libraries in the nation, designed to hold as many as half a million volumes—its capacity would double over time and would include special collections, archives of several film and television companies, a vast array of audio recordings, and a wealth of East Asian collections. The stately Italian Romanesque building remains today as a shining architectural landmark. It boasts exterior statues of William Shakespeare and Dante Alighieri by sculptor Joseph Conradi; windows by renowned stained-glass artist Wilbur Herbert Burnham; bas reliefs by sculptor Robert Merrell Gage; and, in the Treasure Room, murals portraying the history of the printed word by Samuel Armstrong (later one of the directors of Walt Disney's *Fantasia*, *Dumbo*, and *Bambi*), all under the unwavering watch of a marble bust of Ned Doheny by sculptor Mario Korbel.

Her offspring's financial futures and Ned's legacy secured, that same year Lucy married stockbroker Leigh M. Battson, who'd helped sell several of E.L.'s oil lands. They had a small ceremony before the marble fireplace in the Living Room at Greystone—exactly two years and two days after Ned's death—where they'd continue to reside for many years. Battson converted the South Guest Room, the once bloody murder scene, into an uber-masculine study and game room. Soon, the estate transformed back into the spectacular society palace it was intended to be; celebrated guests like Somerset Maugham, W.H. Auden, Jules Stein, Bing Crosby, Bob Hope, and even British aristocracy visited for parties and getaways. Greystone became, with all its expanse, a warm home for the family, which thrived and expanded to include new generations boasting their own accomplishments. Two of Ned and Lucy's fourteen grandchildren even achieved their own celebrity: Dickie Dell's son became the influential science fiction and fantasy author Larry Niven, and Pat's son, also called Ned in honor of his grandfather, became an admired singer-songwriter in the Laurel Canyon music scene. However, the original Ned remained an unknown figure, consigned to the past and rarely discussed among his descendants in anything other than hushed tones, always out of earshot of Lucy, who would live to be 100 years old.

In 1954, the neighboring Doheny Ranch property (gifted to Lucy by her mother-in-law) was sold to subdivision developer Paul W. Trousdale, who turned the expansive 410 acres into tony Trousdale Estates on the expensive condition that the city of Beverly Hills annex the land, where luminaries Frank Sinatra, Dean Martin, Elvis Presley, Groucho Marx, Danny Thomas, Ray Charles, Howard Hughes, and Richard Nixon would soon call home. A year later, with the children gone, the mansion emptier, and the estate's upkeep growing burdensome, Lucy at last vacated Greystone, almost three decades after she and Ned first moved in. She and Battson carved out a ten-acre portion of the property for a considerably smaller, more manageable but undeniably grandiose neighboring estate known as The Knoll, where they would reside. Greystone and its remaining nineteen acres were sold to Chicago industrialist Harry Crown—who owned New York City's Empire State Building—for $1.5 million, but a business merger soon required Crown to stay in Chicago full-time; he never moved in, and the mansion sat unoccupied for years. Battered by inclement weather, looted by vandals, and with its grounds overgrown and untended, the house slumped into disrepair, becoming greyer, gloomier, and ghostlier than ever.

Finally, in 1965, Beverly Hills voters approved the purchase of Greystone for $1.1 million, eager to make use of the grounds for a much-needed twenty-million-gallon municipal reservoir and surrounding park. But in seeking a use for the mansion itself that would convert it into a beacon of civic pride, the city struggled to agree on the right plan, especially as the many uber-wealthy new neighbors who'd settled nearby strenuously objected to any proposal that might bring an unmanageable influx of people, vehicles, and noise.

Finally, Beverly Hills Mayor Phyllis Seaton, wife of esteemed filmmaker George Seaton, hit upon a plan that resonated in the showbiz town: the recently formed American Film Institute, conceived by President John F. Kennedy, would lease the mansion at the bargain price of one dollar per year plus upkeep as a campus for its Center for Advanced Film Studies. The arrangement, composed of a tiny student body of under twenty aspiring filmmakers, an even smaller faculty, and guest lecturers who were among the most revered Hollywood talents, was approved by the NIMBYs. Elia Kazan, Sam Peckinpah, Harold Lloyd, Rouben Mamoulian, Gene Kelly, Don Siegel, Robert Wise, Ray Bradbury, Dalton Trumbo, Budd Schulberg, and Henry Mancini lectured in the very first week in 1969 alone. Some of AFI's earliest students, similarly renowned, included Terrence Malick, Paul Schrader, David Lynch, and cinematographer Caleb Deschanel. Founding director George Stevens, Jr.'s office occupied the infamous South Guest Suite, and the enduring mystery only served to inspire the new cinematic generation: During the fifty-year "class reunion" at the estate, Stevens recalled that "for us, Greystone was a place for storytelling." The estate was named to the National Register of Historic Places in 1976, and AFI would remain at Greystone until 1982, relocating to its current conservatory compound in the Hollywood Hills.

Having launched new generations of filmmaking talent, Greystone was ready for its close-up. While the grounds remained a public park hosting countless public and private events, the mansion became one of the most-used filming locations in Southern California. The Dohenys allowed 20th Century Fox and director Otto Preminger to shoot scenes for 1947's *Forever Amber* there, while Henry Crown frequently leased the property in the 1960s to studios for films like Jerry Lewis's *The Disorderly Orderly* and Bette Davis's *Dead Ringer*. Over time Greystone boasted an impressive array of appearances in films, television series, commercials, photo shoots, and music videos—highlights include *The Big Lebowski*, *The Witches of Eastwick*, *The Bodyguard*, *X-Men*, *Spider-Man*, *Batman and Robin*, *Eraserhead*, *Colombo*, *Mission: Impossible*, *Murder, She Wrote*, *Gilmore Girls*, *Alias*, and, for the 1981 wedding of superstar soap couple Luke and Laura, *General Hospital*. The music video for Elton John's "I Want Love" features a long, lingering look of the mansion's magnificent, if bare, first floor, following Robert Downey, Jr. in one sweeping, continuous tracking shot.

But filmmaker Paul Thomas Anderson took verisimilitude to an entirely new level with his 2007 film *There Will Be Blood*, loosely inspired by Upton Sinclair's novel *Oil!*—itself loosely derived from aspects of the life of E.L. Doheny. The shocking, climactic scene features oil tycoon Daniel Plainview (played by Daniel Day-Lewis) committing a brutal murder in the bowling alley of his mammoth estate, portrayed by Greystone, which

Anderson shot in the mansion's two-lane alley, meticulously restored to its sleek original state for the scene. "Because that mansion has been used so many times in films, it's kind of this notorious location," Anderson, who wondered if he could do something unique with the familiar locale, told *The A.V. Club*. "It's definitely pretty ghostly around there, without question. Daniel called it a pyramid that Doheny built to himself. I think that fits. It's kind of a mad place."

The Dohenys had gone, but against long odds, cloaked and re-cloaked in fresh layers of carefully manufactured glamour, Greystone endured—indeed "as permanent as the pyramids," as its builders predicted. The only thing that might outlive its mystique would be its mystery.

The cynical deputy Leslie White encountered in the morgue as he poured over the bodies of Ned Doheny and Hugh Plunkett proved prophetic: "Old Man Doheny" *was* too big to monkey with. It seemed Buron Fitts had caved to the tremendous political pressure a man as powerful and deep-pocketed as E.L. Doheny could exert, and let the truth be buried with both men. He wondered if Fitts, sitting amid the Doheny's elite circle during Ned's funeral, had even agreed to a payoff or future favor-trade. The D.A. was nothing if not ambitious, and the oil baron was a fine ally to have in his corner down the line. But White would later write he learned his boss had "made a valiant attempt to get at the truth; how valiant it took me a long time to appreciate."

This was, after all, really big stuff.

White stifled his moral outrage and tried to put the case behind him, even as some fellow lawmen and local newshounds ribbed him, even castigated him, for his initial zeal to challenge the Dohenys' script. "I was accused of everything of being a fake to a plain fool," he'd reflect. "I was ready to agree with the latter definition." When his politically adroit captain Lucien Wheeler chided him for not "letting sleeping dogs lie" before definitively proving his suspicions, White snapped, "How can you prove a thing like that unless you're allowed to investigate it?" All Wheeler could do in response was shrug.

But White wasn't the only one who believed a very different version of the officially recorded events had transpired at Greystone Mansion on February 16, 1929. Some mainstream newspapers had gotten wind of the powder wound discrepancies and raised questions—until the coroner's report stifled them. For a while, the local underground press agitated for a closer look at Ned and Hugh's role in the Teapot Dome scandal, until E.L.'s federal acquittal made that pursuit seem like folly. Lucien Wheeler had taken great pains when talking to the press to quash theories that a sinister third party—perhaps a burglar caught in the act, or maybe an assassin paid to silence the men—had actually killed both and escaped. But as the story quickly passed from breaking news into local legend, speculation about exactly what happened between Ned and Hugh began to emerge.

Could the role of the killer and the victim have been reversed? Clearly, the two friends had clashed over Hugh's increasingly fragile physical and mental condition and continued refusal to seek treatment at a sanitarium, or even an extended vacation. But then a probate study of Hugh's financial records revealed that on February 2, two weeks before their deaths and within the period in which Dr. Merrill reported Hugh was significantly improving, the secretary purchased socks, underpants, and undershirts by the dozen from a Hollywood shop, along with an array of supplies suggesting he was planning an extended trip—possibly to a hospital, possibly to Zion Canyon on that planned ten-day trip Dr. Merrill divulged. He also had his Cabriolet serviced, replacing the spark plugs. These appeared to be the acts of a man planning ahead, not contemplating ending his life. While all corners acknowledged his nervous state, allegations of a generally belligerent attitude (suggested by his ex-wife and his houseman) didn't jibe with the impressions of others who knew him best: his family, who idolized him, and his roommate. "He would not intentionally harm anyone," said George Riley. "He was never a man to start an argument."

But *something* ignited a quarrel between Ned and Hugh in the wake of the two February 16 intervention attempts. Based on his reported telephone conversation with Lucy, Hugh had been particularly disturbed by something Ned said to him at his Cochran Avenue apartment. Lucy later tried to dismiss Ned's mystery comment as said in the heat of the moment, but Hugh wasn't satisfied. Was his temper and paranoia really exacerbated by drug use and sleeplessness, or was it possible, with the forthcoming Teapot Dome trial looming over E.L. Doheny, that Hugh was being pressured to become conveniently unavailable to testify by checking himself into a sanitarium, out of reach of subpoenas and federal prosecutors? And if he wasn't willing to commit himself, would Ned do it for him? Hugh knew the power and reach of the Doheny name and unlimited checkbook: would his closest friend have him forcibly confined, possibly indefinitely, to shield the father to whom he owed ever greater fealty? It certainly seemed that Hugh felt cornered in some way, desperate for Ned to grant him some kind of escape.

Hugh also knew, more intimately than anyone, precisely what the Dohenys were capable of in pursuit of their goals. Was Ned pressuring, even threatening, Hugh to give up his freedom? Was Hugh pushing back, insisting on assurances he'd be guaranteed a smooth path out of the asylum? Did he want money for his trouble? Did Hugh actually bring the Colt Bisley into the house to bolster his argument, or was Ned the one to retrieve it? Despite a potentially whitewashed coroner's report, it appeared obvious that, over nearly ninety minutes together in the guest suite, both men had been drinking. Could it have instead been Ned who—under pressure himself and frustrated by Hugh's intractability and the dire consequences it posed for his family—exploded in a fit of rage, further enflamed by scotch, and shot Hugh? Then, in a wave of remorse over snuffing out the life of his dearest friend, turned the pistol on himself, leaving the truth to be sanitized and obscured? With the Dohenys scarcely able to bear another scandal, was Ned's body repositioned by his family's factotums to appear more convincingly the victim, the gun wiped clean of prints, then heated in an oven in advance of the police arrival and stories gotten straight before interrogation?

Perhaps…? Possibly…? Maybe…?

These were all reasonable questions that Les White and his colleagues never got to explore.

The underground press also floated another theory that would gradually gain a foothold and, over the course of one hundred years since the incident at Greystone, would become embedded in the subsequent lore: did Ned and Hugh's much-discussed closeness stem from a secret sexual relationship or concealed romance? "He acted as a secretary to Ned, but their relationship was more than that of friends," Frederic R. Kellogg, one of E.L. Doheny's longtime corporate attorneys, told the press obliquely in the wake of the killings, which some might read as coded phrasing. Certainly the notion of the inseparable secretary-companion was even then a familiar trope to cloak a closeted gay affair.

In the 1920s, Los Angeles, emerging as a cosmopolitan center, boasted a vibrant underground culture of gay and lesbian bars, nightclubs, cabaret shows, and drag performances, especially during Prohibition. The sex lives of Hollywood's often iconoclastic, increasingly wealthy artists tested societal taboos—but sodomy and oral sex were still legally punishable crimes:

discretion, especially among high-profile figures, was advisable. In the case of Ned and Hugh, the rumor mill targeted the pair's final resting places as a tantalizing clue: despite the Doheny family's demonstrated Catholic faith—powered by Estelle's devout piety, famously expressed in her extensive collection of rare religious texts, eventually including an original Gutenberg Bible—if Ned were gay it would be unthinkable to bury him on the consecrated ground of Calvary Cemetery, where all the Catholic power players of L.A. were interred, no matter what the official story was. This could have prompted his placement at Forest Lawn; if so, presumably the family quietly granted the proximity of Hugh's grave there as well as an unspoken concession to keep them as close in death as in life.

It's an evocative scenario, inspiring further theories: that the tragedy was the result of either a dramatic fallout or mutual death pact between tortured lovers; or, more melodramatically, that Lucy discovered them in a compromising tryst and, horrified or enraged, found a pistol and shot both men dead herself (notwithstanding that she continued to reside at the scene of the crime for over two decades despite the means and, in the sympathetic eyes of the public, the rationale to move anywhere else in the world). The concept of a sexual relationship or passionate romance between Ned and Hugh is well within the circumstantial realm of possibility. But in the near-century since that fateful night, no tangible evidence or anecdotal source emerged to concretely substantiate the conjecture—no Doheny or Plunkett family member, confidante, colleague or servant ever testified to any secret relationship; no record suggesting a more intimate connection has surfaced; White's recounting of the forensic discrepancies makes no such intimations, overt or implied. Decades later, the stepson of Hugh's brother Robert said the family was upset by the rumors, adamant there was no such relationship. Ned's namesake grandson, singer-songwriter Ned Doheny, said "Among the ranks of my family, it's held to be a spurious idea. I suspect it arose from all the time that Ned spent alone, away from his family. I can't be any more specific than that." Even Doheny money could buy only so much silence, for so long.

The cemetery arrangement? Suicide, too, was deemed a mortal sin, and if Ned had killed himself he would be denied a Catholic burial, which again could explain the choice of Forest Lawn. Perhaps the Dohenys had stage-managed the death scene to protect his public reputation but decided they couldn't completely shield him from the judgment of their faith.

Perhaps. Possibly.

For everything that was seemingly revealed about Hugh Plunkett in the days following his death, Ned Doheny remained elusive—almost deliberately so. There was virtually no attempt to bring the memory of who Ned actually was to life for his descendants, largely due to Lucy's steadfast refusal to speak of him; even his namesake grandson found him to be "a huge piece to be missing" in the family mosaic. There's some guessing at a possible dark side: rumors, difficult to substantiate, suggest Ned, under pressure from the Teapot Dome trial, was drinking excessively and isolating himself, possibly even spending most of his time at home holed up in the South Guest Room. E.L. was an oft-absent figure for most of Ned's youth; Ned's mother Carrie suffered from depression and committed suicide—also re-staged to look like an accidental poisoning, as it was officially recorded. "Apparently Ned had a great sense of humor and was a lot of fun, but I wouldn't be surprised if there were some issues with depression," his grandson Ned said. "I have a strong sense there was loneliness there. With his dad away all the time and his mom dying like that, I would think there would be some unfinished business."

Perhaps.

Leslie T. White tried to put the Greystone case behind him in the months that followed, welcomed a son, became an expert criminologist, bought a house in Glendale and continued to do standout work for the district attorney's investigation bureau, including landmark cases featuring more high-profile, powerful names, like theater impresario Alexander Pantages and the infamous "Love Mart" prostitution ring. But the Doheny-Plunkett case was just the first of a too-frequent string of his own personal "Chinatown" conundrums in which White found his hands tied by the outside influence of politics, graft or both, while justice went subverted and unserved. He grew increasingly disillusioned and cynical, concerned that one day he too would be infected by the rot of corruption. When D.A. Buron Fitts uncharacteristically stalled the Love Mart case and intentionally let it fall apart, wealthy realtor John P. Mills—who had virgin teenagers delivered to him daily—walked while the ring's procurer Olive Day—who'd cooperated with the D.A. at great peril and whom White befriended and grown to respect—took the fall. White suspected Fitts—the once-crusading reformer who, as politically savvy and ambitious as ever, seemed to be increasingly pulling strings to quash controversies for increasingly powerful film studios like Paramount Pictures and Metro-Goldwyn-Meyer—was likely on the take as well.

White soon resigned. "I like the work, but I hate the politics," he told Fitts. "You can't stay in it and be honest—not really honest…Sooner or later you get seriously jammed up. You know that better than I do."

If Fitts didn't, he would find out: White's superior Lucien Wheeler had quit the department shortly after the Doheny case was buried for a more lucrative career as a private detective, immediately becoming a formidable adversary to the D.A.'s investigators working on behalf of wealthy criminal defendants—including John P. Mills. After the Love Mart case was spiked, it came out that Wheeler paid $18,500 provided by his client Mills to purchase an orange grove in Claremont for twice its value—the property was, not coincidentally, owned by Fitts's sister. Fitts was tried for bribery and perjury; though not convicted, the D.A. never escaped the taint of scandal despite a full, if tumultuous, three-term tenure in office that lasted until 1940. Ever prone to physical danger, Fitts appeared to have an actual target on his back: he was shot at by a mystery assailant in 1937; and while serving in the Pacific as an intelligence officer for the Army Air Corps during World War II he was wounded yet again, earning a Purple Heart for his pain. In 1973, suffering the debilitating aftereffects of his many brushes with death, Fitts, at 78, turned a Smith & Wesson revolver on himself and committed suicide. Curiously, the pistol he used was identical to the long-missing gun used in the still-unsolved murder of director William Desmond Taylor, which Fitts himself investigated back in 1922.

Wheeler fared better, divorcing his wife to marry his office Gal Friday three decades his junior. During wartime he headed the West Coast branch of the Office of Strategic Services, precursor to the CIA, before his death at 73 in 1950. Beverly Hills Police Chief Charley Blair, who may have breathed a sigh of relief after deferring to more experienced detective divisions and thereby sparing his still-fledgling force from facing a compromised role in the Greystone investigation, had many more years of service ahead of him.

After resigning on principal, Les White would see better fortunes than any of them—unlike the prototypical noir protagonist, he evaded being crushed by his disillusionment and doomed by the relentless machinery of the system. Even before he quit the D.A.'s unit, on the advice of his good friend Erle Stanley Gardner he'd launched what would become a prolific and prosperous career as a writer: his second-ever submission sold, and soon his stories—typically smartly plotted, authentically detailed detective yarns starring earnest straight-arrow sleuths who viewed justice in black-and-white terms, as he once had himself, unlike the jaded sophisticates of Dashiell Hammett or the noble but tarnished knights of Raymond Chandler—were in high demand among pulp magazines' editors. His work appeared in *Black Mask*, *Dime Detective*, *Detective Story*, *Dragnet*, *Argosy* and many more, as well as higher-class, higher-circulation publications including *The Saturday Evening Post*, *Collier's*, *Blue Book* and *Better Homes and Gardens*, where he wrote feature articles about more esoteric subjects like flying, deep-sea fishing, dogs, forensics and investigative techniques. "A new sense of power possessed me," he wrote. "I felt that I had at last discovered the work to which I was best adapted." Within a few short years he was thriving professionally, able to return to Ventura County where he purchased a spread in Santa Cruz he dubbed, almost as evocatively as Greystone, "Mystery Ranch."

In 1936—a year after Edward L. Doheny, Sr., died—White published what was likely his most compelling. and most enduring, work: a hard-boiled and candid—blunt, even—memoir centered largely around his experiences with the Los Angeles District Attorney's office. *Me, Detective* was a richly detailed and largely unsparing account of the political obstacles and corrupt hurdles that White faced as he tried to ferret out truth and dispense justice in several sensational cases well known to his reading public—including his previously unrevealed findings in the murder-suicide at Greystone. The book garnered rave reviews and sold briskly across the country, and White's bracing candor, sharp turn of phrase and eye for detail were celebrated with speaking engagements around Southern California.

One reader who had a particularly keen interest in the details of the Doheny case was Hugh Plunkett's brother Robert, still brooding over Hugh's depiction in the press seven years prior. According to his family, Robert—who'd even previously approached White, but the detective was muzzled by dutiful confidentiality while still working for the D.A.—scoured L.A. attempting to find a copy of *Me, Detective*, only to come up empty. He would tell his family he'd been told the same story by several booksellers: the Doheny family had purchased every volume in the area.

As a result of his success, White authored novels drawn from his life experience, police thrillers like *Harness Bull* and *Homicide*. His pulp stories would be optioned by Hollywood studios for film and, eventually, television adaptation—notably Raoul Walsh's *Northern Pursuit* starring Errol Flynn, a pair of original screenplays for Columbia Pictures (*Behind Prison Gates* and *The Unwritten Code*), and an episode of *Vice Squad* based on *Harness Bull*. Eventually—through three more children and two more marriages—White segued into historical fiction, novels, and how-tos on his personal enthusiasms, like *Scale Model Railroading*. He left California behind for the also-Greystone-evoking White Anchors Farm on the Potomac River near Montross, Virginia, living there until his death in 1967 at age sixty-four.

But back on January 11, 1936, Les White was still solidly grounded in the pulp detective genre, invited by legendary *Black Mask* editor Joe Shaw to a soiree for the magazine's West Coast-based regular contributors, held at the handsome Nickabob Café on Western Avenue. Along with White, the gathering included Dwight Babcock, soon to embark on a long, accomplished career as a Hollywood screenwriter; John K. Butler, creator of *Black Mask*'s popular cabbie detective Steve Midnight and soon Republic Pictures's most prolific writers of low-budget Westerns; Eric Taylor, who'd adapt Erle Stanley Gardner's Perry Mason and Chester Gould's Dick Tracy for the screen; Arthur K. Barnes, who'd more fruitfully shift to science fiction within a few years; Herbert H. Stinson, a *Los Angeles Tribune* crime reporter who moonlighted as a pulp writer; W.T. Ballard, former B-movie writer-director-producer whose Hollywood fixer character Bill Lennox was a big hit for *Black Mask*; Norbert Davis, a specialist in darkly humorous hardboiled tales who cut his career short through suicide; and Horace McCoy, an ex-sportswriter and broadcaster who'd just published his first novel, *They Shoot Horses, Don't They?*, later regarded as an essential noir portrait of Depression Era Los Angeles.

And there were the magazine's two superstars. With his commitment to authenticity, sharply drawn characters, and a wearily cynical worldview, Ex-Pinkerton investigator Dashiell Hammett had essentially created the hardboiled form and elevated *Black Mask* as it published his serialized stories *Red Harvest*, *The Dain Curse*, *The Maltese Falcon*, and *The Glass Key*, each of which would become defining novels of the genre—no one knew it yet, but he'd already written his final book, *The Thin Man*, two years prior and embarked on what would be a lucrative but checkered foray into writing for Hollywood.

If Hammett was the reigning master, then Raymond Chandler was the heir apparent, even though he was six years older. Chandler came to fiction writing late in life, after a prosperous corporate career in L.A.'s petroleum industry, where he was well-versed in the machinations of powerful oil barons, including E.L. Doheny, yet his prodigious appetites for alcohol, absenteeism, and skirt-chasing had gotten him excommunicated. But in just three years, he'd established himself as *Black Mask*'s rising star. He was slow and meticulous but wrote with a sly, appraising eye and potent facility for poetic grittiness and biting wit—and Los Angeles, with its inherent blend of the sordid and the sensational, was his muse. He was two years away from publishing his first masterwork novel, *The Big Sleep*.

This was the first and only meeting between the two future literary lions of crime fiction—both were already mutually impressed with each other's craft, though each also craved greater appreciation outside their genre confines, which wouldn't come for either for many years. That night Chandler, a champion tippler, found he admired Hammett's "unspoiled" attitude and "fearful capacity for Scotch." Les White was certainly thrilled to be included in the select fraternity of hardboiled scribes, and to commemorate the occasion, the former photographer brought along his camera and snapped a portrait of the group, staying behind the lens himself. White's shot remains the only known photograph of Hammett and Chandler together.

Though the full extent of White and Chandler's interaction that night, and possibly after, is unknown, their shared professional interest in the volatile, perpetually scandalous L.A. crime scene of the day and, given Chandler's oil industry background, the intrigue involving the Doheny family suggests they had plenty to talk about; from unique insider perches, both had info, gossip, and rumor to spare. White must have mentioned that *Me, Detective* was due to be published in August, and it seems Chandler—even in L.A., where the Doheny buy-out made copies scare—eventually got his hands on the memoir. Because the Dohenys and their showy displays of wealth and dominant exertion of power were catnip to Chandler, his fascination eventually began to find expression in his own writing.

His descriptions in *The Big Sleep* of the estate of the Sternwood family, whose fortune was built on oil, are specifically evocative of Greystone Mansion, closely capturing its overt luxuries and imposing ambiance. Later, through his sleuth Phillip Marlowe's sardonic take on the Grayle estate in *Farewell, My Lovely*, Chandler echoed White's impression of Greystone: "It was smaller than Buckingham Palace, rather gray for California, and probably had fewer windows than the Chrysler Building." Without question, *Me, Detective* and Les White—like Marlowe, a former investigator for the D.A.'s office whose uncompromising moral code set him on his own path—made an indelible impression on Chandler.

Finally, in a passage within his 1942 novel *The High Window*, Chandler went even further than White had, putting forth a full-throated interpretation of what happened at Greystone. Deriving from White's evidence collected and prevailing backroom whispers, the author had Marlowe bluntly and unsparingly recount the "Cassidy case" to a cop named Breeze.

"Cassidy was a very rich man, a multimillionaire. He had a grown-up son. One night the cops were called to his home and young Cassidy was on his back on the floor with blood all over his face and a bullet hole in the side of his head. His secretary was lying on his back in an adjoining bathroom, with his head against the second bathroom door, leading to a hall, and a cigarette burned out between his fingers on his left hand, just a short burned-out stub that had scorched the skin between his fingers. A gun was lying by his right hand. He was shot in the head, not a contact wound. A lot of drinking had been done. Four hours had elapsed since the deaths and the family doctor had been there for three of them. Now, what did you do with the Cassidy case?"

Breeze sighed. "Murder and suicide during a drinking spree. The secretary went haywire and shot young Cassidy. I read it in the papers or something. Is that what you want me to say?"

"You read it in the papers," I said, "but it wasn't so. What's more you knew it wasn't so and the D.A. knew it wasn't so and the D.A.'s investigators were pulled off the case within a matter of hours. There was no inquest. But every crime reporter in town and every cop on every homicide detail knew it was Cassidy that did the shooting, that it was Cassidy that was crazy drunk, that it was the secretary who tried to handle him and couldn't and at last tried to get away from him, but wasn't quick enough. Cassidy's was a contact wound and the secretary's was not. The secretary was left-handed, and he had a cigarette in his left hand when he was shot. Even if you are right-handed, you don't change a cigarette over to your other hand and shoot a man while casually holding the cigarette.

They might do that on 'Gang Busters,' but rich men's secretaries don't do it. And what were the family and the family doctor doing during the four hours they didn't call the cops? Fixing it so there would only be a superficial investigation. And why were no tests of the hands made for nitrates? Because you didn't want the truth. Cassidy was too big. But this was a murder case too, wasn't it?"

"The guys were both dead," Breeze said. "What the hell difference did it make who shot who?"

"Did you ever stop to think," I asked, "that Cassidy's secretary might have had a mother or a sister or a sweetheart—or all three? That they had their pride and their faith and their love for a kid who was made out to be a drunken paranoiac because his boss's father had a hundred million dollars?"

"The Cassidy case" was a ripe metaphor for corruption and a veiled but searing indictment: it took Raymond Chandler's noir fiction to at long last depict the plausible noir reality that unfolded in the hulking, fortress-like estate looming above Beverly Hills, ever-emanating overwhelming privilege and power—though even Chandler skirted the Teapot Dome tie, which he had to have been aware of. But the truth remained as elusive and unknowable as ever. Two men who had shared a deep bond of friendship, one born to the manor, the other invited inside, dwelled together forever in The Big Sleep—death—for reasons perpetually obscured. Ultimately Breeze's question lingers: what the hell difference *did* it make who shot who?

Les White decided that the answer was not nearly as important as the lesson offered: "In the case of extreme wealth, right or wrong, you had to be extremely careful, and there was clearly a defined line beyond which it was professional suicide to trespass," he would write.

And while he was never the literary stylist Chandler was, White succinctly captured the conundrum when justice and money—lots and lots of money—collided: "You can't convict a million dollars."

TO CATCH A THIEF

"I always tried to be a gentleman."
—**Gerard Graham Dennis**

Late on a quiet evening in 1948, Gerry Dennis strolled silently through Bing Crosby's darkened home. The fifteen-room mansion on 594 South Mapleton Drive, designed by architectural master Gordon Kaufman, sat on six acres atop a gently sloping knoll south of Sunset Boulevard in Holmby Hills, the ultra-elite West Los Angeles enclave nestled snugly between Beverly Hills and Bel-Air. The home's opulence reflected the mellow-voiced, forty-five-year-old singer-actor's status in Hollywood as the most popular—and top-paid—entertainer of the day. Even Gerry, who'd been inside some of the area's most extravagant estates, had to be impressed.

Neither Crosby, his wife Dixie, nor their four young sons, who'd been living in the grand home for five years, had greeted their late-night visitor as he arrived. That was by Gerry's design, of course, having bypassed the front door to enter through the garage. Nevertheless, he was dressed for the occasion, clad in a freshly pressed dark blue suit, a crisp white shirt and tie covered discreetly by a black silk scarf, and a black slouch hat pulled low over his handsome face. The hat made it hard to see another, less fashionable sartorial touch: a black silk mask. Inside his suit coat, hidden in a secret pocket, was a loaded .32-caliber semi-automatic Luger.

As he noiselessly made his way through the garage on his way into the house, he passed the custom 1947 Cadillac convertible that the owner had acquired directly from the factory floor in Detroit and caught a glimpse of a driver's license clipped to the steering wheel and found the familiar image of Bing Crosby gazing back at him. Gerry could easily imagine Crosby's baritone crooning one of his signature tunes, something peppy like "Swinging on a Star." He had a soft spot for the pipe-smoking pop idol with the family-man-image. He liked Crosby's records, listened to his Philco radio show, watched him on the siler screen playing likable guys like *Going My Way*'s Father O'Malley, and laughed his head off at the *Road* movies the singer did with Bob Hope. He'd even mixed and mingled with Crosby himself at the swankiest of the Sunset Strip nightclubs they both frequented, where Mrs. Crosby's array of glittery, expensive adornments had caught Gerry's scrutinizing eye. Most of all, he admired Crosby's patriotic spirit, providing entertainment to the troops during the War.

"Bing's too decent a fellow," he decided. "I just can't steal from him."

There were plenty more movie stars on his list of hot prospects: Bette Davis, Charlie Chaplin, Heddy Lamarr, Loretta Young, Ronald Colman, Mary Pickford, Jack Benny, Bing and Bob's "Road" movies co-star Dorothy Lamour, and many others. He wasn't so sentimental about them, except maybe that actor Robert Taylor, who everyone said Gerry looked so much like, with his dark looks and neatly trimmed mustache.

He resisted humming "Swinging on a Star" and slipped out of the garage just as silently as he'd entered, navigating his way back over the estate's walls and through its protective landscaping. He walked back to his own shiny Cadillac convertible, parked several blocks away, utterly unobtrusive in the chic neighborhood. No one would realize he'd ever been there.

Many names on Gerry's "prospects" list were known to everyone in America. But who, exactly, was Gerry? By 1949, that was a question on the minds of several concerned parties.

In New York City, to pretty, blonde twenty-four-year-old Eleanor Harris, he was dashing young Jerry Farrell, her first love and common-law-husband, a medical school dropout who'd swept her off her feet in her native Toronto and whisked her away to America. He took Eleanor dancing at swank spots like the Stork Club and on sun-and-fun getaways to Miami Beach. He showered her with jewels and furs bought, he confided, with money made on the sly converting Canadian currency into U.S. dollars in the black market. They once shared a deep bond: Their daughter Wendie, was too young to remember him since he'd vanished one night in 1947, just ten minutes before the police came knocking on their door.

In Detroit, shapely, raven-haired twenty-two-year-old ex-model Gloria Horowitz thought she had an idea about him, too. He was Jerry Woodruff, a suave and wealthy Canadian she'd been introduced to while waiting tables at the cocktail lounge of Manhattan's Belmont Plaza Hotel in July 1947.

His cash was tied up in various ventures, he confided, and in a bid to make his assets more liquid, he was converting real estate interests into jewelry. He persuaded her to help him skirt international currency regulations by selling several thousand dollars in gems at a Philadelphia pawnshop, promising a 10 percent commission. Gloria soon discovered that smooth Jerry Woodruff was, in fact, a lying, no-good fink who had no problem leaving a girl holding the bag when the police showed up at the pawnshop.

And in Beverly Hills, the twenty-four-year-old former Toronto schoolteacher Betty Ritchie was convinced she intimately knew Jerry McKay, a dapper, successful businessman and a fellow Canadian who she met dancing at the Hollywood Palladium in early 1948. He'd made a small fortune during the war, he'd confided, and sold fine jewelry—which shrewdly appraising Jerry bought and on the cheap at auctions—on the side while prepping a new venture selling an automotive safety device. They fell head-over-heels in love, moving in together almost immediately. Though he'd yet to make an honest woman of her due to a failed but lingering marital entanglement, they'd lived as husband and wife—even calling themselves "Mr. and Mrs. McKay"—for nearly a year. While he insisted that she keep her forty-dollar-a-week job, he'd taken her to posh beach resorts across the country and gifted her with a diamond solitaire ring and a $3,500 mink coat. Betty explained all of this to the two Beverly Hills police detectives at the door of the plush apartment she shared with Jerry McKay on Thursday evening, February 17, 1949. Jerry, she told them, had at last flown back East just a few days earlier to obtain a divorce, and they were on the way to making their loving union legal.

There were other names and other occupations. Sometimes he was Jerry McCabe, a prosperous, jet-setting jewelry salesman. Other times he was a wealthy, champagne-swilling playboy and sportsman, or an up-and-coming Hollywood actor, or an eager real estate agent specializing in showplace properties. Some identities had a shred of truth to them. Many did not.

The detectives opened the secret, hidden closet they found in the Oakhurst apartment, fitted with a reinforced door and special lock, discovering nearly $20,000 in luxurious furs—six minks and a particularly pricey karakul—as well as a locked strongbox they pried open. It was overflowing with a dazzling pile of more than 200 diamonds, rubies, pearls, and other gems, as well as loose gold, silver, and platinum—over $100,000 in precious stones and metals. Secreted alongside the treasure trove were a complete set of pry tools and lock picks, equipment for altering and resetting jewelry, and three pistols.

Now the police knew precisely who Gerry was.

He was Gerard Graham Dennis and, along with being an accomplished liar and an irresistible ladies' man with several beautiful yet gullible young women under his spell, he was the most efficient, daring, and successful cat burglar Beverly Hills had ever seen.

Like a cat, Gerry had lived several lives.

The first began on April 15, 1920. Gerard Graham Dennis grew up in the town of St. Catherines, Ontario, nestled between Lake Ontario and the Niagara River, thirty miles from Toronto and about twelve miles inland from the U.S. border. The youngest of three children born to British immigrants Joseph and Julia Cronin Dennis, he called his early upbringing "better than average"—his prosperous family employed a cook, a maid, a nurse, and a gardener. At an early age, he'd become consumed by three great passions: the care and upkeep of his well-turned-out appearance, in service of his second diversion, the pursuit of the opposite sex; his third preoccupation was pilfering. One family friend's memory had Dennis, charming and good-looking even as a child, dangling over a balcony during one of his mother's tea parties, smiling angelically while adroitly—almost imperceptibly—swiping cookies as trays passed by.

Larceny seemed encoded in his DNA: when he was six, his father, an accountant and auditor, was sentenced to two years in prison in Kingston for embezzlement, draining $80,000 from accounts he handled; his aloof, nervous-natured but always tastefully presented mother, an accomplished opera singer who'd given up her career to marry, taught music lessons to make ends meet during her husband's incarceration. The sins of the father, Dennis later insisted, were visited on the son: his classmates teased and ostracized him, and their parents refused to allow their children to play with the offspring of a convicted felon. He claimed he was convinced he'd been pre-judged as an apple that wouldn't fall far from the tree; many of his contemporaries, however, would later deny seeing any such persecution— indeed, his peers were instructed by their parents to never bring up the sensitive subject of his father's fall from grace.

By age eight, Dennis had fallen in with the inevitable bad crowd as the mastermind behind a series of fruit stand knockoffs; at thirteen, his petty crimes sent him in and out of reform school. A local police detective found precious loot secreted throughout Dennis' room: guns, knives, medical instruments, and cameras, plus stashes of jewelry—gemstones tellingly removed. Family, intimates, social workers, and law enforcement constantly urged him to walk a straighter path; over and over, he returned to his crooked impulses. "He would listen very attentively, taking it all in," the detective recalled of the well-mannered boy. "But it never did any good."

Early on, he was preoccupied with beautiful, exquisite things—young women and fine jewelry, first and foremost. He also cultivated his own increasingly handsome appearance with an assiduous grooming and skincare regimen and fastidiously maintained wardrobe. He filed his fingernails to perfection and absolutely *hated* getting his hands dirty. "He felt that he was an exciting, exquisite creature and that the world owed him a living," a female friend recalled. "He expected the world's riches would be handed to him on a diamond-studded platter. When life didn't turn out that way, he chose an exciting and easy way to get what he wanted."

At fourteen, he admitted to stealing sporting goods equipment from a local store and was sent to juvenile court to be scared straight. The judge ordered him to be strapped, but when his mother revoked permission for the punishment, he was released with a warning. Dennis became so trouble-prone that his mother finally reported him to the police as an "incorrigible," but he ran away before he could be turned over to the authorities.

It would be the first of many such vanishing acts, where the boy would simply disappear for long stretches of time.

When his parents, who'd kept their growing incompatibility from polite company, finally divorced that same year, his mother planned to return to England with his sister Mary but, Dennis claimed to overhear her say, *not* with her problematic youngest son. Fearing he'd be placed in a foster home, he ran away. His father, however, quickly remarried in order to provide a comfortable, stable home for his two remaining offspring. Years later, his mother would contend that Dennis's father "stole" Gerry from her a week before she departed and refused to let her take him with her, or to even say goodbye.

In the absence of his oft-aloof mother—with whom he'd had an alternately dependent and fraught relationship—the opposite sex loomed larger in his life as he flexed the power of his considerable charms. He favored fresh-faced, kind-hearted young *naifs*, whose guileless, inexperienced natures allowed them to overlook his nefarious inclinations as he overwhelmed them with his attentions, dazzling girlfriends with tokens of affection that would invariably turn out to be stolen. "He made you feel that you were the only woman in the world," one paramour recalled. "I could have pictured myself running away with him if he wanted me to."

School, expectedly, bored Dennis, though he was a whiz at cracking the locks on his fellow students' lockers, leading to his expulsion at fifteen. By sixteen, he stole his first automobile, a shiny, brand-new vehicle recently delivered to its new owner with its keys awaiting on the front seat—"The temptation was too much," he'd recall. Promptly caught, he experimented with using an alias for the first time—"James Graham Martin," an English lad who'd stowed away to Canada—to prevent police from exposing his misdeeds to his father. But the gambit backfired: Because he'd given a fake name, the magistrate issued sterner-than-usual punishment, sending him to a reformatory for nine months. Once returned, he seemed a different person at home: more helpful, courteous, and honest. None of the family's valuable possessions went missing, he carried heavy packages for his stepmother, he pulled out chairs for elderly neighbors—his principal fault seemed to be his inability to sustain steady employment.

But two years later, after boosting another car, he earned a yearlong stretch at a prison farm, where he'd finally get an education—the reformatory, he recalled, "was a top training school for thieves and criminals." From a faculty of career recidivists Dennis learned the finer points of a life of crime; upon release, he wound up back behind bars within three weeks, an ego-leveling experience. "I was a far less cocky boy," he'd remember. "I knew by now there was much to be learned, and I decided to take things slowly and surely."

Gerry went to work for his father, helping with his accounting books; he demonstrated an aptitude with numbers, but zero interest in hard, honest work. "You're a sucker," he told Joseph. "You'll work till you have humps on your head and never make real money. I'm going to make my pile an easier way." At age nineteen, he wed Gertrude, a local St. Catherines beauty he'd met on a dance floor; a few years older than Gerry, she recognized his larcenous inclinations but was nevertheless over the moon. "Apart from the one twist in his mind, he was one of the finest men I've ever met," she'd recall. He fathered a son and a daughter with her in quick succession before deserting his new family ten months into the marriage, prompted by another incarceration.

Upon release, he was now prepared to put all his extracurricular lessons into practice. Over the next few years, the cities of Toronto, St. Catherines, and Niagara would be plagued by a series of home burglaries, each more slickly executed than the last. He was not only a quick study, he was also an innovator, developing the patterns that would eventually become his *modus operandi*. Grand theft auto had not proven the most successful venture, so he went after a more elegant and profitable goal: jewelry.

Gerry Dennis had taken a powder. In his place in September 1943 was "Jerry Martin."

By all appearances, Gerard James Martin was a robust twenty-three-year-old who, due to what he cryptically referred to as a "childhood ailment," was unable to serve in the military, but was doing his part for the War effort by working as a tool-and-die maker in Toronto's John Inglis & Co. plant, producing Bren light machine guns for the infantry. With so many of Canada's young men off doing battle with the Nazis, the plant was also populated by patriotic ladies lending a hand in the fight against Hitler…and if they caught the eye of one of the few remaining, eligible bachelors while they were at it, well, wasn't that the kind of thing they were all fighting for?

Dennis had matured into a tall, strikingly handsome young man with matinee idol features, steely eyes, and dark hair. Moreover, he'd become quite the charmer, aided by his courtly speaking voice—"Canadian dainty," the dialect common in the Ontario province. A former medical student, Jerry Martin was, the ladies agreed, the plant's prize catch. Nicknamed "lover boy," he had his choice of escorts, but Eleanor Harris—"Ella" to her family, a pretty eighteen-year-old timekeeper who sang in her church choir—was special. Their dates felt like dreams to the impressionable teenager, dancing and dining in all of Toronto's smartest hotels and nightclubs. She fell hard, and he did too, proposing after a whirlwind two-month courtship.

Eleanor's parents disapproved of Jerry's effect on their daughter, always a model offspring "until Jerry came along and turned her head," her mother bemoaned. Amid a rocky on-again, off-again romance, the young couple skirted the era's conventional mores, resulting in an unplanned pregnancy. When Eleanor gave Jerry the news, he responded with a dramatic revelation of his own: he was already married. There were tears, of course, but he reassured her that she was the true love of his life. His divorce, though messy, was pending and until his prior bond was formally severed, he couldn't make their union legal. Adding a baby into the mix further complicated matters. Fortunately, due to his studies as a "former medical student" before tuition money ran out, Jerry "knew all about" discreetly terminating pregnancies via a potion he concocted.

Along with his day job at the plant, "Jerry Martin" had a highly rewarding sideline on the evenings he didn't share with Eleanor. Even on the nights they hit the cocktail circuit, Jerry was "working": he had a way of charming the society types they mingled with—sometimes it seemed he knew more about them than they did themselves. He had a sharp eye for jewelry, and on occasion, after Eleanor admired some moneyed matron's glittery display, Jerry would later gift her with a similar-looking trinket he'd "spotted at auction" and picked up for a pittance. She was flattered and embarrassed by his extravagances, but the gifts were a *steal*, he assured her.

Gerry Dennis had mastered the final trick of his particular trade: the double life.

His considerable powers of persuasion weren't limited to women: he coaxed a respectable young Toronto college professor at elite, private Appleby College—the son of a London, Ontario, clergyman, no less—into his plots. After bonding while working at the plant over the summer and rooming together in Toronto's west end, Dennis used the academic's social connections and familiarity with swanky homes in Rosedale, the city's fashionable residential district, to target lucrative scores. They timed their strikes to when their victims were summering away, using inside knowledge of the estates and the bounties within to execute break-ins. Although Dennis eschewed formal schooling himself, he was always eager to do his homework when it came to planning the big score.

But the scheme fell apart when a woman romantically involved with Dennis found an unfamiliar brassiere in his room and informed the police of his extralegal activities. Her name was kept out of the papers, but Dennis later revealed the informant was Eleanor. Dennis had sent her to the movies while he, under pressure from his paramour, at last discussed finalizing a divorce with his visiting wife Gertrude. Eleanor returned to discover negotiations had somehow resulted in errant lingerie littering Dennis's bedroom. "Jealousies developed between us and she turned me in to the police," he recalled—she even exposed his role in terminating her pregnancy.

He drew a two-year prison sentence on thirteen breaking and entering counts, plus charges of assisting in an abortion. To shave down his sentence, he wasted no time in ratting out his academic accomplice, who'd returned to teaching in the fall and denied even knowing Dennis. To prove that his outlandish allegations against such an upstanding young fellow were true, he described in detail a stolen silver tray the professor had gifted, post-theft, to his unwitting father, which was recovered in the clergyman's possession. Detectives intentionally placed the professor in a cell with Gerry and listened in as he masterfully convinced the academic to plead guilty.

Only nine days into his term at the Burwash industrial prison farm in an isolated region of Northern Ontario near Sudbury, Dennis added another critical skill to his growing arsenal: the vanishing act. When his estranged wife Gertrude arrived for a visit, an empty cell awaited. Prison officials informed her he'd disappeared two days earlier and likely perished in a blizzard during an escape attempt, his body buried beneath deep Canadian snowdrifts. But those who knew him well suspected that was far too anticlimactic an ending for Gerry Dennis.

"He told me frankly that they wouldn't keep him in Burwash more than a month," admitted Detective Robert Gadd, who'd arrested Dennis. He shared the burglar's confident assertion with the prison farm administration. "They took extra precautions in guarding him, but he was gone in [less than] a month." One day he was behind bars, and the next, inexplicably, he wasn't.

Poof!

Although the means of Gerry's escape was never publicly reported at the time, according to the Dennis family lore, he later revealed that, after joining fellow inmates to venture outside as a labor workforce, he quietly slipped away from the group and made a dash for freedom. Noticing his absence, the guards scoured the region with bloodhounds. Desperate to throw the hounds off his scent—and despite being in the thick of a frigid Canadian winter—Gerry quickly shed his clothes, stashing them near the bank, and plunged into a river, emerging mostly naked to run as fast and as far away as he could. The gambit worked: the dogs lost his trail, and the guards gave up their search as worsening weather and dimming light drove them back inside. Only then did Gerry double back to retrieve his soaking wet, icy clothing, wring them out, and don them again before escaping for good.

Despite the surrounding area being sparsely populated, almost entirely by prison employees and their families, and in defiance of posted signs advising motorists not to pick up hitchhikers, Gerry avoided capture and traveled hundreds of miles to reunite with Eleanor, beguiling her into a reconciliation. He was indeed "a smoothie," she'd later recall. "Life with him was exciting, fascinating, tense. He was the romantic type and had the looks and the manners to match. He simply overwhelmed me." Sometime after their passionate reunion, Eleanor nervously told Gerry she was again pregnant. His divorce was still incomplete, he admitted, but suggested there was no *real* reason that they couldn't otherwise live as husband and wife, with no one the wiser until they could make it legitimately legal.

Thus, they became, to anyone who asked, Mr. and Mrs. "Jerry Langstaff."

By then, Toronto authorities had grown all too familiar with reports of the thief with the handsome mug and light fingers; it was time to seek greener pastures. In March of 1944, they relocated to Montreal, where he said he'd found gainful employment as a gambling house croupier. They were flush—Gerry told his "wife" he'd won $7,000 at the tables (though she never actually saw the winning pot) and found a lucrative sideline converting Canadian currency into U.S. dollars in Montreal's black market. Their daughter Wendie was born in 1944, and they were a happy young family by all external appearances. If Eleanor had concerns about her husband's extralegal activities, which often left her home alone at night with the baby, the occasional gift of a diamond ring here or ruby pendant there apparently quieted them, and he gentlemanly made a point never to introduce her to his more shadowy associates.

Meanwhile, in Montreal, a city then plagued by crime, newspapers reported increasing incidents of a pair of phantom burglars raiding the jewelry boxes of the city's wealthiest residents. Though officially dubbed the "Hooded Bandits," descriptions of the duo repeatedly noted their marked difference in height, leading police to informally nickname them the "Mutt and Jeff Bandits," after the popular comic strip characters of the day. The team evidenced a more brazen, occasionally downright violent approach than Gerry Dennis's prior record ever suggested: gold mine heiress Anne Timmons stumbled across the prowler as he collected a jaw-dropping $75,000 worth of her gems, only to be whacked on the head with a pistol butt and shoved into a bathroom. In another incident, the burglars interrupted a family's home ping-pong match, slugging the mother and tying up the father and daughter as they looted the premises.

Life was good to the Farrells in those early years. Gerry's "business dealings"—and, though Eleanor was none the wiser, his pursuit of another paramour he'd met on the ski slopes of Quebec—frequently brought him to the United States, to places even more affluent than Montreal. His mistress brought him to her home in New York's Westchester County, where the streets were lined with mansions ripe for the plucking and proved far more alluring than any fleeting fling. In the spring of 1946, Gerry planned to relocate his family to New York, a move also spurred by his gnawing suspicion that after Eleanor unknowingly cashed a bond stolen in one of his after-dark excursions, the transaction might soon draw the attention of the law.

Eleanor, who he'd still not officially wed, couldn't have been too surprised when her "husband's" travel plans skirted the formal immigration process. He sent Eleanor and eighteen-month-old Wendie across the border separately, without travel visas, and joined them shortly thereafter. She didn't ask how he'd made arrangements; he'd stolen the identification papers of Royal Canadian Air Force aviator John D'Arcy Shea, passing them off as his own (Shea went on to become an admired virtuoso violinist with symphony orchestras in Montreal and Toronto).

At the time of Dennis's departure, Canadian officials were still trying to determine exactly *who* was responsible for the rash of Montreal's phantom burglaries, resulting in staggering total losses of over $170,000. They zeroed in on a prime suspect, a former "box man" at the *barbotte* tables (the Canadian form of craps) in the west end whom they believed mixed and mingled in the chicest circles, using his vantage point to scout out potential victims. But just as they anticipated a break in the case, their quarry abruptly went missing. And just as suddenly as the brazen crimes had started, they stopped. The vanishing act was still a showstopper.

Poof!

Mr. And Mrs. "Gerald Farrell" had arrived in America.

The family settled into a cozy rented summer cottage on Cornell Place in Rye, New York, a wealthy suburb in posh Westchester County. George Washington slept there twice, and Rye had been home to such august personages as Founding Father John Jay, poet Ogden Nash, Olympic swimmer-turned-movie serial star Buster Crabbe, and aviator Amelia Earhart, another accomplished vanisher. The Farrells took to the new environs with aspirational aplomb: Gerry liked driving by the more lavish estates, noting who had the biggest lawns and fanciest cars parked in their driveways. Committed to expanding his success, he spent countless hours studying at the New York Public Library to sharpen his business acumen, and his professional ventures grew more prosperous—somehow without the benefit of the valid military discharge or rejection papers U.S. employers required during wartime.

Still expected to work, Eleanor got a job as a waitress in a local restaurant. She didn't mind, considering it helped fund the extravagant lifestyle she was becoming ever more accustomed to. Gerry's work often took him to Manhattan, and he occasionally let her accompany him, squiring her to such celebrated café society night spots as El Morocco, 21, and the Stork Club, where famed owner Sherman Billingsley once gifted her with the special perk he set aside for only his most favored patrons, a bottle of the club's signature perfume Sortilege.

Eleanor marveled at Gerry's knack for rubbing elbows with the Westchester crowd, even more wealthy and celebrated than the social circles of Toronto and Montreal, and his encyclopedic knowledge of the elite's every minute movement as if he committed the newspapers' society pages to memory. She felt like they really fit in: Gerry purchased a shiny new Buick, gifted her with a luxurious mink coat and her first real vacation *ever*, a business-related Christmas getaway to Miami, visiting the city's flashy racetracks, casinos, and nightclubs.

To Eleanor, it all seemed like a fabulous dream. Would she ever wake up?

However, not every evening was idyllic. Gerry's work kept him away many nights. Had she been the type to follow police reports in the local papers, she might have noticed that, like Montreal, Westchester County had its own bold cat burglar snatching top-dollar jewelry. Described as silken-masked and wearing a black raincoat and slouch hat by those few who caught a glimpse, the daring prowler discreetly entered darkened mansions with feline grace and always escaped with a choice haul—in his very first strike he made off with $75,000 in jewels, even as the occupants hosted a dinner party in a separate wing of their mansion. An Eastchester job took $8,000 in jewels and cash, a Pelham Manor strike three days later netted $15,000 in baubles and an Oriental rug, and a Mamaroneck heist boasted a bountiful $35,000 score. The thief sometimes made his getaways by boosting the victims' own expensive cars, disappearing without a trace.

But not always: On October 20, 1946, forty-eight-year-old boat building magnate Marshall E. Tulloch surprised the prowler in his stately stone-lined New Rochelle estate. The masked man advised Tulloch that he'd best not attempt to detain him, but a scuffle ensued. In his frantic bid to escape, the prowler pulled out a pistol and shot Tulloch cleanly through the hand, evaporating into the night with $1,200 in cash and $6,800 in jewels.

Eleanor also likely failed to note that the heists took place on the same evenings "Jerry Farrell" was away from home or that the few witnesses who'd glimpsed the tall thief described his features as movie star-handsome, a "dead ringer for Errol Flynn"—not unlike her dashing husband. And she almost certainly missed the reports of a man arrested in Berkshire in nearby Tioga County on suspicion of selling stolen jewelry, a slippery character who somehow vanished overnight from the local jail—*Poof!* Gerry was out that night, too.

While the Farrells enjoyed their getaway to sunny Miami, the cat burglar took a vacation as well: no robberies marred anyone's holidays. As Gerry returned to business as usual in early 1947, so, too, did the burglar, slinking away with $18,000 worth of loot from a rich widow's Bronxville residence on January 17. Eleanor might have been riveted to read of the Long Island Sound incident: the cat burglar, after cutting the main phone line of a wealthy woman's mansion—long surveilled to determine she was the only occupant—believed he had all the time he needed to crack the master bedroom safe, even after hearing her moving about in the far end of the home. But the lady kept a second, private line devoted solely to bedside calls from her beau and used it to ring the cops. Suddenly cornered when fifteen police cars—and a few fire engines—surrounded the front of the estate, the thief tossed a leather footstool out a window and onto the roof of the patio, luring the lawmen to the rear of the house while he dropped off a front-facing balcony onto a row of shrubbery and dashed across the lawn, escaping into the wooded grounds.

Poof!

Gerry's "business interests"—he'd become quite the auction speculator, he told Eleanor—kept him so busy whisking back and forth between Rye to Manhattan that for a while, he pooled resources with a group of fast-rising, well-compensated, and hard-partying young executives to keep a suite of rooms in a hotel for overnight stays, easing his burdensome commute. "We had what you might say was a continuous ball," he later admitted. "Through that suite marched a never-ending procession of lovely young models and showgirls."

But Gerry being Gerry, he also craved a degree of privacy, subletting an apartment in Greenwich Village—not uncoincidentally, after the Tulloch shooting considerably increased the heat on the Westchester cat burglar. According to the lease, the occupant was "Jerry Woodruff," a jewelry wholesaler with an array of tools for cutting, setting, and polishing precious stones, skills picked up over many hours poring over the public library's volumes on the subject of gemology. "I became an expert on jewels, bought and read all the books I could find on diamonds and other gems, and gold and platinum," he later revealed. "Then I bought a complete set of jeweler's tools, including a lathe and also scales to weigh the carats exactly. I also learned to get initials off engraved cigarette cases and lighters."

Gerry's pad also housed a wide assortment of locks he'd collected and the unique tools he'd crafted to practice picking them. "Before long, I could open any type of lock without leaving a mark," he'd boast. "I could separate good jewelry from not-so-good jewelry at almost a glance." Those high-living nights on the town? Fun, yes, but "not only did I get to know many socially prominent people...I was better able to line up many future burglary victims." The variety of methods he used to enter homes kept things lively, certainly, but "this was to avoid leaving a set pattern that could connect all the jobs as the work of one particular thief."

Sure, big, splashy scores provoked police scrutiny and loud headlines, but he believed smaller, more frequent hauls would've brought even greater heat down on him. "If I found no more than $20,000 in jewelry in any one of them, I would take nothing," he revealed—it was better for business in the long term. "They would know a burglar had been in their midst and be on guard. If I left the jewelry and no sign of entry I could return to that same street the next night, confident that I would likely find as much as $80,000 worth in another home."

Dennis would later claim he'd only reluctantly chosen the crooked path yet again, lamenting that his illegal status kept him from obtaining legitimate work in New York; he insisted that he'd even spent $500 on a birth certificate and social security card to get a job, but "it turned out the birth certificate was for a Negro and I couldn't use it. There was nothing else for me to do but steal," he said. "I've been robbing ever since." Embracing his lot, he determined that he was going to be the very best at being bad. "I decided right then and there to fully apply my perfectionist inclinations," he explained. "This, then, was the turning point: the place where Gerry Dennis, the hit-and-miss burglar, faded out of the picture to make room for...[the] debonair society thief."

The haul from Marshall Tulloch's estate was a comparatively minor bounty for the burglar, but one that would ultimately come at a crucial price. The violent encounter set a veteran bloodhound on the cat's trail—namely

Detective Lt. Maurice P. Kelly, the forty-four-year-old head of the New Rochelle police department's vice squad.

Bespectacled, unobtrusive, middle-aged, and married with two sons, Kelly had joined New Rochelle's force in 1928, making detective within his first decade on the job. He'd handled cases both harrowing and high profile. He led the 1938 takedown of a multi-state forgery ring operating a fraudulent Irish sweepstakes scam that reaped as much as $4.5 million from ticket-buying hopefuls; Kelly broke the case by investigating his private suspicions on his days off duty for a year. His police career interrupted by wartime service, Kelly became a much-decorated Naval intelligence officer, breaking Japanese codes and providing security to the war-ending Manhattan Project before returning to the detective bureau. He was instrumental in the 1946 capture of Linwood Magnum, an earlier, similarly elusive residential burglar plaguing New Rochelle for four years: when Magnum, an extraordinarily agile second-story man known as "The Black Cat," narrowly escaped capture after being tracked down at his local bar and grill, Kelly and his fellow detectives cornered him at his girlfriend's home, resulting in a wild chase through alleyways and a dramatic shoot-out; one well-placed shot hobbled the suspect for arrest. Later, Kelly's role in solving a local robbery of $50,000 worth of stolen apparel within fourteen hours would earn him an on-air salute from the popular radio show "Gang Busters," which pioneered the dramatization of cases from real police and FBI files.

Well on his way to becoming the most decorated officer in the history of the New Rochelle police department, Kelly had accrued a stellar reputation for dogged determination and infinite patience when it came to solving cases over the course of his two-decade-long career.

But even with the confidence his previous successes inspired, the detective nevertheless felt intense pressure to put a stop to the mysterious rash of thefts: the town's mayor, Stanley Church, made it clear that the upper-class residents of New Rochelle, one of the cat's favored scratching posts, expected to sleep soundly at night and wake up with their pricey collections of jewelry intact. The thief's exploits were the talk of every local cocktail gathering—he was so brazen and clever that he'd actually once phoned the driver's license bureau, posing as a local detective to request the address of a wealthy socialite whose home was burglarized later that night. Tulloch's shooting further unnerved the locals, suggesting that if the cat were cornered, things might turn deadly as he clawed his way free.

Something needed to be done. And it looked like Kelly just might be the cop to it.

In July 1947, Kelly had just spent some time alone with Gloria Horowitz, a beautiful twenty-year-old aspiring fashion model and actress whose raven hair, smoky eyes, sly smile, and sweater-clad curves made her look every inch a *femme fatale* from the hard-boiled crime films of the day, the kind of girl around which even Humphrey Bogart should watch his back.

But this wasn't the movies, and Gloria wasn't an illicit schemer or a cold-hearted seductress, she insisted to Kelly, who'd joined a succession of law enforcement agents to quiz her. *She* was the one caught in an elaborate web of deception and crime, and now she was a scared young woman— scared enough to talk, with quite a story to tell about the dirty so-and-so who'd left her high, dry, and in handcuffs.

At the center of her tale was the smooth-talking Canadian Jerry Woodruff, whose striking looks, dapper wardrobe, and suave patois captured her fancy as she served him highballs, waiting tables at the ritzy Pine Room bar of Manhattan's Belmont Plaza Hotel the previous spring, after a mutual acquaintance introduced them. Raised near the affluent Detroit suburb Grosse Pointe, Gloria Mitman set out to chase her dreams of a life in the limelight, moving to New York as soon as she graduated high school. But big breaks were not coming at the pace she'd expected, and she'd fallen too quickly for a routinely unemployed, frequently absent actor/model named Arthur Aaron Horowitz, their daughter born shortly after their marriage earlier in 1947. With neither fame nor fortune on their immediate horizons, Gloria had been forced to place their child in a private home while she took a job as a cocktail waitress to make ends meet. "I was living a hand-to-mouth existence," she'd recall.

Jerry Woodruff, too, looked like a heartbreaker, but Gloria couldn't help but be tantalized by him—not only young and handsome but rich to boot, having come into a $25,000 inheritance from his recently deceased father. "Jerry's poise, his apparent wealth and good breeding were so impressive," she later reported. As Gloria lingered at his side, he puffed cigarettes and explained to her that he was freeing up his assets to continue living in the style to which he'd grown accustomed. But he was limited in the amount of Canadian cash he could legally bring into the States. Instead, he'd traded in various long-term real estate investments for something he could convert into cash more quickly: jewels.

His lips moved closer to her ear, keeping the next part just between the two of them—she seemed like the kind of stand-up girl a guy could trust. He had a collection of family jewels with a considerably higher cash value if he could sell them in the States rather than his native country—except for one catch: the international currency regulations and fees he'd have to pay as a Canadian national would put a drain on his profits. Sure, it wasn't *entirely* on the up-and-up, but he was in a pinch, and it was just a matter of making the most money out of his investment, right? If only he had some-one in America he could count on, someone he shared a connection with, a kind, trustworthy soul who could help. And, he confided, a woman as beautiful and sexy as Gloria, with her obvious star quality, would certainly be able to coax and charm any red-blooded jeweler out of a much higher price for his baubles than he could.

Swept up in his story, Gloria quickly took his family jewels in hand.

Around 1 p.m. on July 18, Gloria entered a pawnshop in Philadelphia with a pair of earrings—blue-white diamonds set in platinum—worth at least $3,500. It was the latest of many stops she'd made that day on the city's "Jewelers Row." She'd delivered compelling variations of her cover story, thinking of it as *acting* rather than *lying*. It didn't really matter, as long as it helped Jerry out of his jam. It certainly didn't hurt that he knew all kinds of top people at the fancy clubs he frequented who might help a strug-gling model get ahead; plus, he'd promised her a 10 percent commission, which was a lot more for one day's work than she made toting cocktails. And it would make Jerry as happy as he was handsome. She couldn't see any downside.

Her first outing in New York couldn't have gone more smoothly—she successfully collected between $1,000 and $1,500, delivering the cash to Jerry, who waited for her on the street and paid her commission on the spot. She'd also easily hocked a $500 bracelet Jerry had given her as an extra incentive, taking in a quick fifty dollars. But after Jerry directed her to a new venue, Philadelphia, the plan proved more challenging than she'd anticipated. A few of the jewelers she'd approached balked at her asking price of $1,000 for the earrings—not because it was too high, but because it was *too low* based on their appraisal. Like Gloria herself, they appeared a little too hot to handle, no matter how enticing.

In this latest shop, the pawnbroker grew suspicious enough—perhaps Gloria was a better model than an actress—to discreetly run a check on the jewelry she'd presented, which matched bangles stolen in one of the Westchester cat burglar's raids. "Jerry Woodruff" had probably caught wind that New Rochelle police had been circulating a description of the loot to various area jewelry stores and pawnshops. And he may have even suspected they had a line on the good-looking gem salesman spotted in several such establishments, handing out business cards from the Felix P. Jacobson Co. of Chicago, a legitimate firm whose name, like his wares, he'd simply appropriated. These were principal reasons why he'd taken pains to escort pot-sweetening Gloria all the way to Philadelphia, waiting calmly while she did his extralegal business for him.

As officers escorted her out of the pawnshop wearing a set of less-than-fashionable handcuffs, the downside of Jerry's plan became apparent. Gloria scanned the street corners for any sign of him, but he was nowhere in sight.

She should have known he'd be a heartbreaker.

Philadelphia newspapers couldn't resist publishing prominent, pouty photos of the glamourous dish in police custody, especially when Gloria compounded her woes by being less than forthcoming with police. Initially, she insisted the earrings were hers, originally purchased in Canada, and claimed she was staying at the stately Bellevue-Stratford Hotel. Then her story shifted: she'd purchased the jewelry in Florida and offered a swanky Manhattan address near 47th and Fifth Avenue. Finally, she revealed the gems had come from "Jerry, at St. Francis," presumably the venerable New York hospital or perhaps the famed San Francisco hotel.

Working without a script was not Gloria's forte, and the arresting officers quickly recognized that none of her various versions of events held up against each other. She was held on suspicion of larceny and, due to her disobedience, her bail doubled from $2,500 to $5,000. That maneuver sufficiently broke her resolve after what she called "a miserable, rotten week in jail," and as more investigators took an interest in her—including the FBI, U.S. Treasury agents, and, once the earrings' actual ownership was determined, New Rochelle's Lt. Kelly—she grew less brassy and more fearful. And the more scared she got, the more she talked.

Once she started spilling the real, or at least only slightly sanitized, skinny, her story checked out; Kelly realized Gloria was more dishy dupe than cunning accomplice. "I didn't know a diamond from a broken beer bottle, but I fell for his line—the heel," she'd say, embarrassed at her gullibility. "I never stopped being a chump until I learned what his real business was."

She vehemently denied any romantic entanglement with her manipulator, even insisting he'd taken her out to dinner along with his wife—though she certainly sounded like a woman scorned. "He cast me off as a once-useful toy."

At last, Lt. Kelly had concrete leads on his quarry. Gloria provided a detailed description, introduced a possible Canadian connection, and gifted the detective with one more vital clue to aid his hunt: demonstrating skills honed in her high school art classes, she drew a sketch that startlingly captured Jerry's likeness.

Now Kelly had a face, and after sending the sketch to Canadian authorities, who'd yet to forget the handsome mug with the ugly record, he finally had a name: *Gerard Graham Dennis*. Kelly believed he might have a place, too: Gloria had, after a little searching, pointed him to the Greenwich Village apartment where—just *once*, she insisted—she'd met with Jerry alone. New York police searched the apartment, discovering various items traceable to several Westchester robberies—but no Gerry Dennis. Not in the flesh, at least: a major breakthrough in the case came when detectives searched a desk drawer and found a collection of recent photos of their suspect, which were quickly wired across a vast network of law enforcement agencies.

"He really *is* a good-looking fellow," Kelly noted as he studied the photographs, getting his first good look at the cat burglar who was, at this point, suspected of stealing over $200,000 worth of jewels. "But he should never have gotten so sentimental."

Although it seemed Kelly was at last hot on the tail of his catlike culprit, he should have given Gerry's expertise with vanishing acts more consideration.

After searching Dennis's lair in the Village, police neglected to place the apartment under continuous surveillance. Alerted by a series of broken strips of adhesive tape he'd planted around the dwelling, Dennis realized he'd been discovered. He covertly phoned a moving company, which arrived with a van and loaded up the contents of his den, transporting his belongings, ill-gotten and otherwise, to an unknown location, completely unnoticed by the police.

Poof!

When several Westchester commuters positively identified Dennis's photograph as the dashing man "who always got on at Rye," police planned to corner him in his rented cottage there, only to discover that the occupants had moved out not long ago.

Poof!

Finally, after scouring the records of a Westchester moving company, on August 4, the trail led to a well-appointed Bronx apartment rented by Mr. and Mrs. Jerry Farrell, late of Rye. As Kelly and his fellow officers huddled out front before knocking on the door, he was confident there was no way the cat burglar could have seen them coming this time.

All he found inside, however, was a distraught, teary-eyed young woman and her three-year-old daughter. The woman was desperate to learn why her husband—who'd shown up earlier in the day with a curiously urgent insistence that she join him on an abruptly scheduled business trip and was about to make train reservations—suddenly exited out the back window just ten minutes before the police had arrived.

Poof!

Kelly was getting all too familiar with the vanishing act now. *How does he do that?*

As police removed five firearms, a series of items matching property stolen in the Westchester heists, and a collection of gems later traced back to a Montreal matron, Eleanor Harris Farrell was booked as a material witness and held on $5,000 bail, her daughter Wendie turned over to the care of a children's home. Under questioning, it seemed she was learning more startling truths about the man she'd known intimately for the past four years from Lt. Kelly than he was from her. The dream she'd been living was over—what she was experiencing now was more like "a nightmare," she recalled later.

But her loyalties remained steadfast, and it seemed that even elusive Gerry was worried about her as well: he called the apartment multiple times, her guarded responses ensuring he understood police were still present. Kelly knew then that he'd have to make a calculated, possibly even cruel, tactical gambit to shake Eleanor's faith. He had a photograph of Gloria Horowitz in one of her sultrier modeling poses handed to Eleanor, informing her that the glamour girl was, in fact, Gerry's other woman—a lie of convenience or an as-yet-unexposed truth, the details didn't matter to Kelly in the moment.

As she'd turned on Gerry in Toronto in a fit of jealous scorn, Eleanor did so again: the next time he phoned, she told him the police had finally left; they arranged to meet in Manhattan near the Grand Central Terminal to make their getaway as a family. When Eleanor arrived, Gerry was waiting—and watching from a distance. Realizing several passersby circulating near her were actually plainclothes police officers, Gerry, with little more than his wallet and the clothes on his back, retreated into the shadows and quietly caught a train.

Poof!

Much as he abandoned his "once useful toy" in Philadelphia, the cat burglar had unceremoniously left his wife and daughter holding the bag, and suddenly, Kelly had to admit, he didn't seem like such a sentimental fellow after all.

Gerry Farrell took a powder. In his place was "Jerry 'Duke' McKay."

Fleeing New York in 1947, Gerry, having left everything behind, used his considerable wits and well-honed skills to make his way across the country, stealing a car in Chicago to avoid being spotted on a train by a sharp-eyed porter or an undercover cop. "For the first time since I had launched myself as a society burglar, the police had a description of the wanted man," he knew, shrewdly shedding his well-kempt mustache; the more distance he put between himself and the East Coast lawmen, the better. He just needed a destination, preferably with a population of well-to-do hedonists where the abundance of available surf, sun, and social whirl may have lulled them into a lax sense of security.

California, here I come!

He made a beeline for the state's by-then-famous capital of glamor and decadence, Beverly Hills. If wealthy Westchester County had been a playground for the cat burglar, the even more outrageously wealthy and flamboyant environs of that city—as well as nearby Bel-Air, Holmby Hills, and Hollywood—were a veritable carnival, with wild rides ready to be taken and abundant prizes waiting to be claimed.

"I found myself in a strange new world of pastel shades, flowers, and ever-present sunshine," he would recall of his arrival in the fall of 1947, setting himself up in a modest hotel in Hollywood. He swiftly made *himself* the lure: outfitted in the finest tailored suits and tuxedos he could afford, he slicked back his hair, kept his mustache neatly trimmed, and indulged himself with two shiny new automobiles—a Lincoln and a Cadillac convertible, well-suited for the sun-soaked city where *everybody* drove. He struck the perfect figure of a Hollywood man-about-town, utterly at home among the beautiful people.

He sought out those pretty faces by frequenting the thriving social scenes where they gathered. Everyone else played a part, one way or another, and he proved as talented a performer as some of the marquee names. Sometimes, he cast himself as a wealthy playboy, a footloose, champagne-swilling bon vivant with money to burn and lots of free evenings to party. Occasionally, he played the role of an up-and-coming actor, climbing his way through the studio ranks and networking through the cocktail circuit in hopes of catching that big break.

He hobnobbed with the stars at elegant nightclubs—the Mocambo, the Trocadero, and Ciro's on the Sunset Strip. He drank among the dealmakers at the Polo Lounge of the Beverly Hills Hotel and the privacy-seekers at the Chateau Marmont. He ate alongside power-diners at the Brown Derby on Vine Street and Romanoff's on Rodeo Drive. He chatted up showgirls at the Earl Carroll Theater and the Florentine Gardens in Hollywood. Soon he was a familiar face among the *demi monde*.

With all the tantalizingly perfect famous, soon-to-be-famous, and almost-famous flesh available to him, Dennis had ample opportunity to deploy his lady-killing charms. He recalled an evening on the town when "a very prominent and beautiful redheaded actress tried to pick me up in a club. As she danced with her escort, she stared back over his shoulder at me. In a little while, she slipped quickly toward the exit and motioned for me to follow. It was tempting—very tempting. But I had to ignore the invitation for my own protection." Dennis made a professionally practical decision: "I avoided personal contact with the better-known names of the industry simply because I was in no position to chance the luxury of Hollywood notoriety." He felt certain that if he squired high-profile, gossip-generating stars and starlets on his arm, "inquisitive columnists would investigate my background and find me out for what I was."

Instead, he used his proximity to pick up inside gossip on the heaviest hitters' habits and movements as well as up-close ganders at the choicest jewelry worn by corporate moguls' matrons, box office tycoons' missuses, and power players' mistresses alike. He earned access to places where, for him, the *real* action lay: the private homes of the rich and famous. On the occasions where he didn't score an impromptu invite to a glittering party, he invited himself, his screen-ready looks and freshly pressed tux earning admittance because he looked the part—and that was half the battle in Hollywood.

"I read the society columns," he explained. "I would crash social functions and watch for guests wearing valuable gems. I learned where they lived. I would carefully case their homes during the day." Once inside, he casually worked his way through grand estates, taking mental notes of the layouts, the description and age of each family member, the number of servants, and whether they had dogs, the bane of any cat burglar's existence. He kept literal notes too: maps of the mansions he'd visited, outlines of the ripest prospects and their probable worth in jewelry and furs. He poured over newspaper gossip columns and society pages, jotting down dates that a prospect might be gone for a wedding, birth, funeral, vacation, party, business trip, or movie shoot. And he always kept an up-to-date edition of the Southwest Blue Book, the preeminent social register of Southern California, close at hand. New precautions emerged, like keeping a full change of clothes on hand after prowls to avoid identification—especially brand-new shoes that couldn't be connected to any errant footprints left behind.

"Whenever I set out to loot a mansion, fear was the one thing I didn't take with me," he later reported.

His extensive pains and careful planning resulted in a dramatic payoff greater than Westchester's because his victims' jewelry boxes were loaded with even more opulent and over-the-top treasures. "I knew where the jewels were and what they were," he said, noting that when he arrived at night in his customary working clothes—black shirt, silk mask, slouch hat—he usually found his way inside by climbing up a convenient trestle and accessing an unlocked window. "I liked several people in the house so there were less chance to hear a noise upstairs. I like a house near a golf course for a quick getaway. I'd park my car six blocks to two miles away."

One of his earliest scores, from a home in Hollywood in December of 1947, proved the value of his methodology: he walked off with loot worth over $30,000.

As elaborate as his performances were by night, he played yet another role by day. In New York, he'd finally learned a legitimate trade—though put to illegitimate use—developing a discerning eye for the most valuable of gems and acquiring tools to deconstruct the necklaces, bracelets, and rings he scored, making it harder for pawnshops and professional gemologists to spot stolen swag. He bypassed criminal fences and peddled his wares at top-dollar prices to unsuspecting resellers as "Jerry McCabe," a charming jewelry salesman.

Determined to sidestep the trap that netted Gloria Horowitz, he persuaded a wholesale jeweler to share office space with him, then flew half a country away to Cleveland to have his diamonds cut there. Some of the modified gems returned with him to be sold to and funneled back into the market by the unsuspecting wholesaler. Buyers reckoned they were, like half of the diamond trade, smuggled into the country to avoid pricey tariffs and looked the other way. While in the Midwest, he also bargained with storekeepers who were unlikely to receive L.A. police bulletins with telling details about the stolen gems he was unloading. "I did better financially in California than I had in New York," he'd report. To successfully steal from the jet set, Gerry had become quite the jetsetter himself.

And yet there was one more part to play. In many ways, Gerry was as independent and aloof as a feline, yet also catlike in his appreciation for having another warm body around to feed him and clean up after him in exchange for the occasional affectionate purr.

The latest warm body belonged to Betty V. Ritchie, an attractive, brunette twenty-three-year-old former sixth-grade schoolteacher from the tiny Ontario town of Fenelon Falls. The daughter of a dairyman, Betty escaped the bitter Canadian winter, traveling to Southern California on a six-month visitor's visa—the rigors of educating pre-teens had left her anxious and exhausted, she confessed, and she needed a change of scenery.

In January 1948, fellow Ontarian Jerry McKay swept her off her feet literally and figuratively while dancing at the Hollywood Palladium on Sunset Boulevard. He was dapper, handsome, and educated, he said, at McGill University, cutting an agile figure on the dance floor ("He was very good," she related. "We danced many times that night"). He was also wealthy, having amassed a tidy fortune during the War, now dabbling in the transcontinental gem trade while developing a self-invented automotive safety device he hoped to patent.

Betty and Jerry quickly became more than merely dance partners. "In a little while, he began to make love to me, and I can tell you I was badly smitten from the start," she'd recall. Eventually, on Valentine's Day, she spent the night with him at his Hollywood hotel room; by May, after a brief stint living together in a rental on King's Road in West Hollywood, they'd leased a Beverly Hills love nest in the luxe seventy-five-dollar-per-month Oak Hills apartment building at 322 North Oakhurst Drive—modest by local standards, inconspicuous by his own. Grateful for a life of luxury she'd never known, she agreed to keep her forty-dollars-a-week job to cover her personal expenses, and Jerry generously kicked in another ten to fifteen dollars a week of mad money.

In exchange, she became Mrs. Jerry McKay, in name if not in law. For even as he gave her a gold wedding band for appearance's sake, "so the neighbors wouldn't talk," and a dramatic diamond cocktail ring, Jerry explained that he had a divorce pending back east still yet to be resolved… but the minute it was, he promised, they would formally tie the knot. That was good enough for Betty, who set aside any thoughts of renewing her visa, secure in the belief she'd soon have an American green card. "After I met Jerry, I forgot all about going back to Canada," she admitted. They settled into a cozy domestic routine. "He was the most wonderful of husbands," said Betty. "He was thoughtful, considerate, always asking if there was any-thing he could do for me. Even the little things like helping me with the dishes, going shopping with me so I wouldn't have to carry heavy bundles."

There were apparent quirks to their relationship, however. She never accompanied Jerry on his regular overnight forays to Long Beach several nights a week to visit a pal from his old life with Eleanor in New York—in fact, she never met the unseen crony, who was the only person Jerry appeared close with. He explained that he'd shut himself off from any other friends after his acrimonious split with his spouse—indeed, she noticed that since starting over in Beverly Hills, he never even received any mail. Outside of the occasional music concert, museum visit, or even more infre-quent restaurant excursions, the couple's social circle was limited almost exclusively to their neighbors in the building, the Brucks.

She barely thought to question it when he asked her to register his newly acquired Cadillac under the name of a now-deceased woman she'd known in Canada—to help, he claimed, avoid paying hefty taxes on the vehicle. Doesn't *everyone* fudge a little to keep the government out of their pocket if they can? "He was so kind and attentive I never imagined that he could do anything wrong," she said.

His late-night pursuits had previously been derailed by women who knew far too much when spilling the beans to the police, so he was far more circumspect with his female companion now. Betty wasn't the dish Gloria Horowitz was, nor stirred Gerry's soul as Eleanor Harris had, but she was wide-eyed, naïve, and devoutly respectful of his privacy—she wouldn't even go through his pockets to launder his trousers without asking first, let alone bother him with nosy inquiries about that mysterious double-locked closet he kept, where he told her he was keeping valuable plans and prototypes for that auto safety device he cooked up with his neighbor Julius Bruck. She'd proven far too trusting and compliant to pry. She'd rarely ask questions. She'd cook. She'd clean. She'd do.

Gerry was delivering an Academy Award–worthy performance. In fact, he could've had one of those, too.

In 1948 Loretta Young was one of Hollywood's most popular screen actresses, still radiantly beautiful at thirty-five, and she lived as fabulously as her fans could have imagined. She and her second husband, business-man and fledgling film producer Tom Lewis, lived with their three children (actually, daughter Judy was secretly fathered by Clark Gable, but that's another story) in a magnificent twenty-room Holmby Hills estate at 280 Carolwood Drive. The white-bricked, arch-windowed French Normandy-style home was originally constructed for actress Constance Bennett as a grand "Hollywood-French castle," its winding driveway and surrounding walls of tall great white oaks ensuring the utmost privacy. That March, wearing a jaw-dropping emerald gown and matching opera gloves designed by Hollywood costumer Adrian, Young had collected the Academy Award for Best Actress for her turn in *The Farmer's Daughter*. The Oscar was displayed in a place of honor in the Carolwood home.

The following July, a polite, handsome young man rang the front gate during the day while the family was out. He explained to the housekeeper that he was a real estate agent whom Tom Lewis had asked to inspect the house in anticipation of a future sale. The housekeeper was so enchanted by the realtor—Jerry something or other—that she gave him a guided tour of the entire estate, pointing out relevant details like the location of the burglar alarm and the wall safe. He flashed his winning smile as he bid the servant goodbye, and she went about her duties, never mentioning his visit to her employers.

A week later, Young and Lewis attended a party at the home of con-cert pianist Arthur Rubenstein, along with Irene Selznick, the daughter of studio chief Louis B. Mayer and the recent ex-wife of film producer David O. Selznick. Clad in a brilliant gown, the famously religious Young wore minimal jewelry—including a diamond-encrusted crucifix—but as a gag to cheer up her newly divorced friend, she donned Irene's "consolation prize" from Selznick, an eye-popping pear-shaped diamond bracelet, and wore it throughout the party. Later, Young and her husband were already on their way home when the actress realized she was still sporting the Selznick sparkler. Loretta thought it was far too late to turn around and return the cuff to Irene—it could wait until morning. But Tom insisted, driving back to the party and running it inside as his wife nearly dozed off in the car. Returning home, they quickly retired to bed—*after* Loretta stashed her own jewels safely away.

That night, Gerry returned to Carolwood, this time under the cover of darkness, shimming up a pillar and edging twenty feet along a four-inch-wide second-story ledge until he found a sitting room window that had conveniently been left open—possibly even propped open during his earlier visit—and neatly cut the screen. During his silent prowl through the home in his crepe-soled shoes, he must have caught another glimpse of Young's golden Oscar glittering in the moonlight, the *ultimate* Hollywood accessory. Tempting...but no. Where would he ever sell it? Gerry had no use for trophies: their only value was sentimental. Instead, he consoled himself by making away with $20,000 in furs and jewels, including a rare $5,500 Kohinoor mink coat and the star's treasured crucifix.

The next morning, Young awoke to discover that every one of her most precious indulgences had been spirited away, noting that the tasteful thief made a point of leaving any faux pieces behind. Worse, the newest items had yet to be insured, making them a total loss.

But Loretta Young was always one to look at the bright side and she came away feeling that a higher power was watching over her that night. She thanked God that *something* had prompted Tom to turn around to return Irene Selznick's spectacular bracelet, for it certainly would have vanished as well. The loss of her diamond crucifix she could endure, but the loss of her friend's cuff was a cross she was glad she didn't have to bear.

Though he struck with impunity throughout L.A.'s ritzier residential areas—from the Westside as Hancock Park and the Wilshire District—Brentwood, Holmby Hills, and Bel-Air were Gerry's favored fishing waters. Most homes there were, like Loretta Young's, isolated and obscured from view by lots of leafy foliage and wide property lines. He especially liked homes alongside the Los Angeles Country Club, such as Bing Crosby's Mapleton Drive estate, which abutted the ultra-exclusive, fervently

anti-showbiz golf course (even Bing was denied membership). The shadowy, unguarded greens provided a convenient means of escape if he couldn't
make it back to his Cadillac. He preferred those neighborhoods because
they were part of less police-heavy Los Angeles, unlike Beverly Hills where
the patrol cars routinely cruised the streets and made a point to stop anyone
who looked suspicious or out of place. Producer Louis B. Mayer, dressed
unrecognizably in shabby clothes he used to putter around the yard, was
once detained by officers while on a walk—and the studio chief *thanked*
them for their vigilance.

The city was now under the protection of Clinton H. Anderson, who
was installed as police chief at the end of 1942 when longtime head of the
force Charley Blair finally retired, despite pleas from the devoted citizenry
to continue. Anderson was as notoriously hard-nosed as Blair had been
amiable. A transplant from Providence, Rhode Island, the ex-Marine and
former firefighter had risen through the ranks after joining the force in
1929, beginning by riding a hillside bicycle beat eight hours a day and
gaining an intimate, on-the-ground perspective as the rarefied city evolved.
By the time he took command, he was a veteran of twenty years standing,
tall, imposing, powerfully built, granite-faced, and possessed of a flinty gaze
that stared down gangsters, broke down petty thieves, and kept any privileged attitudes of the rich and often famous locals in check.

A strict, uncompromising disciplinarian—some said martinet—
Anderson ruled his ranks with iron-fisted authority, inspiring devotion
and resentment in equal parts, and steadfastly resisted undue influence
while still zealously protecting the residents' privacy. The people of Beverly
Hills—law-abiding ones, anyway—soon came to revere Anderson for his
devotion to keeping the city as crime-free as humanly possible. By 1949,
his rigid system of vigilance seemed to be working spectacularly: all persons
charged with robbery, burglary, and auto thefts during the year were found
guilty (though some of his detractors would later note that he made certain,
one way or another that the crime statistics played in the force's favor).
Beverly Hills soon had a widespread reputation for being a decidedly risky
place to commit a crime.

But Beverly Hills was also far too alluring, even for cautious Gerry.
He raided the home of powerful talent agent Arthur S. Lyons, who represented luminaries such as Joan Crawford, Lucille Ball, and Jack Benny,
netting $15,000 in gems for his trouble. He struck not once but *twice* at the
Mountain Drive estate of socially prominent heiress Dolly Green Walker,

the perpetually party-throwing forty-two-year-old daughter of city founder Burton Green. In the second instance, Gerry brazenly attended a holiday soiree in her home, making off with a $37,000 diamond-and-ruby brooch belonging to her friend, the wife of a prominent New York builder. Dolly would have been aghast to know her phantom thief lived near the corner of Burton Way; the street named after her father. Gerry even hit the road to loot the Palm Springs Racquet Club suite of William H. Doheny, the scion of the wealthy oil clan and son of one of Beverly Hills's earliest murder victims, absconding with $30,000 in jewels.

Anyone with a big enough bank account was fair game—Gerry's other victims included an auto parts heir, the daughter of a former president of Panama, the wife of Broadway and film songwriter Mack Gordon, and Phillips Petroleum mogul Waite Phillips. He was emboldened by his successes: during a black-tie affair in Frank Capra's Brentwood home, the film director's wife Lu went upstairs and discovered a handsome, tuxedoed gentleman entering a bedroom. She assumed he was one of her guests looking for a bathroom. "I'll be right down," he smiled genially. He was—out the bedroom window with a bagful of her favorite accessories. Back in Beverly Hills, Chief Anderson listened to the bizarre account of one of the cat burglar's female victims, who was reading in her den when she was startled by a black-clad man who quietly crept in looking for valuables. The thief chatted with her amiably for about ten minutes, the perfect gentleman, before making his exit—along with her jewels. One prowl of a celebrity home went amusingly awry when, while creeping onto the grounds, the usually preternaturally agile Gerry slipped and fell into the swimming pool, creating a big splash within earshot of the estate's occupants. Soaked, he managed to escape undetected and, once he was a proper distance from the scene, had a good laugh about it.

By January 1949, Hollywood's high society was abuzz with tales of the mysterious gentleman thief. And as the month ended, tongues wagged even faster when the Bel-Air winter home of Rhode Island oilman and restaurateur Thomas R. "Dick" Winans and his wife Nancy was raided, and the thief made off with a staggering total of $257,775 in jewels, including a 24-carat diamond ring valued at $80,000, and a $60,000 bracelet—all uninsured. The Winans *had* recently hosted a big soiree at their Sarbonne Road estate, one with too many guests to keep track of, but otherwise, there was no sign of forced entry, no fingerprints, no clue of any kind. The puzzled police believed it was the largest single haul ever garnered in a Los Angeles-area home burglary, and the culprit appeared to have simply vanished.

Poof!

At twenty-eight, Gerry had defied the odds. He'd gone Hollywood and hit the big time. He was getting rich. He didn't need to be famous.

Ironically, despite his success as Tinseltown's most elusive society thief, on the very day he impulsively plotted the Winans heist, he'd decided to give up his thrilling but all-too-dangerous exploits. "I'd known for quite some time I couldn't go on making a mess of my life," Dennis later wrote, "but I thought I could make a switch without paying a penalty."

He claimed he'd concocted an ambitious plan to go straight, hung on that auto safety device he actually *had* been working on; all he needed was the proper stake to finance his efforts, that legendary One Big Score so common to career criminals' fantasies. Attending an evening function at a Beverly Hills hotel, he promised himself he'd turn over a new leaf, moments before he spotted Dick Winan and his wife Nan, awash in diamonds, nearby. The Winans had long been prospective marks he'd kept tabs on, and he felt assured that no matter how many glittery baubles adorned Nan at that moment, there was a far greater treasure trove awaiting at the couple's home. Confident the Winans would remain out on the town for a while longer, he slipped away from the hotel and drove to their majestic Bel-Air mansion.

As he explored the master bedroom, he was surprised to discover very few pieces of jewelry significant enough to make a heist worth his while. No matter—he'd simply return a bit later and spirit away the top-tier sparklers he'd seen Nan sporting earlier in the evening. He created an impromptu peephole to spy through from outside by setting a Venetian blind a bit askew, adjusted the bedroom mirrors ever so slightly to allow full views of the space, and left the French window unlatched for silent, stealthy access. Then, unfazed by his previous poolside mishap, he coolly settled in by the swimming pool to relax while awaiting the homeowners' return. "Helping myself to a Coke from the little refrigerator in the dressing cabin, I lay back on a chaise lounge and waited," he'd recall.

Within an hour, the couple pulled into the driveway and Gerry swiftly assumed his vantage point outside the bedroom window. He soon watched Nan Winans shedding her pricey assortment of adornments while she groused indignantly to her husband about a fellow socialite's snide comment referring to her as a social climber. "Here's a woman with everything she needs or wants," Gerry recalled thinking, "and she gets upset because some gossip calls her names." Soon enough, the Winans retired to bed, and Gerry imperceptibly slipped inside and then away with the loot—more than a quarter of a million dollars in gems.

"I'd promised myself this was to be my last job," he later insisted— so much so that he claimed that, when he arrived home, he dumped all his homemade burglary tools into the garbage incinerator. But had Gerry become so skilled at fabrication at this point that he was starting to believe his own lies?

"It takes a thief to catch a thief," the old saying goes. But there was no such criminal available to precipitate Gerry's fall—he worked alone and in secret, leaving any real underworld ties behind long ago in favor of a façade of legitimacy. Even his network of pawnshops and jewelry stores had no idea how hot to handle his wares were. To catch this thief, it would take an odds-defying confluence of coincidences, almost too wildly unlikely for even a hacky Hollywood screenwriter to concoct. It sounded beyond even Gerry's most elaborate yarns.

In early February 1949, Lt. Lawrence Denk of the Cleveland Police Department sat at his office desk and leafed through the latest stack of police bulletins. One report contained the striking image of a darkly handsome young fellow named Gerard Graham Dennis, AKA Jerry Farrell, AKA Jerry Woodruff, and so on. It could have been a Hollywood actor's headshot, Denk observed. *The guy was good-looking enough to star in the movies.* Denk read how Dennis was wanted for a string of big-ticket cat burglaries in Canada and New York, and even though it had been over a year-and-a-half since he'd struck there, some local Westchester County detective—that doggedly determined, infinitely patient Lt. Maurice Kelly of the New Rochelle vice squad—had stayed on the trail, uncovering evidence of fenced gems in Chicago and elsewhere that suggested he might be operating in the Midwest. Denk made a mental note of it—*this guy was quite a character*—and placed the bulletin back atop the shuffle of papers on his desk.

Not long after, Cleveland Heights jeweler Zoltan Greenhut stopped by police headquarters to take care of some routine paperwork, an application for a pawnbroker's license—looking to sell second-hand gold, he needed to supply fingerprints. Greenhut was suddenly transfixed by a poster on the wall that caught his eye: the very same police bulletin featuring Gerry Dennis's handsome mug. "I *know* this man," the surprised jeweler blurted out. "Why, that's 'Duke' McKay!"

Greenhut was sat across the desk from Denk, unspooling a most unusual tale: on Thanksgiving Day, 1948, the jeweler had attended the Ohio wedding of the niece of Irwin Nussbaum, another local gem dealer and also Greenhut's uncle. At the reception at Nussbaum's Cleveland Heights home, Greenhut became acquainted with a young couple visiting from out of town: prosperous jewelry salesman Jerry McKay and his adoring wife Betty. The McKays had generously driven all the way to Cleveland to deliver their Beverly Hills landlord, Nussbaum's brother Frank, whom Jerry had met doing business through Nussbaum's additional office in Los Angeles. McKay thought it would be a lark to "tour the country," and the couple brought ample Hollywood flash with them: Betty turned heads, dripping in jewelry and swaddled in minks luxurious enough for a movie star, and Duke dazzled in his diamond tie pin, platinum cuff links and $800 watch. Such extravagances only added to McKay's dashing matinee-idol aura— when Greenhut showed Lt. Denk the home movies that he'd taken at the reception, the handsome charmer practically *popped* off the screen.

Not long after, when the home movies were screened again for two recent arrivals who'd flown in from New Rochelle, Lt. Maurice Kelly and his partner, Det. Jack Teehan, even Kelly had to wonder if Gerard Graham Dennis had missed out on his truest calling.

Kelly had only just arrived in Cleveland when, on Wednesday, February 17, an urgent phone call came to police headquarters from Zoltan Greenhut, who was shaking with excitement: by an astonishing quirk of fate, he'd just run into Jerry "Duke" McKay at the airport.

"Simply by chance, Dennis flew in from the West Coast," Lt. Kelly later marveled,

Greenhut disclosed that Jerry McKay had flown into town to pay a call on Irwin Nussbaum's fifth-floor office at the Hippodrome Building, a long-time landmark on Euclid Avenue housing the city's own plush Hippodrome Theater—the largest in the country devoted solely to film exhibition—and an eleven-story office tower. McKay set to bargaining with Nussbaum, who still believed McKay was a legitimate wholesale salesman, over a price for the eleven packets of unset diamonds on him worth $20,000; McKay's opening price was $35,000. As the haggling commenced, the jeweler called his nephew to let him know their pal Duke had stopped in; Greenhut dialed the police station.

As the shop bell tinkled, Gerry Dennis turned to the door to see three burly Cleveland police officers filling the frame, pistols drawn. They had a simple instruction: "Reach!"

Gerry, who was in his shirtsleeves drying his hands with a towel, slowly raised his arms above his head, offering a chagrined smile. "Well," he said, "you fellows have got me."

His cool demeanor belied his astonishment. "Before I knew what was happening, a whole platoon of detectives walked into the jeweler's building. It was just like a movie," he recalled. "Outside, the public had been cleared away from the area and another platoon stood on the ready."

Moments later, Lt. Denk arrived, along with a special guest: Lt. Maurice Kelly. After Denk's original phone call, Kelly booked the first available flight from New Rochelle to Cleveland, hoping to finally close his outstanding cases. For the first time, after over two years of pursuit, he stood face to face with Gerard Graham Dennis. "I had never seen Dennis, but after all those months, I knew exactly what he looked like," the detective would recall.

"If you budge, Gerry, I'll kill you," Kelly told him, aiming his pistol through the receptionist's cage.

"What's this about?" Dennis asked calmly.

"We're New York police," Kelly replied.

"Why, I thought you fellows had forgotten about all that," Dennis responded nonchalantly.

The local authorities allowed their dogged colleague from New Rochelle to lock the handcuffs onto their quarry. "Cleveland police gave me the honor," Kelly noted. His patience and persistence had, at last, paid off. And in that moment of satisfaction, seeing his quarry in handcuffs, the detective might have briefly forgotten about the vanishing act.

News reports about Gerry Dennis's capture and his incredible life of crime quickly circulated around the country. Initially, they had an even more outrageous cover story: in the fabricated version, it was a visiting Canadian fishing buddy of Denk's who spotted the police bulletin and recognized Gerry as a fellow angler he'd fished with many times and had just happened to encounter by mere happenstance on the streets of Cleveland. That fish story was presumably concocted and made public to protect Greenhut and

Nussbaum, in the event Dennis were part of any underworld ring seeking to eliminate potential witnesses—for good.

Dennis was already back in Westchester County just hours after his arrest when Clinton Anderson received a call from Lt. Kelly. They'd met some months prior at a gathering of law enforcement professionals on the East Coast and, suspecting that Beverly Hills might make ideal stomping grounds for the cat burglar, Kelly discussed Dennis with the chief then. Now, with the prime suspect in custody, he had something more concrete to convey.

A search of Dennis's Cleveland hotel room revealed $60,000 in uninsured gems, later traced back to the Winans heist. Along with the packets of diamonds and $1,435 in cash, Kelly and the Cleveland police had discovered two very significant items on Dennis's person upon arrest. The first was a handwritten list containing twenty-two names of the burglar's "prospects," among them some of the most prestigious players in Hollywood: Jack Benny, Bette Davis, Katharine Hepburn, Eddie Cantor, Edgar Bergen, Dorothy Lamour, Charles Chaplin, Paulette Goddard, Miriam Hopkins, Alice Faye, Ronald Colman, Louis B. Mayer, Harold Lloyd, Hedy Lamarr, Mary Pickford, William Powell, Kay Francis, Frances Dee and "Olivia De—" (presumably Olivia De Haviland, with Dennis apparently stymied by the spelling of her last name).

If that didn't definitively place Dennis right at the heart of Anderson's jurisdiction, the second item Kelly discovered certainly did: Dennis's home address at 322 North Oakhurst.

Chief Anderson swiftly dispatched two of his leading detectives, Charles Nash and J.D. Alcorn, to the apartment, just three minutes away from the police station. They were admitted by the guileless Betty Ritchie, who believed her jewelry salesman "husband" was away finally untangling the prior marital knot that had kept them from making their union legal all this time. She'd last seen "Jerry McKay" when he kissed her goodbye on Valentine's Day—the one-year anniversary of their first shared night together—and flew East, leaving no lodging address to contact him.

Betty seemed just as dumbstruck as the detectives when—in the absence of any known key—they tore the door off Gerry's always-locked closet and discovered the fabulous treasure trove of jewels and furs within. The coats alone were worth a cool $20,000, while the gems tallied somewhere upward of $100,000. Also secreted with the closet were jeweler's tools, loose metal fittings, the 1949 edition of the Southwest Blue Book social register and, in a rare show of professional sentiment, a damning collection of newspaper clippings chronicling the Doheny theft in Palm Springs. And then there was Gerry's private notebook, filled with the names of even more lucrative targets: Louis B. Mayer was again among them, plus film actress June Haver, socialite Lady Thelma Furness (the aunt of fashion designer Gloria Vanderbilt and the woman who introduced Mrs. Wallis Simpson to the Prince of Wales), automotive titan E.L. Cord, the wives of industrialist Henry Kaiser, Jr. and chewing gum heir Phillip Wrigley and several other prominent local figures.

Betty then shifted from stunned to terrified when the officers discovered three handguns, including a loaded pistol retrieved from the pocket of his raincoat. "I was scared to death," she confessed. "I never saw a gun around the apartment."

Everything was taken into police custody. As was Julius Bruck, the twenty-four-year-old jeweler living in the adjoining apartment, whom the detectives suspected aided Gerry in the disposal of his "wares." As was shell-shocked Betty Ritchie, who thought it was Gerry knocking on the door that day and was stunned to discover the police with their unbelievable tale. "I thought for a little while I was going to go out of my mind," she recalled, exploding in a torrent of tears when the officers suggested that the origins of her diamond "engagement ring" appeared suspect, and Gerry's generous gift of the $3,500 mink five months earlier had in fact been appropriated from oilman Waite Phillips's wife Genevieve. When Gerry gifted it to Betty just prior to their Cleveland trip, he said he'd purchased it secondhand, explaining away the coat's lack of labels.

Arrested on suspicion of receiving stolen property, Betty's plans for an idyllic marriage and the security of American citizenship were evaporating before her eyes. "I overstayed my time here and now I'm in trouble with the immigration authorities—I guess they will deport me when I get out of jail, but I never had anything to do with Jerry's stealing." She fretted to the press, "I do not love him because I realize he was just deceiving me all the time. I know now that he just used me to set up a commonplace background that wouldn't attract any attention to him."

Betty had just learned, like Eleanor Harris and Gloria Horowitz before her, that while being with Gerry might have seemed like a dream, it came with a rude awakening.

Even as his true identity was finally revealed to the world, Gerry Dennis suddenly took on another persona in the headlines: "Raffles."

After his arraignment appearance looking sartorially chic in a natty brown sharkskin suit, brown knitted tie, jaunty fedora, and topcoat, with heavy gold cufflinks gleaming on his shirtsleeves, newspapers and magazines shouted word of his daring crimes, elaborate double lives and way with women from Canada to New York to Beverly Hills, delighting in comparing Dennis to the fictional "gentleman thief" A.J. Raffles, a brilliant cat burglar and "amateur cracksman" posing as a high society cricket champion. In popular culture terms, it was a considerably more flattering sobriquet than being the taller half of "The Mutt and Jeff Bandits."

Raffles was created in the 1890s by British author E.W. Hornung as a criminal counterpoint to the more famous creation of Hornung's brother-in-law, Sir Arthur Conan Doyle. As a deliberate inversion of the deductive genius Sherlock Holmes, Raffles (complete with a Watson-esque accomplice, Bunny Manders) appeared in several adventures in *The Strand* magazine and later starred in several popular novels. Like Holmes, Raffles was no stranger to Hollywood: Bronco Billy Anderson played him in a 1905 short, John Barrymore in a 1917 silent, and there was yet another effort in 1925, with a pre-gossipmongering Hedda Hopper in a supporting role. Filmgoers in 1949, however, were particularly familiar with the character from producer Samuel Goldwyn's 1930 effort starring Ronald Colman and Kay Francis, and Goldwyn's 1939 remake with David Niven and Olivia De Haviland. Ironically, Colman, Francis, and De Haviland each ended up on the *real* thief's all-star roster of prospects. David Niven did not, perhaps spared by something in his performance, the best of the Raffles batch, that came closest to Gerry Dennis's idea of how a debonair gentleman thief truly behaved.

Hollywood—more precisely, Beverly Hills, Bel-Air, and Holmby Hills—immediately took notice of this new "Raffles" as well. His tale was rife with dramatic possibilities, but the most interested parties were primarily concerned with the whereabouts of all their expensive jewelry and furs.

In the days following Dennis's capture, the local glitterati made appearances at the Beverly Hills Police Department, hoping to identify their stolen trinkets among the loot stashed in Dennis's closet, most notably Loretta Young. The Academy Award winner smiled gamely for photographers as she reclaimed her mink and many of her jewels, even as other actresses were added to the cast of characters: the beautiful actress Gene Tierney and up-and-coming Hungarian starlet/ex-wife of hotelier Conrad Hilton Sari Gabor (later better known as Zsa Zsa) joined the list of victims, as did famed ice skater-turned-movie star Sonja Henie when two of her fur coats, stolen from a New York hotel, were revealed among the minks in Dennis's Beverly Hills closet. Fearing implication in the crimes, several East Coast gem dealers made a show of good faith by mailing stones recently purchased from Jerry McCabe to Chief Anderson's office, including a $10,000 diamond lifted from a Brentwood matron.

The headlines wouldn't stop. Gerry suddenly discovered what it was like to be famous. It was better to be rich.

The supporting players took their turn in the spotlight, too: the charges against Gloria Horowitz in 1947 had been dropped when she helped ID Dennis and recovered some of the jewelry she'd helped him unload. After a stint modeling in Tampa, Florida, that went south when her itinerant actor husband finally deserted her for good and their child nearly ended up in an orphanage, Gloria—now Gloria Howard, having legally adopted her ex's stage surname—returned to Detroit, finding part-time modeling work and still looking to break into television while her family helped raise her now two-year-old daughter. She convinced police to cover expenses for her trip to New York, as compensation for potentially lost modeling wages, to testify before the grand jury, turning the heads of reporters and photographers covering the case as she arrived and sending them scrambling for dramatic photographs to capture her sexy, *femme fatale* quality.

This time, Gloria was ready for her close-up.

After telling her tale in closed session, she held court with the press, detailing her interactions with "that skunk" Dennis ("Why, he still owes me commission money!"), offering coquettish *mea culpas* ("I guess I was a little naïve," she sighed. "It took me twenty-two years to find out what a dope I was") and taking pains to correct certain scandalous impressions made in the media ("Some newspapers referred to me as his girlfriend," she pouted. "That's just not so. He never made a pass at me.").

It was her finest public performance yet, but the press only half-heartedly reported (or completely omitted) her sexless spin. Sultry professional modeling photos of Gloria, shot for various male-oriented publications over the years, quickly resurfaced in the pages of national newspapers and magazines, alongside shots of Dennis looking dashing and dangerous, even in custody, with a cigarette clenched defiantly in his lips—indeed, the

White Plains jail was subsequently swamped with amorous missives from around the country after his photos hit the papers. Gloria demurely wrote *LIFE* magazine to protest that friends thought her *femme fatale* poses were snapped in court rather than "perfectly legitimate work" posing for their original source, a pulp detective magazine. By way of "apology," the editors re-ran a 1948 shot they'd published of a swimsuit-clad Gloria frolicking on a Florida beach. Dennis kept his own counsel on the girl he called "Glory," noting only much later that, as far as he was concerned, she was someone he'd been "foolish enough to rely on" and not nearly as innocent as she claimed to be.

Eleanor Harris received a bylined article as "Eleanor Farrell" in the *New York Journal-American*, decrying her years as Dennis's abandoned dupe. "I never dreamed he was a jewel thief during the four years we lived together as husband and wife," she insisted, labeling her love for him an "over-whelming madness" and calling their union "one of loneliness, frustra-tion and deceit." After Gerry's crushing departure, her mother had rushed to Eleanor's side until her charges were dismissed, then took grandchild Wendie back to Toronto with her to give Eleanor an opportunity to set her life back on track.

Gerry may have felt more for Eleanor than any of the other women in his life: remarkably, three weeks after he'd disappeared in 1947, he sent a surprise letter to her attorneys absolving her of all guilt in his crimes. "I suc-cessfully deceived and lied to my wife and family," he wrote, in part. "I have similarly disgraced a previous wife and two children and am now causing misery and disgrace to another. I realize with disgust the extent of my sins."

Photographed in an unflattering floral headscarf at the Beverly Hills jail, Betty Ritchie cried a river to reporters, devastated by the charges hang-ing over her head and heartbroken when she read the words written by Dennis's other "wife." "He used the same suave methods of falsehoods and deceit that he used on me," she said through hysterical sobs, though still managing to use her schoolteacher vocabulary to great effect. "My love for him depreciates hourly. In fact, it's run its full course. How awful can men be? Some men, I mean."

Other men were kinder to her, ultimately. After two terrifying months, Betty was deemed innocent, if hopelessly naïve, and acquitted of all the charges. Still, there was the matter of that expired visa. Facing deportation, she volunteered to leave her once-lush life in Beverly Hills and return to Fenelon Falls, where her parents—who'd immediately sent messages declaring their love and support—welcomed their heartsick offspring back into the family fold. "I guess everyone is entitled to one mistake in life, and I made mine," she'd say.

And Gerry wasn't indifferent to Betty's suffering. Upon his arrest, he had $1,435 in his wallet. Though the cash could conceivably be released by police and applied to any legal counsel he'd care to employ, Gerry instead suggested that the money be used to "meet his obligations" to his abandoned Beverly Hills sweetheart.

As the staggering sum of Gerry Dennis's crimes soared to $1 million, he was suspected of every unsolved high-dollar heist in the region. Greek shipping tycoon Aristotle Onassis's right-hand man Constantine Gratsos flew in from New York hoping to claim $140,000 in jewels stolen at a cottage at the Bel-Air Hotel from his wife Audrey, but flew back empty-handed. Lawmen from over 100 cities inquired about crimes in their localities, and the FBI even eyeballed Dennis for the burglary of a Richmond, Virginia, jewelry shop—a $481,195 job, it was the largest such haul in a decade—but ultimately, no evidence supported the theory.

Even Gerry Dennis couldn't be *everywhere*.

But one thing he managed to walk away with—an extraordinary bounty indeed—was the grudging admiration of Chief Anderson. Beverly Hills had seen industrious burglars and clever con artists before: as a patrol cop, Anderson himself had nabbed "the pet editor," an erudite bandit who, after a lengthy study of domestic animals during a stretch in prison, penned and published articles in various newspapers on pet care even as he pilfered from local homes in broad daylight. There was the rare book expert skilled at befriending Beverly Hills women who collected hard-to-get volumes, inspecting their home libraries only to return by night and raid the bookshelves of the most elite, expensive editions. And there was Frank Fuller, a fifty-four-year-old deaf man from Glendale who'd lifted some $200,000 in jewels and furs from homes in Beverly Hills, Los Angeles, and nearby affluent communities to doll up his forty-year-old paramour throughout the late 1930s. But he made the mistake of leaving fingerprints at the scene of a snatch from industrialist/movie mogul Howard Hughes's home in Hancock Park.

But even those operators couldn't hold a candle next to Gerry Dennis. Anderson—who never, *ever* had a respectful word for any lawbreaker in the gilded city he zealously guarded—appreciated brains and moxie. Dennis had those in spades, and the chief publicly proclaimed him "undoubtedly one of the greatest burglars who ever operated." As was only appropriate for Beverly Hills, Gerry Dennis was a *star*.

But one man outshone the burglar, in the chief's estimation. When Anderson and his detectives were commended by city officials for their work on the Dennis case, he shrugged off the praise, crediting the cooperation of multiple police agencies. He singled out the one man with even more moxie than the celebrity cat burglar: Lt. Maurice Kelly. The chief was notoriously even harder on his fellow officers than he was on criminals, but Kelly was Anderson's kind of cop.

From his jail cell in White Plains, New York, Gerry did something that seemed utterly out of character. He started telling the truth.

On his first day in custody, Dennis gave Lt. Kelly a guided tour of Westchester County, amiably pointing out the many homes he'd burglarized—at least as many as he could remember, he admitted—and confessing to sixteen specific crimes. A few days later, he snitched on his Beverly Hills neighbor, jeweler Julius Bruck, as well as his landlord, downtown Los Angeles gemsmith Frank Nussbaum, Zoltan Greenhut's uncle. Dennis said they'd helped him peddle his stolen goods, but both men were ultimately released due to insufficient evidence. Meanwhile, the FBI was sent an additional $14,000 in jewelry that Irwin Nussbaum had purchased in good faith from Dennis in Cleveland, baubles traced back to Nan Winans and Dolly Green Walker.

He also gave up his diminutive partner in six "Mutt and Jeff" burglaries from 1945 to Montreal authorities: already serving a four-year Canadian prison sentence for burglary following an arrest involving gunfire, Ernest "Little Ernie" Nesbitt earned an additional ten years behind bars. Even if Nesbitt had introduced an atypical element of violence into Gerry's thefts, the cat burglar needn't fear retribution now.

Among the more fascinating revelations was an incident in which he was discovered burglarizing the Brookline, Massachusetts, estate of Dr. James Poppen, a brain specialist. Dennis held Dr. Poppen at bay with his pistol, listening to the medical man's appeal for nearly an hour. "The doctor told me I was a very sick man to be going around committing robberies," he told investigators from Boston, recalling how he exited with only $47 cash and left the physician's other valuables behind. "When I left, I was sorry I couldn't put his advice into practice. I had never known that nice people like that lived in houses like that."

Dennis assiduously plied the court of public opinion, telling reporters how his father's embezzlement conviction shattered his life at a tender age and forced him into a life of thievery and deception. "After that happened, all the other boys in my hometown weren't allowed to play with me," he offered after suggesting that the masses were getting the wrong idea about him. "I guess I was bitter and by the time I was thirteen, I turned to crime."

Despite a sudden pathology for seemingly unabashed honesty, Dennis at first resisted speaking the truth—or anything else, for that matter—to Capt. Emmett Jones of the Los Angeles Police Department. Jones was dispatched to quiz Dennis about the L.A. and Beverly Hills jobs, and was one of more than thirty police officials from around the country sent to White Plains hoping to solve their own baffling burglaries. Dennis may have smiled when he read Chief Anderson's grudging compliment in the papers, but the chief's less-glowing follow-ups were red flags: "When Dennis finishes prison terms for his admitted New York burglaries," Anderson told the press, "he may be brought out here to live rent-free for a long, long time."

But after two hours of intense questioning in which Dennis resisted incriminating himself, the truth won out. He offered up full confessions to thirteen California crimes totaling nearly $400,000—including a handful he was never suspected of—and even drew detailed maps to show where and how he entered each home. He name-dropped his showbiz "connections," regaling Capt. Jones with the story of how he just *couldn't* bring himself to steal from that swell Bing Crosby and expressing remorse for burglarizing another well-known victim. "The only one I ever felt bad about robbing was Loretta Young," he revealed. "I always thought she was nice. But she didn't have much, anyway."

Even stranger truths began surfacing amid his elaborate fictions. Although he'd filled Betty Ritchie's head with a litany of lies, at least one of his seemingly tall tales was on the level. Dennis's formidable defense counsel, Joseph F. Gagliardi—a former assistant district attorney and future New York State Supreme Court Justice—announced that his client was indeed the inventor of an auto safety device which he hoped to place on the market to finance his defense. Yet to file for a patent, Dennis remained mum on the details of the invention, but given his expertise in pilfering cars, one might safely presume it was an anti-theft device.

Yes, the cat let everything out of the bag. Living a life of charade and deception since he was a teenager, it's possible he found the opportunity to finally tell the truth about his astonishing life refreshing, even liberating. "My mind is free of a lot of things that were bothering me," he said. "I am happy that now I can talk freely to ease my conscience." The truth, the saying goes, shall set you free—or at least shave considerable time off a prison sentence.

Being forthright and cooperative was, in fact, one of the only strategies left if he ever hoped to see the outside of a prison again in his lifetime. At one point, Dennis reportedly asked his collective police inquisitors, "Can't you fellows all get together so that I can do my twenty or thirty years and pay my debt to society?" Indicted by the Westchester Grand Jury on twenty-five counts of grand larceny, burglary, robbery, and assault in nearly a dozen burglaries, he faced a combined total of 365 years in prison for the New York crimes alone. "He has shown repentance," Lt. Kelly told police sympathetically. "He has twice broken down and cried like a baby when he's realized how he's disgraced his family in St. Catharine's."

The truth could not, in fact, *entirely* set him free—but it could help. Especially when combined with a liberal dose of his disarming charm, suave patter, and easy smile. Gerry had proven his prowess as a ladies' man, but he was a man's man, too, one who could smooth talk the guys just as easily as he could whisper sweet nothings into a dame's ear. No matter what you knew he was capable of, it was hard not to like Jerry. Just ask Chief Anderson.

And that was the basis of his *real* strategy.

On April 1, 1949—April Fool's Day—Gerry Dennis went to Manhattan, accompanied by three men: Westchester County sheriff's deputy Bruce Johnson, Detective Jack Teahan, and Lt. Maurice Kelly, Dennis's most constant companion since his arrest. He took the lawmen on a long, detailed tour of the network of pawnshops he used to unload his Westchester loot during his stint in New York, offering every detail he could recall about the people who helped him dispose of his spoils. It was a long but highly productive day, and when the officers returned to the Westchester County Court House in White Plains shortly before 8 p.m., they wanted to reward Dennis for his cooperation before returning him to his cell. Even Kelly, who'd only known him as a thieving phantom in the night for years, had learned that Gerry Dennis could really grow on you, once you got to know the guy. He offered to treat Dennis to a hot dinner at the Court Grill, a restaurant across the street from the courthouse.

"He is the most interesting burglar I ever met," Kelly later said, remembering him as "a handsome man…who had a pleasant way about him."

Grateful, Dennis dug heartily into his meal, thanking his captors for their kindness and charming them with jokes and stories like he'd won over the café society at the Stork Club and the Hollywood elite at Ciro's. He casually suggested it was a little tricky to eat with his wrists handcuffed as they were. Sure, the cops agreed: he'd earned an unshackling. Finally, the check came, and as Kelly and Teahan paid at the cashier's station, Deputy Johnson took the prisoner to a vestibule near the exit, preparing to re-cuff him. However, before the restraints clicked into place, Dennis slipped out of Johnson's grip and bolted out the door.

That nice guy act? *April Fools'.* It was time for the vanishing act.

Without collecting their change, Kelly, Teahan, and Johnson dashed out of the restaurant in pursuit. A month and a half in stir hadn't slowed the nimble cat—Dennis quickly outdistanced them. The lawmen fired their weapons, wild shots that sent pedestrians on the crowded streets of White Plains scattering and diving for cover. Keeping pace as best they could, the officers chased Dennis down sidewalks and through alleyways across several blocks, but he was just too fast. A corner turned here, a fence jumped there, and suddenly they lost sight of him.

Poof!

It looked like Gerry had taken a powder once again.

But then the lawmen heard a commotion in a nearby parking lot and hurried over to investigate. There they discovered twenty-seven-year-old rookie White Plains patrolman Cornelius Mullane, who'd heard the gunshots while walking his beat and rushed over to learn what was going on. He saw a handsome young man sprinting through the lot—Mullane didn't know if he was a criminal, a victim or a cop, but he decided to follow his gut and flung himself in a flying tackle. Mullane was wrestling with that handsome young fugitive, now cut and bruised, on the pavement as Kelly and the other officers arrived.

Winded, Lt. Kelly exhaled in relief. "We were lucky then," he'd remember. "And we learned a good lesson." His big catch had charmed his way off the hook and nearly vanished yet again. April 1st or not, the time for fooling around with Gerry Dennis was over.

Dennis spent his birthday behind bars, awaiting trial. Things were not going at all well for him in the spring of 1949 as he entered his twenty-ninth year. The curtain had come down on his fabled vanishing act, and as if to add insult to injury, copycat burglars were stealing his headlines. In the West, his record $258,000 haul from Dick Winans's Bel-Air estate had been resoundingly broken when an enterprising thief burgled a coffee heiress' West Hollywood home and spirited away over $435,000 in jewels, leaving no trace of evidence. Meanwhile in the East, Maureen Elizabeth Murphy, the beautiful, red-haired twenty-two-year-old daughter of a former Wall Street trader, was so taken by the news accounts of Dennis's exploits she set out to emulate him, committing three burglaries—including one at the home of a former victim of Dennis's—before being arrested.

Other women he'd enraptured moved on: in June 1948, less than a year after Gerry's sudden departure, Eleanor Harris married a slightly younger man named Albert "Al" Gedney, a former combat Merchant Marine turned newspaper production foreman she'd met waiting tables in Rye while she and Gerry were still "wed," striking up a romance in his absence. Al became the father to Wendie, adopting her the same year Gerry was convicted. "I feel like I got the best man who ever walked the face of the earth," she wrote. "I want to be a good wife and mother."

As Betty Ritchie picked up the pieces of her shattered life, it was clear she wouldn't lack suitors, either. A Burbank film studio guard, who'd seen her pretty photo in the papers, called her parents—collect—and told them Betty faced three years in jail, offering to hire an attorney and "help her in other ways." The guard's ardor cooled when he was taken in for questioning and sternly reprimanded by the fearsome Chief Anderson. In October, Betty boarded a TWA plane headed back to Toronto, offering advice to other wide-eyed innocents newly arriving to the City of Angels. "Be worldly wise when you come to Los Angeles," she said, "and if you meet someone you like, take him home to mama."

Gloria Howard (née Mitman, formerly Horowitz) hoped to use her newfound notoriety to reignite her bid for fame. Broadway gossip Dorothy Kilgallen frequently peppered her columns with references to Gloria's latest activities: she sold a magazine article, was squired around Broadway by Jackie Gleason's star-making showbiz agent Vic Jarmel, dated a police detective, enrolled in NYU, and peddled her film rights, but police denied her request to cash in on her scandalous ties by dancing in a swanky nightclub. She was briefly engaged to the roguishly charming but eccentric, volatile actor Steve Cochran; in 1951, she instead married Len Golos, the well-connected former *New York Daily Mirror* newspaperman turned press agent for nightclubs, liquor brands, hotels, and independent films. Her union with the publicist—witty and often quoted by top columnists— lasted until Golos's death from a heart attack in 1960. Among Gerry's cast- offs, Gloria alone publicly copped to a sneaking admiration for him. "He was so intelligent," she said. "I'm convinced he could have made as much money legitimately."

When an attorney became the latest to note how closely Dennis's resembled actor Robert Taylor, the once-appearance-obsessed burglar offered a rueful response. "I might have been better off if I didn't."

No, things weren't going so well, finally coming to a head on June 6 when Dennis, previously so free and easy with his confessions when he thought cooperation served his sly plans, stubbornly refused to plead guilty to the charges against him, prompting his lawyer Gagliardi to resign after a futile five-hour argument. In that moment, Gerry must have realized that, despite his solitary inclinations, he was now truly alone. There would be no quick getaway, no reinventing himself in a new locale, no fresh, naïve beauty to tend to his needs, no hobnobbing high society suckers to dupe, no dazzling diamonds to bankroll a new life.

The next day, he asked his attorney to come back, apologized to the judge for the inconvenience, and took his chances with the truth: he was guilty. A week later, dressed in a natty tan summer suit and brown tie, he stood in a sweltering courtroom handcuffed to a deputy sheriff with his head bowed as the judge pronounced his sentence: seven counts of eigh- teen years to life, to be served concurrently at Sing Sing prison in Ossining, New York. He was instructed to hold out little hope of parole before the first dozen years were up, even if his conduct was exemplary; even then, he still faced extradition to Toronto to serve the rest of the term he'd pre- viously been sentenced to there, so abruptly interrupted by the vanishing act. Mercifully, the district attorney in Los Angeles had given up any claim on Dennis, content to clear all the cases and satisfied that his East Coast punishment would suffice for all his crimes.

Many tears had been shed over Gerard Graham Dennis. Eleanor wept after her first love and the father of her child climbed out the window, leaving her to the police's tender mercies. Gloria cried as she was led out of the Philadelphia pawnshop in handcuffs. Betty sobbed buckets before the reporters and photographers surrounded her in the Beverly Hills jail. But their teardrops had long been spent, and only one person was left to cry for Gerry. As he was led from the courtroom to his cell, his icy-cool façade finally cracked as he pulled his crisp white handkerchief from his suit pocket and wiped a few stinging tears from his eyes.

Jerry Farrell, Jerry Woodruff, Jerry McKay, Jerry McCabe, Raffles— They'd all taken a powder. He would be, for the foreseeable future, no one other than Gerry Dennis, inmate.

But the cat had at least one life left: by June of 1950, one year after his conviction, Gerry Dennis was a movie star.

He had not, as he used to claim to unsuspecting Hollywood victims at the Mocambo, parlayed his matinee idol looks into a promising acting career. No, this Gerard Dennis was purely celluloid, the central character of a new Warner Brothers film, accurately if not-so-elegantly titled "The Great Jewel Robber."

Brian "Brynie" Foy, who as a child was one of Broadway's famed family of vaudevillians the Seven Little Foys, had grown up to become a Warner film producer specializing in ripped-from-the-headlines fare such as 1948's *He Walked by Night*. Fascinated by newspaper accounts of the modern-day "Raffles," Foy called his old school chum, Mayor Stanley Church of New Rochelle—Lt. Maurice Kelly's boss. As gossip columnist Louella Parsons, who disapproved of any screen glamorization of Dennis's crimes, reported, "You cannot deny Brynie's initiative in sending [Church] a check for $2,500 " to cinch his cooperation." With the aid of Church and the cat burglar's attorney Gagliardi (who saw an opportunity to actually get paid, quickly, for his legal services), Foy purchased the film rights to Dennis's life story just weeks before he was convicted (in an era before California law prohibited felons from subsequently profiting from their offenses).

Dennis set his initial selling price at $50,000. "Boy, you *are* a robber!" replied Foy, who ultimately ponied up $10,000. Gerry still had a knack for getting money out of Hollywood, though the lion's share went straight to Dennis's ballooning defense fund.

The thief also had an intriguing casting suggestion, reported by gossip columnist Hedda Hopper via Foy: "If you put up $100,000 bail for me, I'll play it myself," Dennis offered. "You could have a couple of fellows watching me." The producer ultimately demurred.

Also snapping up Gloria Howard's rights—and similarly rejecting her own bid to play herself—Foy assigned the respected screenwriter Borden

Chase, known for flag-waving John Wayne war films and top-notch Westerns like *Winchester '73* and *Red River*, to write the script. Accomplished British director Peter Godfrey (*The Two Mrs. Carrolls*) accepted directing duties on the film—originally and evocatively titled "After Nightfall" (initial title "Society Raffles" was nixed when producers holding the rights to the Hornung character objected). Tapped to star was up-and-coming Warner contract player David Brian, a struggling builder whose acting career was championed by Joan Crawford after a fateful dinner party.

When completed, *The Great Jewel Robber* took as many liberties with the telling of the cat burglar's life as Dennis, credited technical consultant, did himself. Eleanor, Gloria, and Betty were morphed and multiplied into a bevy of beauties under Dennis's sway, including a Canadian naïf, a duplicitous accomplice who deserts him during a thwarted robbery (and not, as in reality, he did to his dupe Gloria), a tender nurse ministering to him after he (and not, as in reality, his victim) is shot during a New Rochelle heist who unwittingly betrays him (not, as in reality, the other way around), a vivacious New York fur buyer, a frothy blonde airplane pickup, and a lonely Beverly Hills divorcee who provides his passport into Hollywood society.

On the screen, Dennis gives and gets a few dramatic beatings that didn't actually happen, and his climactic escape attempt after his initial arrest is expanded into a more cinematic set piece in which he flees into a tall office building and then makes a harrowing human-fly-style descent down its exterior before his ultimate recapture.

Nevertheless, upon its release on July 15, 1950 the film trumpeted its real-life credentials ("Headline Hot!" shouted breathless promos. "All True and All Thrills!"): several New York, New Rochelle, and Beverly Hills locations added an air of authenticity, while Hollywood gossip columnist Sheila Graham and *Los Angeles Examiner* feature writer Harry Crocker cameoed. Mayor Stanley Church made his screen debut playing Mayor Stanley Church; as a technical advisor, he even provided Brian with the actual pistol Dennis carried during his robberies. Church donated his acting fees to the Motion Picture Relief Fund, hosted the world premiere in New Rochelle, and scored big P.R. points by squiring around shapely starlet Joi Lansing. Complimented on his ease as a first-time film actor, Church, whose community ran deeply Republican, replied, "Well, what did you expect? Any fellow who can be the Democratic mayor of New Rochelle has to be a pretty fair actor, don't you think?"

Lt. Kelly was not similarly immortalized; though his name was used as the dogged detective in early drafts, he ultimately became the fictionalized "Detective Sampter." Nevertheless, at the premiere, Kelly received a standing ovation from the 3,000 local guests who'd assembled,

Leading man Brian corresponded with Dennis in prison, gathering tips on the well-tailored, freshly pressed suits he wore. "I tried always to be a gentleman," Dennis wrote, as revealed in the film's publicty kit. "Never talked out of the side of my mouth or anything like that. Also I was well-groomed and careful about my appearance. Just thought these little tips from me might help."

In Los Angeles, studio head Jack Warner, who lived on Beverly Hills' Angelo Drive in one of the city's grandest estates, extended a personal invitation to Chief Anderson and several of his officers to attend a preview screening of the finished film at the Warner Hollywood Theater; ironically, while the Beverly Hills force was inside watching the story of the criminal they'd helped put away, a less subtle or sophisticated holdup man robbed the box office outside and made a clean getaway. When informed, the chief confessed amusement—since the theater wasn't in *his* jurisdiction.

The poster tag lines were provocatively purple (*"His evening dress was always white tie…and a black automatic"* and *"He held society in the palm of his hand…and in the other—a gat!"*), and reviews were roundly respectable. *Variety* praised the performances and production values of the "sex-spiced yarn," particularly Brian's "grim, gutty portrayal," while *The Hollywood Reporter* labeled it "an absorbingly interesting drama" that inspired admiration and sympathy for the master thief, predicting boffo box office. Yet the *Los Angeles Times*, while admiring Brian's characterization, found something askance when hearing "audience laughter at times in the wrong places."

Audiences were indeed laughing, but not at *The Great Jewel Robber*, inappropriately or otherwise. Instead, they opted for the wholesome antics of Spencer Tracy as Elizabeth Taylor's flummoxed *Father of the Bride*, the summer's smash hit comedy. After that, *The Great Jewel Robber* pulled a vanishing act of its own, disappearing from theaters and public view for decades until it was finally released on home video in 2016. Dennis's story was revisited in a 1952 episode of NBC's revived television adaptation of the hit radio series *Gang Busters*—the radio incarnation had previously paid tribute to Lt. Kelly for cracking one of his early cases—although the Dennis episode was, again, an extremely loose interpretation of the facts.

There was, of course, one person who might have particularly enjoyed sitting back in the dark to watch *The Great Jewel Robber*, but crime films were strictly forbidden as entertainment for inmates lest anyone get any unsavory inspiration. Even from his cramped prison cell, Gerry Dennis would surely have gotten a kick out of watching Hollywood take great pains to craft the kind of elaborate fabrications about his life that he used to spin so effortlessly for its denizens. At this point, fiction certainly seemed preferable to reality.

But it was not to be. "I never got to see the movie," revealed Dennis. "But the descriptions that have been passed on to me have convinced me that I wouldn't have recognized it as my story. The distortion of the facts was that bad."

And if anyone knew about twisting and contorting the story of his life for a more compelling yarn, it was Gerry.

Transferred from Sing Sing to the notoriously airtight state correctional facility in Auburn, New York, early in his sentence, it became clear there wasn't going to be any invented persona or dramatic change of venue to provide Dennis refuge, with little likelihood of performing his now infamous vanishing act. To escape his current situation, he'd have to take a harder path, and he'd have to do it as Gerry Dennis, and Gerry Dennis alone.

"I suppose my slow transformation in prison started when—for the very first time—I faced the fact that I had unwittingly made an appalling mess of my life," he'd later write, keenly feeling the crushing weight of his reality. He observed so many career criminals inside, looking at lengthy stretches, growing older and even dying behind bars after joyless, stagnant existences. To Dennis's eyes, they'd transformed into "vegetables."

"I sat in my cell wondering if I, too, would become a vegetable," he admitted, "and suddenly my head was buzzing with questions I couldn't satisfactorily answer. They were persistent, nagging questions, not only about myself but about life in general. I knew that if I didn't develop a positive view, I would surely lose my sanity." He realized that he still possessed the most valuable tool that had been in his arsenal: his clever, determined mind. And just possibly, he could further hone it to his advancement.

"I took advantage of the prison school and jumped into my studies with both feet," he recalled, applying the same discipline and dedication he'd once employed while spending hours in the public library learning the vagaries of gems and jewelry. His self-education initially focused on existential topics like religion and philosophy, then expanded to include the social sciences. Page after page, year after year, his appetite for knowledge grew increasingly ravenous: "When I went into Auburn, I had grade nine education," he observed, swiftly accumulating enough credits to formally earn high school equivalency. In time, by his own estimation, he'd devoted over 25,000 hours to his studies, "well past the point required for a [college] degree."

Even behind prison walls, he found outlets for his newly acquired expertise. He taught courses to fellow inmates, emphasizing the importance of mastering proper English to improve their fortunes in life ("I wasn't a reformer—I told them even if it was their ambition to become confidence men they would find English necessary for their success," he explained). He became a trusty, allowed to address a group of delinquent teenagers from wealthy Westchester families involved in a string of gas station hold-ups; they told Gerry he'd reached them on a deeper level than any of the psychiatrists their pampering parents had paid for. He published a prison newspaper, sold articles to men's magazines, even offered ideas for visual gags that were executed by the publications' cartoonists.

In a particularly impressive display of auto-suggestion—and self-discipline, several years into his incarceration—the longtime chain-smoker kicked the habit altogether by posting a magazine photo of a diseased lung on his cell mirror to wean himself off cigarettes. He allowed himself a puff or two a day, followed by reflection over whether he took any true pleasure from the act. After just six days, he'd quit completely. He would similarly address self-identified "personality defects," taping instructional notes on improving his manners and expanding his empathy to his mirror. "I suppose, in a way, I was my own psychiatrist," he mused.

Even despite having indulged in some of the most lavish luxuries the outside world had to offer, Gerry chose not to bemoan the lack of finely crafted cuisine, impeccably tailored clothes or alluring, compliant women once available to him. "Through my studies I was able to adopt a way of thinking that did not permit me to linger on thoughts of things I was missing," he wrote. "To let yourself fret about the things you can't have in prison is nothing short of lunacy. It is best to do as well as you can with what you have." He found solace in a line from William Shakespeare's *Measure for Measure* that resonated with him: "They say best men are molded out of faults, and, for the most, become much more the better for being a little bad."

"Maybe Shakespeare was referring to people like me," he mused. Forget turning over the proverbial new leaf; Gerry Dennis appeared to be working on the entire tree.

Alongside his self-education, Dennis committed to another course of study: law. Through trial and error in his criminal career, he'd nearly mastered the art of escape, and now embarked on a journey to liberate himself by beating the legal system at its own game, zeroing in on an aspect of his conviction he found ripe with loophole potential. "Bothering me was the realization that the sentence imposed on me was unlawful," he wrote. "My record for small-time burglary in Canada was used to make me a multiple offender, and thus subject to the U.S. law that qualifies you for life imprisonment as a four-time loser." Dennis was stunned to learn those crimes had factored into his sentence—no one advised him of that fact—and he'd been found guilty of those Canadian crimes without the benefit of legal counsel.

Availing himself of Auburn's well-stocked law library, Dennis set to perfecting legal arguments that his Canadian record was irrelevant: he believed he should have been tried as a first-time offender in the U.S. and that his eighteen-years-to-life sentence should be overturned. Year after year, motion after motion, he papered the courts with requests for appeals. Rather than finding a way over the wall, he was determined to exit Auburn through its front gates as a free man.

After nine years, on October 23, 1958, Gerry Dennis finally had his day in court.

Dennis's original defense attorney in the 1949 trial, Joseph Gagliardi, had in the intervening decade been elected Westchester County District Attorney, compelled to recuse himself from his former client's revived case in favor of a special prosecutor—which was fine by Gerry, who'd accuse Gagliardi of taking more than his fair share of the cat burglar's movie rights fee in payment for his representation. The U.S. District Court in Syracuse ruled that Gerry successfully demonstrated that his Canadian convictions were indeed invalid: he was to be resentenced. Just in time for the holidays, Gerry was taken to a cell in the Westchester County Jail in the Eastview district near White Plains. While he awaited sentencing, forty-three rookie police officers from various Westchester communities convened for a series of lectures from crime experts; Sheriff John Hoy had a notion that no one was more of an expert on crime than the headline-making master thief himself. Hoy visited Gerry in his cell to inquire about sharing his insights on the methodology and mindset of an accomplished jewel thief.

"Ironically, these were the men who would police the area I once roamed as a burglar," an amused Gerry noted. Always keen for opportunities to offer up his potent charm offensive, he was agreeable. "Why not?" he reportedly replied. "After all, when you want a picture painted, you go to an artist, and when you're sick you go to a doctor."

From the stage of the lineup room, he offered insightful, cautionary tidbits: he advised the rookie cops to keep an eye out for the beam of a flashlight inside darkened manors; suggested wealthy jewelry owners should be directed to periodically check their best baubles to ensure the gems hadn't been replaced with paste facsimiles; and revealed that when stealing fur coats he would redesign the sleeves to render them less recognizable by their rightful owners. And, even after years behind bars, he couldn't resist closing with a little personal flourish, recounting his clever diversionary tossing of an ottoman out a back window to lure police away while he escaped through the front of that Long Island Sound estate. He was revealing, engaging, ingratiating. Sure, he was a little grayer at the temples, but in all the ways that counted, he was still Gerard Graham Dennis, the Great—and, of course, Now Reformed—Jewel Thief.

On January 19, 1960, as he finally entered the Westchester County Courthouse across the street from that ill-fated but nearly successful mad dash from the Court Grill years before, he had reason to believe he was closer to freedom than he'd been since that moment: with his life sentence lifted, he faced a shortened stint in prison, thanks to good behavior. And, having spent nearly a decade behind bars, he was *already* eligible for parole. He let himself entertain thoughts of a life on the outside again, using what was left of that Hollywood payday to pave a path into a new career as a teacher or in social services. "I felt…there was a chance I could equip myself with the necessary knowledge to lead a creative and happy life upon my eventual release," he wrote.

After Dennis's attorney detailed his maturation into "an older and wiser man" in prison—the press noted he was still handsome and charming, but now looked more like "a business executive" than a matinee idol—Judge James D. Hopkins reduced his sentence to fifteen to twenty-three years, giving him the green light to apply for parole immediately. However, there was no clear and easy path to release ahead: California and Pennsylvania issued detainers for his criminal escapades in those states, and there were certain authorities in Canada who were eager to welcome him back to his native land, with two years of room and board paid for by the government.

On April 15, 1960—Gerry's fortieth birthday—he stood before the state parole board after its members were informed in detail about his efforts to educate himself and his fellow inmates, his instructional sessions with law enforcement and juvenile delinquents, his career aspirations, and more. Then the decree came back. "Parole denied," the board chair announced. "The board members do not consider him a good risk. His case will not be considered again for three years."

And just like that, his expectations of release vanished. *Poof!*

"I thought that I was finally free, but I was in for a rude awakening," he later wrote.

On July 3, 1962, thirteen years after his conviction, Gerry Dennis walked out of Auburn prison at long last. It was a year earlier than the parole board chair had predicted, but a change in New York law regarding an increase in credit for good behavior went into effect that year and played in Dennis's favor. With an endorsement from no less authority than the prison warden, the parole board finally granted Gerry clemency. Had he been freed just one day sooner he might have at last caught *The Great Jewel Robber* airing on local television in upstate New York.

Much had changed over the years he'd spent in lockup. On the big screen, "Raffles" had faded into memory; the latest epitome of the suave, handsome, high society jewel thief was Cary Grant, leaping from rooftop to rooftop on the Riviera as John Robbie in Alfred Hitchcock's lush 1955 romantic thriller *To Catch a Thief*. Bing Crosby still sold records respectably, but the listening public had already cycled through musical style-setters like Frank Sinatra, Elvis Presley, and Little Richard, entering the early thrall of Beatlemania. Loretta Young was doing television, still glamorous but on a significantly smaller scale. Curvy pinup Gloria Horowitz set aside her dreams of stardom to play wife and mother again. Several of Dennis's wealthy victims had passed on, their jewelry and furs distributed to other hands.

Even the faces of the lawmen had changed: after a promotion to Captain, Maurice Kelly had retired in 1953 as the most decorated officer in the history of the New Rochelle police force and taken a comparatively cushy, well-compensated position as head of security for railroad car manufacturer and defense contractor ACF. He died at age sixty-one in 1964.

It appeared that Gerry was going to have little opportunity to reacclimate himself to the outside world because his release came with a catch. Immediately upon walking through the Auburn prison gate, Gerry was met by United States immigration officials carrying a deportation order. He was driven over two hours to Buffalo and escorted across the Peace Bridge, the passageway between the U.S. and Canadian border arching over the Niagara River and ending in Fort Erie, Ontario. There, he was handed off to the Royal Canadian Mounted Police, taken into custody on a nineteen-year-old charge: his 1943 escape from the Burwash industrial farm just days into his two-year sentence. After another six-hour drive, he was deposited in a jail cell in Sudbury, where he would await yet another day in court.

It was not, to say the least, the homecoming he'd hoped for.

This time, Gerry was determined to disappear from confinement without ever having to look over his shoulder again. He petitioned for a trial by jury and recruited lawyer Frank J. Keenan, his friend and high school classmate from St. Catharines, to represent him pro bono. His case drew the attention and support of the Law Society of Upper Canada, and the celebrated Ontario defense attorney and ex-Parliament member Arthur Maloney, the principal author of the Canadian Bill of Rights, provided additional legal artillery. Once again, much was made of Gerry's ostracized youth, a result of his father's conviction, his own youthful indiscretions leading to imprisonment turning him further toward crime, his subsequent efforts to better himself, and the headlines that prejudiced others against him. "He is being tried by the notoriety and the late show," argued Keenan, nodding to the fact that *The Great Jewel Robber* had aired on Canadian television just days before Gerry's court appearance.

If the arguments prevailed, one of these days, he might actually get to see it himself.

Initial testimony from Sgt. Charles Leigh, a guard who oversaw work gangs at Burwash during Dennis's brief stint there, seemed damning: "He worked in my gang," Leigh recalled. "There was a snow blizzard and at 6 p.m. he was missing." After Keenan insisted it was cruel and unusual punishment to invoke the old charges, Justice H.A. Aylen sympathized. "No one can help being sympathetic for this man," the justice said. "I don't know why the crown saw fit to lay these escape charges after all these years." But sympathy only went so far in court: the judge nevertheless rejected Keenan's legal argument.

Yet the prosecution was unable to ultimately produce any physical documentation proving Gerry had ever been either convicted or committed to Burwash in 1943—and thus no evidence that he hadn't exited the facility by legal means either. It was a technicality that, on December 6, 1962, led a jury to deliberate for approximately three minutes before acquitting him. The once-notorious playboy jewel thief Gerard Graham Dennis, the "international Raffles" of hundreds of headlines, was finally free. And just as he had back in 1949 when he was first sentenced, Gerry allowed himself to shed a few tears in the courtroom upon his release.

As he exited the courthouse, Gerry reiterated his hopes to find work in sociology, preferably in rehabilitation and prison reform, calling penitentiaries "continuous criminal conventions" that were "manufacturing crime."

But first, he told reporters, freedom "was going to take some getting used to."

"When finally, a few days ago, I was free of the law at last and walked the streets of Toronto a free man, it was cold and raining," Gerry Dennis wrote in the first of a nine-part series of articles under his byline in *The Ottawa Journal* in the waning days of 1962, providing an extraordinarily intimate window into his life of crime. "I needed an overcoat, but as I walked along I didn't mind the rain. There were times, before I went to prison, when I had closets full of clothes, and I didn't care then, either, whether it rained, because my biggest decision about rain in those days was whether I'd take the Cadillac with the top up or drive the closed Lincoln."

"I went from store to store in search of an overcoat without seeing anything I liked at a price I could afford," he recalled. "Then suddenly, it hit me." Gerry was struck with the realization that, even after spending the better part of fourteen years behind bars, "my taste was still what it was when I was when I was living high as a jewelry thief. With only fifty dollars to spend I was looking for a $150 coat. I had to come down to earth in a hurry. But I didn't compromise my taste. I simply settled for a good gabardine topcoat instead of an expensive heavy winter coat."

Purchasing clothes was just one of a slew of once-familiar, long-denied experiences Gerry reveled in, including "the sight of women and children…the chance to breathe fresh air at will…to choose a meal of my own liking…to dial a telephone."

The forty-two-year-old also admitted that, after that long stretch in stir, the opposite sex ranked just below a new topcoat on his list of priorities. "I've gathered, in the past, somewhat of a reputation as a ladies' man," he noted, "and I'm sure all my old friends would assume that on my first day out of jail I'd be chasing a woman." Stopping into a bar for a drink, he caught the eye of two women "whose profession I'm sure I recognized" entertaining a client a few tables away. But when invited to join their party, Gerry demurred, surprising himself by deciding that his standards in feminine companionship remained as steadfast as his taste in outerwear, preferring "the civilized company of intelligent women in decent surroundings."

Thus began Gerry's latest confessional offense, a newsprint attempt to rehabilitate his tarnished but still fascinating reputation by copping to his offenses in the most charismatic manner, casually unspooling dangerous, sexy tales of his outrageous escapades. His yarns were peppered with tangents of being reluctantly led astray by forces beyond his control and how, if only things had gone just a bit differently, he was often one good choice away from following the straight and narrow path. He revealed his calculated methodology, patted himself on the back for his ingenuity, settled old scores with the likes of Gloria Horowitz and Joseph Gagliardi without naming them, and shrewdly altered or excised various details and incidents that might leave him vulnerable to future prosecution. In a gentlemanly gesture, he avoided any direct mentions of Betty and Eleanor that might haunt—or even incriminate—them years after moving forward in their lives. But obliquely, amid boasts about his womanizing prowess, he tenderly referred to Eleanor as "the Toronto girl with whom I had fallen in love."

Such revelations were in service of "setting the record straight before I make a fresh start," he explained in print. "I was 28 when I was sent to prison 'for life'…I am 43 now, reasonably healthy and eager to discover if, with the added advantage of 14 years good education, I can't do as well at some useful pursuit as I did as a professional burglar." It was also a canny P.R. campaign, embellished with repentant flourishes: "I honestly hope that my story may have some influence on others, especially youngsters who are tempted to foolishly try, as I did, to have a life of ease and luxury."

While the payment for the articles would smooth his reentry into the world, it was clear he hoped that being straightforward about who he had been and who he was now, hat in hand, would pave the way for a new kind of future. "Just what [the] world holds in store for Gerard Graham Dennis is something that no one knows at the moment—least of all Gerard Graham Dennis," he admitted. "I will have to wait and see if someone—somewhere—has the courage to take a chance on me. With all my heart I hope so. For I feel that I have as much to give back to this old world from which I have taken so much."

A handful of people were already waiting in his corner: his family. His mother Julia and sister Mary had returned to Canada from England in 1948, just months before Gerry's name was splashed across international headlines. His first wife, Gertrude, after moving to Buffalo, where she remarried and raised Dennis's two children, kept in close contact with Gerry's family as well. "We were accepted wholeheartedly," recalled Gerry's daughter Anne, though her father's notorious past remained a secret to her and her older brother until their early teens. During a quarrel, a neighborhood boy spat out a shocking revelation: "Your father's in jail!" and the family finally explained the truth; not long after Gertrude drove Anne to Auburn prison, where she was introduced to her father for the first time. The environment was frightening, but Gerry, of course, quickly ingratiated himself to his daughter, and they remained in touch during his incarceration.

While Anne was living with roommates in New York City, she was briefly mortified to come across *The Great Jewel Robber* on television and recognize her father's name amid the film's otherwise distorted depiction. "I couldn't talk to anybody in those days about it—it was just too embarrassing," she recalled, snapping off the TV before her roommates noticed the similarity between the central character's surname and her own. Anne would not see the film again, in its entirety, until it was released on DVD in 2016.

Cleared of the Canadian charges, Gerry made his way back to St. Catharines, where, despite his mother's inherently aloof nature, he was reembraced by his family. Although not legally allowed to cross the border into the United States due to his criminal history, he managed to sneak in frequently to visit his ex-wife and their children, who became deeply fond of him. He even established a surprisingly convivial relationship with his former common-law wife Eleanor Harris Gedney, still married and living in Rye and once again an active church choir soloist—he was even allowed to have occasional contact with his younger daughter Wendie. Anne believed her own mother Gertrude, despite remarrying, continued to carry a torch for her ex-husband; in one dramatic instance of jealous ire, she even called immigration officials on him.

Where the women in his life were concerned, Gerry's charismatic twinkle and potent powers of persuasion barely dimmed over the long interlude since they'd last seen him. The hearts he'd stolen remained, to degrees, in his possession. "He was just delightful to be around," Anne said. "And he was *really* good looking. I mean, you wouldn't believe how good-looking."

Indeed, as proof of his still-potent magnetism, Gerry eventually attracted a new paramour: a British-born driving instructor he'd met in Toronto named Maureen, who, by outward appearances, seemed to be the kind of woman of substance he'd envisioned. His family members approved of her, and for a long while, Gerry and Maureen appeared blissfully happy. But their union was ill-fated: she was adamant about wanting children, yet despite having rebuilt amiable ties with his previous offspring—more like a favorite, rascally uncle than a father—Gerry believed he wasn't temperamentally built for real, meaningful fatherhood, especially in his forties. After several years together, they went their separate ways.

While Gerry's family was willing to offer him a second chance, employers, once they caught wind of his criminal record, were less embracing; it perhaps didn't help his cause when, in his first year of freedom, his public profile remained high after discussing his burglary career on *The Pierre Berton Hour*, the widely watched national daily talk show hosted by the popular Canadian author. After that limelight dimmed, Gerry sold encyclopedias door-to-door, regularly sought backing for various inventions (that fabled auto safety device never came to fruition), then opened a tastefully curated gift shop in downtown Toronto, but he was soon forced to shutter it. As promising opportunities first melted away and then simply failed to materialize at all, Gerry realized he was going to have to get creative. "Nobody in Canada would hire him, so he just had to fall back on what he knew," Anne Dennis recalled.

Ever entrepreneurial, he revived a skill that he'd mastered a lifetime ago: painstakingly disassembling and reconstructing jewelry into innovatively designed rings, bracelets, and necklaces—*legitimately*, this time. His creations were, family members agree, impressive. "They were really beautiful, high-end, one-of-a-kind, interesting, ultramodern designs," said Anne. He further resurrected well-practiced, pre-prison skill sets, deftly slipping back and forth across the U.S.-Canadian border and making successful sales calls on gift shops up and down the East Coast. While he wasn't quite prosperous enough to reclaim the life of luxury and decadence he'd once savored, he established a comfortably profitable niche, especially in the States—enough so that he eventually took up permanent—if illegal—residence near his former prowling grounds, New York City, in the early 1970s.

By the time he'd relocated to an oceanside berth in Rockaway Beach in Queens, Gerry had entered his fifties, but his rugged yet enduringly youthful face and still-trim, muscular physique—aided by faithful applications of black hair dye—allowed him to pass as a man nearly a decade younger. He flaunted his genetic gifts before the bikini-clad sunbathers and surfer girls packing Rockaway's grungy, post-hippie, proto-punk scene, strutting down the boardwalk wearing little more than a Speedo and a pair of fringed, knee-high suede boots. He caught the eye of one impressionable sunworshipper, a young woman named Roseann. Twenty-eight years his junior, she was born the same year his incredible criminal enterprise was flourishing in Beverly Hills. She was intrigued enough to quietly ditch her rock-carving artist boyfriend and follow Gerry back to his apartment. When he answered the rapping at the door, the barefoot woman he discovered there informed him, inexplicably, that she'd lost her shoes.

"Well, come right in," said Gerry, unfazed, casting an intrigued glance back at a visiting relative. "Look what the gods have brought us." It was love—or at least lust—at first knock.

It wasn't a luxe bachelor apartment in the Village or a swanky rental cottage in Westchester County, but the glorious double-sized lakeside log cabin Gerry discovered on Deal Lake in Interlaken, New Jersey, was an ideal fusion of his outdoorsy Canadian roots and his appetite for elegant accommodations. Set back from Windemere Avenue on a quarter-acre lot with a spectacular view of the lake, the cabin was originally a Canadian hunting lodge built in 1927 and transported to its locale near Asbury Park in the 1930s. Previously used as a corporate retreat for Bethlehem Steel, a headquarters/exhibit hall for a local art society, and a long-and short-term rental property, the two-story, ten-room structure, nicknamed "The Lodge" was simultaneously grand and cozy. With high beamed ceilings, hardwood flooring, and charming faux-rustic décor, it offered ample space for his jewelry designing equipment and supplies. A swath of surrounding foliage provided privacy, and a pair of snarling stone lions at the top of the dirt driveway discouraged uninvited guests.

Just how he negotiated a favorable and lengthy rental agreement remains a mystery, especially after his business began suffering due to a sustained spike in gold and silver prices that ate away at his customer base, increasingly reluctant to pay the escalating rates he needed to charge to make a profit. Nevertheless, the cabin became home to Gerry Dennis.

Or more precisely, "Grae Dennis," as Gerry had added yet another sobriquet to his roster of identities. Since earning his freedom, Gerry adopted a perhaps less notorious moniker with increasing frequency, especially because Roseann—who didn't really see him as a "Gerry," a "Gerard" or a "Graham"—preferred "Grae" as an affectionate alternative, so much so that it became the name by which he'd be known, socially and privately, from then on.

But Gerry and Roseann's romance proved downright volcanic, marked by blowouts, separations, and tempestuous reconciliations. It was so intense that, once Roseann moved in with him in between spats, Gerry would tell his family with a poker face that he kept a boat moored by shoreline outside the cabin, saying, "so I could always have a getaway." His family members made little secret of their distaste for his paramour, deemed insufficiently classy for their polished sort-of patriarch. Some encouraged him to seek out a more stable and especially wealthy "sugar mama" to help underwrite his taste for the finer things, especially while his looks still made such a scenario viable. "He said, 'Yeah, I know, but I don't really have much money, and Roseann loves me for all of what I am,'" his daughter Anne remembered.

Maybe not *all*, but at least the parts he told her about. For the duration of their relationship, Roseann reportedly had no idea that her handsome Grae was nearly three decades her senior; she genuinely believed they were considerably closer in age, and he did nothing to disabuse her. Some habits, like withholding vital personal information from the woman in his life, apparently went uncorrected during those self-improvement experiments in prison.

Family members believed Roseann held back her own share of information from her romantic partner, particularly in the realm of birth control. After making it abundantly clear he had no desire to be a father, he was reportedly livid when she revealed she was pregnant. Gerry became a new father yet again—well after becoming a grandfather—when their son was born in early 1978. But much to his own surprise and chagrin, he discovered that, this time around, he absolutely adored the experience.

"He said, 'Wow—this is great! I should have done this a long time ago,'" one family member confided. But he was not so utterly transformed that Roseann didn't trust him not to fly into a rage again when she became pregnant a second time—so, as he traveled around selling his jewelry, she stayed with her mother in New York City until their second child, daughter Tara, was born in the fall of 1980 and, at last, revealed to Gerry.

"He was fucking *pissed*," chuckles Tara Dennis today. "He's like, 'No—you've got to be kidding me!'"

Although he may have been tempted to board that boat outside his cabin and stage another one of his signature vanishing acts, Gerry "Grae" Dennis instead leaned into this new phase and the responsibilities that came with it. In letters to his family, he brimmed with optimism about the future as 1980 gave way to 1981. "This was going to be the year that his whole life was going to turn around, and everything was so exciting," his daughter Tara recalled.

But fate had thrown Gerry curveballs in the past, and now it hurled an unexpected, shattering twist. Shortly after Tara was born, he was diagnosed with pancreatic cancer, a notoriously swift, aggressive, and lethal form of the disease. This was despite Gerry's near-fanatical adherence to a healthy lifestyle—he was roughly the same weight as when he entered prison decades earlier and had not picked up smoking again after release. His family, kept in the dark about his diagnosis until it was irreversibly terminal, suspects that if he'd felt poorly beforehand, Gerry may have put off seeking medical attention until he could take advantage of Canada's universal health care system. But it had been increasingly challenging for him to cross the border with his usual impunity, and by the time he knew just how sick he'd become, it was too late.

Gerard Graham Dennis died on June 14, 1981. He was—much to Roseann's reported shock—sixty-one years old.

Tara Dennis was barely nine months old at the time of her father's death. She never knew him—nor was she told, for most of her early life, much about him at all; certainly nothing about his outrageous history as one of the most notorious yet glamorous society cat burglars of his era. But over time, she grew curious, unraveling bits and pieces of his backstory on her own, eventually discovering and forming warm bonds with siblings twice her age. I'd been slowly but steadily uncovering facets of her father's history since discovering his story while working as a rookie reporter at the *Beverly Hills Courier* newspaper when Tara and I made virtual and then in-person contact.

As Tara and I shared details about Gerry Dennis, she was taken by the unique parallels that marked their lives. Having always felt more than a bit out of place in her family throughout her upbringing—"I was always, like, 'What planet did I drop out from?'" she told me—she discovered familial connections she never expected: to support her college education, she worked in the jewelry business, becoming as schooled at the purchase and sale of diamonds as Gerry did; she initially planned a career as an English teacher, recalling how her father educated his fellow inmates on the value of mastering the language; and in the same way Gerry had evidenced an aptitude for legalese in his bid to cut short his prison sentence, Tara became an attorney practicing in New York City. Today, she marvels at the similarities. "I have the same handwriting as he does," she says. "It is a weird nature-versus-nurture thing."

The day after he died, Gerry was cremated and—according to unsubstantiated but accepted family lore—buried somewhere on the grounds of the Interlaken rental cabin overlooking Lake Deal. As it had so many times before, his abrupt departure left his paramour rudderless, with little sense of where to find any remaining resources to face the future. "Not a dime was left behind, that we know of," said Tara. Despite their oft-tempestuous romance, her mother would, Tara recounts, suffer his loss for many years to come. "This was the love of her life." And was she his? "I don't know. He had a lot of lives."

"Michael G. Graham" appears to have been one of these lives. As did "Grae Gerrard," "Graham Dennis," and other playfully deliberate alterations of his name.

Throughout uncovering further fragments of information about her father, Tara discovered a cachet of official identification documents—social security cards, passports, driver's licenses, bankcards—featuring Gerry's photo and signature under a variety of different names. Among the more tantalizing was an Ohio license issued to Michael G. Graham in April of 1978, at a condo address in Middleburg Heights, about twenty miles from the site of his capture in Cleveland in 1949. This paired intriguingly with a customer photo ID card from the Cleveland Trust Co. bank (today known as AmeriTrust) issued to Grae Gerrard.

His datebook reveals that Gerry appeared to have several jewelry clients in the region, as well as throughout the East Coast, Canada, and the United Kingdom. But the Ohio license presents a more elaborate, detailed fiction, begging the question: had Gerard Graham Dennis, the cunning, cultured, jet-setting "Raffles" of Westchester and Beverly Hills, actually committed to life on the straight and narrow, living in the New Jersey suburbs, after his release from prison?

Indeed, evidence suggests Gerry never entirely put his colorful past behind him.

"I think he *tried* to go straight," said his daughter Anne, recounting the many obstacles her father encountered while trying to carve out an honest living and the later struggles of his jewelry business. "He didn't tell me anything that he was doing that was illegal…But he had to have been doing something on the side just to exist."

There was a barely concealed air of pride about his notorious past: after reconnecting with his family, Gerry was a decidedly open book about his criminal life, spinning wildly entertaining yarns about his more cleverly achieved scores and self-deprecating anecdotes about moments where things nearly all fell apart. He suggested that filmmaker Alfred Hitchcock and screenwriter John Michael Hayes may have taken direct inspiration from his own methods and appearance when crafting Cary Grant's suave cat burglar in *To Catch a Thief*. For the record, they didn't; David Dodge, the author of the 1952 book the film was adapted from, was influenced by an acrobatic thief who raided the mansion next door to the villa Dodge was renting along the French Riviera—a crime the writer himself was briefly suspected of committing.

For a period, Gerry even hung an enlargement of the striking photograph of himself taken after his 1949 arrest—the one that had him casting a steely gaze at the lens while dangling a cigarette defiantly between his lips—prominently, cheekily, on his bedroom wall in Toronto. And he poked fun at his long list of alternate identities, signing at least one letter to a family member "Love, Gerry Graham Gerrard Grae, etc."

As his esteem for his larcenous accomplishments never fully dimmed, neither it seems did his impulsive desire to claim someone else's finery for himself. Anne recalled an incident in 1978 in which Gerry traveled to Philadelphia for the funeral of her mother Gertrude's aunt, a woman Gerry admired and who was very fond of him. After he'd departed, Anne was picking out some items she'd been bequeathed for shipment to her home in California, including a set of fine, quite expensive Limoges china on display in a glass-doored cabinet. She noticed that where she expected to see the set's massive gold-trimmed turkey platter, all that remained was an empty space where the platter, used maybe once or twice annually, had sat for years.

"I looked at my mother and she looked at me, and we thought, 'Oh no—he didn't!'" Anne recalled. Word filtered back to Gerry that his daughter suspected he'd helped himself to the platter. "He wrote me a real combative letter," Anne said. "It went on and on and on…He was really upset that we would think that he would do such a thing." The resulting friction caused an estrangement between the two that wouldn't be smoothed over for years.

"I *know* he took it," Anne chuckles today, noting that whenever her family has a big dinner spread, her husband still faux-apologizes to guests for not getting a larger turkey because his father-in-law swiped the biggest platter.

Harder to laugh off was an instance in the early 1970s when Gerry accompanied then-flame Maureen on several trips to her native England, where he also mined sales contacts. His family members recall how, while shopping on one such excursion, a comforter set caught his eye; he brazenly attempted to walk out of the shop with it but was intercepted by the store's security. How he escaped arrest and prosecution remains unknown, but the unpleasantness of the situation and Gerry's continued inclinations to flout the law proved to be as critical a breaking point for Maureen as their clash over having children. When they returned to the United States, Anne recalled, "she said, 'That's it,' and that's when she broke it off. She couldn't deal with this anymore. He couldn't hide everything." Nevertheless, Maureen—who would soon have a daughter on her own—would remain a regular presence in the lives of Gerry and his family for several years, often ferrying items from him to family members in New York prior to his relocation to the United States.

Those close to Gerry looked the other way when it came to his multiple personas. The numerous fake IDs were, they understood, forged for him by a former fellow inmate at Auburn living in New Jersey to help him move back and forth between countries without detention, even as international security escalated. "Every time he went across the border, he used a different name," said Anne. If there were other uses for the phony ID cards, Gerry kept them to himself.

There was additional intrigue: Gerry kept a cachet of belongings secreted in a family member's cellar on the U.S. side of the border. One evening, the usually unflappable Gerry arrived, urgently needing to clear out the contents of the cellar, which included a large amount of expensive fur coats and other suspect items, reminiscent of his mink-filled locked-closet cachet in the Oakhurst Drive apartment in Beverly Hills.

Gerry confided to at least one family member that his Ohio visits involved a mysterious mistress, "my plump girlfriend in Cleveland," reportedly a millionaire's daughter with her own interior design business—one Gerry hoped she'd expand to include small home décor items that he'd specialize in crafting. Whether his paramour knew him as Gerry, Grae, Michael, or any other alias remains unknown.

Exactly where Gerry obtained the diamonds and other gems he used in crafting his jewelry—and how, during leaner times, he paid for them—is also a mystery. His children wondered if, somewhere along the way during his cat burglar heyday, he'd hidden a reserve of pricey stolen jewelry or pilfered stacks of cash somewhere and was dipping into it as needed. "We never could figure out if he had a stash or not," said Anne.

The log cabin in Interlaken was grand enough that his intimates wondered how he financed such a desirable set-up—especially one in high demand. When queues of eager summer renters offered the owner significantly higher rent, Gerry somehow wrangled an even longer lease nonetheless—a curious victory, even for the accomplished smooth-talker.

Was that "getaway" boat moored in the back merely reserved for fleeing relationship dustups, in jest or otherwise, or stationed there as part of a more strategic escape plan?

Upon Gerry's death, his sister Mary—deemed near saintly by her nieces and nephews—debarked for Interlaken to assume responsibility for his effects in the log cabin. In particular, he kept a workroom there housing his jewelry-making tools, as well as the gems and precious metals used in their construction. However, when Mary arrived, the entire cabin had already been completely stripped of its contents (the Dennis family suspected Roseann and her family arrived ahead of Mary and cleaned the cabin out).

Years later, after Gerry's daughter Tara learned of the cabin's existence, she couldn't resist exploring it during a trip to New Jersey. Peeking through the windows, she discovered that while it still had a certain fairy tale appeal, the cobwebs covering the door and the empty interior suggested that it had gone uninhabited for quite some time—indeed, she thought it looked untouched, inside and out, from photos taken during Gerry's stay there decades earlier. Fascinated by the connection to the father she'd never known, she noticed a "For Sale" sign and decided to make an offer on it.

Despite repeated attempts, she never got a response and couldn't get a showing. "I begged for five years: 'Can I buy your house?' And they just ignored me," said Tara. "It was the strangest thing. And then they sold it. I had to think it had something to do with my name."

Clearly, so much of Gerard Graham Dennis's life after his incarceration remains cloaked in mystery. But there seems to be little question that, following his release, he did not entirely give up a life of crime.

More likely, he got considerably better at not getting caught.

Who, exactly, was Gerry?

"Gerry, Graham, Gerrard, Grae, etc." Through all the guises and all the artifice, there were constants, to be sure: Gerry, the boy who sneakily plucked cookies from a serving tray with the skills of a magician. Gerry, the chameleon of ever-shifting identities, to be used and discarded as necessary. Gerry, the ladies' man, so fond of less-worldly women who didn't ask too many questions, also used and discarded as necessary.

Gerry, the charmer, who could seemingly smooth talk his way into and out of any situation. Gerry, the indulgent, who always found a method to exist lavishly beyond his means. Gerry, the meticulous, plotting his movements down to the tiniest detail. Gerry, the gentleman. Gerry, the penitent. Gerry, the incorrigible.

Gerry, the maestro of the vanishing act, who, even as he exited the mortal plane, left nary a trace—including a definitive resting place—behind him.

Gerry, the Great Jewel Robber.

Poof!

THE RECKLESS MOMENT

"Did I hit what I was aiming at?"

—Walter Wanger

Veteran film producer Walter Wanger waited calmly in the parking lot of the gorgeous white Colonial-style headquarters of the Music Corporation of America. Fifty-seven, silver-haired, polished, and patrician, Wanger looked every inch the epitome of Hollywood success, if a bit disheveled on this occasion. The Music Corporation of America was the most powerful talent agency of its day, representing a lengthy list of top-tier stars, including Wanger's beautiful wife, actress Joan Bennett, a screen star of over twenty years and still radiant at forty-one. It was a locale the producer visited countless times to broker deals for his long and enviable list of prestigious film projects. But despite the often-intense professional enmity that could arise between producers and agents—where negotiating tactics sometimes resembled all-out war—Wanger had never come to MCA literally armed. Until that day, December 13, 1951.

His .38 still warm in his hand, Wanger—an honorary county deputy sheriff since 1933—greeted two warily approaching Beverly Hills police officers with a succinct summation of his business at MCA that afternoon: "I've just shot the son of bitch who tried to break up my home."

Despite the lack of a body, the officers took Wanger at his word and escorted him to the police station—about fifty paces across the street. This was the fallout of a classic love triangle gone wrong, a star-studded variation on one of the oldest stories known to civilization, with all the requisite ingredients of a true crime of passion: a faith betrayed, a reckless act and a smoking gun. It was unique in the fact that the three sides included a highly respected movie producer, his glamorous screen actress wife, and her Hollywood agent. And, of course, the fourth angle that disrupted this particular geometry: a battalion of press ravenous for all the sordid details.

If any couple embodied the utmost expression of the Hollywood Dream, at least on the glossy surface, it was the husband-and-wife team of Walter Wanger and Joan Bennett.

Born Walter Feuchtwanger on July 11, 1894, to a wealthy San Francisco knit goods manufacturer, the Dartmouth-educated—although he never graduated—Wanger (rhyming with "ranger") shortened his surname and broadened his horizons by entering the theatrical world as a "glorified office boy" for British playwright Harley Granville-Baker. He swiftly rose to become a wunderkind stage producer, his career briefly interrupted by a distinguished tour of duty as an Army Intelligence officer during World War I, including a staff role on President Woodrow Wilson's negotiating team at the Paris Peace Conference. Possessed of a decidedly European sensibility when it came to the arts, Wanger returned to New York's Theater Guild, where in 1919 he met his first wife, the glamorous Ziegfeld Follies Girl and silent screen actress Justine Johnstone; billed as "the most beautiful girl in the world," she was also an intellectual on par with Wanger and later became a respected medical researcher. He was eventually lured to the burgeoning film industry by pioneering executive Jesse Lasky, joining Famous Players-Lasky studio—subsequently Paramount Pictures. Migrating west to Los Angeles, he served as a top production executive for Paramount, Columbia Pictures, and Metro-Goldwyn-Mayer.

But after cutting a glorious swath to studio success, Wanger truly made a name for himself when he struck out on his own as an independent producer, fueled by the desire to create popular entertainment with at least a smattering of artistic sensibility after seeing the value of film as both a teaching tool and propaganda vehicle during his war service. Craving approval from the intellectual arbiters of taste, he was determined to put cinema to what he felt was its loftiest purpose: not exactly high art, but a medium with deep, meaningful undertones, elements of social critique, and calls for progressive change, even enlightenment—all packaged in the dazzling gloss of Hollywood. The first film released under his imprint was an impressive knockout—1933's *Queen Christina* starring Greta Garbo— and he'd go on to shepherd a host of successful convergences of art and commerce to the screen, including the classic John Ford Western *Stagecoach* and Alfred Hitchcock's *Foreign Correspondent*.

He joined and revitalized United Artists just as its founders Douglas Fairbanks, Mary Pickford, and Charlie Chaplin peaked professionally, developing the careers of many top stars, including Rudolph Valentino, Clara Bow, Claudette Colbert, Charles Boyer, Sylvia Sidney, Henry Fonda, and the Marx Brothers (at Wanger's suggestion, Groucho at last dropped his greasepaint mustache in favor of a real one). Almost as glittery was the array of sexual conquests the relentlessly flirtatious producer amassed (he and Johnstone had a quietly open marriage), Tallulah Bankhead and Louise Brooks among them. "When he arrived on the set for a conference with the director, he always found time to check out the new females," Ginger Rogers would recall. "He'd spot a starlet and look her up and down like a horse trader." But if his intentions were less than subtle, Wagner was famous for his ability to charm his way into the bedroom of any woman he set his sights on, possessing an innate understanding of the opposite sex, or at least what they wanted to hear.

While some of his cohorts never knew exactly how genuine his intellectual aspirations really were—he produced his share of crowd-pleasing popcorn entertainments built on easy, exploitive hooks—by 1939, the distinguished, pipe-smoking producer had achieved such an abundant combination of success and respect that he was appointed president of the prestigious Academy of Motion Picture Arts and Sciences. He held the post for six years until 1945 and would even receive an honorary Oscar a year after leaving office in tribute to his service and accomplishments.

By Hollywood standards, Walter Wanger had it all. Recklessly, he would want something more.

Joan Bennett led a similarly charmed existence. Born on February 27, 1910, in Palisades, New Jersey, to a prominent theatrical family eight generations strong, Bennett was the youngest of three daughters to the acclaimed yet volatile stage actor Richard Bennett—one of the most popular and critically hailed performers during the early twentieth century, also known for his erratic onstage tirades against various perceived enemies, typically theater critics—and his actress wife Adrienne Morrison Bennett. Unlike older sisters Constance and Barbara, who'd both go on to Hollywood success, Joan initially balked at pursuing the family business, feeling she wasn't a natural fit for the limelight. "I was definitely the mess of the family," she explained. "Connie and Barb were beautiful, even as young girls. I was near-sighted and wore glasses. The most obvious thing about me was my inferiority complex." The acting life often left her family's home life chaotic, exacerbated by Richard's chronic alcoholism, infidelity, and frightening outbursts that came with the threat of violence, all ultimately contributing to her parents' divorce. Joan believed she was temperamentally better suited to a more stable, home-centered life. "I wasn't going to have acting rammed down my throat," she'd recall. "I wanted marriage and a family."

Even as a child, her reserved nature left her far less prone to the rash, imprudent behavior her father and sisters would become infamous for. Still, on occasion, she'd display a streak of recklessness: after she'd blossomed into an undeniable beauty, the abiding pull toward family and stability led her, at sixteen, to bolt from finishing school in Paris to run off to London with Seattle high society scion John Marion Fox. In quick succession, she became a wife, then mother to daughter Diana, and, when Fox's unabated alcoholism proved too much to bear, ultimately a divorcée and single mother at eighteen. Out of necessity, she made her Broadway debut opposite her father, which caught attention in Hollywood. She'd accumulated a wealth of life experience in just a few short years, but it was her fresh-scrubbed beauty that launched her film career in 1929, when she was chosen to star alongside Ronald Colman in his first talkie, Samuel Goldwyn's smash action-adventure hit *Bulldog Drummond*, based on the popular hero of pulp fiction.

Less ambitious than her sisters and with a child to raise at home, Bennett slowly and surely built her screen career in a series of standard sweet-but-bland girlfriend roles. "When I went to Hollywood the first thing they did was bleach my hair," she'd recount. "I was the blonde ingénue type, short on brains and always involved in some kind of triangle." But she received praise for standout roles here and there, including a comically petulant turn playing pot-stirring sister Amy opposite Katherine Hepburn's Jo in 1933's *Little Women*, and as a mentally unraveling young wife in the Walter Wanger-produced psychiatry melodrama *Private Worlds* in 1935. Her personal life offered more spice due to a smattering of high-profile romances with the likes of film executive John Considine, Jr., actor Lew Ayers, and dime-store heir Woolworth Donahue, leading Hollywood scandal-scouters to target Bennett, like her sisters, as a potential provider of eyebrow-raising gossip.

Intensely private and as outwardly gracious and poised as she was stunning, Bennett resented the muckrakers' attentions, giving as good as she got: on Valentine's Day, 1950, the actress sent gossip columnist Hedda Hopper a live, de-scented skunk bearing a note—"Won't you be my valentine? Nobody else will. I stink and so do you."—to illustrate her disapproval over one particularly offensive article, along with buying $800 worth of trade paper ads mocking the ex-bit player-turned-columnist as "a frustrated and jobless actress." A delighted Hopper snarked back, "I didn't know she had that much money," and named the reportedly well-mannered skunk "Joan." Along the way, her Hollywood colleagues struggled to get a bead on exactly who Joan Bennett was. Mary Pickford, herself a dichotomy of sugar and spice, dubbed Bennett "Pollyanna Borgia," noting, "She looks so quiet and sweet, but underneath that gentle exterior, *watch out.*" Despite her turbulent love life, Bennett was professionally more respected by film crews than her oft-erratic sisters, deemed "the good Bennett."

Domesticity, she always felt, suited her: after her on-off relationship with Considine finally fizzled and a long recuperation after a bone-shattering fall from a horse, Bennett was courted by novelist and screenwriter Gene Markey, whose ladies' man charms made up for his lack of leading man looks. The couple married in 1932 and set up housekeeping on Beverly Hills's Tower Road, where they welcomed their daughter Melinda and Markey formally adopted Bennett's elder daughter Diana. Settling into a semi-quiet routine, Joan recognized that, even with Markey's attraction to Hollywood's social whirl, he was easily the most reliable partner she'd found.

And yet, she soon wondered if she had entered into her marriage to Markey because she was in a particularly vulnerable state, especially when a certain dashing, dignified producer took a more active hand in her career—and other aspects of her life.

Even though he'd once rejected her earliest screen test on the grounds that "she'd never photograph," on the strength of her performance in *Private Worlds*, Walter Wanger developed a keen interest in Joan Bennett. Many noticed that during the filming the famously hands-off producer began showing up on set every day—at least, every day Bennett was on set. It was a habit he'd uphold in their subsequent collaborations over the next few years, adding her to his recurring stable of screen players.

It was Wanger who substantially reinvigorated Bennett's film career in 1938 by changing her image from plucky good girl to sultry *femme fatale* for the film *Trade Winds* by simply concealing her blonde locks under a jet-black wig. The transformation, reminiscent of the re-making of another star in the Wanger stable, Hedy Lamarr, was so dramatic—and welcome, based on the audience response –Bennett was soon being considered for more plumb roles, including the coveted Scarlett O'Hara part in *Gone with the Wind*. When the highly hyped search narrowed to Bennett and one other contender, she lost out to Vivian Leigh. But with her smoldering new look and coolly sexy screen persona, she emerged as a leading siren of the emerging *film noir* genre.

"I turned my hair dark and have received much better parts ever since," she enthused. "I liked the idea of escaping from all that bland, blonde innocence." Welcoming the shift, Bennett was quick to let her own dark locks grow out. "It wasn't black, but it was dark enough to classify me as a brunette and for the next ten years I was the smoldering brunette, slinky and husky voiced." With her smoldering new screen look and attitude—some friends believed her icy, detached air, on screen and off, was due largely to the fact she remained, as in her youth, blind as a bat without her glasses on—Bennett's film fortunes shifted dramatically. Her romantic life would soon follow, both thanks to the same man.

As her allure to moviegoers intensified, so too did her spell over Wanger. Though both were married and she was aware of both his permissive union and reputation as an inveterate womanizer, Bennett spent more and more time in the producer's company. Something was missing in her marriage to Gene Markey—yes, he provided stability and was a wonderful father to the girls, but he was too eager for social status, an artistic dilettante lacking in the serious substance she craved. Conversely, the polished, sophisticated, impeccably dressed Wanger, with his seemingly inexhaustible depth of knowledge of art, literature, culture, and politics, practically *exuded* substance, especially when waxing poetic about the societal enlightenment and progressive benefits he believed were possible through cinematic storytelling. Soon, they were spotted keeping company off-set as well, and though she rationalized her eventual split from Markey in 1937 as the result of their marriage simply becoming "lusterless," the entire industry knew full well that Joan Bennett and Walter Wanger, who split from his own spouse a year later, had fallen deeply, if perhaps recklessly, in love.

On January 11, 1940, the two were discussing an upcoming project over the phone when Wanger, who for two years had been determinedly gun-shy about entering into marriage again, impulsively popped the question. The next day they were married in Phoenix, the union witnessed by Bennett's close friend and press agent Margaret Ettinger (who also happened to be cousin to Hedda Hopper's rival gossip maven Louella Parson).

Wanger telegrammed his plight to his cronies with military allusion: "Impossible to withhold any longer. Front lines gave way completely." A Hollywood power couple, before the term was coined, ascended, but there was a dark postscript: three days after the wedding her first husband Jack Fox, still plagued by drink and money woes, who'd said in the press "I don't like the idea of Joan being married to that other fellow," died of a prescription drug overdose (Gene Markey fared somewhat better post-Bennett: ever the charming social climber, his subsequent wives included Hedy Lamarr, Myrna Loy and wealthy thoroughbred heiress Lucille Wright).

But the Wangers were determinedly on the ascent: they settled into the $150,000 fifteen-room French Provincial manor designed for Bennett two years earlier by famed architect Wallace Neff at 515 Mapleton Drive in Holmby Hills, the chic L.A. enclave just outside Beverly Hills, reserved for those even wealthier than the above-average denizens of 90210. Neighbors on the street, one of the most elite in L.A., would include Humphrey Bogart and Lauren Bacall, Bing Crosby, and Alan Ladd, as well as the rear entrance to department store heir Arthur Letts, Jr.'s massive estate, later known as Hugh Hefner's Playboy Mansion. The home's exterior was distinguished by a white brick facade, peacock-blue shutters, twin chimneys, an abundance of flora, and a decided lack of security gates, which Joan found gauche; behind the house was an enormous lawn boasting a pool, dining area, gardens, a greenhouse, flowerbeds hedged by boxwood, and a resplendent magnolia tree outside the master bedroom. Inside, a glittering crystal chandelier Bennett brought over from France floated above the two-storied circular entry hall; the fastidiously kept living space was filled with shelf after shelf displaying her elaborate collection of miniatures, Wanger's voluminous library of first-edition books, and *objects d'art* from around the world.

The couple shared certain qualities in abundance, especially a passion for the movie business, and other seemingly opposite traits that were actually quite complementary: he fawned over famous people and extolled exciting projects, while she was hard to impress; he liked simple daily routine and retired to bed early, she lived to host extravagant dinner parties—featuring guests lists that read as a who's who of Hollywood—and was a late riser; he was a determined, unyielding, occasionally ferocious negotiator, she was considered an authority on beauty and good manners, penning an instructional tome called *How to Be Attractive* in 1943, to aid women who'd stepped into the working world during wartime. A devoted mother who gloried in grooming her girls to be as elegant, tasteful, and glamorous as herself, she had it written into her contracts that she would be released from work in time to get home and tuck her daughters into bed.

They developed a series of private hand signals to communicate wordlessly at chic functions and help each other avoid embarrassment (although her poor vision often made awkward situations worse). They hobnobbed with a more rarefied breed of celebrity than the typical Hollywood variety, intellects like Carl Sandburg and political powerhouses like Wendell Willkie, Franklin and Eleanor Roosevelt, and Harry and Bess Truman. At Mapleton they weathered the end of the Depression, the entirety of wartime, and the postwar recovery; active in Democratic circles, Walter was even named county and city chair of the anti-Communist Crusade for Freedom in 1950. And while Wanger had never fancied himself a family man, he genuinely adored Bennett's daughters and became a dedicated, doting father with the arrival of their own subsequent offspring, Stephanie and Shelley.

Joan Bennett had, at last, found the stable home she'd long craved. Walter Wanger discovered the one he'd never known he wanted.

If life on Mapleton Drive seemed idyllic, Bennett and Wanger's careers similarly soared during the first decade of their union, which featured some of his most commercially rewarding productions. She, too, triumphed when working on two crackerjack *noir* thrillers, 1940's *Manhunt* and 1944's *The Woman In the Window* with the German expatriate filmmaker Fritz Lang, whose work was suffused with moody, atmospheric expressionist flourishes. For the latter film, the director steered Bennett into more erotically charged territory than she'd ever navigated, lavishing almost fetishistic attention on shooting her for carnal effect—many colleagues and crew members wondered if Lang and Bennett were similarly intimate when the cameras weren't rolling, but a lack of further evidence led most to conclude that, at best, the filmmaker was hopelessly enamored with the newly transformed screen goddess.

For her part, Bennett experienced an even greater on-screen metamorphosis than *Trade Winds* had provided. The collaborations with Lang proved foundational in the developing *noir* genre, and Bennett's sex-drenched yet icy, domineering, ultimately man-destroying performance in *The Woman in the Window* created a vivid template for the *femme fatale* archetype that her contemporaries—Barbara Stanwyck, Lana Turner, Rita Hayworth and Ava Gardner among them—soon expanded upon. Her newfound, provocative incarnation as a dangerous dame, Bennett said, "was much more fun to play than the insipid ingenues I had been doing."

Though later she learned to diffuse the perfectionist, frequently dictatorial Lang's oft-mercurial moods when she arrived on set by announcing, with uncharacteristic bawdiness, "Hello, Fritz, you old son of a bitch!" she always spoke glowingly of Lang, proud of the work they did together. The combination of filmmaker and star proved so potent that, once Wanger forayed into his career as an independent producer, two more *noirs* followed: the brilliant *Scarlet Street* (1945), in which Bennett brings her *femme fatale* image to full fruition as a soul-crushing succubus, and the less effective *Secret Beyond the Door* (1948), each directed by Lang, produced by Wanger and starring the increasingly bankable Bennett, through the trio's co-venture Diana Productions.

Bennett's success was celebrated in the dining room of the Wangers' Mapleton Drive home, where at the end of the dining table, behind the chair that Joan habitually took hung a mesmerizing oil painting of the glamorous star: the original portrait of Bennett as her character in *The Woman In the Window*, created for the film by artist Paul Clemens, who painted portraits of celebrities for *LIFE* magazine and later married actress Eleanor Parker. Rendered in Clemens's gauzy, romantic style, the dreamlike image elegantly captured Bennett's exquisite beauty while conveying a more seductively dangerous edge.

Even as Bennett matured beyond the era's leading lady status at the end of the decade—her oldest daughter already married and with a baby of her own—the actress, still in her early forties, became hailed as one of the screen's "Glamorous Grandmas." "I was made a grandmother at thirty-seven and I didn't like it," she admitted. "Marlene Dietrich, who was being called 'Hollywood's most glamorous grandmother,' sent me a wire saying 'Thanks for taking the heat off.'"

Nevertheless, Bennett made a smooth transition into witty, nurturing but still head-turning maternal roles, such as in Vincent Minelli's 1950 comedy *Father of the Bride*, playing Spencer Tracy's wife and young Elizabeth Taylor's appropriately stunning mother. Though ambivalent about sacrificing a degree of sex appeal in this latest transformation—"After a few mother roles, I was fit to be tied," she confessed. "I didn't know whether to go back to being sultry or to get a blonde wig." But it kept her firmly planted in the upper echelon of Hollywood, always important to both Bennett and her husband.

Simply put, the Wangers were at the top of the world. An easy place to topple from, they'd soon discover, and a very long fall.

It was another Joan who in 1948 instigated the first shove prompting Wangers' precipitous plunge from grace: *Joan of Arc*, Walter's no-expense-spared effort to tell the legendary martyr's story on a scale both epic and intimate, with Ingrid Bergman, who'd been reliably minting box office gold with her most recent films, in the title role. The producer had believed the $4.7 million, 145-minute film would be his own *Gone With the Wind*, a defining career milestone. *Joan of Arc* was well-received critically in many circles, nominated for several Academy Awards, winning three—including another honorary Oscar for Wanger ("for distinguished service to the industry in adding to its moral stature in the world community" for his work on the film). And it *did* sell tickets—just nowhere near enough to recoup its extravagant price tag. It was deemed a commercial disaster of historic magnitude, the kind of monumental flop that left aftershocks rattling Hollywood for months.

Worse, it left Wanger in considerable financial straits since he had bankrolled the project personally, with some of the funds borrowed from his wife. He blamed its dismal showing on Bergman's highly publicized adulterous liaison with Italian director Roberto Rossellini, after leaving her husband and child, which produced a public backlash so severe Bergman expatriated from Hollywood for years. The producer, a serial philanderer, even had the nerve to wire Bergman and take her to task for putting the film—and especially him—in fiscal jeopardy. Indeed, by the time *Joan of Arc* opened nationwide—forty-five minutes shorter—the actress had been roundly condemned by religious groups, media outlets, and even on the floor of the United States Senate; to many, casting Bergman as a virginal saint carried a blasphemous taint that kept them away from movie theaters. Wanger even tried advertising the film, which was not nominated for Best Picture, as "Academy Special Award Picture," until the Academy's Board of Governors warned him of what he, as a past president likely knew well: that the award was bestowed on *him* and not the film. Not that it mattered; ticket sales still slumped.

Yet one failure, even a resounding one, does not destroy a respected career overnight, and he began to take out a series of loans from the Bank of America to keep churning out pictures, including Max Ophuls 1949's prophetically titled *noir The Reckless Moment* starring Joan as a fiercely protective mother trying to safeguard her daughter from a lowlife criminal paramour before and after his demise. Her performance marked a significant bridging of her established persona as *noir* goddess and still-glamorous matriarch. It was also, her daughter Diana noted, the role closest to the woman she knew at home, ever caretaking, giving of herself for her family, repressed and committed to maintaining order and control. "She was exactly like the role she played in the film," Diana explained. "It's almost as if she wasn't acting."

But encroaching chaos could only be staved off so long: Wanger's behind-the-scenes money problems continued to accrue, causing the producer to lose out on a much-hoped-for reunion vehicle with Garbo due to lack of capital. By January of 1951, Bank of America charged Wanger with involuntary bankruptcy after he failed to make good on 20 percent of the money borrowed for *The Reckless Moment*—approximately $178,000. Hoping to recoup its losses, the bank set its sights on the Holmby Hills estate Joan so treasured (she'd even had it meticulously restored after a fire nearly consumed it on Mother's Day, 1943, an incident that left her weeping at the curbside); the couple was forced to fight for their dream home in court. Although the producer still had a three-picture contract with Monogram Studios, a haven for "B" films, it was a far cry from the prestigious associations to which he'd grown accustomed. The same week, at a New Year's Eve party at Romanoff's restaurant on Rodeo Drive, an over-served Oscar Levant, feeling umbrage with Wanger over some perceived slight, took a swing at him, missing when the producer ducked; the pianist instead decked their would-be peacemaker, movie tough guy George Raft ("I see trouble and I try to break it up," noted Raft. "I'm in the middle and I'm the guy who gets poked. Usually I do the poking. This was a new one on me.").

Though he and Levant quickly mended fences, Wanger endured stage-whispered rumors that screenwriter and novelist Budd Schulberg—whom Wanger had hired as a fledgling scribe to bolster the work of his hero, then-imploding literary giant F. Scott Fitzgerald, on the 1939 film *Winter Carnival*—fashioned a withering, thinly disguised portrait of the producer in his 1950s' bestseller *The Disenchanted*. The novel depicted Hollywood movie magnate Victor Milgrim as a domineering, self-important, ultimately soulless man, too commerce-oriented to mesh with artists and too emotionally volatile to function well in business, a sensibility that was reflected in his sentiments about show business agents. "These goddam agents are going to put us out of business," says Milgrim in the novel. "Three years ago Monica Dawson was starving to death on Broadway. Now these agents get her so worked up her feelings are hurt if she's only offered a hundred thousand dollars for five weeks' work."

Meanwhile, Hollywood columnists piled on, taking veiled jabs at how Bennett was now the household's breadwinner, resorting to TV and radio jobs while Wanger, as Earl Wilson framed it, sounded "like a frantic house-wife minding the kids." Wilson also reported how on her birthday, Bennett lost a precious diamond cigarette case given to her by her husband on their anniversary, with the *sub rosa* implication amid Wanger's concurrent bank-ruptcy headlines that she shouldn't hold her breath waiting for a replace-ment. Others alternately hinted at or pooh-poohed increasing friction in the marriage. Worse, the couple's two-year-old daughter Shelley had to be rushed to the hospital to have her stomach pumped after she ingested a mix of stimulants and opiates in a pillbox she discovered at home; a few weeks later, teenager Melinda, on the brink of embarking on her own act-ing career on the summer stage, also ended up in the emergency room with a viral infection.

As Wanger's stresses and miseries mounted, each new film announce-ment met with a setback. He'd just about signed the up-and-coming (thus affordable) screen *femme fatale* Barbara Payton to headline a gender-bend-ing take on Dumas titled *The Lady In the Iron Mask*, but yet another public sex scandal upended the plan—actors Tom Neal, Payton's lover and—he thought—fiancé, and Franchot Tone, her suddenly announced *new* fiancé, duked it out in a bloody brawl in the actress's Hollywood front lawn in September 1951; Tone, face beaten to a pulp, ended up unconscious in the hospital. The tsunami of lurid headlines signaled career declines for all three stars and resulted in Wanger dropping Payton, who'd gotten a literal black eye in the incident. Wanger long nursed a simmering resentment toward the gossip press, grousing, "This is the only industry that finances its own blackmail."

Once again, ill-considered trysts scuttled one of his more promising projects, this time before it even got off the ground.

Over and over, Wanger tried to right his listing ship, unable to make the right deals fall into place to effectively salvage his situation. At age fif-ty-seven, his luck, he felt, had run out. And the situation was growing even worse in the Wanger household, spiraling as steeply as the gossip columns had forecast.

Though Bennett told the press, "I think Walter gets handsomer every year—we've been married twelve years and it couldn't get better," her already cool manner plummeted several degrees to downright frosty as early as 1950—even earlier, she'd later reveal. "My relationship with Walter had become filled with untenable problems," she wrote. "The decline of our marriage had begun much earlier than his professional decline." As they drifted further apart, she adopted a hard, distant, even formal demeanor with her husband. Over the years, she'd become aware that the affairs and flirtations he'd pursued during his unconventional first marriage had not been suspended during their own union—including a dalliance occurring so shortly after their wedding that Bennett nearly left him immediately. Once wed, she'd ceased casual affairs with passing fancies—flings which were, after all, largely motivated to stoke Wagner's jealousy and inspire him to put a ring on her finger—but he continued his extramarital pursuits. "Throughout the years that followed, there were any number of other amorous misdemeanors, and finally I couldn't overlook them any longer." Now, as external stresses added further pressure, their marriage teetered on the brink.

Joan's continued ability to find work during his hard times—*Father of the Bride*'s success prompted a 1951 sequel, *Father's Little Dividend*, and she had a well-received run on the stage opposite daughter Melinda—left a bitter taste in Wanger's mouth, especially when she was giving him $500 every week so he'd have money in his pocket. For a while, he did little to forestall the alienation of his wife's affections, but, nearing the end of his professional rope, he grew increasingly restless to find a situation he could do something—*anything*—about, and began to obsess over their dwindling love.

"It was quite obvious to me that our marriage had entered a new phase, and a dire one," he later said. "I…was ready to do all I could to stop it."

But there was now a new obstacle in Wanger's path, an obstruction named Jennings Lang.

Handsome, curly-haired, and rakish, Jennings Bentley Lang was born in New York in 1915 and educated at St. John's University, entering the entertainment field as an attorney specializing in motion picture law. In 1938, after becoming the youngest person ever to pass the bar exam in New York City, he struck out for Los Angeles with forty dollars in his pocket, finding work as a clerk in a Thrifty drugstore until he could break in as a talent agent. Swiftly amassing a respectable stable of clients, he was snatched up by the prestigious Sam Jaffe Agency, making a winning impression with his deft handling of the firm's legal matters. Lang rose to become a vice president, offering legal and business advice to agency clients including Joan Crawford, Humphrey Bogart, Lauren Bacall—and Joan Bennett.

Within a year, Lang became Bennett's official representative, taking his clients with him in 1950 when the Jaffe Agency was absorbed by Jules Stein's powerful Music Corporation of America in Beverly Hills. As the agency's West Coast executive in charge of television accounts and highly effective in his business dealings, Lang was doing well enough to find a fine home in Brentwood on North Bristol Street—just steps away from Joan Crawford's front door—for his wife Pam (the former Flora Pam Friedheim, a publicist) and their two sons, Bobby and Mike.

For a dozen years, Lang brokered deals for Bennett, and by the fall of 1951, he secured a potentially lucrative NBC radio and television contract for the actress, still lovely at forty-one—though she hoped to forestall the move and keep her name on movie marquees as long as possible. But their close professional relationship had evolved into something much deeper. Whenever Bennett made a television appearance in New York, Lang—eighteen years her husband's junior and, while younger than Bennett herself, much closer to her own age—squired her around town, much to Wanger's growing consternation. During one of Wanger's many business trips abroad in his scramble to secure financing for proposed film projects, the agent tenderly ministered to Bennett when she was hospitalized with a mysterious, never publicly disclosed condition—decades later, her family members speculated that Bennett had suffered a miscarriage—thus cementing their bond and sparking a secret love affair. Wanger's past indiscretions provided a powerful justification in Bennett's mind, compounded by her husband's increasingly brusque, frustrating behavior.

"Suddenly I was offered the sympathy and gentleness I found lacking at home, and I turned to Jennings more often," she later wrote, "with feelings that went beyond our business relationship." The movie star and agent dove headlong into what became the first of an extended series of reckless moments together.

Already feeling his world slipping away, Wanger was quick to suspect that Lang was now getting a percentage of more than just Bennett's income, but—in the all-too-common double standard of the times—he failed to equate her fling with his loveless dalliances and began to brood miserably. Rather than confront his wife, however, Wanger focused his discontent directly in Lang's direction, even though the agent had helped him secure his own potentially lucrative TV deal with ABC. During a meeting in Manhattan in January of 1951 in which Bennett discussed taking on a television series to bring in more money, Wanger bitterly complained that the deal was all a ruse to keep her in New York—away from him and free to carry on with Lang.

Finally confronting the agent, Wanger did not mince words: "If any man breaks up my family, I'll kill him; I'll shoot him."

Lang protested his innocence, but the affair continued unabated. He and Bennett devised ever more furtive schemes to slip away together under the (sometimes legitimate) guise of business, jetting off to places like New Orleans and the West Indies for their rendezvous. When Wanger complained to Bennett, she insisted she was working on deals; Lang's presence was sometimes necessary, sometimes coincidental. The Hollywood social set noticed the paramours' not-so-discreet habit of making well-synchronized exits from parties they'd arrived at separately.

The pair also established private trysting spots in tucked-away little corners of Beverly Hills. For several months, the lovers clandestinely convened for lovemaking sessions at least once a week in a luxury apartment at 141 South Bedford Drive, just a few blocks from MCA headquarters. Lang typically arrived first and let himself into the swanky, Spanish-style balconied suite, followed minutes later by Bennett, who'd park a few blocks away and stroll up to the door in darkened sunglasses. Although the rendezvous usually took place in the afternoon, they didn't adjourn until after dark. On the rare occasion that she arrived first, Bennett would walk around the block until Lang arrived. He had the key, borrowed from fellow MCA agent Jay Kantor.

After leaving the Navy, Kantor had been feeling a bit rudderless; living nearby the MCA offices, he found himself drawn to the stately building, its windows revealing silhouettes of bustling people working inside at all hours. Finally, he worked up the gumption to walk inside and ask what kind of operation it was. He has no idea what an "agency" did—*maybe espionage?* he thought—but he was intrigued enough to apply for a job, and bright and energetic enough to get one. Kantor was taken under Lang's wing as he found his footing. One day, the senior agent asked his young protégé, always eager to ingratiate himself in any way that might move him another rung up the corporate ladder, if he might borrow the apartment down the street Kantor had leased for an actor friend of his who was currently based in New York but was beginning to make waves in Hollywood. Kantor was confident his actor pal, Marlon Brando, wouldn't mind if Lang "entertained" there every so often.

Their recklessness grew, along with the frequency of their trysts. The neighbors noticed. MCA colleagues noticed. In Hollywood, secrets spread quickly.

Bennett would return home to Holmby Hills for dinner with Wanger, who later confessed that he could barely stomach sitting at the same table with his wife and their children, knowing where she had been all day—the added gaze of Joan's *Woman in the Window* portrait likely compounding his torment. He knew, of course, thanks to the briefcase full of information provided by the private detective agency he'd hired to follow her in Beverly Hills and New York.

It wasn't the first time that a cuckolding panic had Wanger considering desperate measures. Actor David Niven recalled a foreboding, portentous moment in the late 1930s when he rented a Beverly Hills residence at 601 North Linden Drive with his close friend and fellow rising star Errol Flynn. The home quickly hosted some of the most rollicking gatherings of Hollywood bachelors and their intended conquests of the moment. Returning home from shooting at the studio one evening, Niven spotted a somewhat menacing figure in a camel-hair overcoat with turned-up lapels lurking on the property.

After hurriedly entering the home and failing to find his famously athletic housemate—who, like his swashbuckling screen characters, would merrily dash headlong into dangerous confrontations—Niven summoned his courage with a shot of whiskey and went outside. He was shocked to recognize the well-appointed lurker as Walter Wanger (Niven starred in the Wanger-produced *Eternally Yours*, and the two were on each other's holiday gifting lists), in a state of nervous agitation in stark contrast to his familiar unflappable, patrician-producer persona. Wanger confessed that the source of his distress was his then-faltering courtship of Bennett, whom he was convinced was at that very moment luxuriating in Flynn's bedroom in the arms of the notorious swordsman.

"I was able to tell him with truth that Flynn was not in the house," Niven wrote in his second memoir, 1975's *Bring on the Empty Horses*, "but I withheld the information that downstairs in the living room awaiting

Flynn's arrival was Joan. Wanger, mollified, left and Joan, rather precipitately, left soon after."

Over a decade later, having sunk deeper into a similar morass of jealous desperation and with his warning to Lang unheeded, Wanger purchased a .38 caliber Colt police pistol from a Los Angeles County sheriff's deputy in August of 1951. He made no secret about his new acquisition, registering it openly and using his honorary commission to legally carry it in his briefcase or his car. Perhaps attempting to signal to his wife that she was playing a dangerous game, he sometimes displayed it for her. She told him not to leave it where the children could get at it, confessing that it made her nervous.

It should have.

Wanger was already talking—to the seasoned, hardened Hollywood journalist Florabel Muir, no less—like a man with very little left to lose. "Hollywood is a strange, cruel place," he said. "When you're down on your luck, you run out of friends."

Finally, as December arrived, he made his feelings explicit to his wife: "If you see any more of Jennings, I'll kill him." It was a last, ominous prologue to the most reckless moment to come.

Wanger's jealousy had grown nearly unbearable for Joan—particularly in the midst of a protracted battle to keep the Bank of America from taking over their home. Still—"for the children's sake"—she had no intention of throwing Wanger over in favor of Jennings Lang. The agent, whose home life seemed tranquil on the surface but had quietly hit a rocky stretch, perhaps had stronger romantic inclinations towards his glamorous client. For Bennett, their fling was a sexy, validating diversion as her marriage disintegrated, to be sure, but far from a passionate love affair for the ages. However, when Wanger's covetous attitude began threatening her ability to provide for her daughters, she made it clear she would not hesitate to take the necessary steps to keep her income intact. "I was taking anything and everything that came in the way of work," she recalled, and it was Lang, not her husband, bringing opportunities her way. Indeed, her most recent career successes owed nothing to Walter, so she seemed perfectly capable of moving on without him. The dark clouds of divorce gathered on the horizon. Now, Walter decided, it was time for action, to do what he decided any red-blooded man would do when the sanctity of his family was about to be torn asunder.

On Thursday, December 13, 1951, Wanger drove to the magnificent MCA headquarters, a gleaming white Georgian Classical Revival-style marvel designed by prominent Black architect Paul R. Williams—one of the most spectacular buildings in Beverly Hills, even among the city's wealth of staggering structures. Built in 1938 to house Jules Stein's exploding music booking firm and soon-to-be talent agency, the building was an elegant yet powerful convergence of high profit and exquisite taste. It instantly elevated the deal-closing company—by the 1950s, the largest and most powerful broker of film and TV talent in the world—into an elite sphere, heretofore unoccupied territory when agents were looked at as having an air of vulgarity. Standing at the intersection of Rexford Drive and Burton Way, the building also, coincidentally, sat directly across the street from the similarly grand Beverly Hills City Hall, which housed the headquarters of the local police department. Wanger arrived at the serene setting toting a small suitcase full of reports from his private eyes divulging that Bennett often parked at MCA and went for long afternoon drives around Beverly Hills with Lang. The suitcase also contained his pistol.

As if to spur him to action, that very morning, Hollywood columnist Jimmy Fidler, syndicated in newspapers across the country, dropped another oblique reference to his discordant union into print for all the world to see: "Persistent is the word for those rumors about a rift in the marital bliss of Joan Bennett and Walter Wanger."

Wanger drove by around 2:30 p.m., spotting his wife's Kelly green 1946 Cadillac convertible unoccupied in the MCA lot, returning an hour later to find the car still parked there. Never taking his eyes off the convertible, he parked his own car in the lot, reached into a box in the back seat, and pulled out his gun. For two hours, he remained in place, awaiting the arrival of Joan Bennett and Jennings Lang.

Finally, after the sun had set and the lot was illuminated only by dim lighting, the two lovers arrived in Lang's car at 5:30 p.m. Wanger watched intently from 275 feet away as Bennett exited Lang's vehicle and slipped into the driver's seat of her Cadillac. Lang, who'd been out of town until the previous day, leaned casually against the driver's side door as she started the car. Gripped by a jealous rage, Wanger revved his engine and raced up alongside the convertible. Gun in hand, he leapt out of his car and strode purposefully toward the couple. He forgot to set the parking brake, and his car kept rolling onward, traveling off the lot, across Burton Way and finally crashing into the curb.

Samuel Richard "Rick" Scott, a forty-year-old attendant/mechanic employed in the parking lot, was distracted from his duties by the sound of a heated argument several feet away. He looked up and spotted Wanger, Lang and Bennett engaged in a tense war of words for several minutes. Lang, in fine agent tradition, tried to finesse the situation: "Don't be silly, Walter, don't be silly," he urged, hands raised in submission. But Wanger, who later said he didn't hear Lang's words because "he was in no mood for listening," had always been able to recognize a dramatic moment, and slowly, deliberately, almost hypnotically leveled the gun at Lang.

"Don't, Walter! Don't!" screamed Bennett.

Wanger squeezed off two shots, close enough to leave powder burns on Lang's Shetland gray suit. One bullet grazed the agent's thigh and lodged in the side of Bennett's Cadillac; the other, however, struck Lang high in the groin, missing his vital organs but tearing through several muscles in his right leg. When Lang crumpled to the ground, Wanger dropped his gun. The agent grabbed it as blood soaked into his clothes. Wide-eyed with horror, Bennett cried out hysterically, "Now will you go and leave us alone?" She reached out to comfort her newly ventilated lover and tossed the gun into the back seat of her car while. As if in a trance, Wanger said nothing and simply stared at his handiwork.

Alerted by the gunfire, Sid Holtzman, the owner of the service station on the lot who leased the parking space to MCA, came running onto the scene. The bloodied Lang pleaded for Holtzman to take him to his personal physician, Dr. Robert Riemer, whose office was several blocks away at 6333 Wilshire Boulevard, even though the Beverly Hills Emergency Hospital was only a short ride down the street and police headquarters stood just steps away.

Holtzman and Bennett lifted Lang into the convertible, and Holtzman took the wheel, racing away from the scene. As she tended to her wounded paramour, Bennett regained her famous composure almost immediately; indeed, she practically seemed to summon the cool *femme fatale* persona she had conjured so effectively on the screen. She gave Wanger's pistol to Holtzman and calmly told him to wrap it in a towel so as not to disturb any fingerprints, instructing him to wash out the car's blood-soaked interior when he returned to MCA. She and Lang then discussed how they might best avoid a torrent of publicity. Although they at first had difficulty locating Riemer at his office, once found, the physician accompanied them in an ambulance to Midway Hospital on San Vicente Boulevard, where Lang was pumped full of painkillers, underwent ninety minutes of emergency surgery, had his right leg set in a cast and later received a blood transfusion to offset shock at the loss of his vital fluids.

Walter Wanger remained immobile in the parking lot, as if waiting for a punishment he knew could not be avoided—especially since the police station was literally within earshot. Although motorcycle officer Edward Gaba had been in the vicinity when the shooting took place and even heard the gunfire, he inquired at the station and was told that what he had heard was merely a car backfiring, so he didn't bother to investigate (Later, when ever-flinty Police Chief Clinton H. Anderson heard of this lax response, he suspended Gaba for a day). Eventually, however, eyewitnesses and passing motorists alerted the police, and Lt. D.R. Beckwith and Sgt. A.J. Gebhart were dispatched to see what had caused all the commotion. They were greeted by a shaken but remorseless Wanger, who cut straight to the chase: "I've just shot the son of a bitch who tried to break up my home."

The officers were left scratching their heads. Although they had an apparent murder confession on their hands, they were missing two key pieces of the puzzle: the weapon and the victim. Still, they took Wanger's story seriously and issued an all-points bulletin for a green 1948 Cadillac carrying "a man who might be bleeding to death for want of medical attention."

That was all the local media, closely monitoring their police radios and taking calls from paid tipsters within the force, needed to hear. The scent of blood was fresh, and all hunting parties immediately descended upon Beverly Hills.

As the officers took Wanger into custody, he made a modest request, asking that police call the servants at his home and tell them not to turn on the radio, so his children would not discover the shocking news so impersonally. The officers then confiscated the private detective reports discovered in Wanger's car, along with the producer's green, leather-bound private diary and appointment book; the car was sent to a local garage. When Gebhart frisked Wanger and found a sharp hunting knife in his coat pocket, the producer shrugged and said he only used it to open envelopes and sharpen pencils. He was booked, fingerprinted, and relieved of all his personal items, including a gold money clip holding thirty-five dollars, a gold notepad holder and matching pencil, a pocket picture folder, and his platinum wristwatch. Finally, he was escorted in to face the intimidating

Chief Clinton Anderson himself, where he was allowed to make a phone call to his attorney, Mendel Silberberg, interrupting his dinner.

"Mendel, I'm in the office of Chief Anderson," Wanger told his lawyer. "They're holding me for shooting Jennings Lang. I want you to come down here." Ever the gentleman, he added one more thought before hanging up. "Finish your dinner first." Silberberg didn't heed Wanger's admonition. Within seconds, he was on the phone with another learned legal mind, soon *en route* to the police station.

Before the new player could arrive, however, Wanger was already spilling everything to Chief Anderson, detailing how his wife's affection for him had chilled, how his financial woes had compounded, how he had warned Lang to watch out, how he'd set the private detective on Bennett's tail when he suspected hanky-panky, when and how he purchased the pistol, how he'd lay in wait for the couple and purposefully shot Lang, how Lang had grabbed the gun and sped away with Bennett at his side. His version of events, however, had him approaching the couple without a word and squeezing off the rounds without warning. And then he made a telling admission. "I didn't intend to kill him," he reported. "I just wanted to wound him."

Anderson nodded grimly all the while, taking down the producer's every word in a stenographer's notebook. He was well familiar with the pitfalls of police involvement in marital discord. "We would prefer to steer clear of such entanglements," he later wrote in his memoir, "but sometimes warring couples toss their troubles right in our laps and we have no choice but to intervene." This, though currently lacking the proverbial smoking gun, was one of those troubles.

Pandemonium broke out at the police station as a legion of photographers, reporters, press agents, and a small cadre of Wanger's intimates arrived, creating a mob scene with popping flashbulbs and a torrent of prying questions. The chaos gained sharper focus with the simultaneous arrival of District Attorney S. Ernest Roll, Wanger's lawyer Silberberg, and another learned presence, the fabled defense attorney Jerry Giesler. Known as "The Great Mouthpiece," Geisler was the newly appointed president of the Beverly Hills Bar Association with the reputation as the patron saint of seemingly lost legal causes among scandal-stricken superstars—including past clients Robert Mitchum, Charlie Chaplin, Alexander Pantages, Benjamin "Bugsy" Seigel, and Wanger's old romantic rival Errol Flynn—

had inspired the famous rallying cry for every famous face in trouble with the law: "Get me Giesler!"

That's when the newshounds knew something *really* serious was going down.

Giesler was at the height of his notoriety, having within days of the Wanger incident gotten the famous exotic dancer Lili St. Cyr freed from indecency charges stemming from her enticing bathtub burlesque act at the glitzy Sunset Strip nightspot Ciro's. In court, the puckish but poker-faced attorney argued strenuously for the act's artistic content, asked Ciro's owner, husky Herman Hover, to demonstrate St. Cyr's supposedly lewd bump-and-grind to illustrate that obscenity was in the eye of the beholder, and disproved claims of full nudity by delicately displaying St. Cyr's flimsy net bra and G-string for all to see. The case was literally laughed into acquittal.

Theatrical stunts like that were among the reasons why Giesler was known as "the man who could beat the rap"; his razor-sharp intellect, exhaustive research and keen use of logic were others. And while he had on occasion beaten tough charges against hard-core criminals like Bugsy Siegel, he was best known for handling cases much more in Wanger's vein: crimes of passion.

One 1937 trial made the Wanger incident particularly well-suited for the attorney: The so-called "White Flame Case," in which Union Air Terminal manager Paul Wright telephoned Glendale police and openly confessed that he had shot and killed both his beautiful young wife and his closest friend after coming home from a bender with his buddy. After passing out, Wright was awakened by the taping of piano keys and groggily went downstairs to discover his missus and his pal making vigorous love on the piano bench. As Wright put it, a "white flame exploded" in his brain. He grabbed his gun and fired nine shots into their bodies. Giesler had the piano bench brought into court to enhance the adulterous betrayal committed by the victims and characterized Wright's actions as Almighty Justice meted out by a man driven temporarily insane. His "heat of passion" argument resulted in a reduced verdict of voluntary manslaughter. When Wright's sanity was debated by the court, Giesler successfully argued that since he had the burden of proof, the defense should be allowed opening *and* closing arguments—something never before heard of in California law. The lawyer not only got his temporary insanity ruling but also had Wright deemed sane. The defendant walked out of the courtroom a free man.

With cases like that in Giesler's win column, all this new, violent love triangle needed to more perfectly suit him was a piano bench.

Arriving about twenty minutes into the interrogation, the first thing Giesler did was interrupt Anderson's interview with Wanger and advise his new client to keep his mouth shut, although most of the beans had already been spilled. The lawyer immediately went into a private conference with the producer, which was fine by Anderson, who had new business on his plate. Bennett and Lang had been located, Wanger's pistol had been recovered, and Holtzman was at the station for questioning (the lot owner would be held for five hours before being released, deemed an "uncooperative" witness). Lang, still in surgery, was allowed to remain at the hospital.

It was then that Joan Bennett made the most dramatic entrance of her career, clad entirely in black, with dark glasses barely concealing eyes swollen red from tears and her usually pristine lipstick slightly askew. The woman whose closest friends sometimes found her simply too perfect to be believed was watching her carefully constructed world crumble as she made her appearance at the police station, escorted by her trusted friend and P.R. representative Margaret Ettinger and two detectives who met her at the hospital. Confronted by an unceasing barrage of questions and popping flashbulbs, her trademark poise threatened to desert her at any moment, her dismay apparent to everyone—in stark contrast to Wanger's blank demeanor.

Bennett was escorted in to see Anderson. The chief had a history with her family: as a police detective lieutenant, he'd been dispatched to arrest her father Richard in 1934 when his then-wife Aimee Hastings accused her husband of battery, only to discover the Bennett household was frustratingly just outside the city limits—and his jurisdiction.

Now, the second-generation celebrity described a new, even more violent confrontation: her husband, distraught from financial troubles and on the verge of a nervous breakdown, must have gone berserk. Yes, Wanger's jealous tendencies had escalated dramatically, but there was certainly no rational reason for him to attack Jennings Lang, she explained. Her relationship with the agent was strictly professional; the two had only gone out driving to discuss business away from Lang's constantly ringing telephone.

"If Walter thinks there is any romance between us, he is wrong," she asserted, unaware Anderson had already gotten a peek at the private detective reports. Like her husband, she also neglected to mention the brief argument that preceded the shooting, insisting there had never been any previous consideration of divorce or separation between the couple (Wanger's version disputed this claim). Anderson assumed his best pitiless, hard-boiled cop persona, once even stopping the grilling to assess her glacial demeanor. "You're pretty cool about all this, aren't you?" he remarked; perhaps the chief, too, had been irrevocably bedazzled by her *femme fatale* persona on screen. "Go ahead, barbeque me on both sides," Bennett told him matter-of-factly. "If you think I'm going to break into hysterics for your benefit, you're very much mistaken." Just to see if he could rattle her, Anderson unceremoniously marched Bennett in front of reporters again when he turned her over to D.A. Roll for another round of questioning, when he just as easily could have led them quietly to an interrogation room. "The police chief led me directly into the jaws of the press," she'd recall. "He thereby gathered no little publicity for himself." She correctly pegged Anderson as a pretty cool customer himself: if he couldn't crack Bennett's icy façade, he made sure to score instant publicity points touting how he already had yet another sensational Beverly Hills crime under control.

After repeatedly reiterating her story, an exhausted Bennett was finally released and allowed to go home, accompanied by Maggie Ettinger, her eldest daughter Diana, and Rev. J. Herbert Smith, the Wangers' clergyman from All Saints' Episcopal Church in Beverly Hills, who had earlier been allowed to confer with Wanger in his cell. Appearing on the verge of collapse as she navigated the flashbulbs, all she could offer to the detail-starved newshounds was a weak, "No comment." But at least one reporter claimed to hear her say that Wanger would not be welcome in the home if he were to be released. It was almost 1 a.m. when she finally arrived in Holmby Hills, collapsed in bed, and—with the help of a good dose of sedatives—finally drifted into the oblivion of sleep.

Earlier, another shaken woman also tossed into the fray faced a throng of inquisitors at Midway Hospital. Pam Lang, Jennings's wife, had arrived on the arm of her friend and dinner party companion that evening, actress Jane Wyman—both still in full cocktail dress. Joan Bennett herself had called Wyman and alerted her, knowing the actress was hosting the Langs at her home that night. Following a brief visit with her husband as he was prepped for surgery, Pam held a devoted vigil outside the emergency room. Later, flanked by two publicity agents, she held a mini-press conference in the hospital cocktail lounge, assuring reporters she was confident "the only relationship between Joan Bennett and my husband was that of good friends." Jennings was soon out of surgery in stable condition but—even more so than Bennett—had to be substantially tranquilized with painkillers, much to the dismay of Deputy District Attorney Adolph Alexander, who wanted to question the man who, it turned out, was expected to recover nicely from wounds that were more painful than life-threatening.

As word of the nascent scandal spread around Hollywood like wildfire, many of Wanger's friends were devising ways to distance themselves from the now-notorious shooter. But some loyalties endured: Harold Mirisch, vice president of Monogram Studios—where Wanger had his current production deal—showed up at the station ready to post bail, as did Beverly Hills realtor Sam Genis, actor and later U.S. Senator George Murphy, and actor Clifton Webb. "Prince" Mike Romanoff, hearing the news at his eponymous Rodeo Drive eatery, first sent his head chef over to the station to prepare a gourmet meal for Wanger, then arrived to personally serve it himself (Romanoff was no stranger to nights spent behind bars, thanks to a colorful youth of con artistry passing himself off as the heir to the Russian dynasty). Paramount's Y. Frank Freeman made an appearance, as did Wanger's business manager George Mereader, Rev. Smith, and Wanger's friend Eugene Frank. (At least one of the producer's visitors anonymously quoted Wanger as saying shooting Lang was "the only thing I could do.")

Aware of the Wanger's economic woes, some of the most powerful forces in Hollywood rallied around their longtime colleague, when only months before they had turned thumbs down to his movie projects. Studio heads Samuel Goldwyn, Daryl F. Zanuck, Joseph Schenck, Warner brothers Harry and Jack, and agent Charles Feldman each contributed $1,000 to his legal fund. Hal Wallis, Spyros and Charles Skouras, Sol Lesser, Y. Frank Freeman, Clifford Work, and even Walt Disney pitched in $500 or more—a boon for the producer, as legal acumen like Giesler's did not come cheap.

Humphrey Bogart made an appearance to visit his Mapleton Drive neighbor Wanger as well. Years earlier, when Wanger was an assistant serving under producers Jesse Lasky, Samuel Goldwyn, and Cecil B. DeMille, Bogart—then envisioning a career as a screenwriter—submitted a rather lurid, gory screenplay called *Blood and Death* for consideration, but none of the three had time to read it and passed it down to Wanger for coverage. Wanger, put off by the abundant, visceral violence, tossed it into the trash. Later, after both men's careers had skyrocketed, Wanger sometimes shamelessly boasted, "Bogie used to write for me." During Bogart's visit to the Beverly Hills jail, Wanger confided gruesome details about his assault on Jennings Lang, Bogart's own agent, including his intended target on the agent's anatomy.

"So what in the hell was the matter with my screenplay?" Bogart responded.

In addition, dozens of telegrams from friends, business associates, and well-wishers began pouring into police headquarters, prompting the lead detective, Captain Walter W. White, to remark to reporters that he hadn't seen action like this in the station house since Bugsy Siegel was gunned down on Linden Drive four years earlier.

By morning, everyone in Los Angeles, Hollywood, Beverly Hills, and even proverbial Peoria had heard about the love triangle and its disastrous consequences.

Eighteen hours after his arrest, a bleary-eyed Walter Wanger was released on $5,000 bail posted by Mirisch and allowed to leave the station. D.A. Roll ensured the press understood that even if Lang was unwilling to press charges—which the D.A. anticipated after learning of the adultery in the detective reports—there was no question the producer would be prosecuted. Accordingly, Capt. White announced the police department's intent to file a charge of assault with a deadly weapon with intent to commit murder, whether there was a complainant or not.

Dressed impeccably in a gray flannel business suit, Wanger was nevertheless unable to conceal profuse perspiration as newspapermen and television cameras watched him leave the station, Norma Desmond-style. Noting he'd had a good night's sleep, he commended the staff for their fine treatment, as if he were checking out of the Beverly Hills Hotel, and even paused to shake hands with a jailer. He then left the station with Giesler and Silberberg, retrieved his car from the impound garage, and went into a lengthy conference at Giesler's office before retiring to a secluded apartment on Lasky Drive donated by a friend.

D.A. Roll recommended Wanger avoid returning to the home in Holmby Hills "because of the children" (he even offered to provide Bennett with a police guard), and the silver-haired filmmaker agreed to make only a brief stop to pick up some clothes. He called ahead to Bennett's secretary and inquired about his seven-year-old daughter Stephanie, who'd been sick with a virus, but he did not ask to speak with his wife. The next day, in

Bennett's absence, he slipped in, played with the children briefly, then left with a small cache of personal belongings.

At some point during that first day, Wanger asked his friend, *The Thing from Another World* producer Edward Lasker, "Listen, tell me the truth. Where did I hit him? No one will tell me. Did I hit what I was aiming at?"

After a long, restless night calmed only by sleeping pills, Bennett rose around noon to face the press firestorm again. But this time, she regained some of the ice water-veined cool of her screen personas, ready to launch a full-on counterattack to prevent the damage Wanger had so recklessly inflicted on their lives and reputations from spreading any further. If her resolve ever wavered, it may have been when she received the first phone call of the day; her longtime friend Pam Lang was on the line. Whatever words were exchanged between them—kind and supportive or hostile and accusatory—remain a mystery. Her famous sisters Constance, who lived around the corner on Carolwood Drive but was staying in New York, and Barbara, who relocated to San Francisco, rallied behind her. Despite Joan's attempts to downplay the direness of the situation, Barbara was on the first available flight to Los Angeles.

At 1:45 p.m., accompanied by attorney Grant Cooper, whose growing reputation was rivaling Giesler's—years later, he defended Robert F. Kennedy's assassin Sirhan Sirhan—the actress appeared at the patio of her now-broken Mapleton Drive home, which was brightly decorated for the advancing Christmas holiday. Bennett was brightly decorated herself, and while the trying night was still evident, she was otherwise gorgeously made up and attired in a chic checkered Hattie Carnegie suit with a hint of demure white lace at the throat and a pair of sensible black pumps, as well as her clearly visible wedding band—every sartorial detail thoughtfully selected to send a message of dignity and marital devotion to counter the sordid scenario she was starring in. She was prepared to face the music, but on her own terms this time. A score of reporters had assembled for the command performance, nibbling on cookies and sandwiches provided by the Wangers' servants. She apologized for the delay and made sure everyone had gotten enough to eat before she got down to the business at hand: spin control.

"I hope that Walter will not be blamed too much," she told them, recounting the past unhappy months of forestalling bankruptcy and battling to hold on to their home. She painted a sympathetic portrait of her husband and all his tribulations, described their twelve-year marriage, and recalled their long friendship with Pam and Jennings Lang. "I feel confident that Walter would never have given voice to the suspicions expressed by him in the newspapers," she offered floridly, "were it not for the fact that he has been so mentally upset with the complexities of the financial burden he has been carrying for such a long time." She ended her speech with a calculated crescendo, practically a public service paean to the wonderfulness that was Tinseltown. "Knowing Hollywood as I do, knowing how good, wholesome, and sincere by far and away a majority of motion picture people are, I want to express my deep regret that this incident will add to the erroneous opinions entertained by so many."

One photographer asked her to assume an air of mystery. Another wanted her to dab at her eyes with her handkerchief. Attorney Cooper, who offered little hope of reconciliation between the estranged couple, shooed them away. Bennett smiled as she retreated into her home, satisfied with her performance as a defender of not just her own virtue but of all Hollywood's. Later she advised her daughter Melinda to soldier through her live television debut on *The Arthur Murray Show* in New York that night with a stiff upper lip—but Melinda was summarily dismissed by the scandal-averse Murray prior to air.

Wasting little time, Bennett had also given an exclusive telephone interview on the night of the shooting to Maggie Ettinger's cousin, the deeply sympathetic gossip queen Louella Parsons (likely because Joan so detested Parsons' rival Hedda Hopper), who merrily outlined the marital discord and mounting debts Parsons had, she insinuated, known about all along. Bennett played to Parsons' ego: "Nobody knows better than you, Louella, the necessity of my having to work to support my children," the actress commiserated. "Walter has been jealous of everybody. Even when I was in New York and Jennings took me to my TV shows, he objected."

"To think I should be the one to bring all this terrible publicity on Hollywood," Bennett lamented, pooh-poohing allegations of adultery. "Walter's jealousy of Jennings Lang is so absurd that it borders on temporary derangement. Why, Pam Lang, Jennings, Walter and I spent a lot of time together. Jennings has been wonderful to me. He's the one who got me TV jobs, which, goodness knows, I've needed."

She'd given an Oscar-caliber performance for the press. If only somebody had told her, however, that the police had those troublesome detective reports tracking her trysts with Lang, and they were already telling the newspapers about them.

Jennings Lang was no actor, but even doped up on opiates he, too, knew the role he was supposed to play. "I am bewildered by the unfortunate and unprovoked event that has occurred," he said in a press statement the day after the shooting as criminal lawyer Jake Ehrlich—the celebrated defense attorney rumored to be an inspiration for Perry Mason who coached Raymond Burr in his television portrayal—flew down from San Francisco to take up his cause. "Walter Wanger misconstrued what was solely a business relationship," Ehrlich asserted. "Since there are families involved and children concerned, I hope that this whole regrettable incident can be forgotten as quickly as possible."

That was all D.A. Roll needed to hear—it was obvious, attempting to quell bad publicity, Lang would not be pressing charges. Roll was already annoyed enough that doctors had continually barred his deputy Alexander from questioning the agent (Alexander only half-sarcastically offered to transfer Lang to a prison hospital, if need be, but relaxed his stance when told of the agent's need for a blood transfusion). One of the reasons they were eager to hear Lang's story was to check how it gelled with that of witness Rick Scott, who'd described in detail the heated argument the Wangers had conveniently forgotten. Threatening to "get tough," the frustrated Roll—who felt he'd been more than considerate—waited one more day for Lang to mend. Then on Saturday, December 15, he stormed Lang's hospital room with Alexander, Chief Anderson, and Capt. White in tow, but found his path blocked by attorney Oliver Schwab, Ehrlich's lieutenant, and a protective nurse. After a heated discussion involving potential subpoenas and a county grand jury, Schwab relented; Roll entered Lang's room only to find the agent asleep under sedation.

Instead, the D.A. grilled an uncooperative Pam Lang until her husband finally came to a few hours later. A brief 15-minute recounting of the incident ended when Lang, overwhelmed with pain, dissolved into tears. Still, Roll told reporters "We got what we wanted" but didn't reveal if the agent's story varied from the Wangers'. He visited Lang again the next day, but by then Ehrlich had arrived and insisted his client was in too much pain to give a complete account.

That same day Anderson began focusing his investigation intently on the detective reports and Wanger's diary, looking for any clue that might indicate premeditation on the producer's part. He hinted to the press he might reduce the official charge to felonious assault with a deadly weapon in hope of outmaneuvering Jerry Giesler's "high-powered legal artillery," which threatened to blow away the attempted murder charge. Surprisingly, it took a Los Angeles County grand jury just five minutes of deliberation on December 18 to conclude that the original assault with intent to commit murder charge—even absent a formal complaint from Lang—was appropriate enough for indictment. Wanger, laying low in Palm Springs, now faced five to fourteen years behind bars if convicted.

If was the operative word, because public sentiment suddenly shifted in Wanger's direction when on December 20 Los Angeles newspapers broke the news of Lang and Bennett's reported romps in the Brando apartment. Suddenly the actress' protestations of innocence seemed like the calculated acts of one of the indiscreet maneaters she played on screen. A day later, Bennett's television deal was called off "by mutual consent" and her commercial endorsements for Colgate-Palmolive-Peet were in question. At the same time, more witnesses came forward to corroborate Rick Scott's story of the angry row preceding the shooting. Bennett was glimpsed praying at All Saints' Church, while in the hospital Lang endured a nasty infection.

Meanwhile, a supporter sent Wanger a sharpshooter's medal. He dined out with friends and attended movie premieres. Monogram Pictures confidently announced the producer would establish headquarters in a newly remodeled studio bungalow within a week of his indictment and start to work on a new picture.

The surprising groundswell of industry support for the once beleaguered producer owed in part to a patriarchal postwar view that, after being cuckolded, Wagner had somehow acted reasonably—perversely, even nobly—to preserve his marriage. Sympathies were further bolstered as word spread of the stresses from his dire financial circumstances—many knew all too well what it felt like to be down and out in Hollywood, and recognized the desperate extremes one might be resort to. When one couldn't get arrested in their professional life, they just might end up with a real-world mug shot. "Walter was in a turbulent state of mind," as one anonymous Hollywood insider put it in the press. "He didn't shoot Jennings Lang—he shot the millions of people who didn't see *Joan of Arc*."

The press hungrily devoured the news when word broke on Christmas Eve that Wanger would spend the holiday with Bennett and their daughters.

The producer arrived overloaded with gifts for the girls just after dawn and stayed throughout the day, sharing dinner with his wife for the first time since the shooting. Bennett was more tolerant than might be expected, though in her nervousness she'd forgotten to apply half of her lipstick. It had been a nightmarish Twelve Days of Christmas, and Wanger's rash act—publicly approved as it may have been—had effectively, if not purposely, destroyed the actress' career: the studio heads felt no need to protect Hollywood's investment in a middle-aged actress with a twenty-two-year career behind her. But Bennett was always one to make sacrifices for her girls, and if it meant breaking bread with Wanger she would gladly do so. Christmas would prove to be only the beginning of her magnanimity.

Wanger was arraigned the following day in Santa Monica Superior Court, and the master showman Jerry Giesler demonstrated exactly the brand of hardball he intended to play. He insisted the judge issue a $2,500 bench warrant for Jennings Lang, by then recuperating at home, to ensure he'd be present for the trial whether he wanted to be there or not. Then the Great Mouthpiece made certain he would be granted access to the detective reports and Wanger's "thick as a Bible" private diary with, he said, the full intention of entering them into evidence. As he left court, Giesler said Wanger would fight the charges against him. Reporters practically licked their lips at the revelation, anticipating a gloves-off, no-holds-barred slalom through a uniquely Hollywood mudslide.

They were not disappointed. On January 7 Wanger, solemn-looking and pale, entered a not guilty plea. Giesler's master plan became clear as he unveiled his defense strategy in court: while not a wholly original plot, at least Giesler was ripping off a classic of his own, as followers of the Paul Wright case were quick to point out. Adding a second plea, Giesler proclaimed with characteristic hyperbole that Wanger was also not guilty by reason of temporary insanity, a condition that seized the jealous producer after a "vicious circle of deception culminated in a bluish flash through a violet haze in the shadows of the early evening," prompting Wanger to fire his .38. The "temporary" part of the insanity plea was proven, the Great Mouthpiece reasoned, because Wanger was rational enough to realize the seriousness of his actions and remain on the scene for police to arrest him without attempting to flee. "The fact that this defendant fired low and that the gun contained unused bullets, with ample opportunity to fire, clearly demonstrated the defendant was at that moment restored to full competency and normalcy," Giesler reasoned in court.

The "White Flame" defense proved effective in 1938. Why not a "Bluish Flash?"

Jennings Lang did not attend, and when Giesler made noises about it, Lang's lawyer Jake Ehrlich announced the agent may be permanently crippled as a result of the gunplay. D.A. Roll, as anxious as Giesler to hear Lang's version of events under oath, promised to bring him to court in a stretcher if need be. Giesler also went after MCA agent Jay Kantor, who lent out the Brando apartment and was conveniently transferred to the New York office following the shooting.

No one was clamoring for an appearance by Joan Bennett quite yet, however—except the canny producers of a Chicago-based stage production of *Bell, Book and Candle*, who gave the actress her first job since the scandal broke, replacing departing lead Rosalind Russell in hopes of reaping a box office bonanza from the controversy. In her first stage role since before her marriage, Bennett was simply being the consummate "trooper" to provide for her kids, knowing that Wanger's finances weren't likely to improve anytime soon. The public disgrace had completely humiliated her, and she'd never been comfortable in live performances—even ones where they weren't whispering about her marital infidelities. But she knew the show must go on.

And that spirit, in the end, was what kept Wanger from allowing Giesler to unleash what Chief Anderson called his "full legal artillery." By the time his case was ready for trial, the producer could not, ultimately, subject his wife to the kind of courtroom muckraking sure to ensue. And so, on April 15, Wanger—this time tanned and cheerful-looking—appeared before Judge Harry Borde, waived trial and threw himself on the mercy of the court. The plea had been earlier approved by the judge, D.A. Roll—who decided the county could do without the expense of the trial—and Wanger, who wanted to spare his family (and, he claimed, the entire movie industry by association) from an excruciating trial.

Lang would not have to appear in court after all, and neither would Bennett—but that didn't stop her from making a jaw-dropping surprise appearance in Wanger's corner, adding fuel to rumors of reconciliation that began buzzing when the couple were seen acting very warmly at All Saints' Easter service. They didn't exchange a word in court, just a single soulful glance that lingered until Giesler hustled his client away. A reunion seemed almost certain several days later when the media spotted Bennett giving three "long and tender" kisses to Wanger at Los Angeles International Airport as she departed to assume her theatrical duties.

While Bennett was treading the stage of the Great Northern Theater in the Windy City, Judge Borde returned his verdict based on the grand jury inquiry on April 22, after Giesler read glowing testimonials on Wanger's behalf from Sam Goldwyn (who said his friend "had never chosen the easy way"), Rev. Smith (who confirmed he was working with the Wangers toward reconciliation) and others; it sounded like an awards dinner at the Beverly Wilshire Hotel.

"I am of the opinion there was great provocation for what happened," said Borde. "What that provocation was I don't know, other than from rumors and newspaper reports, but I'm sure it existed." He also announced that he did not believe Wanger intended to kill Lang in his assault—however, as the judge pointed out, "the law of the six-shooter went out in California many years ago." Reducing the charge to assault with a deadly weapon, Borde sentenced Wanger to four months in the Sheriff's Wayside Honor Farm in Castaic, fifty miles north of Beverly Hills—the lightest possible consequence short of acquittal.

"The past must be done with, for the sake of the future," said Joan Bennett in Chicago upon hearing of her husband's fate. She was good to her word, although it was not easy.

Trading his tailored suits for a blue denim inmate's uniform, Walter Wanger began what he wryly called his "summer vacation" when he returned from a visit with Bennett and was admitted into the honor farm on June 6 as prisoner No. 22487 after two days in County Jail. Perhaps because of his celebrity status, he shared his twelfth-floor cell with another prisoner with dubious notoriety and his own tenuous Hollywood pedigree: Evan Charles Thomas, a former railroad switchman who had murdered one woman and wounded four other people during an assault with his .22 rifle, inspiring the 1952 film *The Sniper*.

Still brimming with movie ideas, the producer served as the prison librarian, managed requests for athletic equipment in the recreation building, and was reported to be an excellent worker. He was allowed to conduct film business with the help of his visiting secretary, signing papers and even taking meetings with fellow producer Bryan Foy. Frequently he would write his old colleagues in the industry, signing his missives "Yours on location," but often, his good humor masked a brooding, solitary existence in which he grew to feel dehumanized and victimized. In August, after serving sixty-two days—half of his sentence—Wanger appealed for parole, claiming good behavior and financial hardship. He told the media he'd grown close with some fellow prisoners, most of whom he viewed as victims of circumstance or bad luck. He announced he would head a new organization called the Phoenix Foundation—with the appropriate mythological allusion to rebirth—dedicated to helping ex-cons find jobs (his efforts eventually resulted in the creation of a job training program at Castaic). Perhaps inspired by Bennett's foray into self-help authorship, he was also planning to write a book called *How to Behave in Jail*, a decidedly different set of rules from her *How to Be Attractive* volume.

He would have plenty of time to put pen to paper when, after only twelve minutes of deliberation, the parole board rejected his appeal and sent him back to the prison farm. Finally released in September with a mere twenty-one days knocked off his sentence, he announced that his first order of business would be, true to form, to educate the public through his movies on the appalling condition of the modern penal system—"the nation's number one scandal." He would prove good to his word.

The four months of Wanger's incarceration had, in some ways, been even worse for Bennett, for while her husband was shut away from the eyes of the world, she still had to face it every day. During her nerve-wracking *Bell, Book and Candle* stint, otherwise well-received critically and commercially around the country, she was occasionally booed and once even had tomatoes tossed her way. Her Holmby Hills home was ransacked on June 10, with every appearance that the burglars sought juicy personal dirt about her affair with Lang—her belongings and letters were scattered about her bedroom, personal cameras inspected and strewn about in Wanger's room, but nothing appeared to have been taken, her jewelry safely locked away in a safe deposit box before she went on the road. And while some Hollywood friends—like James Mason, Humphrey Bogart and Lauren Bacall—stuck by her, even fought for parts for her, jobs simply evaporated. "Without question the shooting scandal and the resulting publicity destroyed my career in the motion picture industry," she later wrote of the period.

Despite her all-too-public humiliation, Bennett stood by her man. She allowed Wanger to stay with their children while she was on the road with *Bell, Book and Candle*. He moved out again upon her return, but soon her daughters asked her to allow him to come back, and the ever-dutiful mother could never refuse their wishes. By June of 1953, the couple stopped being coy with the press, announcing that they had indeed resolved their differences and were living again under the same roof. It was far from a completely peaceful accord, however: the union was really only salvaged for the sake of their children, the wounds from the shooting more enduring on their marriage than they were on Jennings Lang.

For the rest of their mostly separate lives together, Bennett never stopped needling her husband and made sure her children understood her indiscretion was prompted by Wanger's multiple infidelities. Wanger was often forced to communicate with his wife through written notes in front of dinner guests—a harsh reversal of their earlier teamwork—and he suggested that in Europe, his crime of passion would never have been punished at all. And while their personal lives headed in separate directions, Wanger stubbornly refused to acquiesce to a divorce without a messy public fight.

Within a year of their reunion, the couple managed to save their Mapleton Drive home from foreclosure, but by 1954, even after constant winnowing of the domestic staff, it was apparent that Joan's tastefully appointed haven—the place where she felt so comfortably in command that she'd welcomed in the press during the most out-of-control twenty-four hours of her life—had to be sold. After handing off the keys to producer Hal Wallis, the Wangers departed for their new, smaller address at 1423 Stone Canyon Road in Bel-Air. It had its charms, and the girls were happy there, but it would never be the tranquil home Mapleton had once been.

Things were not always grim, though—at least for Walter Wanger. His producing star was unexpectedly on the rise again after a string of small but respectable films including *Navy Wife*, in which he successfully lobbied for a part for Bennett. While his own prison tenure was certainly in one of the most comfortable, lenient institutions available, the producer had funneled his resultant outrage and bitterness into his 1954 film *Riot in Cell Block 11*, a hard-hitting, melodramatic indictment of life behind bars modeled after a 1952 uprising at a prison in Jackson, Michigan, and directed by Don Siegel. The film, fueled by savvy publicity proclaiming Wanger's "firsthand" experience within a penal system in need of reform, was a critical and commercial smash—just the kind of progressive-spirited prestige statement film Wanger always aspired to make. Suddenly, the industry power players who'd passed his table by, eyes averted, when he dined at Romanoff's or the

Polo Lounge were dropping by to convey congratulations—in Hollywood, as sure a sign as ever that he was back in the game.

That success was followed in 1956 by the then-uniquely highbrow science fiction film *Invasion of the Body Snatchers*, also helmed by Siegel, a smart and artfully crafted allegorical tale of Cold War paranoia that paralleled the personal one Wanger's cuckolding and imprisonment fueled: writing in prison, he once compared MCA agents to Communists. The film not only spoke to the conspiratorial times, it endures as a classic of the genre today.

Wanger completed his moral outrage trilogy triumphantly with 1958's *I Want to Live*—a three-hanky biopic melodrama directed by Robert Wise chronicling the case of beautiful Barbara Graham, a juvenile delinquent turned indigent party girl/prostitute who was arrested, convicted, and executed in the San Quentin gas chamber after three male associates accused Graham of the 1953 bludgeoning death of an aged Burbank widow. San Francisco journalist Ed Montgomery had investigated the case and found compelling holes in it, gaps that greatly appealed to Wanger's sense of injustice. He related to the media's sensational depiction of the case of "Bloody Babs." Over lunch in the Beverly Hills Brown Derby, the producer recruited Wise to tell the tale sympathetically in Graham's favor.

With Susan Hayward, a dead ringer for Graham, in the lead and a script penned by Nelson Gidding and Don Mankiewicz, *I Want to Live!* became a colossal, if controversial, hit despite minor censorship problems with the Legion of Decency and a backlash from police organizations for the film's support of a convicted killer. Clinton Anderson later wrote that he found the film to be a surprising slap in the face to his department, considering Wanger's relatively benign treatment at their hands, feeling it was "an unfair, untrue and biased attack on police methods." But *I Want to Live!* was nominated for five Oscars, and Hayward took home the Best Actress statuette, offering her first thanks to Walter Wanger. It was a rousing comeback of dynamic proportions, the type Hollywood adores.

Wagner took his resounding rebound, fueled by bitter alienation both personally and professionally, in stride, almost as an inevitability. "This is my fourteenth career," he offered matter-of-factly. "What people here don't realize is that I'm the perennial man-who-came-back."

However, as Wanger, his confidence restored, scaled to his greatest career heights, he once again forgot a Hollywood truism: once you're at the very top, you have nowhere to go but down. A reckless moment loomed ahead.

Like *Joan of Arc* before it, another overly expensive film about famous woman from the history books paired with another all-too-of-the-moment case of high-profile Hollywood adultery, brought an end to Walter Wanger's remarkable comeback—and his storied career.

Wanger's next film would be his last: 1963's grand, gaudy *Cleopatra*, with an out-of-control $37 million budget that caused frequent financial and creative skirmishes between Wanger and many others involved in the film. The producer was also put in the ironic position of handling damage control involving yet another very public love triangle starring the film's leads, Elizabeth Taylor and Richard Burton, and Taylor's then-husband-turned-odd man out, singer Eddie Fisher. Burton and Taylor's seemingly flagrant liaison—only the latest act of an ongoing offscreen melodrama that began when Fisher left his own spouse, perky actress Debbie Reynolds, for the sensuous Taylor, widow of Fisher's best friend, the late producer Mike Todd—consumed the media's interest for months and created a tense atmosphere of distraction during an already difficult and protracted European production.

When a reporter pressed Wanger for comment on the scandal as it played out, he dryly noted, "I once made my views on the subject of marital infidelity quite clear." But the producer—under fire from studio executives who unfairly blamed him for letting things balloon out of control—admitted that dealing tolerantly with *l'affaire Taylor* caused him to take a more mature and understanding view of Bennett's liaison with Lang. Though he knew others might scoff at the notion of him gently handling a situation so similar to the one that had made him pick up his pistol, he chalked it up to wisdom gained with the passage of time. "As I reach my more mature years, I realize there is nothing that can be done to control a man or woman's heart."

Although personally enlightened by *Cleopatra*, Wanger—who'd battled for years to will the would-be epic into production, wrangling studio interference, a change in regimes, a switch of directors, Taylor's always-fragile health, and his own nearly failing heart, only to be iced out of hands-on control at the eleventh hour—was professionally done in by the film. The jettisoning prompted him to pen *My Life with Cleopatra*, one of the earliest and most revealing books chronicling a film's production, to salvage his reputation—and those of the film's cast and crew—in advance of release. The book wowed critics and became a bestseller; the film's reception was more polarizing, and its box office receipts were calamitous.

The spectacular commercial failure of *Cleopatra* made *Joan of Arc* look like a bump in the road. Though Wanger soldiered on in an effort to make more movies, his career effectively came to an end. As nearly did 20th Century Fox, forced to sell much of its Beverly Hills-abutting backlot to developers who created high-rising Century City, ironically now an epi-center of top agencies, in its stead. In the way the historic Egyptian queen reshaped the world of her age, Wanger's *Cleopatra* irrevocably changed the face of the region surrounding Beverly Hills.

The producer retreated to New York City. In 1961, a decade after the Lang incident, he joined Bennett and their children in Holmby Hills for Christmas and agreed at long last to an amicable divorce. But the couple, citing the fact that their schedules barely allowed for them to be in the same city at the same time, didn't finalize their split until 1965, with Joan jetting off to Juarez, Mexico, to at last call it quits. Wanger found love again with Aileen Mehle, best known as the widely read society columnist Suzy, and while the two never married, they remained companions until his death from a severe heart attack at age seventy-four in 1968.

A postscript to the Wanger/Bennett/Lang triangle also provided one other substantially significant contribution to the world of cinema.

Several years after the shooting, filmmaker Billy Wilder—whose masterful films *Double Indemnity* and *Sunset Boulevard* endure as pillars of Hollywood's *film noir* genre—and his frequent screenwriting collaborator I.A.L. Diamond were attempting to crack a new project long brewing at the back of Wilder's brain: an updated take on director David Lean's 1945 British film *Brief Encounter* (penned by Noel Coward, based on his 1936 one-act play *Still Life*) in which a man and woman embark on a secret emotional affair, considering consummating their extramarital romance in a flat belonging to a friend. Years before, Wilder was unable to figure out how to tackle the subject matter in a way sexually prudish American audiences would accept—and more pointedly, that censors would allow. He found himself drawn to a facet unexplored in *Brief Encounter*, as he later explained it: "Who was that guy who owned that flat where those lovers meet? Who is the friend who would let himself be exploited that way?"

By 1959, in the wake of Wilder and Diamond's wildly successful sex farce *Some Like It Hot*, the duo was eager to further push past comfort zones and the notion came back around again. Equipped with a concept and a situation, they found themselves searching for a plot until discussions turned to that scandal that had rocked Hollywood in 1951 and Lang and Bennett's use of the unoccupied Brando apartment for their secret rendezvous. Taken by the notion of a low-ranking agent offering a trysting place to his superior, as Jay Kantor had, they built their scenario around a lowly employee lending his apartment not out of friendship but as a transactional act of professional ambition.

With an ideal hook, Wilder and Diamond tweaked and re-tweaked the scenario until the two men devised a dark comedic gem, *The Apartment*, starring Jack Lemmon as the ladder-climbing corporate drone who lends his flat to his philandering boss (Fred MacMurray), only to discover the executive is cheating with the sweet but gullible elevator operator (Shirley MacLaine) Lemmon is smitten with himself. The hugely successful film— produced by Walter Wanger's old boss Harold Mirisch and his brothers Walter and Marvin—received ten Academy Award nominations in 1960 and captured five Oscars, including Best Picture.

Susan Hayward had paid homage to Wanger collecting her award, but when accepting their shared Best Original Screenplay trophies, Wilder and Diamond simply thanked one another.

The Wangers were put through a painful emotional wringer, personally and in the press, but Jennings Lang suffered the most physical agony as a result of the shooting. Although plenty of people thought Wanger's vengeful, calculated shot exacted a price for infidelity that could be considered poetically just, the emotional fallout was considerably worse.

The forgotten victim of the debacle was Lang's wife Pam, who died at age forty on October 23, 1952—almost one year after Wanger's assault on her husband. Dr. Riemer, the physician whom the agent sought out while there was still a bullet in him, reported that Pam—the subject of tremendous sympathy in the Hollywood community as the innocent victim of the affair—suffered a heart attack related to a toxic thyroid condition, a condition wags like Louella Parsons overtly suggested was exacerbated by the stress of the scandal. After the shooting, the Langs reportedly repaired their flagging marriage, and the agent, at last fully recovered from his gunshot wounds, was devastated by her passing. "I don't know when anything has hit this town as hard as the passing of Pam Lang," Parsons eulogized in her column. "Everyone who knew Pam loved her and felt the way she stood by her husband at the time…was magnificent."

Approached for comment, all a distraught Joan Bennett could offer was, "I'm so sorry."

Humiliated by the revelations of his indiscretion with Bennett and non-stop buzzing about Wanger's below-the-belt assault, Lang was initially reluctant to resume his professional and social life at the eye of Hollywood's gossip-mongering storm—he felt he might have become a laughingstock. But his close friend Greg Bautzer, the handsome entertainment attorney who handled everything from profitable business deals to contentious divorces and—with romances that included Lana Turner, Dorothy Lamour, Ginger Rogers and Joan Crawford—one of Hollywood's most prolific playboys, insisted Lang step back into the social whirl. "You have to face them sometime," Bautzer told him, taking him to dinner at Romanoff's where they would be on prime display among the Beverly Hills glitterati. "When people see that I'm behind you, they'll stop laughing" (At the same time, Bautzer refused to sever professional ties with his longtime legal client Walter Wanger).

Throughout it all, his employer MCA—more specifically, his powerful, influential boss Lew Wasserman—rallied behind Lang, deeming his value far more significant than a bout of embarrassing headlines. Lang rebounded from the incident, even more prosperously than Bennett or Wanger. By 1952, he'd risen to become vice president of MCA's television division, shepherding the development of such popular shows as *Wagon Train* and *McHale's Navy, Alfred Hitchcock Presents* and *The Virginian*, the first ninety-minute weekly drama. Later, after marrying singer/actress Monica Lewis in 1956, he would pioneer the concept of made-for-television movies.

When MCA absorbed Universal Studios in the 1960s and had to divest its talent agency to satisfy antitrust laws, Lang transitioned to the studio side. At Universal, he developed a "wheel" of recurring monthly series requiring fewer commitments from name stars, like Peter Falk's deal for *Columbo*, successfully transformed several TV series into motion pictures and helped champion Steven Spielberg's directing career at the studio. Branching into features as a producer in the 1970s, he made further innovations, including the Oscar-winning Sensurround sound systems that were the hallmark of his big-budget, all-star disaster films, including *Earthquake* and the *Airport* series. After multiple collaborations with stars like Clint Eastwood and

Walter Matthau, Lang's long string of successes were finally halted when he suffered a debilitating stroke in 1983, although he would live for another thirteen years before dying of pneumonia at age 81 in 1996.

In addition to the two sons he shared with his first wife Pam, Lang and Lewis welcomed his third child, son Rocky Lang in 1958, seven years after the reckless moment—which should have settled some of the talk of his post-shooting physical condition. But for years, it would be whispered—sometimes too loudly—that Jennings Lang had sacrificed a costly percentage over his dalliance with his client: one testicle, maybe both.

Even Rocky couldn't escape the ever-churning Hollywood rumor mill even on the playground when, in front of several classmates, his sixth-grade best friend told him, "My mother said your father was shot in the balls!" Stunned—and suddenly questioning his own parentage—Rocky returned home, his queries put off by both his mother and the maid. Finally, he faced his father, who'd been alerted and was prepared to provide an answer. "I'm not going to tell you much about it because it wasn't a very happy time, but I am going to show you something," he said, revealing the lingering scar where Wanger's bullet had pierced his upper thigh.

"The guy was a lousy shot," Lang told his son. "But Hollywood is Hollywood, and getting shot in the balls is a better story than getting shot in the leg."

Walter Wanger often appeared to be most bitter toward Jennings Lang's employer MCA—the first of the super-agencies, popularizing package deals and star bargaining power which sounded the death knell for the studio system—believing the powerhouse had orchestrated the media feeding frenzy that followed his trial, rather than sordid dalliances or violent confrontations. He even believed MCA's "persecution" continued in his business dealings long after his release from Castaic.

In many ways, the shooting became as symbolic of the age-old enmity between producers and the talent brokers that continually threaten to drive up their costs as it was representative of a love triangle gone awry. Indeed, Wanger, who saw himself as the ultimate maverick producer with an eye on the bottom line, seemed more incensed about being cuckolded by the enemy, a nefarious 10-percenter, than he was about the actual cuckolding itself.

Or, as Wanger himself once remarked to a group of top film executives, "You chaps just talk about agents. I'm the only one who ever *did* anything about them."

Whether she wanted to or not, Joan Bennett had to get a new agent. Still, she would recall Jennings Lang fondly and appreciatively in her 1970 memoir/family history *The Bennett Playbill*, reflecting on his gracious move not to press charges against Wanger. "He made a statement that must place him among history's most forgiving victims."

As the target of an unstated moral blacklisting by the studios, film roles were scarce for Bennett; her old friend and neighbor Humphrey Bogart, who always followed his own moral compass and whose box office clout overruled nervous executives, lobbied ferociously for her casting when an actress was need to take over Irene Dunne's role in 1955's *We're No Angels*, incensed that studio suits held her responsible for her husband's "lunacy." Bennett, who equated herself splendidly, was grateful that Bogie "had made the stand to show what he thought of the underground movement to stamp out Joan Bennett."

"Bogie, who lived on the same street I did, insisted that I be in *We're No Angels* or he wouldn't do it," Bennett revealed. "Now *that* is a good friend."

She soldiered on professionally, achieving her greatest post-scandal successes starring as matriarch Elizabeth Collins Stoddard in the enduring cult favorite vampire-themed soap opera *Dark Shadows* from 1966 to 1971—a role that earned her an Emmy nomination—as well as in influential Italian filmmaker Dario Argento's belatedly embraced 1977 horror film *Suspiria*. Otherwise, she did what she'd always done: put her head down, did the work that came her way—TV movies, series guest spots, summer stock, touring companies—and continued providing for her family with gratitude and perseverance. Though she wasn't above musing wistfully about the glossy off-screen world she'd once so thoroughly inhabited. "I don't think much of most of the films I made, but being a movie star was something I liked very much," she admitted.

There remained room for romance in her life: in the early 1960s she grew close to journeyman actor John Emery, ex-husband of Tallulah Bankhead; he divorced his subsequent wife in hopes of marrying Bennett, but tragedy struck: she tended to him through a lengthy cancer treatment until his life was cut short by the disease at age fifty-nine. Four years later, while shooting *Dark Shadows* in New York, she met and became involved with David Wilde, a prominent writer, publisher, and critic seven years her junior.

After ten years together, the couple married in 1978; by then, Bennett was aware that, like her previous husbands, Wilde had an inherent characteristic that would, on occasion, challenge their relationship: though resolutely straight, Wilde long found profound satisfaction dressing in women's clothes, adopting a female-presenting persona known as Gail and taking a prominent position in transvestite circles. While this posed complications for Wilde in his previous marriage and relationships with his children, many of his friends found the calmer, more relaxed Gail better company than his masculine identity. The revelation caused initial friction with Bennett, but Wilde assured her that during their relationship he'd moved past, at least for the time being, his need to cross-dress. Bennett—ever true to her pursuit of a stable home life—made her peace with the situation. They lived a quiet life in her home in Scarsdale, New York, until her death from a heart attack at age eighty in 1990—her funeral took place on December 13, exactly thirty-nine years to the day of Walter Wanger's reckless moment in MCA's parking lot in Beverly Hills.

For nearly five decades, she'd held on to the striking Paul Clemens portrait from *The Woman In the Window*, vividly juxtaposing her own outward allure with the cool menace of her *noir* bad girl persona, always displayed prominently in her subsequent homes. Long after the complications of her fraught romantic life were trumpeted in breathless headlines, that double-edged image endured beyond celluloid and canvas. The actress burnished her screen image as a *femme fatale*, only to be undone by a skewed perception that she was just as dangerous, duplicitous, and potentially deadly in real life. She noted the lingering sting of disappointment she felt when so many in Hollywood turned their backs on her over her own moment of recklessness. "Suddenly I was the villain of the piece, the apex of a triangle that had driven my husband to a shocking act of violence," she'd reflect.

"Before December 13, 1951, I'd made sixty films in twenty-three years, while, in the decade that followed, I made five," Bennett pointed out, noting that social mores had significantly shifted. "If it happened today, I'd be a sensation. I'd be wanted by all studios for all pictures."

But as far as the Hollywood of her heyday was concerned? With a hint of one of those hardboiled noir dames in her repertoire, she said, "I might just as well have pulled the trigger myself."

RING-A-DING-DING

"The only one who can call me dago is Frank. I call him dago too. With anybody else, there's a fight."

—Dean Martin

It was Dean Martin's forty-ninth birthday. The drinks, as you might suspect, were flowing, and in the wee small hours of the morning, Frank Sinatra was buying.

Dino, as he was known to his intimates, and his closest "pally"—whom he'd christened The Chairman of the Board on the first episode of his TV series *The Dean Martin Show*—were marking the occasion at a location that was as nearly iconic as they were: the posh Polo Lounge of the Beverly Hills Hotel on Sunset Boulevard. Both had plenty to celebrate on Dino's birthday—June 7, 1966—with a late-night bash just after midnight.

Earlier in the year, Martin's series had debuted on NBC, and Dino's breezy, unrehearsed approach had struck ratings gold with viewers all over America. *The Silencers*, his first Matt Helm spy-spoof film, had been a smash at the box office, and the first of three sequels, *Murderers' Row*, was in the works. His albums remained solid sellers, and, even in the era of rock and roll ascendence, his singles still regularly cracked the charts—he won a bet with his teenage son Dean-Paul after successfully predicting, with a bit of braggadocio, that his tune "Everybody Loves Somebody" would dethrone their musical heroes The Beatles in Billboard's number one slot two years earlier; it did, becoming his signature tune and TV theme. "Dean Martin & Friends"—namely Frank and comedian Joey Bishop—had brought down the house playing the showroom of the Sands Hotel in Las Vegas a few weeks earlier. Between movies, television, records, and concerts, Martin was well on his way to becoming the era's highest-earning entertainer in show business.

For Sinatra, it was also a "Very Good Year." At the end of 1965, he'd celebrated his fiftieth birthday at the Trianon Room of the Beverly Wilshire Hotel at the apex of then-emerging glamour center Rodeo Drive; the conspicuously absent Sammy Davis, Jr., surprised him by jumping out of the giant cake. His daughter Nancy's debut single "These Boots Were Made for Walking" became his record label Reprise's second number-one hit (Martin supplied the first)—earlier in the week, Sinatra had hosted a soiree to welcome her back from a successful European tour. Better yet, the old saloon singer's songs still boasted some big action in the post-rock-and-roll landscape, too: his single "Strangers In the Night" was on its way to becoming a chart-topper; the subsequent album would stay at number one for seventy-three weeks and win four Grammys. He'd spent the past two days in Burbank taping the second of his popular and critically heralded TV specials, *A Man and His Music*, in which he ebulliently belted out future classics like "That's Life" and "Fly Me to the Moon." His film career continued to thrive: a year prior, his wartime action-caper hybrid *Von Ryan's Express* had been a box office smash, his highest-grossing film of the decade, giving him a substantial profit-sharing windfall. Along with all the professional triumphs, Sinatra had another reason to be in good spirits: he was in love with twenty-year-old actress Mia Farrow. Thirty years his junior, Mia was five years younger than his oldest child, Nancy, and their sometimes turbulent May-December romance had caused tidal waves in the press and concern among Sinatra intimates for the past two years. But somehow, they were making it work.

Farrow was absent on Martin's birthday, as was Mrs. Martin, the former beauty queen Jeannie Biegger. So was the hardest working man in showbiz, Sammy Davis, Jr.: fresh from his acclaimed Broadway run in *Golden Boy*, Davis had hit the road on tour, beginning at the Sands's Copa Room. The ruggedly handsome B-movie leading man Richard Conte, who also appeared with Sintara, Martin, and Davis in 1960's *Ocean's Eleven*, stood in for Sammy this night. A Jersey boy like Frank and the son of an Italian barber like Dino, "Nick" Conte, fifty-six, was a favored fellow Hollywood *paisan*: three years earlier, he'd co-starred with Martin in *Who's Been Sleeping in My Bed?* (with scenes shot at the Beverly Hills Hotel's storied pool), and his latest film opposite Sinatra, *Assault on a Queen*, would be hitting theaters in eight days. Joining the party was Sinatra's close friend Ermenegildo "Jilly" Rizzo, the beloved owner of the popular New York nightspot Jilly's. A thick, burly rhinoceros of a man with a glass eye (the source of much lurid speculation, Jilly's damaged "blinker" was the result of an errant paperclip flick while horsing around with his brothers). Jilly, who spoke in a *Guys and Dolls*-esque parlance of "dese, dems, and dose" liberally laced with enough expletives to make Damon Runyon blush, affectionately called his friend "Sinat." The Sinatra-Martin party also included a trio of women, two of whom were Black.

The group had been out celebrating and arrived after midnight at the luxurious, dimly lit cocktail bar. The revelers settled into a large booth and continued having a typically raucous "Ring-a-Ding-Ding" time (a signature turn-of-phrase claimed by Sinatra—via has favored songwriters Sammy Cahn and Jimmy Van Heusen—with the 1961 song and album of the same name), the centers of attention in the most rarefied watering hole in the city, glittering like 24-carat diamonds in a solid gold setting.

Or, as the birthday boy reportedly told Sinatra, "If looks could suck cock, we'd be wilted by now in this joint."

And as the celebration stretched on to nearly 2 a.m., it was with just *that* kind of racy repartee—not to mention the casual use of various self-depre-cating ethnic slurs and epithets tossed around the table—that started the trouble that quickly followed, drawing the ire of a nearby diner who, while not nearly as famous, was at least as wealthy and possibly more influential. As Frederick R. Weisman rose to complain, he had no idea that he would soon be carried out of the hotel on a stretcher, comatose.

Dean might have warned Weisman. "It's Frank's world," he once philosophized. "We just live in it."

Forget for a moment the term "Rat Pack," that hand-me-down 1950s nickname for a debauched bunch of Humphrey Bogart's Holmby Hills drinking buddies. Frank Sinatra was only a satellite in Bogie's group. By the 1960s, the singer and his closest cronies, a consortium of the top tal-ents of the day—including Martin, Davis, Bishop, Peter Lawford, and their revolving supporting cast of showbiz luminaries, as well as one political icon, Lawford's brother-in-law John F. Kennedy, whose path to winning the presidency in 1960 was bolstered by Sinatra's group's support—preferred to be referred to as "The Summit," as in The Summit of the entertainment mountain, the loftiest of the lofty, masters of all they surveyed. Kings of the Hill, Tops of the Heap. Music, stage, screen, tube, comedy, Hollywood, Broadway, Las Vegas—between them, they conquered the whole shootin' match and all points in between. In 1966, though the press couldn't help returning to Rat Pack references, to call themselves The Summit was neither exaggeration nor hubris—it was *right*.

Freely blending their on- and off-stage lives in a heady cocktail of Hey-Hey hijinks served up for all the world to sample, the members of The Summit wowed and amused audiences with talents and shenanigans that made them appear to be at once a rarefied breed and regular Joes, glamorous gods and naughty little boys. Booze—or Gasoline, in hipster Summit-speak—was the fuel that revved their engines—Dino built his entire on-stage persona, post-Jerry Lewis partnership, around over-imbibing—as they followed "The Leader" (Sinatra) and raced past the Clydes (the losers) to the bar and toward the dangerous curves of whatever koo-koo broad was ahead. It was crazy. It was a gas.

Frank Sinatra. Where does one start? The Voice. The Leader. Ol' Blue Eyes. The Chairman. The premiere popular vocalist of the twentieth century. Volumes can, have, and will be written about him, but to cut to the chase: Once the idol of legions of bobby soxers who screamed, swooned, and worshipped at his every velvety note during the 1940s, the Hoboken-bred ex-boy crooner had beaten off mid-career doldrums, scandalous headlines, and shattered romances in the 1950s to become the most phenomenally popular singer of his day and an Oscar-winning actor, all with undeniable style and swagger. The story goes that on the night of his comeback triumph, winning the Academy Award for Best Supporting Actor for *From Here to Eternity* at the Pantages Theater in 1954, yet in the midst of another heated, heart-wrenching breakup with second wife Ava Gardner, Sinatra slipped out his own celebratory bash at Romanoff's restaurant on Rodeo Drive, where his dear friend the ersatz Russian royal "Prince" Michael Romanoff reigned, and took his trophy for a reflective late-night stroll around Beverly Hills' deserted streets, his adopted home town since debarking from the East Coast to pursue his silver screen ambitions. "I ducked the party, lost the crowds and took a walk. Just me and Oscar," Sinatra recalled. "I think I relived my entire life as I walked up and down the streets of Beverly Hills." He likened his victory to "your first kiss" and "the first time you hit a guy and he went down." His reverie, the legend goes, was interrupted when he was approached by a member of the ever-vigilant Beverly Hills Police Department, who wanted to know just where the moonlight wanderer had gotten that golden statuette.

With that trademark trilby hat tilted just so, that smartly pressed Sy Devore suit, whether swingin' or singin' an achingly sad saloon song, it seemed that suddenly every red-blooded American male over twenty-five wanted to be Frank Sinatra. Except maybe that *other* Italian crooner Sinatra got chummy with on the set of *Some Came Running* in 1958.

Dean Martin wasn't doing too bad, either. In the early 1950s, he and his anarchic nightclub partner, the outrageously spastic man-child Jerry Lewis—"the organ grinder and the monkey," they called themselves off-stage—had risen to Hollywood superstardom; their outrageous antics on stage and screen ignited a frenzy in fans unseen since Sinatra's bobby-soxers. But clashing, escalating egos—mostly Jerry's—ultimately led to an acrimonious split in 1956. The handsome, laid-back man's man with pleasing mozzarella melodies and ever-present cocktails remarkably sustained his career despite the break-up of the most popular comedy team of all time. In real life, unshackled from the straight-man shtick and adopting the devilishly good-natured persona of a dedicated boozer, he was to many tastes even *funnier* than his ex-partner. Everybody loved him, and not just sometimes—all the time. If one couldn't be perfectly Frank, it was just as keen to be Dean.

Through Bogie's Holmby Hills Rat Pack, Sinatra and Martin had casually socialized for years, but their shared time on the remote set of director Vincente Minnelli's *Some Came Running*, shot largely in Madison, Indiana—drinking, gambling, carousing, wise-cracking, and playing juvenile practical jokes on each other—sealed their friendship. Though they had their differences—Frank hated to be alone, Dean preferred it (social creature Sinatra was driven to always go-go-go every night, all night, only retiring in the wee-est small hours after he had worn out everyone else, while the more aloof Martin would just as soon stay home watching Westerns on TV before bedding down at ten)—they clearly complemented one another, intensity tempering mellowness. Sinatra had found a rare someone he felt on par with, maybe even envied a little, and Martin loved Frank as long as things were kept light; Dino humored him but never kissed his ass. They always knew where they stood with each other. Their lives became so intertwined they were "Uncle Frank" and "Uncle Dean" to each other's children. "They were buds—'pallies,'" Frank's youngest daughter Tina once told me. "Dean was a kind of the reverse, the antithesis of Frank, but somewhere down in that Italian lineage, they all kind of came together anyway...Their work was important, but so was home, and they had that much in common."

"We cut the tops of our thumbs and became blood brothers," Martin once recalled. "He wanted to cut the wrist. I said, 'What, are you crazy? No, *here's* good enough!'"

Together with longtime pally Sammy Davis, Jr.—who was just as multi-talented and worked twice as hard, breaking color barriers through sheer talent and occasional assists from his buddies—they formed the central triumvirate of their rechristened The Summit (briefly known as the Clan, but changed to avoid association with *that* Klan), with actor Peter Lawford, all dashing, debonair British charm, as their wingman. Soon they were all recording for Sinatra's nascent Reprise label, campaigning for Lawford's brother-in-law JFK (though Martin didn't much give a shit about the politics of the briefly rechristened "Jack Pack") and performing at Sinatra's Las Vegas casino of choice, the Sands.

Their camaraderie went very public in 1960 when the guys simultaneously decided to appear in the caper film *Ocean's Eleven* to be shot in Vegas, and, during filming, perform together on stage at the Sands along with stand-up comic Joey Bishop, who proved adept at tossing off sly wisecracks that often deftly punctured his comrades' outsized personas without pissing anyone off. Thus was born the legendary "Rat Pack" image of a brotherhood of staggeringly talented middle-aged men in tuxedos to whom the rules of society no longer applied, telling off-color, politically incorrect jokes between song sets, slugging down Jack Daniels, playing pranks and generally living out their boys-will-be-boys friendship on stage as much, or more, for their own amusement as to thrill the audiences. "We ain't figured out ourselves what we do up here," Sinatra once told an audience, "but it's fun, baby."

The Rat Pack was known, in their off-hours in the steam room at the Sands, for wearing matching white robes monogrammed with their nicknames: Frank's alternately bore his initials "FAS" or "The Leader"; Dino's was "Dag," short for "Dago"; Joey's had his catchphrase, "Son of a Gun"; Peter's said "Brother-in-Lawford"; and cigarette-puffing Sammy's said "Smokey"—or at least it did when one of the guys hadn't swapped it out for a chocolate brown robe in one of their attempts at ethnic humor.

Similarly, Frank and Jilly Rizzo would often don matching orange jackets, the backs emblazoned with the logo "Living Well is the Best Revenge, F.T.A."—the initials standing for "Fuck Them All." An unofficial, unbilled but ever-present Rat in the Pack, the mountainous, Greenwich Village-bred Rizzo was already a successful nightclub owner whose hulking, intimidating appearance was balanced by an earthy charm, salty humor, and boundless generosity of spirit when he began rubbing shoulders with Sinatra. He first caught Sinatra's attention around 1956 when both were in a New York nightclub where Rizzo once served as a doorman: a patron got out of hand, and despite having elevated himself to restaurateur, Jilly handily tossed the troublemaker out without incident. For Sinatra, it was love at first bounce, impressed by Rizzo's savvy mix of street smarts and Old World wisdom, not to mention his intense love of music. They further bonded during a 1958 trip to the Fontainebleau Hotel in Miami, where Sinatra was filming *A Hole in the Head* and Jilly hosted an elite party for Sinatra's guests, NASA's original Gemini astronauts. They became more than fast friends—they became as close as brothers, nearly inseparable.

Jilly's at 52nd and Eighth in New York was a clubby little piano bar and restaurant that lured an intriguing mix of celebrities, politicians, doctors, lawyers, Broadway chorines, working girls, and unsavory characters by serving, depending on who you asked, either the best or the worst Chinese food in Manhattan. Jilly's became a Sinatra shrine, known for its napkin endorsements ("My Favorite Bistro—Frank Sinatra"), a dominating oil portrait of The Leader, and a flashing sign proclaiming it "The Home of the King." Jilly even installed a private restroom for Sinatra in the back, a "throne" to do his business without being crowded by an unwanted entourage.

Sinatra returned the compliment and immortalized Jilly's in song with a mention in his kicky duet with Davis, "Me and My Shadow," and in film with a brief exterior shot in *The Manchurian Candidate*. By 1962, Sinatra also invited Rizzo to "Come Fly with Him" around the world as his preferred right-hand man with a mean right hook who tackled a wide range of duties, from muscling away overzealous fans to procuring comely companionship to accompanying Sinatra to meet Queen Elizabeth II of England ("If anyone ever hits you, call me," Jilly told Her Majesty).

And when the singer's famously volcanic temper boiled over, as it too often did, Sinatra intimates knew Jilly was the only man who carried enough heft—in respect and muscle—to stand up to him effectively. Tough love was his forte: when a very inebriated Johnny Carson, aggressively hitting on a gangster's girlfriend, belligerently resisted Rizzo's warnings to flee when said gangster was en route to the nightclub, Jilly simply said, "Sorry, John," knocked the talk show host cold with one punch, carried him over his shoulder out the back door and loaded him into a taxi, presumably saving his life.

Of course, not all the gang's Hey-Hey happened at the Copa Room or around the bar at Jilly's. They often brought it home to Beverly Hills, where most of the guys lived just a few minutes from each other in 1966. When he wasn't staying at his lavish Palm Spring estate, Sinatra resided primarily in Trousdale Estates in an enviable hilltop manor melding Midcentury Modern style and a bold Japanese aesthetic, designed by the renowned architect Paul R. Williams, one of the few Black visionaries of his era who'd risen in the discipline, nicknamed "The Teahouse" overlooking Coldwater Canyon at 2666 Bowmont Drive, which he fashioned as the ultimate swinging bachelor pad after his split from Ava Gardner in 1957; he and Williams shared a love of gadgets, and the architect crafted the home as his vision of the future, incorporating a plethora of high-tech toys offering every convenience at the press of a button, and, at Sinatra's direction, conceived the home entirely around the singer's cutting-edge hi-fi system, resulting in the finest home acoustics in town. Even at the very pinnacle of Beverly Hills, literally and figuratively, however, the splendid surroundings didn't ease Sinatra's inherent restlessness and melancholy; his *Ocean's Eleven* co-star Henry Silva once recalled leaving a party there around 3 a.m. and watching a wistful Sinatra survey the glittering lights of the suburban San Fernando Valley and muse "Many nights I've looked down there and envied the people who live there."

Later, when the neighbors put the kibosh on a planned helipad that Sinatra wanted to whisk him between engagements and tighten his relentless schedule, he sold the home and—spending increasing amounts of time in Palm Springs, Las Vegas and New York, on location and abroad—made his local residence just across the Beverly Hills city limits in a luxury gated compound at 882 North Doheny Drive in West Hollywood, in a comparatively modest two-bedroom apartment previously owned by his late friend Marilyn Monroe. Sinatra stashed his girlfriends *du jour* within the compound, and in-the-know circles dubbed it "The Sinatra Arms." A quick drive away was another party pad employed by the Rat Packers en masse, a second-floor apartment in the Frank Lloyd Wright-designed Anderton Court building at the heart of Rodeo Drive (years later, when celebrated hairstylist Fernando Romero made over the space for his salon, he told met he discovered an entire wall full of autographs signed by Sinatra, his pals, and their many celebrity guests hidden behind a mirror).

Meanwhile, Sammy Davis—when he wasn't on the road, which was rare—had recently purchased a Georgian-style estate originally built by famed producer David O. Selznick nearby at 1050 Summit Drive—after many attempts thwarted by racist real estate practices, he became one of the earliest Black homeowners in the city. Further down the Hills of Beverly, Martin and his large brood had been dwelling in a family-friendly mansion just above Sunset Boulevard at 601 Mountain Drive since 1953—far less ostentatious than its neighbors, the Martin residence, luxurious to be sure, was a warm and cozy ranch-style abode on an acre-and-a-half of property, and over the years, the family expanded the house to better suit their growing, boisterous clan.

Even as Beverly Hills was the home where the members of The Summit hung their snap-brim hats, it was also, like the rest of the world, these titans' playground. And occasionally, their indulgences in good, semi-clean adult fun—as it was viewed in a more permissive time—couldn't escape the attention of local law enforcement.

During this period, Beverly Hills patrol officer Mike Cangelosi was making late-night rounds in his black-and-white when he spotted a sleek, limited-edition black Dual Ghia. He clocked the sportscar doing fifty-eight miles per hour in a thirty-five zone, then watched it race through a red light to turn onto Coldwater Canyon Drive toward Bowmont, so he lit his flashers and siren and roared off in pursuit. After the Ghia pulled over, a familiar-looking face squinted out from the driver's window and growled, "What did I do, officer?" Frank Sinatra had nursed an attitude toward authority figures ever since his youth when he was harassed by Hoboken cops who, because of his Italian lineage, suspected his always-natty clothes had been stolen.

Irritated by the testy, entitled tone, Cangelosi snapped back. "You were going pretty fast and you ignored the signal," he replied, as recounted in the book *Echoes from the Beat: Beverly Hills Cops Tell Their Stories*. "But I'm not going to write you a ticket—go ahead, kill yourself!" As the officer turned on his heel and strode back to his patrol cruiser, Sinatra jumped out of the Ghia to follow him, suddenly penitent and grateful for the concern. "I've got it coming—go ahead and write me a ticket." Cooling off, Cangelosi told Sinatra that newshounds perpetually staked out the police station; he'd spare him a major media-feeding frenzy over a minor infraction and give the singer a pass this time.

A relieved Sinatra apologized again, saying he'd been daydreaming and not watching his speed; hearing the patrolman's Italian surname, he inquired when Cangelosi's shift ended, and when the officer told him he got off at midnight, Sinatra made what sounded to him like a surprisingly sincere offer: "Come up when you're through and have a drink. You know where I live?"

Cangelosi admitted he was familiar with the singer's Bowmont Drive digs, especially the conspicuous sign at the front gate that read, "*If you haven't been invited, you better have a damn good reason for ringing this bell!*" Sinatra laughed, repeated the invitation, and was on his way. Cangelosi never did drop by, but later would run into him again at Puccini, the Italian restaurant at 224 South Beverly Drive co-owned by Sinatra and his Rat Pack pally Peter Lawford (similarly, Martin lent his name and likeness to the even more popular Dino's Lodge on the Sunset Strip just a few blocks out of Beverly Hills, for a hefty percentage—half of the profits), where to the officer's surprise, the star remembered him and welcomed him hospitably.

In another after-hours misadventure recounted to the admired celebrity journalist Bill Zehme, Sinatra and Martin were driving home from a fun-filled evening at the Villa Capri nightclub on Hollywood's Yucca Street, a regular meeting place and after-session hangout among A-list singers, musicians, songwriters, composers, record executives, and their Reprise label-mates. Slightly more sober than his pal, Sinatra argued that he should take the wheel of Dino's shiny red Ferrari, but Martin wouldn't hear of it. Inevitably, flashing lights appeared in the rearview mirror after they entered Beverly Hills, and Martin had to pull over. Sinatra devised a plan and instructed Martin: *Don't look at the cop, and don't say a word or he'll smell the booze on your breath. Let me do the talking.* Dean agreed.

Sinatra stepped out of the sports car and turned on some high-wattage charm as two officers approached. They recognized him and were suitably impressed—even in Beverly Hills, where celebrities were commonplace, a Sinatra encounter always promised some thrill—but they insisted on seeing the driver. Sinatra did his best to intervene, but one of the cops aimed his flashlight at the shadowy driver. Perhaps the spotlight made Dino think it was his cue: he got out of the car and began to warble: "Everybody Loves Somebody" as if he'd stepped right onto the stage at the Sands.

Sinatra shook his head, defeated. The officers asked Martin to walk a white line. "No way, pally," he replied. "Not unless you put a net under it." Amused, the officers made sure the two singers got home safely without citing them, a gracious payback for the impromptu "performance"—and, in typical fashion, Martin wasn't nearly as soused as he appeared.

"The one thing Dad knew how to do was get people out of scrapes," Martin's daughter Deana believed. "He had a great relationship with the Beverly Hills police, who were his number one fans." This proved helpful when Dino's elderly father, Guy Crocetti, was arrested for allegedly stealing a pad of prescription forms and passing off a faked scrip to feed an addiction to sleeping pills—in exchange for Dino performing at a police benefit, Guy was delivered safely home, and the story never made the press.

On yet another occasion in 1964, Dean and his second wife Jeannie hosted a fifteen-year anniversary party for themselves at their home on Mountain Drive, a major black-tie blow-out under a tent in the backyard with lots of eating, drinking, and making merry. As the party was in full swing around 11 p.m., police sirens could be heard outside over the orchestra. When Jeannie searched for her husband and couldn't find him anywhere, Sinatra assured her he'd take care of things. Sinatra met Beverly Hills police officers at the door, curious about the matter. The officers told him they had received a complaint call about a loud party. It was time, they decreed, to call it a night.

Sinatra was shocked—virtually everyone in the neighborhood was in attendance. Who was left to complain? The cops demurred, not at liberty to disclose the neighbor's identity, but Sinatra persisted. He poured on the charisma again. Meanwhile, the band had been stopped, and Jeannie finally located Dean upstairs in his bedroom. She told him the police were shutting down the party. "Oh, too bad," he said in dismay.

At last, Sinatra coaxed the source of the complaint out of the officers outside. "To be totally honest with you, Mr. Sinatra, the call came from *inside* the house."

Sinatra politely thanked the officers, assured them everything would be taken care of and excused himself. He marched up the stairs directly to Dino's bedroom, where he found his pal lying in bed in his pajamas, watching the late news on TV and fiddling with a golf putter.

"Did you call the cops on your own party?" an irate Sinatra demanded.

"Hey, they ate, they drank," shrugged Martin. "Let 'em go home. I gotta get up in the morning."

It was an era that was more accepting of such alcohol-soaked antics; folks even found it amusing if no harm was done. But it was difficult even for these two titans to laugh off the late-night misadventure that went sorely awry that night at the Polo Lounge in 1966.

The Beverly Hills Hotel was itself no less a luminary than its Rat Pack patrons, with a sweeping, sun-dappled, mission-style Mediterranean Revival grandeur that became so evocative of the region that David Alexander's photo of the structure at twilight would a decade later grace the cover of the Eagles' "Hotel California," one of the bestselling albums of all time, eternally cementing the resort in the public consciousness as *the* quintessential Southern Californian hotel. Designed by architect Elmer Grey and opened in 1912 to stand majestically above the city along Sunset Boulevard, the hotel predated the establishment of Beverly Hills as a city by two years. In truth, Beverly Hills might never have come to be had the owners of the surrounding territory not constructed it: they'd purchased lands comprising the territory in hopes of finding oil underneath, but when that plan largely went bust, the abundant water they discovered instead inspired the landowners to develop the property for residential use. The hotel was conceived as a lure for wealthy travelers journeying from downtown Los Angeles and the Pacific Ocean, an ideal halfway point stopover. Outfitted with every imaginable luxury in a region so bucolic, the monied vacationers visiting the hotel couldn't help but fall in love with the area and purchase their own property nearby.

The gambit worked: not only did Beverly Hills emerge—an early master-planned city populated almost from the outset by deep-pocketed elites—the hotel became the central hub of the nascent community, where locals gathered for hobnobbing, worship, education, holiday activities, and society events. Surrounded by twelve acres filled with gardens lush with tropical foliage including bougainvillea, banana plants, hibiscus, and spiring palm trees, the grounds featured an elegant array of freestanding private bungalows that dotted the rear of the property, swelling from five in 1915 to a total of twenty-three, enticing famous occupants including Howard Hughes and Marilyn Monroe to make their homes away from home there.

El Jardin, the hotel's original bar and restaurant, had emerged as the preferred watering hole for Hollywood's original bad boy imbibers, a debauched silver screen version of the Algonquin Round Table that included Errol Flynn, John Barrymore, and W.C. Fields, and where Table One was perpetually reserved for Charlie Chaplin. By 1941, under the auspices of new owner and soon-to-be world-class hotelier Hernando Courtwright, the bar had become the favored hangout for a gang of tipplers that included humorist Will Rogers, studio chief Daryl Zanuck and Spencer Tracy, who knocked drinks back after a day on the polo field at

Rogers' Pacific Palisades ranch; Courtwright thus rechristened the resplendently swanky bar the Polo Lounge. Soon, the grand Brazilian pepper tree on the patio would bear witness to decades of Hollywood power dining and star-making—there wasn't a famous name in the entertainment industry who hadn't entered its environs to see and be seen. So many landmark deals were struck at the hotel that its staff installed trademark pink telephones alongside every plush green banquette, just in case agents and producers concocted a career-making pact so huge over lunch that the deal couldn't wait until they returned to the office. Hotel guests, tourists, and visitors from all walks of life descended on the Polo Lounge to bask in its one-of-a-kind ambiance, the epitome of glamour in the unofficial capital of show business. The exterior of the hotel adopted its signature pink-and-green color scheme, which earned it the enduring nickname "the Pink Palace," by 1948; a year later, Paul R. Williams, who'd soon realize Sinatra's gadget-laden temple on Bowmont Drive, crafted the distinctive signage and Crescent Wing addition. Its corridors were made instantly recognizable by the famous Martinique banana leaf wallpaper selected by famed interior and film costume designer Don Loper, especially after its visual splendors were on display in movie magazines and as splashy settings in films like *The Bad and the Beautiful* and *Designing Woman*. By then, the iconography was complete.

It was against this extravagant backdrop that Frank and Dean—two of Hollywood's loftiest stars and most notorious party boys of that or any era—convened.

At about 1:40 a.m. early Wednesday morning, twenty minutes from closing time, another Beverly Hills resident arrived at the Polo Lounge, as was his custom. Frederick Rand Weisman, then fifty-four, was the son of Russia-to-Minneapolis immigrants who'd relocated to Los Angeles. He'd risen from selling wholesale produce to become the president of Hunt's Foods when he was just thirty-one and, after a uranium investment ballooned his fortunes, retired in 1958 to pursue a peripatetic assortment of business ventures, remaining director of the company's executive board. His middle name was self-invented, inspired by Minneapolis' soaring Rand Building as a symbol of his own lofty ambitions. A well-known patron of the arts—his wife Marcia was the sister of multimillionaire philanthropist Norton Simon—he kept one of the region's top modern art collections in his showplace Angelo Drive home, Cézannes, Picassos and Kandinskys joined by early works from postwar standouts including Rothkos, de Koonings, and Giacomettis. He hosted instructive classes for novice collectors and was a booster of the West Hollywood Ferus Gallery, which was crucial in cultivating artists like Frank Stella, Ellsworth Kelly, and Roy Lichtenstein. Two years hence, the Weismans' central role in the L.A. art scene would be commemorated on canvas by David Hockney in his dual portrait work *American Collectors (Fred and Marcia Weisman)*.

Accompanying Weisman was a guest of the hotel, seventy-four-year-old Franklin H. Fox, a prominent businessman from a Boston furniture company. The two men had just driven over from dinner at Chasen's restaurant to prep for an engagement reception at the nearby Bel-Air Hotel celebrating the impending wedding of Weisman's son Richard and Fox's daughter Elizabeth, a former Miss Teenage Boston, scheduled later that month in Boston. Stopping in for a nightcap, they took the booth alongside Sinatra and Martin's. Weisman and Fox chatted over drinks for about ten minutes, barely able to hear one another over the rowdy laughter and salty conversation from the celebrity celebrants. Eventually, Weisman grew annoyed, leaned over to the party, and, as Sinatra concluded a call from one of the boothside telephones, asked them to lower the volume because there were other people in the room. Weisman also scolded them for their vulgarity—there were ladies present in the Polo Lounge, after all.

Despite Weisman's objection to blue language, Sinatra later quoted him as saying, "You talk too fucking loud and you have a bunch of loud-mouthed friends." There may have also been the use of a certain d-word and a certain w-word that Italian Americans typically object to.

Taken aback, the singer—who said at first that he thought Weisman was kidding but quickly realized the man was serious—fired off a testy "You're out of line, buddy," and turned back to the merriment at hand.

This is where the details become rather hazy, depending on whose account you believe:

It's possible, as Sinatra would state to police, that Weisman suddenly decked the singer in the right eye, giving him a near-instant shiner, then apparently slipped and fell—though no one had touched him—breaking the base of a cocktail table as he crashed to the floor with a thud.

It's possible, as Franklin Fox would tell Sinatra biographer Kitty Kelly decades later, that Sinatra uttered an anti-Semitic remark at Weisman, following up with a crack about his glasses, then stormed out of the room with his friends before things came to blows, only to return moments later in a fit of rage. Martin, Fox, and hotel security guard Forrest Henry tried to hold Sinatra and Weisman apart as Martin pleaded, "Let's get out of here, Frank!" Then Sinatra may have grabbed one of the boothside telephones and hurled it viciously at Weisman—Ring-a-Ding-*DING!*—knocking him cold and sending him to the floor with a thud.

It's possible that after trading insults, "everybody started grabbing everybody else," as one eyewitness reported, and in the melee, Weisman suddenly fell to the floor with a thud.

It's possible that Dean Martin really didn't see what happened, as he related, but some Clyde who had taken a poke at his pally suddenly hit the floor with a thud.

In the end, the thud was one constant element in each of the stories. Weisman had landed on the floor and was flat on his back amid an upturned ashtray, a cast-off tablecloth, and a clutter of broken crystal. It sounded as if he were snoring. And he wasn't getting up.

Security officer Forrest Henry had separated the combatants, and Martin, Conte, Rizzo, and the rest of the party hustled Sinatra—who, Henry said, kept "hollering" about his sore eye—out of the cocktail lounge as Fox tried to revive Weisman, to no avail. The Beverly Hills Police Department was alerted, and an ambulance from the local Fire Department's Emergency Division was dispatched. Paramedics took Weisman out on a stretcher as police interviewed the Polo Lounge staff and eyewitnesses. The executive was transported to the Beverly Hills First Aid Station, where he was treated, revived, and released, then taken home and put to bed. No formal complaint was made by the hotel or the parties involved, so an investigation was not pursued.

When Martin returned to his home a few blocks away on Mountain Drive, he stopped in the living room and perched glumly on the sofa next to his eighteen-year-old daughter Deana, who was surprised to see her father home so early on his birthday.

"Frank blew a fuse tonight," he told her. "He can't let it go."

"Was anyone hurt?" Deana asked.

"I don't know," her father replied as he rose to go to bed. "I don't know anything."

Almost twenty-four hours after the incident, when Weisman again failed to awaken, an ambulance was called to his home at 8 p.m. to speed him to the intensive care unit of nearby Mt. Sinai Hospital, where Weisman was on the board of directors. He remained there in critical condition for forty-eight hours. Then he was rushed into surgery, where he endured a two-and-a-half-hour operation to alleviate a skull fracture. Weisman emerged in serious condition, still comatose, and doctors could not guarantee he would survive.

As soon as Police Chief Clinton Anderson learned just how grave Weisman's condition was, he ordered Beverly Hills detectives B.L. Cork and Robert Estell to launch a full-scale investigation immediately. Anderson had known Sinatra since at least 1954, when the singer was involved in a fender-bender and immediately reported to police headquarters to file an accident report and check on the welfare of an elderly woman injured in the crash. He'd likely kept an eye on Sinatra long before that, given the persistent rumors of his shoulder-rubbing with the kind of gangland figures that Anderson detested within his city limits. Later, there were surely encounters at galas and social functions within the tight-knit, small-town-feeling Beverly Hills community and, of course, the chief took an active hand in security measures when Senator John F. Kennedy frequently visited the Beverly Hills Hotel—a favorite pre-presidency trysting place—during his candidacy and, as president, the Beverly Hilton Hotel, JFK's unofficial "Western White House," frequently with Sinatra in tow.

Anderson's detectives rounded up more hotel employees and bystanders who might have seen something. Still, the stories were only consistent in that nobody knew for certain if anyone had pushed or struck Weisman. Anderson, who was told Weisman had been drinking and was taking prescription medication that might not have mixed well with the liquor, may have been willing to hold off on any conclusions until he heard everyone's stories: "He *could've* fallen and hit his head on a table," mused the chief to the press, "but somebody might have slugged him, too." His suspicions were fueled when he discovered that two of the principal players—Frank Sinatra and Dean Martin—had flown the coop. Quite literally, as it turned out.

"Sinatra has been in hiding," Anderson told the detail-hungry press, "but we'll get him."

Dean Martin was located in Lake Tahoe and interviewed by telephone but "had nothing to say, as you might expect," Chief Anderson reported. Martin claimed that as his party was leaving the Polo Lounge Weisman punched Sinatra. Fox then jumped in between them, allowing the group to leave. When Martin looked over his shoulder, he saw Weisman on the floor.

All he knew was that he didn't witness anyone striking the man. "He said he didn't see anything, but you know how that goes," said Anderson. "We'll keep working on the case and get to the bottom of it."

Meanwhile, Sinatra's press spokesperson Jim Mahoney told reporters the entertainer had indeed suffered a black eye at Weisman's hands, indicating the singer "was the aggrieved party, not the aggressor. If Mr. Sinatra threw any punches, they would have been entirely a reflex under the circumstances."

Eventually, police headquarters received a telephone call with a familiar voice at the other end: Frank Sinatra, who had hightailed it out of town with Martin around 6 a.m. in his private Lear jet *Christina II* (after briefly diverting it from a loan to the Air Force to photograph a prototype military plane, which coincidentally crashed later that day). Dino, the pilot recalled, suggested that they leave the country, but Sinatra—who carried his left arm in an improvised sling made from a pillowcase—said, "We'll hide out for a few days. It'll be fine." While Martin continued on to Tahoe, Sinatra holed up in his landmark two-and-a-half-acre home, called The Compound, on Wonder Palms Drive in Palm Springs after a sixteen-minute flight.

If the singer seemed quick to duck out of the public eye, his reaction was understandable: he had been plunged into this kind of hot water before. "Trouble just seems to come my way—unbidden, unwelcome, unneeded," he once lamented. Just a year earlier, the volcanic-tempered Leader was accused of punching a prominent socialite during the Bing Crosby Golf Tournament in Pebble Beach. In 1947, in the middle of Ciro's nightclub, Sinatra famously clobbered Lee Mortimer, a tart newspaper columnist who constantly baited Sinatra in print, branding him a Communist and a mob crony. Over the decades, there had been other skirmishes, large and small, and there would be yet more in the years ahead. Sinatra was known as a man with a short fuse, quick fists, and a long memory for vendettas. There's a reason Paul Anka wrote "My Way" with him in mind.

As actor and equally notorious tough guy Robert Mitchum once put it, "The only man in town I'd be afraid to fight is Sinatra. I might knock him down, but he'd keep getting up until one of us was dead."

Slurs on his ethnicity especially made his blood boil at molten temperatures. Sure, he jokingly dubbed his previous private jet *Il Dago*, and sure, he and Neapolitan cronies like Dino affectionately called each other "Dag" in abbreviation. But if any non-*paisan* hurled pejoratives like "Guinea," "greaseball," "wop," or "dago" in his direction, they quickly "became punched," as Sinatra said. Worse yet was to call him a "dirty" anything; obsessed with cleanliness, "dirty" was an adjective the singer wouldn't abide.

Sinatra himself succinctly summed it up: "When a guy bothers me, I belt him."

Or sometimes he had a guy belt a guy for him—namely Jilly Rizzo. Remarking on Rizzo's skill for roughly clearing a swath through an adoring crowd to allow Sinatra to pass through unmolested, comic Don Rickles once asked Jilly, "How's it feel to be Frank's tractor?" *Bulldozer* might have been a more apt description: Rizzo and his mammoth associates were frequently accused of being *overly enthusiastic* in their duties protecting the Chairman, taking matters into their own meat hooks as roughly as they saw fit. In 1964, Rizzo was alleged to have stomped on the hand of a French paparazzo, crushing the bones, during an altercation in Europe.

So Sinatra was no stranger to this kind of publicity. But he needed it like a hole in the head. He'd lit out of town to lick his wounds and put steak on his eye in Palm Springs, but after he heard of the seriousness of Fred Weisman's condition, the singer—by then well-aquatinted with Chief Anderson's flinty demeanor—knew it was best to face the music sooner rather than later. "The guy was cursing me and using four-letter words," Sinatra explained to the detectives. "I told him 'I don't think you out to be sitting there with your glasses on making that kind of conversation.' The guy got up and lunged at me. I defended myself, naturally." He contended that after Weisman had slugged him, Fox tried to separate the combatants and the executive fell without anyone laying a finger on him. "I at no time saw anyone hit him—and I certainly did not," he said, noting that on his way out "I looked behind me and as I left and saw a man on the floor." His statement echoed Martin's, almost verbatim.

The police noted Sinatra's version of events and advised him they would be in touch as the investigation warranted. Left to sweat out the situation and pray that Weisman recovered, he was joined at his home by the Sands's general manager Jack Entratter, who'd had the hotel-casino's luxe Copa Room showroom designed specifically as a central showplace for Sinatra and his A-list contemporaries, and his future wife Corrine Cole, a Playboy Playmate, showgirl and actress. Mia Farrow flew in as soon as she could to provide consolation and wait out Weisman's fate as if they were on a deathwatch.

By June 12, Fred Weisman had started to regain consciousness. The next day, he was awake and able to recognize his family members. His doctors called him "vastly improved" but remained guarded about the outlook for a full recovery. Detectives hoped to question the executive, the last witness on their list, on June 15 and see if they could fit the final piece into the puzzle, but Weisman's doctors held them off because their patient "was confused and could not answer questions intelligently." It became obvious Weisman was having trouble with his memory when he repeatedly kept introducing his wife to his physicians.

Such ambiguity caused even more nail-biting in Camp Sinatra, where the mood was already tense. No one ever left the house; they just sat inside, occasionally playing backgammon and frequently staring at the walls. Sinatra was genuinely repentant over the whole affair, but many of those close to him believed the singer was less concerned about Weisman's survival than he was about how *he'd* be affected if the man didn't pull through. He told friends, "Now I've gone and done it... If this guy croaks, I'm finished." Corinne Cole (later Corinne Sidney, wife of the late film director George Sidney, who helmed Sinatra's "Pal Joey") later said it was the first time she'd ever seen the man genuinely scared.

As someone who once referred to himself as a "24-karat manic depressive," Sinatra's mood continued to sink to ever-darker depths as the days dwindled by. He and Farrow reportedly got into a heated row when, in an attempt to be supportive, she told him the fight was "probably" not his fault—"*probably*" not being deemed sufficiently supportive in the Summit's lexicon.

Meanwhile, in Lake Tahoe, Dino played golf.

On June 27, Beverly Hills detectives were at last allowed to interview Fred Weisman, who was recovering at home. But if they were hoping for a conclusive revelation, they were disappointed. Weisman told them that he could remember everything leading up to the altercation but nothing else—the whole incident was a blank. Doctors called his condition "retrograde amnesia."

Weisman's family had been incensed and initially wanted to press assault charges against Sinatra, but thought better of it. Sinatra biographer Kitty Kelly claims an anonymous family member told her they were scared off by the singer's intimidating reputation and anonymous telephone threats from ominous-sounding figures. Famed Hollywood attorney Grant

Cooper announced that the Weismans wanted to close the case, forget the incident, and move on. "A further investigation as to whether he was hit, pushed, or fell is not necessary," Cooper said.

The police detectives could do little but shrug their shoulders. On June 30, the Los Angeles County District Attorney's office decided not to pursue the investigation, and the case was closed.

A few weeks later, after rumors circulated around Hollywood that Sinatra's shiner was actually caused by an errant elbow thrown by Dino while attempting to shield his pally during the melee, Hollywood columnist Earl Wilson put the question directly to Martin during a phone interview as the star commenced filming on *Murderers' Row*.

"Not true," Martin laughed off the theory. "The fact is, I hit Frank in the eye myself, intentionally. I've been wanting to do it for 26 years."

Yet another theory was floated, decades after the birthday braining, by George Jacobs, Sinatra's personal valet from 1953 to 1968. In his 2003 memoir *Mr. S: My Life with Frank Sinatra*, Jacobs offered still another scenario in the already splintered narrative: it wasn't Frank Sinatra who bashed Weisman in the head with the telephone; the culprit was Jilly Rizzo.

According to Jacobs, as Sinatra and Weisman's sparring over who was offending whom that night escalated, Rizzo—who, as Jacobs put, "would stand up for Mr. S's honor even when there was none to stand for"—took umbrage, picked up the phone, and rang Weisman's bell of his own accord. Then the "dagos got out of Dodge, pronto," as Jacobs put it. The valet accompanied his famed employer on his escape trek from Beverly Hills to Palm Springs, where Jacobs claims Sinatra was absolutely livid over Rizzo's imprudent, hair-trigger explosion—but nevertheless chose to keep mum on Jilly's involvement, firm in the belief that if the situation were reversed, Rizzo would take the fall for Sinatra. Jacobs also implies that the Weisman party was offered—and accepted—a vast sum of hush money from Sinatra and his attorney, Mickey Rudin, to dissuade them from pursuing the matter further.

In his memoir *Get Mahoney!*, Jim Mahoney, Sinatra's public relations manager during the row and for many years before and after, bolstered that assessment, naming Rizzo as the actual assailant, though he points to a heavy glass ashtray as the weapon of choice. Mahoney also suggests that the "n-word," another anathema to Sinatra, was uttered, aimed at the women in his company, further enflaming the singer. "Rizzo, with a legendary short fuse, was ferociously protective of Sinatra," Mahoney wrote. "It's at times like these when you need to pull in favors. From the bartenders to the waiters, maitre'd, and nearby customers, they were all kind enough or smart enough to keep the details to themselves."

"They got their asses out of there," Mahoney—who, with additional clients like Steve McQueen and Lee Marvin, became quite skilled at crisis management during his career—told me in 2023 of his clients' flight from the hotel, with Rizzo's hand bloody from shattering whatever tool he'd used to clobber Weisman. "His hand was severely cut, supposedly, and required stitches," the publicist remembered. "Jilly went to the doctor—I don't even know if he went to the doctor in L.A. or in Palm Springs, but he got his ass out of town, that was for sure."

For Mahoney, who'd initially been invited along to the party at the Polo Lounge, it was both a stroke of good fortune and business as usual that he hadn't been on the scene himself. "I didn't want to spend a hell a lot of time hanging out with the guys," chuckled Mahoney. "The position was enviable, but I wanted to be somewhere safe where if they got their ass in a situation like the Beverly Hills Hotel, I could come in and hopefully calm everybody down."

It certainly wouldn't have been the first time Rizzo would be accused of aggressively and violently intervening on behalf of his beloved friend—or the last. In 1972, he reportedly assaulted a young student suspected of snapping shots of Sinatra in Monte Carlo, then was whisked out of the country on the singer's private jet. In 1973, Rizzo was found guilty of assault after he and members of Sinatra's entourage, reportedly at Sinatra's behest, rained brutal blows on a guest at a Palm Springs hotel, chanting the refrain "Respect the man!" He paid the plaintiff $101,000 (the verdict was later overturned, and the case was settled out of court).

If Rizzo sometimes took his role as Sinatra's guard dog too seriously, Sinatra loved "that bum's" pit-bull-like loyalty and otherwise jolly demeanor too much to care, seeing him as the brother he never had. The rest of Hollywood embraced Jilly as well, and he was a beloved, respected figure in the show business community for years to come. Sinatra continued to reference Rizzo in song (in his unlikely cover of "Mrs. Robinson" he proclaimed, "*Jilly loves you more than you can know!*") and gave him cameo roles in several of his films—the big man even enjoyed a brief moment of national celebrity in 1970 when he regularly delivered mangled poetry readings on *Rowan & Martin's Laugh-In*. After thirty years at Sinatra's side,

Jilly Rizzo died tragically in 1992 on his seventy-fifth birthday when a drunk driver moving at 85 mph. collided with his borrowed car, trapping Rizzo inside as it burst into flame. In the end, all that was left of him was his jewelry. When informed of Jilly's demise, a devastated Sinatra literally fell to his knees.

The revised, Rizzo-centric version of events is definitely plausible, though it doesn't jibe with most other accounts. And given that it was Rizzo who typically took the blows (as well as dished them out) when "Sinat" wanted things done His Way, one wonders why it wasn't it Jilly—and not the boss who would face the music in the case? Singer Paul Anka wrote in his memoir *My Way* that Rizzo, "never one to rat on any situation," had confided in him one night about the brouhaha, alluding that it was Sinatra's volatile response that had ignited the situation, with a hint that an additional complement of Sinatra's "goons" had finished the job. Anka—who was close enough to Sinatra to pen one of the singer's defining, seemingly autobiographical songs—had seen similar eruptions. "Frank had a terrible temper, especially when he was drinking, but he suffered great remorse for his actions."

"Sinatra don't need no protection," Jilly, who repeatedly denied serving as Frank Sinatra's bodyguard in any official capacity, once explained. "He's man enough to stand up and defend himself in his own way, like any man should."

Frederick Weisman would recover and go on to live a long, prosperous life as a businessman and one of America's foremost art collectors—and his storied history as one of the nation's preeminent art benefactors can be attributed, apparently, to having his bell rung at the Polo Lounge. He was plagued by amnesia for months following the incident, struggling to recall simple, everyday details, until one day when his wife Marcia brought a small painting to his room, and he was startled to recognize it immediately: "Jackson Pollock, I remember when we bought that," he recalled. From then on, the fog seemed to lift, his memories came rushing back, and he was so grateful he established the first in a series of significant art endowment programs that would characterize his later years; he was particularly inspired to establish a visual arts program—including temporary exhibitions and gifts of art—at the hospital.

In the early 1980s, Weisman proposed a plan to turn Greystone Mansion—the epic Beverly Hills estate that had gone largely unlived in since the Doheny family moved out in 1954 and had subsequently been purchased by the City of Beverly Hills—into a public art museum, where he and other collectors could display their fine works for all to see. The plan was never realized; meanwhile, the Weismans amicably divorced, divvying up their art collection in a fifty-fifty split. Fred Wesiman would purchase a showplace Gordon B. Kaufmann-designed home on Holmby Hills' Carolwood Drive just minutes outside of Beverly Hills, which, in 1986, he decided to convert into a private museum. Upon his death in 1994, the estate continued to house redubbed The Frederick R. Weisman Art Foundation; items in his collection toured the world and also found homes at places like Malibu's Pepperdine University, the San Diego Museum of Art, the New Orleans Museum of Art, and the Frank Gehry-designed Frederick R. Weisman Museum on the campus of the University of Minnesota.

In his twilight years, Weisman delighted in giving non-stop personal tours of his by-then astonishing assortment of modern art at Carolwood. The man who was scandalized by Frank Sinatra's bawdy language would lead visitors into an upstairs bathroom, where they would be stopped in their tracks by the sight of a nude couple in a passionate embrace—in actuality, a life-sized, realistic sculpture by artist Duane Hanson. "Oh, I guess they didn't check out yet," he'd say in mock surprise.

Frank Sinatra was so elated that the whole thing was over that he returned to Beverly Hills, went to Ruser's jewelry store on Rodeo Drive, and purchased an $85,000 nine-carat engagement ring, presenting the sparkler to Mia Farrow on the Fourth of July. The two were swiftly married on July 19 in a private ceremony in Jack Entratter's suite at the Sands in Las Vegas. Dean Martin got the thankless task of informing the Sinatra children—so much closer in age to Mia than their father was—of the nuptials just as the ceremony was taking place.

Perhaps the Weisman incident had shown Sinatra how fragile life could be and prompted him to grab all the happiness he could with Mia. He told his daughter Nancy, "Maybe we'll only have a couple of years together… but we have to try." His words were sadly prophetic as their union was ultimately doomed to fizzle out in 1968 after a contretemps over her star-making turn in *Rosemary's Baby*. She wasn't going to be the traditional stay-at-home spouse he'd imagined she'd become.

And there were more noisy incidents involving Sinatra's incendiary temper: just three months after the Polo Lounge brouhaha, the singer legendarily got into an ugly public row in Las Vegas with the casino staff at the Sands when the new owner, Howard Hughes (who sparred with Sinatra in the 1950s over possession of Ava Gardner—as if either of them could possess her), refused to extend him any further courtesy credit at the gaming tables. After issuing various threats of physical injury and fairly accurately reminding the staff he'd "built this hotel from a sand pile," Sinatra deliberately crashed a golf cart through a casino window, tried to light a stack of chairs on fire with a gold lighter and, during a subsequent attempt to settle the issue, upturned a table in fury only to have his two front teeth knocked out from a punch by burly, connected Sands V.P. Carl Cohen. "You make one move and they won't know which part of the desert to find you," Cohen hissed at Sinatra's looming lackeys, who wisely retreated. There were some men even Frank Sinatra couldn't safely screw with, and Cohen was one of them.

Some intimates would later claim that the Polo Lounge incident was really the beginning of the end of the Sinatra-Farrow relationship, as Sinatra reportedly looked for the first time at all of young Mia's gentler, more tender qualities and saw only his own shortcomings reflected back at him—his fiery temper, his violent impulses, his petty squabbles. From then on, things were never the same between them. Still, even after they split, they remained very close throughout the epic saga that was Sinatra's life (she would even later intimate that her son, journalist Ronan Farrow, whose father of record was filmmaker Woody Allen, was actually the result of a decades-later reunion fling with Sinatra).

With so many legendary dramas yet to be played out, what *really* happened at the Polo Lounge that night seemed fated to remain shrouded in mystery.

Leave it to Dean Martin, the guy who didn't see a thing, to shed at least a little more light on the matter over a year later during an interview with *Look* magazine at his Mountain Drive home. As he waxed enthusiastic about his Italian heritage, Dino let slip a juicy little tidbit about just what might have gone on that night:

"On my birthday, Frank and I were at the Polo Lounge over here. We were with six other people, mindin' our business, and we were a little loud. When we were goin' out the door, there is a couple of guys, and one of 'em says: 'There goes two loud dagos.' Well, Frank got there one split second ahead of me, and he hit one guy, I hit the other, picked 'im up and threw 'im against the wall. The cops came. We said we didn't know who did it, and walked out. But we did, yeah."

Martin, briefly an amateur prizefighter as a teenager, would go on to recount how, since his youth, he was known to jump anyone who used anti-Italian slurs—from barbershop customers making fun of his father's broken English to patrons sitting in the audience of one of his early shows—and how it used to cost him a lot of jobs. "The only one who can call me dago is Frank. I call him dago, too. With anybody else, there's a fight, 'cause I never call anybody a Chinaman or a Jew, so why should they call that to me?"

On the night of the actual fight, he told his daughter Deana a similar version of events, but one infused with slightly less machismo, in which Sinatra was the more pugilistic member of the duo. "Some drunk called us wops and Frank got mad. I told him 'Frank, just let it go, who cares? I call you wop and dago all the time.' But he got mad anyway."

Either way, if Dino was serious—and how often was that?—the incident was all a matter of ethnic pride. Or as Sinatra once noted, "If my name didn't end in a vowel, I wouldn't have had all this trouble."

Martin and Sinatra would remain bonded to the end. When Martin entered into a brief, ill-fated marriage to his own much-younger paramour Cathy Hawn in 1973, he gifted best man Sinatra with a gold plated lighter inscribed "Fuck You Very Much" during the reception held—where else?—at the Beverly Hills Hotel. Sinatra helped engineer a memorable surprise public reconciliation between Martin and Jerry Lewis in 1976—on national television during Lewis's Labor Day telethon for Muscular Dystrophy. Their friendship endured even through Dino's emotional withdrawal from those closest to him following the 1987 death of his adored singer-actor-fighter pilot son Dean-Paul Martin when his Phantom Jet crashed into the San Gorgino Mountains—the same range, ironically, that claimed the life of Sinatra's beloved mother Dolly in a plane crash ten years prior.

They even endured a brief falling-out in 1988 when Martin abruptly bowed out of the Rat Pack's "Together Again" reunion tour Frank and Sammy had engineered to try to snap Dean out of his grief. They announced it at Chasen's, where Sinatra bristled at a reporter's use of "that stupid phrase" *Rat Pack* and Martin was already half-joking about calling the tour off. Sinatra had expected Dino to jump back into the usual all-night revelry, but those days were long over for Martin. He resented Frank's behind-the-scenes demands and constant pestering to join the after-hours partying. Frank resented his pally's blasé attitude, and after four half-hearted performances, Dean jetted back to Beverly Hills, claiming kidney problems, replaced on the tour by Liza Minelli. The personal rift between the pallies lasted all of two weeks, and within a month, when Martin resumed his more comfortable solo act in Vegas, the whole imbroglio was merely fodder for another throwaway Dino quip. "Frank sent me a kidney," he told his first audience at Bally's, "only I didn't know whose it was."

Toward the end, as old age and ailments inevitably ravaged their once-godlike frames and Sammy succumbed to throat cancer in 1990, the two saw one another in person infrequently but spoke on the phone three or four times a week. "Frank, who loved to talk, and Dad, who didn't." Martin's daughter Gail told me, noting that Sinatra was among the select few who could keep her father on the line for long. "Dad says, 'I'm watching something here! I'm trying to watch the game!' But I think they both became, as they got much older, sentimental and just as sweet as could be."

On Christmas Eve, 1995, as both were in their Beverly Hills homes just three minutes apart, Sinatra placed a call to his increasingly fragile ol' buddy.

"What did one casket say to the other casket?" Dino asked. "*Is that you coffin?*"

Sinatra was still chucking when he hung up the phone. "That cuckoo bastard is still telling jokes," he grinned. "I love him."

In that last telephone conversation, their final words to each other were identical.

"Goodbye, Dag."

Hours later, Dean Martin was dead. Overwhelmed with grief, Sinatra collapsed while preparing to attend the funeral, which he simply couldn't face. "Dean has been like the air I breathe—always there, always close by," he said in a statement to the press. "He was my brother, not by blood, but by choice."

Frank Sinatra endured three years longer when in 1998—in Summit-speak—he finally cashed in his chips at age eight-two and joined his old "crony-type buddies" in the Big Casino. They were all waiting for The Leader: Dino, Sammy, Peter, Jilly, Nick Conte and so many more. And as Martin told Sinatra biographer J. Randy Taraborelli shortly before he checked out, "we'll all be together again. And *god damn it*, we're all gonna have some fun then."

Whatever *actually* happened that fabled night in 1966, in the end, it was Chief Anderson who best summed up the fisticuffs: "It was a typical barroom brawl." Then he added a caveat: "Of course, we don't have any barrooms as such in Beverly Hills."

And ain't that the truth, baby?

Alfred Hitchcock is escorted into a holding cell by the legendary
Beverly Hills police chief Clinton H. Anderson.

(Bettmann Collection / Getty Images)

Palatial Greystone Mansion patrolled by security guards in the immediate wake of the shocking murder-suicide in February 1929.

(Los Angeles Times Photographic Archive / UCLA Library Special Collections)

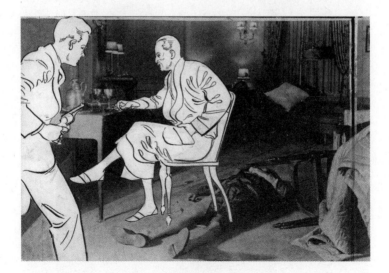

The Los Angeles Examiner dramatically illustrated the prevailing theory behind the murder-suicide based on accounts from within Greystone Mansion.

(Herald Examiner Collection / Los Angeles Public Library Photo Collection)

Ned Doheny, left, leaving the federal court in Los Angeles with his stepmother
Estelle and father Edward L. Doheny during the Teapot Dome trial in 1924.

(Everett Collection Historical / Alamy Stock Photo)

D.A.'s office investigator Leslie T. White, right, examines the vintage Colt Bisley that
took the lives of Ned Doheny and Hugh Plunkett with fellow detective Ed King.

(Herald Examiner Collection / Los Angeles Public Library Photo Collection)

Leslie White photographed his fellow Los Angeles-based Black Mask crime fiction writers in 1936: the only known meeting of Raymond Chandler (top row, second from left) and Dashiell Hammett (top row, far right).

(Black Mask Magazine / courtesy Steeger Management LLC)

Gerard Graham Dennis' live-in girlfriend Betty Ritchie breaks down after police detectives raid their Beverly Hills apartment and take her into custody.

(Los Angeles Times Photographic Archive,
UCLA Library Special Collections)

Dashing high society burglar Gerard Graham Dennis, center, is finally apprehended
by dogged New Rochelle police detective Maurice Kelly, right
– but the thief had one more daring escape up his sleeve.

(Anthony Camerano / Associated Press)

Loretta Young identifies her glamorous Kohinoor mink jacket as Beverly Hills detective J.D. Alcorn guides her through Gerard Graham Dennis' trove of stolen treasures.

(Los Angeles Times Photographic Archive, UCLA Library Special Collections)

Walter Wanger, questioned at the Beverly Hills police station after shooting Jennings Lang, confers with attorney-to-the-stars Jerry Geisler, one of the shrewdest legal minds of his era.

(The Everett Collection)

Hollywood agent Jennings Lang undergoes emergency surgery at Midway
Hospital to remove the bullets Walter Wanger fired into his body.

(Los Angeles Times Photographic Archive / UCLA Library Special Collections)

Clutching her cigarettes, Joan Bennett is escorted into the Beverly Hills police
station by publicists Chuck Cochard, left, and Margaret Ettinger, rear.

(Ira W. Guldner / Associated Press)

Outfitted in denim prison blues, Walter Wanger boards the bus
to the Castaic honor farm to serve out his sentence.

(David F. Smith / Associated Press)

Beverly Hills locals Frank Sinatra, left, and Dean Martin enjoy their distinctive brand of boozy
hijinks—but a barroom brawl and an errant telephone upended the good times in 1966.

(Pictorial Press Ltd. / Alamy Stock Photo)

In 1975, nine years after the fracas at the Polo Lounge, Jilly Rizzo, right, remains faithfully at Frank Sinatra's side, the singer's closest companion and, when necessary, informal bodyguard.

(The Everett Collection)

The chic Polo Lounge at the Beverly Hills Hotel was the see-and-be-seen epicenter of Hollywood power-dining and deal-brokering.

(Marc Wanamaker, Bison Archives)

Established in 1912, predating the city itself, the Beverly Hills Hotel was already a glamorously iconic Southern California landmark by the Rat Pack's 1960s heyday.

(Marc Wanamaker, Bison Archives)

A Los Angeles County Sheriff's Department helicopter drops SWAT team members atop the roof of Rodeo Drive's Van Cleef & Arpels jewelry boutique, where a gunman held store employees hostage in 1986.

(Kevork Djansezian / Associated Press)

Los Angeles County Sheriff's Department SWAT team shield themselves after placing a package of food demanded by the gunman at the doorstep of Van Cleef & Arpels.

(Doug Pizac / Associated Press)

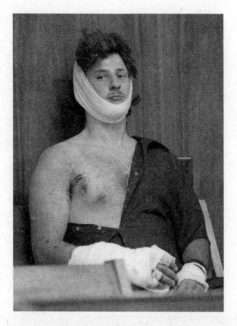

Swathed in bandages after the violent climax of the hostage standoff, gunman Steven Livaditis faces felony charges in Beverly Hills Municipal Court.

(Lennox McLendon / Associated Press)

Cameras crowd in too close as Winona Ryder exited a shoplifting and drug possession hearing in 2002, it causing a chain reaction that reinjured the fractured arm that had initiated the actress' reliance on prescription painkillers.

(Ric Francis / Associated Press)

Security video reveals Winona Ryder, laden with shopping bags, engaging in suspicious behavior during a shopping spree as items disappear from Saks Fifth Avenue's racks.

(EXTRA / ZUMAPRESS / Newscom)

Winona Ryder enters the Beverly Hills courthouse on her 30th birthday in 2002, chicly adorned in Marc Jacobs couture.

(Globe Photos / ZUMAPRESS.com / Alamy Stock Photo)

While Winona Ryder remained even-tempered in court, her
temper finally flares during the climax of her trial.

(Nina Prommer / Globe Photos / ZUMAPRESS.com / Alamy Stock Photo)

DOG DAY AFTERNOON

*"My intention was to take the jewelry and leave
with nobody hurt. It didn't work out that way."*

—**Steven Livaditis**

10:02 a.m., June 23, 1986: Just minutes after posh Van Cleef & Arpels opened for business on Monday morning, the first customer of the day walked into the jewelry boutique's gated entryway on Rodeo Drive and pressed a buzzer, requesting admittance. Following his unvarying routine, Hugh Skinner, the store's silver-maned, always impeccably dressed general manager, looked up at the security monitor. The twenty-ish-looking man caught by the camera in the caged entry waited.

He was a bit younger than Skinner's usual clientele and clearly scruffy around the edges, but he was smartly dressed, clad in a blue pinstriped suit and carrying a business-like briefcase. And in his many years on Rodeo Drive, the sixty-four-year-old Skinner was not likely to practice what would just a few years later be called the street's "*Pretty Woman* Syndrome": judging a book by its cover in the way Julia Roberts's hooker-with-a-heart-of-gold was so summarily dismissed in that film despite having gobs of Richard Gere's cash to unload.

This was Beverly Hills, after all, where even a rumpled young person clad in ripped jeans, a wrinkled t-shirt and dirty sneakers might be worth—and willing to spend—millions. This was the apex of Rodeo Drive's heady retail heyday, the big-spending, have-it-all 1980s, when the three-block commercial stretch of Rodeo stood squarely at the center of the Material World everyone wanted to be living in, a shopping mecca for moguls, monarchs and movie stars from every corner of the globe, lined with more limousines, Rolls Royces, and Ferraris than any two episodes of *Lifestyles of the Rich & Famous* combined. Equal parts glamorous and gaudy, it was, as the old Bing Crosby song went, the Street of Dreams, where every extravagance imaginable seemed obtainable—at an equally extravagant price.

The then-eighty-year-old Parisian jeweler Van Cleef & Arpels had been an integral part of those dreams since 1969, serving as the first international jewelry boutique to open on the street, just one year after Gucci had instant success ushering in a bold new era of globally brand-conscious, status-symbol shopping to the city. Co-founder Julien Arpels's son Claude opened the salon in one of the city's oldest commercial buildings, located at the prestigious corner of Rodeo Drive and Dayton Way. Previously, the venerable jeweler Ruser had catered tasteful trinkets to the area's elite since 1947—notably founder and master designer William Ruser's intricate, sculptural pieces: swans, hummingbirds, poodles, skunks, even feisty looking cherubs—with a then-innovative use of baroque freshwater pearls. The baubles were much favored by Hollywood actresses like Marlene Dietrich, Lana Turner, Ava Gardner, and Joan Crawford, both on and off screen.

In assuming Ruser's longtime berth, Van Cleef & Arpels also folded its devoted customer base into its own long-cultivated following, which included the Duchess of Windsor and the crown families of Iran and Iraq. The jeweler had already enjoyed a high-profile history with Hollywood: Marlene Dietrich made the company's *manchette*-cuff bracelet famous, while Grace Kelly's wedding jewels from Monaco's Prince Ranier had dazzled the world. Signature butterfly- or clover-shaped ornaments quickly became the traditional "first fine jewelry" gift that every young Beverly Hills girl's well-heeled parents purchased for her as she came of age. By the 1980s, the least expensive item in the store cost $30,000, while the highest-priced escalated well into the millions. Amid neighbors that in 1986 included Chanel, Sotheby's, Giorgio Beverly Hills, and Jewels by Edwar, Van Cleef & Arpels was a local institution.

So, too, was Hugh Skinner. He'd worked at the Rodeo Drive location for two decades, the first for Ruser and the last managing the Rodeo berth for Van Cleef & Arpels. Skinner was known as a jeweler who appealed to the over-privileged. Genteel, elegant, and known for never, ever forgetting a name, his customers—which had included Cary Grant, Frank Sinatra, and Jerry Lewis—valued "Hughie" for his discriminating taste. And even more so for his unwavering discretion: in a city where many of his clients purchased the same gorgeous gems for their secretaries and girlfriends as they did for their wives, he steadfastly kept his confidences.

The young man at the door looked okay to him. Skinner buzzed him in.

Upon entering the main sales area, the man was approached by salesclerk Ann Heilperin. Still strikingly attractive at forty, Annie, as friends called her, was a Swiss émigré who faced her recent landmark birthday with a positive attitude. Rather than grow melancholy over the encroachment of middle age, she instead committed to self-improvement with a new workout regimen and a beauty makeover, and her friends believed she was looking better than ever. The nearby apartment on Elm Drive in Beverly Hills she shared with her dog Cyrano reflected her outlook: filled with plants, birds, and fish, it was brimming with life.

After the customer told her he was interested in seeing some men's watches, Heilperin escorted him to Time Boutique, an adjoining room lavishly appointed with an array of Van Cleef & Arpels's timepieces. Then he opened his briefcase, reached inside, and pulled out a .357 Magnum. He pointed the weapon at her head. "Shut up and get on the floor," he ordered.

In a moment of panic and terror, Ann Heilperin screamed.

And over the next thirteen and a half hours, the Street of Dreams would transform into Nightmare Alley, where it seemed everything that could go wrong—tragically, horribly wrong—did, and the price was measured in human lives.

"I've always had a little theft in my blood," twenty-two-year-old Steven Livaditis would recall, looking back at his life. "Nothing serious. I was always rebellious. I never liked taking orders."

Born and raised in Brooklyn, his issues with authority may have stemmed from his early life with his abusive father Louis Livaditis, a Greek immigrant who owned several family restaurants in New York. Livaditis's parents' marriage had been arranged in their home country, and it was a never a successful union. The elder Livaditis routinely took his frustrations out on his wife Sophia, Steven, and his older siblings, a brother and two sisters. Indeed, Steven's aunt would later recall Louis as "a monster in the house" who brutally beat his offspring and wife, including one instance when she was pregnant. Sophia came with her own built-in traumas: she'd essentially been sold to American relatives who mistreated her and brokered the marriage to Louis; never wanting children, she attempted self-induced abortions—including while she was pregnant with Steven. Unhappy as a mother, she too beat the children; she suffered nervous breakdowns and was diagnosed with possible dissociative disorder. Through either abuse, genetics, or a tragic combination thereof, some of the Livaditis children would later exhibit symptoms of mental illness themselves. By the time Steven turned five, his mother had grown protective enough that she could no longer endure the violent assaults on her children and divorced her husband, though it meant that she and her brood would struggle with poverty and frequently rely on welfare to survive. After the split, Steven would have little to no contact with Louis, whose impact lingered nonetheless.

His mother favored Steven among the children, and when he was in grade school, he was sent to a Greek Orthodox Church orphanage in upstate New York—he would characterize it as a "private school," a claim that seems unlikely given the family's dire financial situation. Unhappy away from his family, he acted out in school, feeling deserted. Hoping to provide her son with more structure and discipline, Sophia sent Steven to live with relatives in Greece for his seventh-grade summer, but when he thought it was time to return home for school, he learned that there was no plan to bring him back. He remained in Greece for three years, constantly chafing against the very discipline he was sent to receive.

When he finally returned to Brooklyn at age seventeen, he managed to obtain a high school equivalency and then did something surprising for someone with a pronounced distaste for taking orders: he enlisted in the Army Reserve. Upon joining, he was trained as a field equipment repairman at Fort Lee, West Virginia, and subsequently transferred to Nevada in 1982, serving at a combat support hospital in Las Vegas, where his older brother George had also landed.

Thin, quiet, and topping six feet, Livaditis initially seemed to get along well enough with his fellow reservists, but he was continually plagued with financial woes. On one occasion, a supervisor recalled, he nearly burst into tears while trying to collect a late paycheck for less than $100. As his money frustrations escalated, so too did his irresponsibility and unwillingness to fulfill his commitments, and after being deemed "flaky" by his superiors, his active status was terminated within the year. In Las Vegas, menial jobs came and went—waiter, cab driver, and the like—and it was often a contest to see whether Livaditis would quit or be fired first. Co-workers found him alternately hyper or moody, his demeanor turning on a dime.

But if Sin City didn't offer much by way of gainful employment, it abundantly delivered on a familiar fantasy that Livaditis would quickly, wholeheartedly embrace: making that One Big Score that would leave him set for life.

Falling in with what his brother George called "the wrong kids," Livaditis got his first taste of easy money when he and his friends stole an antique slot machine that they imagined would be filled with quarters.

They found four; however, Livaditis was able to sell the slot for $100. "A hundred-dollar bill was like a thousand dollars to me," he would explain. "I thought that was easy. That's how I got started."

Steven Livaditis had finally found a steady gig he could stick to: small-time crook. Unfortunately, he wasn't especially good at *that* job, either.

In 1984, he was arrested in a crowded Las Vegas computer store after attempting to sell $22,000 worth of hardware he'd boosted in a recent burglary. As a police officer attempted to handcuff him, he struggled free, broke through a sliding glass door, sent several customers falling to the floor, and escaped after frantically tearing the store's front door from its hinges. He was subsequently arrested—resisting less successfully this time—and sentenced to five years in Nevada State Prison for burglary and possession of stolen property. After a couple of months behind bars, he was released and placed on probation—which he violated within six months by failing to check in with his parole officer, as well as being arrested on suspicion of possessing cocaine. During the latter incident, Livaditis fled on foot, then kicked and struggled fiercely against several officers when he was eventually captured. He clearly placed a high value on his freedom.

Despite his pronounced lack of success in his criminal enterprises, it was then that Steven Livaditis decided to get ambitious for the first time in his life. Broke and jobless, with his rent overdue and his probation officer constantly on his back, he felt squeezed by the mounting pressure. He was looking for an easy way out and devising a plan, thought he'd "take a shot."

And to take a shot, he needed a gun.

On February 12, 1986, Livaditis—his beard and mustache neatly trimmed, and clad in a gray polyester suit and alligator shoes—walked into a Zales Jewelry in a shopping center two miles from the Vegas Strip and confronted two salesclerks, armed with a large caliber revolver. He bound a male clerk's hands and feet with tape in the back room while forcing a female clerk to collect merchandise from the display cases. He strolled coolly around the store, acting as if he were the manager; for forty-five minutes, he turned customers away, telling them the store was closed temporarily while the cases were being rearranged. But despite that calm bit of bluffing, something had snapped inside Livaditis, unleashing a brutal side he had not previously displayed. He began verbally abusing his victims, threatening to kill them and kicking them repeatedly, savagely, before escaping with a haul worth between $250,000 and $400,000.

It wasn't quite a clean getaway: his palm print was found on a roll of discarded tape he'd left behind, and the clerks subsequently identified him from a police photograph. The FBI swiftly issued an arrest warrant in his name.

But after upping the ante to armed robbery and assault, as far as Livaditis was concerned, what had happened in Vegas was staying in Vegas. Adopting his brother George's name as an alias, he left Nevada behind in favor of a new address: Hollywood, California. Livaditis rented an apartment on Franklin Avenue, living off the cash he reaped fencing the stolen goods from Zales. He avoided his neighbors, partying after sundown for several months with what his landlord described as "scummy friends," as well as an unidentified woman. He was kicking back, comfortable in California's warm embrace…until, inevitably, his liquid assets began to dry up. By May, delinquent in his rent, he voluntarily left the apartment to avoid a formal eviction. It was time to go back to work.

His next robbery, he decided, had to be the One Big Score, something so lucrative that he'd never, ever have to risk staging another. And when Livaditis started thinking big, no place was the living larger than on Rodeo Drive. All the most expensive, exclusive jewelry stores were conveniently located on that elite three-block stretch in Beverly Hills. A plan, such as it was, quickly formulated: He would steal $2 million in jewelry from one of them and escape to Australia, where he would buy a yacht, invest the rest, and live the good life for the rest of his days. "I figured that Beverly Hills job would have set me for life," he reasoned, "and it would have."

On May 19, the drifter embarked on a reconnaissance mission to Rodeo Drive in his yellow Plymouth, which still bore Nevada plates. When he made an abrupt lane change directly in front of Van Cleef & Arpels, Beverly Hills motor officer Russell Sharp, who'd been eying the car's slow, deliberate crawl down the street, pulled the Plymouth over. The man behind the wheel identified himself as "George Livaditis" but did not offer a driver's license, prompting Sharp to run a DMV check. The search turned up a California driving record for a man with the same name, but the driver insisted that he was a different individual altogether. When the driver failed to provide sufficient proof that he owned the Plymouth, Sharp was obliged to arrest him for giving false information to a police officer and driving without a license. He was booked at the police station, but with no real reason to suspect that Livaditis was guilty of anything more than a run-of-the-mill traffic misdemeanor, Beverly Hills police did not run a check on their arrestee's fingerprints and never became aware of the FBI warrant for his arrest. He was released on a $150 bond.

It would not be the last time the Beverly Hills Police Department would encounter Steven Livaditis.

A little over a month later, on June 23, he was back on Rodeo Drive. He'd driven his Plymouth part of the way and—to avoid making another traffic blunder that might catch the watchful eye of the police—made the rest of the trip by bus. He casually strolled up the street in his natty navy-blue polyester pinstriped suit, clean-shaven and carrying an attaché, looking for all the world like he belonged at the heart of 90210.

Inside the briefcase was a survival knife with a six-inch blade, a switchblade, rolls of heavy tape, cord, gloves, ammunition, a pair of quick-loading devices, and his nickel-plated .357 Magnum revolver.

"After years of just trying to make ends meet, I just decided to go all the way that day," he explained. "I had a lot of anger inside me. I felt I was cheated and kept getting the short end of the stick."

Arriving at 300 North Rodeo Drive, he entered Van Cleef & Arpels's gated foyer and pressed the buzzer.

10:08 a.m.: Ann Heilperin's scream pierced the air at the usually tranquil jewelry store. "Please don't hurt me!" she cried.

Bookkeeper Julie Stipkovich was one of thirteen employees working that morning, out of sight in a basement office. She heard a man shout, "Everybody on the floor! Now!" and wasted no time dashing up to the store's second-floor offices, where she alerted her co-workers: "Get out—we're being robbed!" One of her fellow employees quickly activated the three silent alarms wired directly to the police department, while another who had spotted the gunman on another security monitor hastily dialed 911. He alerted police to a robbery in progress, giving a brief—and, it would turn out, not entirely accurate—description of the culprit. Hearing Heilperin scream again, Stipkovich and seven of her co-workers then sprinted out the store's rear exit to safety.

At age fifty-four, security guard William Richard Smith was a committed churchgoer and a devoted son who lived with and cared for his elderly parents. A decorated veteran of the Korean War, he sprang into action when he heard Heilperin's cries and Livaditis's orders to drop to the floor. In the main showroom, Smith ran towards the gunman, his eyes fixed squarely on the .357 as Livaditis forced Heilperin back into the main room. Smith's hand reached for his own weapon, but Livaditis placed his Magnum on Heilperin's temple. "If you draw your gun, I'll shoot her," Livaditis said.

Smith froze and stared for several long seconds. His hand moved slowly away from his holster and, at the gunman's order, he sank to his knees. Livaditis quickly disarmed him.

At that moment, fifty-year-old shipping clerk Robert Taylor—who'd worked in the Rodeo location for three decades, predating its Van Cleef & Arpels incarnation—ran into the main showroom from his office in the rear of the building, concerned when he heard Heilperin scream. Livaditis caught sight of him and demanded that he join the rest of the employees who had been unable to flee—Hugh Skinner, Bill Smith, Annie Heilperin, and another saleswoman, forty-two-year-old Culver City resident Carol Lambert—in the Time Boutique, where he ordered everyone to lie down on the floor except Lambert and Taylor, whom he instructed to bind the hands and feet of the others with the thick tape from his briefcase. The gunman returned to the central showroom and had Lambert and Taylor clean out the store's displays, filling his attaché with Val Cleef & Arpels's treasures. He was rattled, even angry—he hadn't expected Heilperin's panicked reaction, which spooked the other employees into evacuating before he could stop them—but he was determined to keep his composure and see his mission through. It was the One Big Score.

At last, his briefcase was near to overflowing with glittery watches, bracelets, and necklaces. It all seemed to be coming together. Using Taylor as a shield, Livaditis began to make a cautious exit through the front foyer. He stepped past the security gate and peeked out the door.

10:16 a.m.: Eight minutes had passed since Beverly Hills police had received the 911 call. The force, headquartered less than a mile away on Rexford Drive, mobilized instantaneously, some arriving on Rodeo within seconds of the alert. The Los Angeles County Sheriff's Department, with its Special Weapons and Tactics Team, had also been summoned: due to its small size, Beverly Hills routinely called upon LASD for assistance during potentially large-scale crises. Since its emergence as the premiere shopping destination for the jet set in the late '60s and early '70s, the most frightening incident to strike Rodeo Drive occurred in 1973, when five armed hold-up men posing as shoppers took over the Tiffany & Co. boutique at the Beverly Wilshire Hotel in the middle of the day. They posted a "Closed Until Monday" sign, smashed display cases, terrorized sales staff and customers—including comedian Dom DeLuise—and critically wounded a sixty-three-year-old security guard with a brutal gunshot to the chest before escaping with $500,000 in loot. It had all happened so fast that police had to settle for systematically rounding up members of the gang over the next year. This time, it was thought, would be different.

Scores of officers were already surrounding the store. The street was cordoned off (along with several blocks of adjacent Wilshire Boulevard, causing traffic repercussions throughout the Westside) and was lined with black-and-white patrol cars. Startled shoppers were hastily escorted off the sidewalks. Storekeepers were instructed to remain inside their shops. Soon, over eighty law enforcement agents—some in fatigues and carrying high-powered weaponry—would converge on the scene. Police were already setting up a command post mid-block on the west side of the street in front of the Polo by Ralph Lauren store at 323 N. Rodeo Dr., when Livaditis peered out of the store. Officers raised their weapons and ordered him to surrender, but he quickly ducked back inside, shaken.

Now what?

He was nervous, and though he tried not to admit it to himself, he was scared. But moreover, he was *angry*. The screaming saleswoman had screwed things up. Things weren't going the way they were supposed to go. His plan was foiled.

But as he and Taylor retreated into the main showroom, Livaditis began to realize that all hope was not necessarily lost. He couldn't know the particulars, but it was clear that Van Cleef & Arpels was one of the most impenetrable locations in all of Beverly Hills—indeed, it was now a virtual Fort Knox. The elaborate state-of-the-art security system and the gated foyer effectively prevented any unauthorized entry, bolstered by the closed-circuit cameras and alarms that kept each entryway under close scrutiny. The doors were bulletproof and soundproof, as were the store's few small windows, which were designed solely to showcase attractive jewelry displays and did not allow police to observe what was happening inside. Further complicating matters, the main showroom was set in the building's center court, which made direct entry from the outside even more difficult.

Livaditis might not be able to get out, but the police couldn't get in, either. And he possessed something that, for the moment, was even more valuable than the jaw-dropping pile of diamond-encrusted booty in his briefcase: five hostages.

He was upset, but he'd made last-minute getaways before, right? He might just get out of this okay, after all.

10:34 a.m.: Beverly Hills police officer John Edmundson fielded a 911 phone call placed from within Van Cleef & Arpels by Carol Lambert, who subsequently turned the phone over to Steven Livaditis, identified only as "John." Edmundson patched the call directly to his superior, Lt. Robert Curtis, who would serve as the robber's principal point-of-contact for the remainder of the standoff. The department had never, at that point, needed to employ a hostage negotiator, and Curtis had no formal training in such negotiation, but his inherent cool-headedness and even-handed demeanor marked him as the best officer for the task.

Livaditis informed the police that he had five hostages inside and immediately began issuing demands, first and foremost being the withdrawal of the officers surrounding the store. He also had an unusual second request: he wanted media coverage, insisting on access to television crews, and a TV set to watch himself broadcast live on the air. He made it clear that if his demands weren't met, he would "execute these people one at a time." He took particular pains to pointedly describe security guard Bill Smith as "an old, weak, fragile man."

Smith had stoked Livaditis's growing rage when the gunman had herded his hostages back into the Time Boutique, where Lambert bound Robert Taylor like the other prisoners. Livaditis insisted that they all lie prone on the floor, but Smith would get no further than his knees. Glowering at his captor, Livaditis put his gun to Smith's head, telling him he had three seconds to comply. Cocking the trigger, he began counting down the seconds until Smith finally relented. Moments later, Livaditis moved the prisoners again, back into the main showroom as he prepared to call 911, and again, it had taken a gun to Smith's head to get him to cooperate. His accusing scowls and under-the-breath utterances were getting to Livaditis.

Lt. Curtis coolly took note of "John's" demands but balked at allowing access to a news crew—the last thing police wanted to do was provide the gunman with even more hostages. After several minutes of negotiation, the force agreed to withdraw. However, peering out of a window on the Dayton Way side of the address, Livaditis caught sight of armed officers still stationed outside the store and grew increasingly agitated, though he was assured those officers would also retreat. A few minutes after 11 a.m., he slammed the receiver down.

Their contact with Livaditis had confirmed the police's worst fears, and it became clear that the situation was not likely to end simply or any time soon. As a Sheriff's Department helicopter arrived, hovering in the skies above Beverly Hills, officers immediately began a full evacuation of the neighboring businesses. Across the street at Giorgio Beverly Hills and Chanel, customers who had been previously hustled to each store's windowless second floors in case a gun battle erupted were escorted out of the building, while SWAT team personnel set up a vantage point atop Chanel's roof. A manager at Van Cleef & Arpels's neighbor Battaglia, who had been about to go next door to have an earring repaired when police first arrived, scurried away in high heels with the rest of the staff. Employees and customers caught inside fine china and silver purveyor David Orgell, who had been calmly sipping tea and coffee and nibbling cheese, scrambled away in a panic when officers evacuated them.

Tensions were rising outside the store; inside, they were boiling over.

As he bound Carol Lambert's hands and feet with tape, Livaditis glared furiously at Bill Smith, who returned his scorn with a steely, condemning gaze.

"You're too old to be a security guard," he told Smith. "That gun of yours is outdated, just like you."

Smith didn't waver. "You think you're a big man with that gun. I'd like to see you without a gun."

"You talk too much," Livaditis fired back. "Shut up, or I'm going to kill you."

Smith mumbled something under his breath, straining against the tape that bound him.

"Then I just clicked," Livaditis recalled. "My fuse went off."

He made the hostages face the wall, calling Smith a "useless old man." Fuming, Livaditis stormed over to his briefcase and set his revolver aside, retrieving the six-inch survival knife he'd stashed within. Ordering the other hostages to look away, he plunged the knife violently into the center of Smith's back. Blood spurted from the stab wound into Robert Taylor's face. Smith gasped hard for breath, choking on his own vital fluids, and struggled to rise onto his shoulders. He appeared close to freeing himself from his bounds—close enough that Livaditis retrieved his gun and aimed it at Smith—but then slumped in a heap face down on the floor, still. Powerless to do anything but watch in horror, the other hostages trembled together as Bill Smith slowly died before their eyes, splatters of his blood on their clothing, their faces, and their shoes.

A palpable dread filled the room for everyone except Steven Livaditis, whose growing list of offenses now included homicide. As he draped his suit coat over the body of the man he'd just murdered, he was oddly relieved.

A burden was lifted, he thought. He didn't feel good about the slaying, but he was convinced it had been merited. He had been fair to the security guard, he reasoned, and had given him several warnings. But he was losing control of the situation and needed to show everyone that he was still in charge.

He moved the four remaining hostages to another side of the showroom, and further covered Smith's lifeless form, the blade still protruding from his back, with display case sheets. He imagined he was being courteous to his other prisoners: "It wasn't their fault I killed him. I didn't want them to see him in a pool of blood with a knife in him."

11:59 a.m.: Lt. Curtis was on the phone with "John" again when the Sheriff's Department's Hostage Negotiation Team arrived. Along with an added request, delivery of food and soft drinks for himself and the hostages, the suspect's demands remained the same. He insisted on speaking with a television crew, asking for a newswoman to come to the caged front entryway and interview him there. He told Curtis that he wanted to make a personal statement about hunger and poverty in America, the struggles of the economically disadvantaged, and the false promises of politicians, things he'd become bothered about during his jobless periods. "I feel it's okay to steal from the rich," he believed. "At the same time, I'm generous to the poor—if anyone wanted money, I'd give them money."

The police were still unwilling to allow the gunman access to a reporter, and the negotiations waged on for an hour-and-a-half, with Livaditis continually threatening the lives of the hostages inside. At some point, he revealed to Curtis that he had already taken the life of Bill Smith. But something about his tone did not ring true—he was so light-hearted and casual about the admission that it seemed difficult to believe, a fact made more confusing by his subsequent retraction: "No, I didn't, really." Livaditis continued with a contradictory series of confessions, threats, and denials that flummoxed the negotiators and the psychologists on hand.

Normally, when police believed a suspect to have slain a hostage, they are likely to attempt a forced entry to save the lives of the remaining captives. However, Livaditis had promised by phone that at the first sign of an assault, he'd kill them all and use the rest of his energy to shoot it out with the invading officers and deputies. Hostages are typically killed to make a point to the authorities, and unlike most hostage-takers, he had not offered any clear or visual evidence that he'd taken a life. The negotiators ultimately concluded that Livaditis's claim was in all likelihood a bluff.

However well-reasoned, the police judgment was mistaken. Although they did not realize it at the time, there had been a second, crucial oversight: at the outset of the standoff, the police believed they had taken control of all the telephone lines leading into Van Cleef & Arpels. But they had not been aware of the store's unlisted, exclusive line for its elite VIP customers, registered to the address of the adjacent Dayton Way entryway. That line was not shut down. As a result, whether the police authorized it or not, Steven Livaditis was about to be granted the media access he'd been craving.

1:30 p.m.: Inside the store, the private line rang. During a break in his negotiations, Livaditis answered, as "John," and found himself being interviewed by a journalist from the news agency United Press International, which had discovered the unlisted number. Livaditis described the events leading up to the standoff. "My intention was to take jewelry and leave with nobody hurt. It didn't work out that way."

Then in a moment of bravado, he told the UPI reporter that he had killed one of the hostages. "He was a security guard in here. He was talking back to me. I asked him to keep his mouth shut, and he kept talking, so I killed him." After Livaditis described the stabbing matter-of-factly, the reporter asked if he felt any remorse. "Absolutely not," he replied. "I do not regret it. It was the appropriate thing to do at the time. He failed to obey my order."

He insisted he had no intention of killing anyone else—unless the police stormed the store, in which case he would shoot all the hostages and worry about his own safety later. "I have no fear of death. It's just the type of person I am. It's me. I don't care about dying," he explained coolly. "I'm going to reach the point soon where I'm going to have to execute someone else if my demands are not met."

Livaditis then handed the phone to a shaky Annie Heilperin, who confirmed that her captor had indeed slain Bill Smith while he was lying on the floor next to her. She said while the surviving hostages were "all very scared," they had not been mistreated. She believed their situation was "hopeless" if the gunman's demands were not met. "We want TV cameras, please!" she implored the reporter. "Please do as he says!"

Taking the phone from her, Hugh Skinner gave the UPI reporter his first name and told him that all was quiet inside the store. "The main thing is to get the TV in here, and get the news," Skinner said. "He wants to get on television and make a speech,"

Livaditis then concluded the phone call. "Have a nice day," he told the reporter.

Along with fielding calls from Lt. Curtis every ten to fifteen minutes, Livaditis would continue to answer the private phone line while the police remained unaware of his access to the outside world. He seemed to enjoy playing twisted pranks on the store's clientele, which he thought eased the tension among the hostages inside the store. One female customer inquired about dropping off a ring to be cleaned. "Only if you're good-looking," Livaditis told her, pretending to be the store manager. "We don't allow customers who aren't good-looking inside the store," Another caller was apoplectic when she was told that her $100,000 rings and necklace had been misplaced, and worse, "our new policy is there are no refunds if we can't find your jewelry."

"I was playing head games over the phone," he said.

Those games were extended to the media: About an hour after the UPI interview, another media outlet, the Mutual Broadcasting Company, had discovered the private line, and Livaditis found himself being interviewed again. Where he had been relatively truthful before, he now began weaving an elaborate fiction designed to justify his actions. "Van Cleef & Arpels cheated me out of some jewelry a long time ago," he lied. "They gave me fake jewelry and I tried to return it, and they wouldn't accept it. So I got very irritated and I came back here to collect."

But despite his fabrications, twisted attempts at humor, and constant posturing, Steven Livaditis was far from relaxed, far from in control. After his explosive, deadly confrontation with Smith, his nerves continued to fray, and he would obsessively fixate on how quickly his One Big Score had gone south and why.

One of those reasons, he believed, was Annie Heilperin. When this escapade had started, he was practically on a high, feeling like he was "the President of the United States." Now, his mood had shifted: feeling like he'd been "at a party having a good time and somebody does something to ruin it." He hadn't expected her to scream as she had when he first pulled his gun, and her panicked reaction had alerted too many of the store employees, causing the silent alarms to be tripped and the law to disrupt his master plan. It was *her* fault he was trapped in here like this, he believed, and her continual terror throughout the standoff was making things worse. Aside from Smith, the other hostages had been cooperative, even helpful, but not "Big Mouth Annie," as he'd begun to call her. Her constant crying and whimpering were *pissing him off*. He had wanted her to stay quiet from the beginning, and he wanted her to shut the hell up now.

"Somebody is going to die," he repeated several times to his prisoners. "Somebody has to die."

3:00 p.m.: Outside the store, the mood veered between tension and tedium as the standoff stretched on. As police and media helicopters droned above Rodeo Drive, car horns sounded in all directions as a snarl of traffic was diverted around the area. A horde of reporters stood at the street's median, occasionally stepping on a marigold. Waiters would frequently trot over from Café Rodeo at the Beverly Rodeo Hotel, just outside the area cordoned off by police barricades, carrying a tray of drinks for the newshounds, while a cluster of evacuated employees, stranded pedestrians trapped in Beverly Hills due to several parking lot closures and the usual crowd of the morbidly curious lingered further up the street, taking ringside seats at the café. With no customers to service, the Rodeo shopkeepers who hadn't yet thrown in the towel and closed their doors wandered out of their stores to check on the progress. "I'm losing $20,000 an hour," lamented the director of the deserted Upstairs Gallery, an elite art store. Bernini rang up a single transaction when police allowed one customer through to pick up a suit he desperately needed for a formal affair that evening.

One block south of Van Cleef & Arpels, at the foot of Rodeo Drive on Wilshire Boulevard, stood the lavish Regent Beverly Wilshire Hotel. On a private visit to Southern California, Nancy Reagan, the First Lady of the United States, had checked into the Presidential Suite shortly after the standoff had begun. Zealously guarded by Secret Service agents, her schedule would no longer include a shopping trip to Rodeo Drive, a favorite locale since her days as a Hollywood starlet. Indeed, as she watched the situation unfold on television in her suite, she recalled that it had been at Ruser's, the jewelry store that preceded Van Cleef & Arpels in the Rodeo-

Dayton location, where her husband Ronald Reagan had purchased her platinum diamond wedding ring in 1952.

At police headquarters, 911 lines were flooded with well-meaning calls from people around Los Angeles and other parts of the country who were watching the scene on TV and had suggestions to resolve it, including drugging the food left at the doorstep or flooding the building with invisible knockout gas. A tank-like assault vehicle idled outside City Hall.

Marvin Iannone, the Beverly Hills Chief of Police, had arrived at the scene to oversee the standoff. It was the rare situation indeed that would draw the department chief out into the field; on any other occasion, it might have been difficult to ascertain whether his presence was more reassuring or only added to the edginess of his officers, particularly as Iannone had taken the helm of BHPD just a year earlier.

Veteran officers would recall in awe another hostage situation during Chief Clinton Anderson's tenure in 1959, where the fearsome top cop personally faced down an amateur gunman in a black tie and dinner jacket who'd taken nine prisoners in a suite at the Beverly Hilton Hotel. With only four officers as backup, Anderson coolly ignored two narrowly dodged warning shots in his direction and, after a stern and uncompromising thirty-minute face-off, broke the gunman's will to the point that he meekly tossed his gun over to one of the hostages (local cop legend morphed the story over the years into one in which the chief testily snatched the gunman's weapon away, handed it to an officer and walked back down the hall as if nothing had happened). The times and the circumstances had changed radically, however, but the officers on the scene breathed easier: he may not have presented himself as God Almighty, like Anderson, but if there was any department leader who was abundantly qualified to take the reins of a large-scale crisis, it was Marv Iannone.

He began his law enforcement career in 1956 as a rookie LAPD cadet, graduating at the top of his academy class, and using the time afforded him by his less-than-desirable first duty working at a city jail to earn advanced college degrees. He would go on to work virtually everywhere in Los Angeles, with some twenty-eight different assignments over twenty-eight years with the force. As a patrolman, Iannone was one of the first officers on the scene when Marilyn Monroe was discovered dead in her Brentwood home in 1962; he would succeed ex-cop and future *Star Trek* creator Gene Roddenberry as the principal speechwriter for Chief William Parker; as the leader of LAPD's field command post cadre he managed crises including the Watts riots and the Sylmar earthquake; he oversaw all policing and security for the 1984 Olympics and ultimately rose to become LAPD's assistant chief and head of operations, responsible for managing 85 percent of the entire police force as what the press called the "number two man" under Chief Daryl Gates.

By 1985, however, Iannone believed that his career in LAPD had reached its zenith, as the youthful and energetic Gates did not appear to be going anywhere any time soon. He retired from the force to take the chief's seat in Beverly Hills, only the sixth man in the city's history to hold the office. After the end of Chief Anderson's twenty-seven-year, iron-fisted reign in 1969, the "Mom-and-Pop"-style Beverly Hills force had struggled with growing pains as the city's profile as an international destination grew. The chief's office had something of a revolving door in the post-Anderson era, and the department was in turmoil: its officers were often confused and dissatisfied with the city's Byzantine internal politics and sometimes ill-equipped to handle the increasingly complex level of crime that was striking the city.

As someone familiar with both the concerns of the rank-and-file patrol officers and the intricacies of high-powered politics, Ianonne was well-suited to upgrade BHPD into a sophisticated, state-of-the-art police force. But in this, his first year, Iannone had not yet implemented Beverly Hills's own special tactics unit, so he assumed command of the Van Cleef & Arpels situation in concert with his colleague, Los Angeles County Sheriff Sherman Block.

Chief Iannone, along with Lt. Bill Hunt, a fourteen-year-veteran of the force, addressed the assembled media's questions about the gunman's claim to have murdered the security guard. Police were still unconvinced that "John" had told the truth. "Our feeling is that we haven't had anyone hurt, that they are all alive," said Hunt. "We think he's pumping information to the hostages, telling them what to say to the media. Negotiators feel he's probably orchestrating this."

"It is my firm belief that no one is injured inside," Iannone told the press. "I hope and pray that it is true."

But it had been a bad day for hopes and prayers, and it was about to get worse.

3:30 p.m.: Police had finally taken control of the private phone line into the store and had agreed to grant one of "John's" demands and meet another halfway. A team of four Sheriff's Deputies huddled behind handheld bulletproof shields that had slowly inched towards the front door, leaving two bags filled with white bread, bologna, and cold sodas outside the door before retreating. Though he'd insisted on the food for himself and the hostages, Livaditis never retrieved it.

Livaditis was also allowed to place a series of telephone calls to the Los Angeles station KTLA-TV Channel 5, while the hostage negotiating team surreptitiously orchestrated the station's responses. Again, Livaditis explained that he had not planned on taking hostages when the day began, again he accused Van Cleef & Arpels of selling him phony jewels "a long time ago," and he matter-of-factly reiterated that he had killed security officer William Smith several hours earlier. And he was still insistent on getting a television set. "I'll make a statement when I'm put on the air," he told KTLA. "I want it taped and put on television and aired at a later date. And I'd like it to be put on television live."

As the station responded, Livaditis interrupted. "One man has died already, okay? And I will execute someone else...Within the next few minutes."

"What can we do to prevent you from doing that?" the station asked.

"That is final," said Livaditis curtly. "There is absolutely nothing you can do to prevent me from doing that, unless I see a TV camera outside the door right now coming inside." He agreed that the standoff would come to a peaceful end if his demands were met. "I want to see myself on network television, live."

Police were still unwilling to allow a crew to approach and possibly add to the gunman's hostages. Suddenly, there was a brief flurry of apprehension outside the store when a shirtless, bearded forty-three-year-old man clad in a pair of tiny blue running shorts broke past the police barricade and sprinted down Rodeo Drive. He was arrested for interfering with police and resisting arrest, taken in for questioning, and ultimately deemed to be a crackpot who had no connection to the standoff. Police had the media circus under control, but L.A.'s contingent of attention-seeking eccentrics now threatened to add a freak show.

Meanwhile, KTLA's conversations with Livaditis—which police replayed for him to prove they were televised—continued until shortly after 5 p.m., when he abruptly paused the exchange. "Quiet. Just a minute."

A half-hour earlier, to punish her for her perceived offenses, he had forced the bound Ann Heilperin lie on the floor next to the body of Bill

Smith and face the wall. She hadn't been like all of the other hostages, he felt. She hadn't done anything to help him. She had been crying, and Livaditis had finally reached the breaking point with "Big Mouth Annie," banishing her to lie with the dead man. Now, however, she was silent, her eyes closed, unaware of what was about to happen.

He told the other hostages to look away, walked up behind her, aimed his .357 at the back of her head, execution-style, and squeezed the trigger.

The soundproof walls kept the blast of the gunshot from being heard outside the jewelry store, and while he had decided it was time to end Ann Heilperin's life, he wasn't quite ready to tell the police. But he didn't know if the caller had heard the shot on the line. He picked up the receiver and told KTLA that his gun had "misfired. No one was hurt. The bullet went through the wall." And then he hung up.

He pulled the jewelry sales display cloth from Smith's body to cover Heilperin's lifeless form. To the other hostages, he appeared relieved that she was dead. Livaditis immediately shifted the responsibility onto the police, who he claimed could have prevented the murder if they'd only acceded to his demands. He would question his deadly decision, if only for a moment, but then, despite realizing "it didn't feel fantastic," he reasoned that it was something he *had* to do, to demonstrate that it was he, not the police, who was in control of the situation.

6 p.m.: Livaditis allowed Hugh Skinner, whom he had bound back-to-back with Robert Taylor in two chairs to serve as human shields if police stormed the store, to tell the police that a second hostage was dead. Again, everything was delivered in such measured, unemotional tones that the police found it difficult to believe that the hostages had witnessed such horrors— and no one outside the store had heard the gunshot. The psychologists on the scene now suspected that the hostages inside had fallen victim to "Stockholm Syndrome," that the gunman held such power over them, that they were so desperate to survive, they would say anything to please him, perhaps had begun to relate to him—even side with him—on some level. "They were not convincing at all, just the things they said," Chief Ianonne later explained, and Sheriff Block had agreed—to him, it seemed as if the suspect was "talking to his staff." Lt. Curtis continued to stay in contact, pleading with him to release the hostages unharmed.

There was some strange truth to the growing connection between the hostage-taker and his victims. Killing Annie Heilperin had, oddly, taken some of the edge off Steven Livaditis. He grew calmer, feeling comfortable enough to free his prisoners from the tape that bound them. He was trying to like them. They were, he deemed, good people.

Indeed, they were trying to help devise a course of action that would allow all of them—Livaditis included—to escape unharmed. Robert Taylor was convinced that the only chance of survival was for everyone to somehow leave the building. Livaditis was skeptical, until Hugh Skinner suggested a plan: a company car was parked in the lot to the rear of the store on Dayton Way, and Taylor had the keys. Carol Lambert owned a cabin far away in an isolated locale north of Los Angeles; they could drive the store's car there, with Livaditis squeezed in the front seat between her and Skinner and Robert Taylor in the back, each hostage forming a shield around him. Livaditis would then release them somewhere along the way to the cabin.

Perhaps softened by their cooperation, Livaditis agreed that he did not want to hurt them, but he was afraid that the police were unpredictable and would open fire on him regardless. But then Skinner presented a seemingly foolproof idea: the hostages could sew several of the black velvet jewelry display cloths together to form one large blanket that would cover all four of them as they exited the store. The police would not be able to distinguish between Livaditis and the hostages, and thus be prevented from shooting. They would make it safely to the car and drive off, unharmed.

Livaditis was not fully convinced, but agreed the idea was feasible. He would put it to a vote: All three hostages were in favor; his was the only dissenting voice. But Skinner was one of the most experienced, savvy and persuasive salesmen on Rodeo Drive, an expert in making his customers understand what it was that they really wanted, and skilled at making the "up-sell." Whether he was truly invested in the plan's foolproof qualities or secretly holding out hope that the police would somehow be better able to rescue them and apprehend their captor on the outside, Skinner cannily sweetened the pot: using the same discerning eye he shared with Cary Grant, the store manager would collect items of jewelry from throughout the Van Cleef & Arpels's displays and vaults that were *considerably* more valuable than the many watches already filling that briefcase.

And with the renewed possibility of the One Big Score—the *Even Bigger* Score—once again dangling tantalizingly within reach, Livaditis agreed to the plan. Hugh Skinner had, as he always did most elegantly, sold him.

11:25 p.m.: Hours after the sun had set on Beverly Hills and the last of the Rodeo Drive shops closed for business, the police had extinguished most of the streetlights in the area and prohibited the news crews from using their camera lights for illumination. Beverly Hills police had been stretched to the limits of their resources, as had the Sheriff's Department, trying to employ enough officers to relieve those who had been on the vigil throughout the day. Chief Iannone still suspected that the best bet was to wait the situation out, but the gunman had become increasingly reluctant to speak with Lt. Curtis. At some point, BHPD attempted a clever but risky gambit: one of its most effective and accomplished officers, Det. Tom Edmunds, who'd spent nearly twenty-five years on the force, was dispatched to the jewelry boutique's entryway in disguise as a television reporter, microphone in hand and requesting an interview, in attempt to lure the publicity-craving gunman within striking distance. "I could have taken him into custody. Or I could have shot him," Edmonds later recalled. "But he didn't take the bait."

Finally, a glimmer of hope: Livaditis was on the phone again, and after thirteen and a half long, tense hours, he finally agreed to release the hostages. But because night had fallen, he was reluctant to end the situation immediately, fearing something might go awry in the darkness. Before hanging up, he assured the police that everything would come to a peaceful end at 6 a.m. the next morning.

"It's getting late," he told them. "Might as well relax, and perhaps in the morning we'll resolve this."

Carol Lambert had spent the past several hours sewing together the display cloths using a ballpoint pen and the cord from Livaditis's briefcase, and once her work was finished, the hostages and their captor practiced walking underneath it. Livaditis had reloaded his .357 and stocked his briefcase with even more of Van Cleef & Arpels's finery, even stuffing several loose gems and rings into Hugh Skinner's pockets. With more of the cord, he now bound Lambert and Taylor together at the hands and at the waist and tied himself to them. The cool-headed Skinner, it was now decided, would be left free to drive the car.

"Everybody ready?" he asked as he pulled the improvised draping over the group.

"We're ready. Let's go."

Leaving the lifeless bodies of Ann Heilperin and Bill Smith behind in the showroom, the group exited out the side entrance along Dayton Way.

The strange, obscured mass emerged from Van Cleef & Arpels, immediately drawing the surprised attention of the many officers still stationed outside. As his prisoners stuck close to the building and moved toward the rear parking lot, Livaditis could hear the cops murmuring in the darkness. Skinner, Lambert, and Taylor cried out, warning the officers that they were hostages and begging them not to open fire. From under the cloth, Livaditis shouted to his unseen observers, "If you try to stop me, I'm going to kill them all!" Then, just as the group had maneuvered their way between a blue Honda and the store's white sedan, Livaditis heard something strange as he unlocked the escape car's rear door:

"It's the guy in the grey pants."

"I see him."

It didn't make sense to Livaditis. But before he could try to decipher the meaning, his world exploded in a fiery flash of blinding white light and a thunderous BOOM! He was knocked backward off his feet, falling hard to the ground, the hostages tied to him dragged with him. Plumes of flame licked the air. Carol Lambert began to scream and didn't stop.

At that moment, it seemed as if Hell itself had erupted on Rodeo Drive. And for all intents and purposes, it had.

As he struggled to keep his senses, Livaditis could only wonder, "Where am I shot?"

11:30 p.m.: The County's SWAT team was prepared for a sudden escape attempt. It had been decided that the suspect could not be allowed to "go mobile" in a vehicle, and two of the deputies watching the Dayton Way entry had been equipped with "flash-bang" grenades, diversionary concussion devices that explode like giant firecrackers when deployed. The deputies were instructed to hurl the flash-bangs to disorient the suspect, even if he was shielding himself with hostages, and prevent him from successfully entering any of the cars parked behind the jewelry store.

Even with their tactics outlined, the deputies were surprised by Livaditis's sudden attempt to flee. They made the split-second decision to deploy the flash-bangs just as the group approached the store car. The force of the hot, blinding flashes hitting the parking lot pavement knocked the group off their feet, and one of them—a man—emerged from the concealing drapery.

Sheriff's Deputy George Johnson was stationed in the "long rifle position," high atop a seven-story parking structure at the southeast corner of

Dayton Way and Beverly Drive, seventy feet above and 100 yards east of the Van Cleef lot. The thirteen-year veteran officer had been a member of the Special Weapons team for over three years and, at forty-three, was a highly trained marksman. Stationed on the scene twelve hours earlier, Johnson had watched the group make its way from the store through the night scope of his high-powered .308-caliber rifle and spotted the legs of three men and a woman underneath the dark cloth that obscured them. Two of the men were wearing dark pants, while the third man's pants were grey. Nearby, Deputy Jon Rhodes had come on the scene at 9:30 p.m. to relieve Johnson's previous spotter. Both men had been informed that, according to the reports of the store employees who successfully escaped at the onset of the standoff, the gunman was a Caucasian male in a grey suit.

In the smoky, hazy aftermath of the flash-bang explosions, Johnson saw the man in the grey suit tumble free from the cloth. The man raised himself into a sitting position and extended his arms toward the rest of the group, shouting something. As the smoke wafted away, Johnson locked the crosshairs of his rifle on the man's chest "like a heat-seeking missile."

"There's a shiny object in his hand!" Rhodes shouted to Johnson.

Another officer stationed nearby yelled, "Gun!"

Johnson had the authority to fire at will. The man matched his description of the suspect. The parking lot was brightly lit. He had a clear shot. The man was pointing something at the hostages, most likely a gun. The suspect had sworn to kill the hostages. In a heartbeat, Johnson made his decision.

CRACK!

The bullet whizzed through the air, covering 100 yards in a microsecond, and penetrated the heart of the suspect, dead center. He slumped to the pavement.

Seconds later, Johnson saw officers descend upon the remaining hostages and pull away the cloth. Along with a Black man and a white woman, a *second* white male lay on the ground underneath. "Where did he come from?" Johnson's heart suddenly sank—he'd been advised that both male hostages were *Black*.

Hugh Skinner fell dead on the grounds of the store he'd managed for the past decade, his impeccably tailored grey suit now soaked with his own blood.

He had been trying to point out Steven Livaditis to the police. "Here he is!" he'd cried. Whatever it was that glinted in his hand—The car keys? One of the rings or gemstones Livaditis had stashed on him?—it was not a gun.

11:35 p.m.: Pandemonium had exploded in the parking lot. Not only had Hugh Skinner been killed by the sharpshooter's bullet, but the flash-bangs also landed too close to the group. Carol Lambert couldn't stop screaming because she was aflame: her face, chest, and arms burned in the explosion. Robert Taylor clutched at his chest: his heart could no longer take the strain; a diabetic, he appeared to be suffering a cardiac arrest.

Initially, Steven Livaditis couldn't figure out why he couldn't feel the pain of his gunshot wound, but quickly realized it was because he hadn't actually been shot. But pain would come soon enough—he, too, had been burned in the explosion, seared on his arms, chest, and face. But in those first stunned moments, Livaditis remained both calm and calculating. He closed his eyes and lay as still as stone, feigning death. His gun and his bounty-loaded briefcase, dropped in the melee, were just a few paces away.

There was always a way out, right?

This time, however, there would be no last-minute getaway. Dozens of police officers dog-piled Livaditis, restraining him as he erupted in a frenzied attempt to fight them off. The police responded in kind, wrestling him into submission. During the restraint, if Livaditis's account is to be believed, several of the officers bluntly described what they would like to do to him if justice were *really* in their hands. At last, he was cut free from Taylor and Lambert and handcuffed.

His attaché and its precious contents were being collected by the police. His weapon had been confiscated. Three of the hostages were dead; two were being loaded into ambulances in critical condition. And his fantasies of freedom, of sailing around Australia in a yacht, were just that: extravagant flights of fancy that now, even on Rodeo Drive, no amount of money would ever be able to buy.

As he was taken into custody, his words from earlier in the day still hung in the air. "My intention was to take the jewelry and leave with nobody hurt. It didn't work out that way."

June 23 had been a day of tragedy, trauma, and confusion. And, not surprisingly, the aftermath of the standoff was ugly and hurtful as well, as everyone involved sorted out what had gone wrong, struggling with regrets and recriminations.

The Los Angeles County Sheriff's Department launched an immediate investigation into the circumstances surrounding the shooting of Hugh Skinner, who was pronounced dead on arrival at Cedars-Sinai Medical

Center. At first, there was some confusion over whether Livaditis had shot him during the flash-bang explosions, but his weapon had been recovered with a full load of ammunition. It quickly became apparent that Deputy Johnson had fired the fatal shot following a search for the bullet that passed through Skinner's body, which was discovered by a young boy the next day in a nearby parking lot. It was also speculated that Livaditis might have switched clothes with Skinner to create confusion about his identity. Per standard regulations for personnel involved in fatal shootings, Johnson and his spotter, Deputy Rhodes, were taken off field duty for five days and underwent psychological counseling.

What was revealed was that while Deputy Johnson acted appropriately based on the information about the suspect he'd been given, but that information was faulty. The early description of Livaditis and the hostages that Beverly Hills police had provided to LASD based on the initial eyewitness accounts inaccurately placed Livaditis in the grey suit and erroneously indicated that the hostages included two Black males, two white females, and possibly one other undescribed captive. In reality, Taylor was Black and Skinner and Smith were not, but Johnson believed the gunman was the only white male in the building.

Johnson's team leader said that sometime between 2:30 and 4:30 p.m., he transmitted an updated description that included the fact that two "elderly white males" were trapped within the building. But the update was sent over the multi-channel police band radio. After being instructed by his command post to turn off his general police radio to conserve its batteries, Johnson had left his backup radio on, which was tuned only to a special SWAT frequency, as he awaited the delivery of new batteries, which came at 10:30 p.m. The updated descriptions were never issued over the SWAT radio. Further adding to the confusion, Rhodes was given a description when he arrived that meshed with Johnson's, and their accounts were supported by other deputies on duty. When the results of the investigation were made public two months after the standoff—though the 300-page report was kept confidential—no criminal charges would be brought against any of the officers involved.

It had all been yet another of the day's heartbreaking miscommunications.

Carol Lambert was rushed to Brotman Medical Center's Michael Jackson Burn Unit near her home in Culver City, where she underwent treatment for second- and third-degree burns over 17 percent of her body, as well as corneal abrasions. She was stabilized and prepped to undergo, among a myriad of painful skin graft procedures. Upgrading her condition to fair—she was, thankfully, in excellent health prior to the standoff—her doctor said that while she would suffer some permanent scaring, she would probably not have cosmetic damage to her face. She would ultimately be released after nineteen days in the burn ward.

Robert Taylor was taken by ambulance to Cedars-Sinai after complaining of chest pains and admitted to the cardiac care unit for observation. His wife Willie met him there—throughout the entire day, her faith never wavered that he would emerge alive from Van Cleef & Arpels. "I was holding my breath but I always believed he would be fine," she told reporters as she arrived at the hospital. "I said so many prayers—I am truly a believer in miracles." Taylor was discharged after a week of observation.

Those who didn't make it out alive—Ann Heilperin, Bill Smith, and Hugh Skinner—were laid to rest in the days after the incident, remembered with warmth and sadness: Heilperin for her kindness and love of animals, Smith for his bravery and devotion to faith and family, and Skinner for his infectious *joie de vivre* and ability to make people happy. Most who knew Skinner never thought the genteel gentleman jeweler the type to be a hero, but in the end, he had certainly tried.

The day after the siege, the doorstep of the locked and gated Van Cleef & Arpels store was awash with mournful flowers, beginning early in the morning with three red roses to symbolize the lives lost there. As the afternoon approached, the collection of blooms grew by the hour: near a hand-lettered sign that read "Closed," coral orchids hung from the door handle; "God bless the innocent who had to suffer," read the card on three thick clusters of white and yellow chrysanthemums. The colorful petals stood in relief to the yellow police tape that still enclosed the rear parking lot.

"Life is more important than money," said David Orgell, whose eponymous fine china and silver shop of thirty years stood four doors down from the jewelry salon. "It's a terrible way for it to end."

The mood on the Rodeo Drive was not entirely funereal. As police continued to circulate through the crime scene, shaking off reporters' questions, curious bystanders peered into the jewelry store's windows. The more black-humored among them struck the action-style poses they'd seen on TV, snapping photographs alongside patrol cars and Rolls-Royces alike. Members of the Los Angeles Raiderettes strolled the street, hoping to provide their trademark cheer by handing out their team calendars. Tour buses made their usual rounds up the Drive. And though several retailers began the morning fretting about the standoff's impact on their business, there were shoppers. Some stores did brisk, if not overwhelming, business, while others reported their best sales days in recent memory.

"It was a horror story," one woman told a friend, discussing the siege as they strolled past a shop window. "A horror story...*Ooo*, look at that beautiful soap!"

A day earlier, the street had looked like a war zone; now, it was, for the most part, back to the glamorous business as usual.

Except, of course, for Van Cleef & Arpels. The store's doors would remain locked for two weeks—nevertheless, the victims' fellow employees gathered together there every day. "We don't want to go off on our separate ways," said the reluctantly promoted new store manager Larry French, one of Ann Heilperin's closest friends. "The people who died in that store were not employees—they were family."

The Beverly Hills merchants, of course, had concerns other than sales—namely: could and would a copycat crime happen here? How could they better protect themselves? And should the situation have gone down as disastrously as it did? Many, especially the jewelers on the street, accepted that the risks came with the pricey territory. But even some storekeepers with the highest opinions of the Beverly Hills police began to question, some quite publicly, if the scenario had been handled properly.

"I look at the whole situation in retrospect and I wouldn't have done anything differently," Chief Iannone assured the public in a crowded press conference held in the City Council chambers the day after the standoff. The chief and his officers—as well as Sheriff Block and his deputies—were clearly troubled, even haunted, by the horrific turn of events and looking for answers as to what went wrong, but Iannone was steadfast in his refusal to second-guess their decision-making. He addressed all the issues that his force had faced but was unequivocal in his belief that they had pursued the only course of action that was available. He characterized Livaditis as "a ruthless mad-dog, a killer who had no compunction to do what he did."

As expected, the finger-pointing commenced, and the famed, controversial attorney Melvin Belli led the charge. Known as "the King of Torts," Belli earlier gained nationwide fame for his role as defense attorney for Jack Ruby, who was on trial for killing President John F. Kennedy's assassin Lee Harvey Oswald. Belli also served briefly as something of a media and police go-between for the Bay Area's notorious Zodiac serial killer. His array of high-profile clients included gangster Mickey Cohen, actor Errol Flynn, rockers The Rolling Stones, and comic Lenny Bruce (achieving his own degree of celebrity, Belli also occasionally moonlighted as an actor, including on an episode of *Star Trek*, the iconic series created by Chief Iannone's old LAPD colleague Gene Roddenberry).

Just five days after the standoff, on behalf of Hugh Skinner's nephew and nieces, the notoriously pugnacious, mellifluously voiced litigator filed $2.5 million claims against the City of Beverly Hills and the Los Angeles County Board of Supervisors that called the police actions "unjustified, unreasonable, unfair and unprofessional...The result was a wrongful death." Belli then threw fuel on the fire by tossing off a particularly acidic aside, even by his standards: "When you call a cop, you don't call an executioner."

This incensed Chief Iannone, who though prevented from commenting on the case, called the remark "unforgivable." Sheriff Block was positively apoplectic, calling Belli's words "a disgusting exhibition by an individual whose actions and morals, if they could stand in comparison to those of the officers in this situation, would come off second best—if not worse."

Within two months, Carol Lambert and Robert Taylor had filed $2.5 million claims against the city and county—as well as also planning a suit against the makers of the flash-bang grenades—alleging a "complete mishandling" on the part of the authorities. In addition to recovering damages, their attorney said, the impending suit would hopefully assure "this type of tragedy will not happen to other families...[and] will improve the competence and planning of the Beverly Hills police force" (The City of Beverly Hills and Los Angeles County settled the lawsuit with Skinner's family in 1990, paying out $130,000 for their loss. In 1993, however, Lambert and Taylor's lawsuit was dismissed because it had not come to trial within the five-year statute of limitations).

"Who would have thought anyone would attempt a robbery here?" wrote *Variety's* Army Archerd in his must-read column, as if wondering on behalf of all of the showbiz community. "It just wasn't in the script."

Blame had been tossed around, accusations had been made, and tempers had flared, but ultimately the bulk of Beverly Hills rallied around its police force, as it traditionally did. That gilded community, always on the lookout for a silver lining, instead put their faith in Iannone's leadership, and the chief kicked off a series of meetings with local merchants—more than fifty retailers attended the first gathering—to discuss ways in which they might work more closely with law enforcement to safeguard their assets. The result was a long-standing, unusually tight-knit, and communicative relationship between the commercial district and the police force that evolved over the years and still exists today.

Meanwhile, the siege itself had provided the City Council with all the evidence it needed to establish BHPD's own special tactics unit and lessen its dependence on the Sheriff's Department. Within a decade, precious few cities of comparable size could boast a police force as tactically trained, strategically skilled, and well-equipped as Beverly Hills, its officers studying and consulting the most state-of-the-art methods and equipment from agencies worldwide.

Somehow, something positive had been salvaged from that grim and bloody day.

And then, of course, there was a matter of justice.

"I was hoping they'd shoot me," said Steven Livaditis, "and get it over with."

When it became obvious that his burns needed medical attention, he was taken to the jail ward of Los Angeles County-USC Medical Center, where he was booked shortly after midnight. Once his wounds had been attended to, detectives questioned him the next morning. They were, by then, fully aware of his identity. Livaditis remained in agonizing pain, and during their interrogation, the detectives showered him with empathy and compassion, feeding him ice chips to ease his burned, parched lips, no matter how much it personally rankled them, as they methodically sought to draw out statements they might use to convict him for murder.

Throughout the questioning, the captive made no attempt to deny his crimes. He freely confessed to killing William Smith and Ann Heilperin, and did little to help his cause by using cold, casual turns of phrase when describing the murders, like when he told them the knife he'd killed Smith with "went in just like butter."

Disoriented during the flash-bang conflagration, Livaditis had been unaware that anyone had been shot until police revealed that another hostage had died during the escape attempt, mistaken for Livaditis (erroneously told that it was Robert Taylor who was killed, he would discover the next day that the victim was actually Hugh Skinner). It wasn't until he learned of the death of one of the cooperative hostages he had joked with and supposedly grown to like that the enormity of his misdeeds appeared to finally begin sinking in.

Details about Livaditis's life began to be made public, and even those who knew him and his hustling ways, including his former attorney from his prior burglary trial, seemed unable to process that he was capable of such heinous acts. "I never thought he had something like this in him," his brother George said dourly. "He had me fooled completely...I never even knew he knew how to use a gun."

On July 30, one week after the botched robbery and following days of continued questioning, Livaditis was taken from the county jail to Beverly Hills Municipal Court. Making his first public appearance beyond recycled, scruffy-looking mug shots from his 1984 arrest, he made for an eerie sight. Brought into the court in chains and shackles, his arms were wrapped in thick bandages, and another swath of gauze encircled his face, covering his jaw to the top of his head. Even more bizarrely, his blue jail jumpsuit had been opened and pulled off his right arm, exposing his chest and right shoulder and giving him an even more savage appearance—the prisoner had been allowed to appear so disheveled in court because the jumpsuit was irritating the burns on his chest and neck. He looked like a caged beast, every inch the "mad dog" Chief Iannone had described—only one that had bitten off far more than it could handle.

Looking dazed but lucid, Livaditis responded to the judge's questions clearly, and he was arraigned on fifteen felony charges, including three counts of murder with special circumstances—which meant that he'd be facing the death penalty if convicted.

He hadn't said much in court, but the man who had insisted on media coverage was about to earn even more ink.

"*I'm guilty*," shouted the *Los Angeles Herald*'s July 7 headline over a courtroom photo of the bandaged Livaditis. "*I'd rather they just executed me and get it over.*"

Over the preceding weekend, *Herald* reporter John Crust dramatically scooped the competition when, rather than fill out a special media request form which would no doubt be refused by Livaditis's attorney, he skirted procedure by waiting patiently in line at the county jail to speak with the accused—there were no regulations barring a reporter from talking to a prisoner as a member of the general public. Crust met with Livaditis, who immediately agreed to the interview. The journalist insisted on notifying the jail officials, who subsequently sat in on a series of conversations.

Livaditis, who admitted that he dreaded living a life behind bars because he "appreciated freedom," would go on to give a lengthy, wide-ranging account of his life and what led him to Van Cleef & Arpels that fateful day, as well as an intricate, chillingly detailed description of what happened inside the jewelry store—including the slayings of Smith and Heilperin, Though his account was clearly slanted, emotional, and overflowing with justifications for his actions—he never varied from the belief that his crimes "seemed appropriate" at the time—his version of events hewed closely to the particulars, and he did not deny committing the many transgressions he was accused of.

"I want to plead guilty because I don't want this thing to drag on," Livaditis revealed, just two days before he was to return to court and enter his plea. "I'll accept any punishment they give me. If it's the death penalty, so be it…I realize I violated one of the most important laws. I took other people's lives."

When the story saw print a day before the plea was due, the *Herald*'s readers were shocked and enthralled, but Michael Demby, Livaditis's public defender, was stunned: his client had spoken without his awareness, let alone his approval. Livaditis was not fond of his lawyer and believed he didn't have to listen to him, but under the California penal code, the attorney's approval of *any* plea was mandatory in a capital case—if only to prevent a defendant from seeking a state-assisted suicide. "I don't have an urge to go on with life," Livaditis told Crust.

Demby had another concern: "My feeling is that the case should be tried in the courtroom and not in the press," the displeased public defender said. "Maybe the press should look at some of their ethics,"

Didn't he realize that Livaditis had invited the press to a ringside seat from the very beginning?

Or did Demby remember the notation he made when Livaditis mused about his ability to convincingly act crazy in the courtroom, because he had heard "they could not execute an insane person?" The attorney entered a plea of not guilty to all fifteen counts. But when the judge delayed the trial date to give Demby adequate time to prepare a defense, the impatient accused—now clean-shaven, fully clothed, and only sporting a bandage on his right wrist—spoke out.

"I'd like to have it sooner, your honor, if it's possible."

Ten months would pass before Steven Livaditis would get his wish to stand before a judge and admit his sins. Shortly after jury selection had begun, he entered a series of guilty pleas in Santa Monica Superior Court, freely admitting his responsibility for the murders of William Smith and Ann Heilperin. But he hesitated when he was charged with the death of Hugh Skinner. It was explained that under the law, first-degree murder was applicable whether or not he himself had pulled the trigger. He also briefly quibbled over a charge that he robbed Carol Lambert, until further legal intricacies were explained to him. He held his arms tight against his chest, fist clenched. "I guess I'll have to plead guilty."

Something was different. Didn't he want to, as he said, get it over with?

"He's hoping for the best," Demby revealed. "He does not want to die." Given the preponderance of evidence against him, it was unlikely that Livaditis could escape conviction. But while he was willing to accept a prison sentence, he had changed his tune about being put to death. In pleading guilty, his trial would go directly to the penalty phase, and he hoped that would help him avoid the gas chamber in favor of a life sentence without the possibility of parole. "He has shown responsibility," Demby argued, "and he has shown remorse."

The jury did not agree. Almost a year to the day after he rang the buzzer at Van Cleef & Arpels, twelve Los Angeles County residents recommend the death penalty for Steven Livaditis. On July 8, 1987, he appeared before Judge Laurence J. Rittenbrand, his last hope for leniency. Rittenbrand was not exactly known for dispensing overly merciful justice and was no stranger to high-profile cases, having presided over director Roman Polanski's statutory rape case, Elvis Presley's divorce, Marlon Brando's child-custody battle, and a paternity suit against Cary Grant.

"I've disgraced my family," Livaditis had said a year earlier. "I suspect they don't want anything to do with me." But his mother had traveled all the way from Athens, Greece, to speak to the court in the hopes of saving her youngest child. "I want everyone to forgive my son," she said. "He did a terrible thing, and we're all very sorry. We want the victims to forgive him."

Livaditis had certainly forgiven *himself*, according to a probation report that was made public. "In the beginning I felt a tremendous amount of guilt and regret that it happened…I realize what I did and how horrible it was," he told a probation officer during a routine interview. "Then I started reading the Bible and learned I could be forgiven." Livaditis still believed in the last-minute escape. Not only did he believe his soul would be saved, but he also thought the verdict would fall in his favor, leaving him years of life left to live, if from behind bars. He was even considering marrying a twenty-two-year-old girlfriend and studying law. "Ever since I accepted Jesus, I have a clear conscience."

A little too clear, perhaps. His probation officer believed Livaditis did not truly accept responsibility and accountability, instead justifying his actions as necessitated by the behavior of the victims and the police. "He has not shown any remorse or regret except one: that he got caught," prosecutor Dona Bracke told the court in a fiery summation. "I firmly believe he is not sorry to this day."

After deeply weighing the option of a life sentence against the "ruthless, monstrous and premeditated" crimes that were committed on June 23, 1986, Judge Rittenbrand could find "no single redeemable virtue" in the defendant to merit a shred of mercy. As Livaditis sat emotionless before him, Rittenbrand did what the gunman had failed to do for William Smith or Ann Heilperin: he looked him in the eye as he sentenced him to death.

The young drifter's big dream of fine living and unfettered freedom had been perverted into a nightmare. "I thought that Beverly Hills job would have set me for life," he had imagined. Instead, it had delivered him to Death Row. He joined 210 inmates at California's San Quentin prison, where, due to ongoing constitutional challenges to the death penalty, no one had actually been put to death since 1967, twenty years earlier.

At the time of this writing, nearly four decades after his conviction and after exhausting his appeals (his most recent was denied in 2019), with the gas chamber replaced by lethal injection and the ranks of California's Death Row swelling to nearly 650, Steven Livaditis—now over fifty years old, with no legally compelling diagnosis of mental illness, still a stated believer in capital punishment for crimes like his own yet convinced he would be allowed into heaven since embracing God—remains behind bars, in a secured room not much larger than that barred entryway at Van Cleef & Arpels, the captive of men with guns, at the mercy of men with knives. Told what to do. No way out. No "getting it over with."

Waiting…Waiting…Waiting. For salvation, or for execution. Hostage to his own acts.

CHARADE

*"You'd think if he was going to raise hell and
steal things, he would've done it long ago."*

—**LAPD Det. Don Hyrcyk**

I arrived in Los Angeles at the intersection of Celebrity and Crime.
I moved to the city in the spring of 1994, virtually sight unseen—
no job, no family, just one close friend. I rented a single room in a
Mar Vista apartment to get a toehold in L.A., hungry to write. I originally came from Grand Ledge, Michigan, a classically American small town
outside the more urban state capital, Lansing. I'd studied film and television along with English and journalism in college, and my long fascination with Hollywood's personalities, inner workings, rich history, and juicy
lore marked L.A.—glitzy, sun-drenched, and with excitement seemingly
around the corner—as a most logical destination. I'd missed the Rodney
King riots by a couple of years and the Northridge earthquake by mere
months. Timing, they say, is everything.

But my plan to take L.A. by storm stalled out of the gate: transmission
trouble sidelined my planned job search and exploration of my sprawling
new home for a few weeks, and I ventured little further than Tito's Tacos
two block down the street until my car was repaired—as Missing Persons
had assured me, nobody walks in L.A., especially then. But the city was
practically vibrating after an almost incomprehensible scandal: on June 12,
Nicole Brown Simpson, the beautiful ex-wife of the handsome, charming NFL Hall of Famer, commercial pitchman, and occasional actor O.J.
Simpson was found murdered alongside the body of waiter/aspiring restaurateur Ron Goldman at her condo in the tony enclave of Brentwood—
just fifteen minutes from my new, far less chic neighborhood. Even more
unthinkable: Simpson himself emerged as the prime suspect. Five days
later, on June 17, still carless, I sat down to eat lunch, turning on the after-

253

noon TV news to discover Simpson was expected to turn himself in to the police at any moment. That sounded like good TV to me, and I settled in to watch.

Anyone who was alive and aware in 1994 remembers what unfolded over the next several hours on live television as channels across the country shifted to cover Simpson's bizarre, desperate fugitive flight from the law on the 405 Freeway. Behind the wheel of his white Ford Bronco was his friend and former teammate Al "A.C." Cowlings, fielding cell phone calls from the police while Simpson hinted at killing himself. More and more police vehicles joined a sprawling parade in slow-speed pursuit.

Toward the climax of the outlandish spectacle, I notice an increasingly loud whir of helicopters in the air outside, growing nearer. Studying the live shot on the TV screen, I realized the Bronco was now whizzing past recognizable landmarks. I peered out the window of my second-story apartment overlooking the 405, just a block to the east: not only were news choppers circling, but dozens of cars had pulled to the side of the freeway; motorists were spilling out of their vehicles, even climbing atop to get a fleeting glance at the famous running back during the most peculiar dash of his life.

I called my parents in Michigan: Like much of America, they were watching, too. With one eye on the freeway and another on the TV, I saw the white Bronco carrying Simpson roll past to a surprising chorus of cheers; I spotted the roof of my new home on the screen. "There's my new apartment!" I said.

"You're moving back home," my mother deadpanned.

"I don't think so," I chuckled. "This place is going to be interesting."

That would be an understatement.

Within a few weeks, I landed a job as a reporter for the *Beverly Hills Courier*—in its twenty-ninth year, the longest-running newspaper in the fabled city. Having cruised through college largely avoiding hard-news coverage, I was slightly nervous about the responsibilities, but I also remember thinking, "*This is going to be hilarious.*" My pop culture consumption had included a steady diet of Hollywood products depicting—and usually satirizing—the glitzy city over the years—*The Beverly Hillbillies*, *Shampoo*, *Beverly Hills Cop*, Johnny Carson monologues, Merv Griffin theme shows, *Pretty Woman*, *Beverly Hills 90210*, and, that very year, *Clueless*—so I felt prepared for a veritable phantasmagoria of over-the-top glamour, wealth, power, celebrity, designer labels, grand mansions, fine dining, and cosmetic surgery spanning the gamut of quality.

Beverly Hills certainly delivered on the fantasy, but I was surprised to discover that the splashy city still retained the tight-knit bedroom community character that uniquely defined it for many decades, even in the mid-'90s when the biggest contemporary film and TV talents of that period had migrated to even more spectacular compounds in Bel-Air, Malibu, and Pacific Palisades, and the classic stars retired to Palm Springs. But in its very specific way, Beverly Hills was a funhouse mirror version of my own small-town origins: along with Rodeo Drive, the Beverly Hills Hotel, the Academy of Motion Picture Arts & Sciences, and top-tier talent agencies like CAA and WME, there was a city council, municipal employees and activist civic leaders, neighborhood organizations, a school board, a PTA, a teachers union, a business community, a chamber of commerce, a Rotary Club, a League of Women Voters, mom-and-pop shops and restaurants, and of course, a police department.

Located at the southeast border of the city in a nondescript one-story office on Olympic Boulevard, *The Beverly Hills Courier*, too, was a reflection of that Everytown territory—and plugged into all of it. Founded in 1965 by publisher March Schwartz and his wife Wendy Lee, the newspaper was prosperous—March alternately drove a bronze Rolls-Royce, a creamy yellow Cadillac, and a white Chrysler convertible and lived a few minutes away in a tony Century City condo community with celebrity neighbors—but decidedly no-frills and old school. When I started in 1994, the tiny editorial team still wrote copy on typewriters, using typesetting machines so ancient there was only one person in all of Los Angeles and Orange counties combined who knew how to repair it. Articles were printed out into inches of columns, waxed, X-acto knifed, and pasted onto old-fashioned publication boards (mercifully, after a few months I was allowed to computerize the office and drag the staff—absolutely kicking and screaming—into the digital age).

March Schwartz was as colorful as they came in Beverly Hills: Born in Philadelphia in 1917, he'd daringly stowed away on a literal slow boat to China as a teen, becoming fluent in Mandarin and attending college there before the Japanese invasion. Back in the U.S. to serve in the Army during World War II, he snared a prestige duty as the public relations officer for First Lady Eleanor Roosevelt. A career in newspapers followed, first as editor of the *Los Angeles Mirror* and sales manager for the West Coast edition of the *New York Times*. But he truly found his niche when his wife, former B-movie actress turned restaurateur Wendy Lee—one in a series of many spouses, but the standout he clearly regarded as his soulmate—convinced him to launch a free weekly community newspaper in the town where they were raising their family, Beverly Hills. Early on, it was an operation so thoroughly mom-and-pop that once when a distributor failed to show at the printer, thinking the couple's order was a joke, March and Wendy loaded their large brood—a dozen kids between them—into a convertible and made a game out of tossing 20,000 newspapers onto every lawn and business doorstep in the city. "The greatest and most accurate delivery we ever had," he recalled to me, laughing.

Wendy died of breast cancer in 1968, just a few years into *The Beverly Hills Courier*'s run. But her brainchild thrived: scrappy, opinionated, and stacked with columns by veteran writers recognizable to local readers—typically retired colleagues from Schwartz's prior jobs, or admirers like journalist/screenwriter Paul Yawitz, who contributed pulpy short fiction—giving the *Courier* a patina of high-end respectability to offset its upstart outlook. It would earn the slogan printed below the nameplate on every front page: "The Best Read Paper in Beverly Hills."

The paper's rise paralleled Beverly Hills's escalating profile in the zeitgeist as Rodeo Drive captured the public imagination; local ad sales boomed—bolstered by creative exchanges of goods and services for free ad space—making March both a wealthy man and a political kingmaker. Local candidates for office vied feverishly for his endorsement, while state and national politicians courted his favor for his access to the city's reservoir of deep-pocketed donors. By 1978, the publisher of a local newspaper serving a city of about 33,000 people joined the White House Press Corps, traveling with U.S. presidents over the years, including Jimmy Carter, Ronald Reagan, George H.W. Bush, and Bill Clinton, to far-flung locales around the world—including returning to his beloved China. I would marvel when March would bring back photos of Clinton beaming as he held up an issue featuring headline stories I'd written, or simply gift me with a box of specially branded M&Ms he'd copped from Air Force One.

At seventy-seven, silver-haired and pear-shaped, March was flush with success when I came in to interview for the job, though at first glance you'd never know it, given his penchant for wrinkled t-shirts and jeans—I mistook him for a *janitor* when he came out to greet me (though his dress clothes were impeccably tailored and monogrammed at the shirt cuff). A framed wartime photo of himself and Eleanor Roosevelt hung in his lavish but cluttered office—the only thing lavish at *the Courier*—alongside contemporary shots of Sharon Stone flirting with him, his friend jazz legend Lionel Hampton embracing him, a giant blown-up portrait of March with a casually dressed Ronald Reagan, and of course a shot of his late wife Wendy in the smashing $1,500 Halston suit he put on his credit card when they were broke so she'd look the role of a chic Beverly Hills businesswoman. Past the most colossal '90s-era big-screen TV I'd ever seen was, inexplicably, a barber chair—office scuttlebutt suggested it was a regular prop in March's still-active dating life. March was charismatic, charming, gossipy, and quick to share the latest off-color joke he'd heard; I'd also discover that he could be mercurial, subject to petty personal and political feuds, and paranoid that various challengers would steal away his prized fiefdom.

I found it all both dazzling and deliriously amusing. *This is going to be hilarious.*

From my first bylined story on July 29, 1994—a write-up refuting that screen icon Gene Kelly, who lived in the residential portion of Rodeo Drive, was not in ill health as recent reports had claimed—I quickly got a taste of the sublimely surreal nature of general assignment reporting in Beverly Hills. For every often snore-inducing city council ceremony, school board meeting, and business luncheon, there was some gloriously unexpected and oh-so-90210 moment.

The everyday constantly mingled with the extraordinary: I found myself chatting on the phone with Charlton Heston about civic issues that concerned him; watching Jack Lemmon address the City Council, dramatically protesting a billionaire neighbor's plan to erect an oversized mega-mansion on Tower Road; lunching with concerned parent Valerie Harper at her Restaurant Row eatery to discuss the state of the school system; encountering fun-loving Tony Curtis and his Amazonian, half-his-age paramour at boutique openings seemingly every other night; sitting behind the wheel of Hollywood car customizer George Barris's 1966 Batmobile outside the grand opening party for Crustacean restaurant; learning from film critic Roger Ebert in the Academy Awards press room how much he *loved* that his syndicated reviews, which I curated in the *Courier*'s pages, ran in the local newspaper read by industry insiders; being hugged by Buddy Hackett at a party at the Beverly Hills Hotel because the notice I'd written up resulted in the joyful return of his lost dog; receiving a message from

Jimmy Stewart's publicist offering Stewart's appreciation of my story about his valiant wartime service; hearing Slash shredding his way through "Jingle Bells" from a Rodeo Drive rooftop as the Beverly Wilshire Hotel lit up its holiday tree, all under a flurry of soap-bubble "snow."

More surreality ensued: I interviewed the manager of the Lladro boutique while Michael Jackson discreetly shopped on the second floor, surrounded by his private security; met fashion designers Mark Badgley and James Mischka as they excitedly prepared their first-ever boutique for its grand opening on Rodeo Drive; listened to blacklisted Hollywood Ten screenwriter Ring Lardner, Jr., lecture about his experience to an auditorium of high school students; had a table setting card signed by comic book legend Stan Lee during a Friars Club tribute dinner honoring my publisher as Keeley Smith sang in the background; wondered who might afford the $3 million Modigliani on display at Sotheby's before noticing Steve Martin immediately to my right, carefully appraising the painting; toured the iconic studio chief and film producer Robert Evans's stunningly gorgeous estate on Woodland Drive—formerly Greta Garbo's—as he contemplated suing the city over its plan to erect a water tower in the empty lot next door, conjuring his very British butler, bearing historical records and blueprints, with the merest wave, even as my presence caught a quite well-known, quite naked actress quite off-guard as she emerged from the bedroom; and shook hands with Prince Charles, the future king of England, on Rodeo Drive as he arrived for a screening of a film about one of his ancestors, *The Madness of King George*.

The glamor of the mundane even spilled directly into the office: March's close friend, the prolific film director George Sidney, who, in a lifetime in Hollywood, helmed everything from *Our Gang* shorts to classic musicals like *Anchors Aweigh*, *Pal Joey*, *Bye Bye Birdie*, and *Viva Las Vegas*, held a tongue-in-cheek "Staff Photographer" credit in the *Courier's* masthead. George would drop by once or twice a week to hand off a stack of star-filled point-and-shoot photos he'd snapped at social gatherings, regaling me with stories of working with Sinatra, Ann-Margret, or Elvis.

It was all just bonkers. Yet every day was just another day in Beverly Hills.

At that point in its history, Beverly Hills had regularly dominated headlines and watercooler buzz after minting a new, more notorious kind of household name: the celebrity criminal. Heidi Fleiss—the famously flashy young "Hollywood Madam" who arrogantly drew too much attention to her wildly successful high-end prostitution enterprise providing impossibly gorgeous, $1,500-an-hour "Heidi Girls" to an elite crop of corporate titans and A-listers like Charlie Sheen—was arrested in a sting operation by undercover Beverly Hills police working in concert with LAPD and the FBI. Two years earlier, young brothers Lyle and Eric Menendez were charged with the brutal 1989 shotgun slaying of their parents, entertainment executive Jose Menendez and his wife Kitty, in the family's home on North Elm Drive. If the premise of parricide in such a pampered, privileged environment wasn't sensational enough, the shock factor skyrocketed when the brothers alleged they'd been pushed to murder after years of suffering horrific sexual abuse at their father's hands while their mother turned a blind eye, instantly adding the "abuse excuse" into the pop psycho-legal lexicon.

Both cases were instrumental in sparking a wave of furious interest in the scandals of the rich and famous, living high until brought low by crime. The double murder of Nicole Brown Simpson and Ron Goldman, ostensibly at the hands of O.J. Simpson, was the *ne plus ultra*: all of Los Angeles, most of the country, and much of the world obsessed over every new twist in the investigations and subsequent trials. At the *Courier*, I fielded numerous outlandish calls claiming knowledge of the "real story" and encountered many of the trial's players, both in courts of law and the social whirl of 90210. I vividly recall walking to my parked car after escorting March from the celebrity-packed funeral of Eva Gabor at the Church of the Good Shepherd, directly behind fabled high society crime writer Dominic Dunne—holding *Vanity Fair*'s coveted seat at the Simpson trial, he was the toast of L.A.—and nonchalantly eavesdropping as he shared hot court gossip with Angie Dickinson and Roddy McDowall. On the day of the trial verdict, I was set to ride-along with Beverly Hills police in anticipation of Rodney King-like potential protest riots in the streets until Simpson's jaw-dropping acquittal so stunned, even stupefied, the populace that no cautionary patrols were required.

An abiding fascination with high-glam crime consumed the cultural air, and I was not immune. Recognizing Beverly Hills as a nexus for those types of stories, currently and historically, I eagerly took ownership of *The Courier*'s police and crime beat, covering then-trending crimes in the city like follow-home Rolex robberies. I was unaware the *Courier* had, prior to my hiring, developed a contentious relationship with the Beverly Hills Police Department, a political imbroglio stemming from, of all things,

Sylvester Stallone's May 1991 arrest there following the climax of a two-mile high-speed car chase through West Hollywood.

After leaving Sunset Boulevard nightclub Bar One around 2 a.m., Stallone, an unidentified female companion and his bodyguard Gary Compton alleged that a rented Honda Civic—occupied by the six-foot-three ex-Green Beret-turned photographer E.L. Woody, a ubiquitous presence outside celebrity hot spots as the self-proclaimed "King of Paparazzi," and studio musician Phillip Norris—struck Stallone's Mercedes Benz 500 SL. Per Stallone, the Civic sped off without exchanging insurance information, prompting the actor to pursue, his bodyguard close behind in a Nissan 300ZX. During the chase, winding through the hilly streets above the Sunset Strip and down Doheny Drive into Beverly Hills, Stallone claimed the photographer intentionally crashed into his Mercedes at least three times, ultimately causing him to spin out of control and crash near the intersection of Santa Monica Boulevard and Doheny. "It was like an excerpt out of *The French Connection*," Stallone told the Associated Press.

But Woody and Norris, who'd fled to the West Hollywood Sheriff's station on Santa Monica Boulevard after calling 911, offered a decidedly different version of events: sensing Stallone's ire as he exited Bar One and walked toward them amid the pop-pop-pop of Woody's flashbulbs, they retreated and drove around the block, only to discover Stallone and Compton in their respective vehicles waiting to pursue them. As the chase ensued, Woody contended, *Stallone* was the one who Rambo-ed his Mercedes into *their* Civic multiple times, as did Compton's Nissan. "What kind of a nut uses a $100,000 battering ram?" Woody, who filed an assault with a deadly weapon charge against Stallone, asked the *Los Angeles Times*. He and Norris also filed civil suits seeking damages.

Incumbent Beverly Hills city council member, attorney Robert K. Tanenbaum, who'd served a recent rotation as mayor, was a former congressional counsel and ex-New York prosecutor on cases ranging from the assassination of John F. Kennedy to the Hillside Strangler with a successful sideline as a bestselling novelist penning dozens of legal potboilers inspired by his courtroom experiences; he'd also just lost a bid to be elected Los Angeles County District Attorney. When Tanenbaum took on Stallone's case, Beverly Hills police deemed his involvement a blatant conflict of interest—further, Tanenbaum was accused of meddling in their investigation.

The D.A.'s office declined to file charges against Stallone, and the civil lawsuits were quietly settled, but in Beverly Hills the tussle waged on as Tanenbaum hit back: he was the lone holdout on the city council approving funds to hire more police personnel, urging his colleagues "not to add more police desk jockeys in suits." That enraged the police union, which vigorously campaigned against Tanenbaum's reelection; in a place and time where public safety spirit ran sky-high, it was little surprise he was defeated—except to March Schwartz, who'd given his full-throated endorsement. Not only did March and Tanenbaum fall out, but each also blamed the other for the political loss, creating an icy, extended divide between the police department and the newspaper.

The dust hadn't yet settled when I entered the scene, and the police department warily regarded my blissfully ignorant, probably overeager interest in the force's cutting-edge tools with some skepticism. But 1994 saw three separate homicides in the city when *any* murder was rare, all in the last six months of the year: the body dump of a prominent gay rights activist from Chicago, murdered while vacationing in West Hollywood; the shooting of a gown rental shop owner in her store a block from the *Courier*'s office; and the execution-style murder of a Brink's armored car guard during an ambush robbery. As a rookie reporter who'd never covered violent crime before, I took the responsibility very seriously, which I suspect convinced BHPD that I had no hidden agenda.

Before long, I was getting an almost-insider's view of the force, accompanying officers on ride-alongs, sampling their self-defense training in the Israeli martial art Krav Maga, experiencing their high-tech targeting range, observing K-9 unit training and allowed rare face time with the revered Chief Marvin Iannone (aware of my penchant for classic Hollywood lore, he shared that, when as an LAPD patrol officer he was the second officer to arrive on the scene of Marilyn Monroe's Brentwood home on the night she died in 1962, he did not register anything indicating foul play).

Fascinated by how the police force operated in this most singular landscape, and after countless hours at the Beverly Hills Public Library—conveniently next door to the police station—digging into dusty volumes and scanning microfiche spools exploring the history of the city, I developed a passion for the distinctive, unconventional, and often bizarre crimes that occurred almost from the city's inception, those "only in Beverly Hills" stories where the city's celebrated cachet of wealth, fame, power and luxury was tainted by lawlessness. During my tenure in Beverly Hills and long after, crimes that couldn't have happened anywhere else regularly emerged. Because of the city's perpetual pop cultural cachet, a few stories—like those involving pop star George Michael and actress Winona Ryder—made headlines around the world. But I harbored a sneaking fondness for oddball crimes with less of a global or national impact but just as outrageous, if not more so—more Elmore Leonard than James Ellroy.

These crimes, though never victimless, allowed me a lighter touch telling them while writing full-time for *The Courier* and later, as a freelancer for a subsequent local paper, publisher Josh Gross's *Beverly Hills Weekly*, and *Los Angeles*, the long-running glossy lifestyle magazine covering the region. I would amuse myself by dubbing some of the strangest cases with memorable names straight out of vintage pulp crime magazines. I was especially struck by stories involving the elaborate lengths some local lawbreakers would go to in assuming another identity—sometimes wholly fictional, sometimes built on a kernel truth, sometimes borrowed without permission from another person. Digging into my case files to recount a few of the most memorable, I realized Beverly Hills's status as a showbiz town, home to some of the most accomplished actors in Hollywood history, rubbed off on its criminal element, many of whom proved just as committed to delivering convincing, immersive performances.

THE F/X FELONS

From the moment the two men entered Wells Fargo Bank in the middle of the day on June 19, 1998, they immediately drew attention to themselves. In Beverly Hills, customers walking into any business might routinely turn heads, but this was something altogether different.

At a glance, the men appeared professional and polished, sharply dressed in business suits as they entered the busy lobby of the branch anchoring the first floor of the four-story office building at the southeast corner of Wilshire Boulevard and Crescent Drive, straddling the city's commercial and residential districts. Yet to an even casual observer taking a second look at the two white, bald men, there was something decidedly *off*—even disconcerting—about their faces. There was an odd, unnatural sheen and bloodless pallor to their skin, an almost rubbery, translucent quality to their facial features. To employees in the high-traffic branch, always alert for possible red flags, both men read…artificial. And not in the cosmetically enhanced way that was commonplace in 90210.

Bypassing the teller windows, the duo confidently approached a customer service agent and insisted on speaking to the bank manager, growing increasingly impatient and antsy as they waited to be seen. But they had already been *seen*: the unnerving Uncanny Valley vibes they were giving off quickly escalated the suspicions of the bank staff, and silent alarms were activated—with police headquarters just blocks up the street and a heavy patrol presence roaming the city during the day, the response would be momentary.

But the plasticine-looking men in the snappy suits were also on high alert and immediately felt their own warning bells blaring. With a sense of impending catastrophe overwhelming them, they bolted out of the bank in unison, scrambled across the sidewalk down Crescent Drive, and dove into the brand-new, shiny red Lincoln Navigator they'd left parked streetside in the residential neighborhood.

Irwin Salgado, a traffic control officer for the city of Beverly Hills and a lifelong resident, was on duty, idling at the red light at Crescent and Wilshire, when a call of a 211 in progress at Wells Fargo came over his radio. He instantly spotted two very odd-looking men with skins that looked to him like "miscolored zebra." The robbery suspects had caught sight of him, and although he wasn't a sworn police officer, he felt a responsibility to pursue the fugitives and keep them in the city so they could be captured, even as he instinctively recognized why they were running with their hands in their pockets: "I go 'Shit, those guys are carrying guns,'" Salgado remembered. Sure enough, as Salgado maneuvered his vehicle to investigate, one of the men aimed a semiautomatic pistol in his direction and fired off a round—missing Salgado, the bullet lodged in the outer wall of the Ramada hotel across the street.

The SUV roared recklessly into the streets of Beverly Hills, disregarding pedestrians and the steady flow of vehicles in both directions—Wilshire was a heavily trafficked east-west artery through the city at any time of day, with seven traffic lanes at the Wilshire-Crescent intersection. The Navigator tore across the boulevard and shot northbound on Canon Drive, tailed by a rattled Salgado, who'd radioed in their location, even as one of the men fired another round in his direction.

Almost instantly, a pair of Beverly Hills motorcycle patrol officers blocked the intersection of Canon and Dayton Way. Swerving onto Dayton, the Navigator fled down the alleyway running parallel to Crescent and Canon, traveling in the wrong direction—narrowly missing an elderly Beverly Hills matron driving the other way who pulled over and shouted at the fleeing driver to correct his course.

Growing increasingly aware they lacked the firepower to escape capture, both gunmen tossed their pistols out of the windows of the speeding vehicle just as it zipped past the expansive rear dining patio of Caffe Roma, a classy but louche Italian bistro within the Le Grand Passage shopping center, which also housed the trendy Giuseppe Franco hair salon and Nazareth's Fine Cigars, an elite cigar shop and lounge. The entire courtyard was an antithesis of see-and-be-seen hotspots of the day like The Ivy and Spago: there was an abundance of Hollywood power players, yes, but lunching in much more of a clubby, under-the-radar ambiance. Since its opening in 1985, Nazareth's had counted cigar enthusiast Arnold Schwarzenegger among its biggest boosters. He, along with Mickey Rourke—who'd bankrolled Franco's salon—held court regularly at Caffe Roma over Roman cuisine made by the founders, brothers Gigi and Gianni Orlando and Stefano Orsini, since 1980. Despite its trendy neighbors, the restaurant's eclectic, devoted tribe skewed in the direction of an earlier generation: mellifluous crooners like Al Martino and Jerry Vale, comics like Shecky Green and Norm Crosby, and Beverly Hills habitues like Zsa Zsa Gabor, superhero scribe Stan Lee, and superstar realtor Elaine Young.

As the gunmen's semiautomatics struck the pavement in the alley behind Caffe Roma, one of the weapons discharged. A bullet hurtled through the courtyard, lodging in the wall of Giuseppe Franco's salon—no bystander was harmed by the errant projectile, though the incident did offer one diner among the lunch crowd, actor Don Adams, famed for the 1960s spy-spoof sitcom *Get Smart*, a prime opportunity to use his character Maxwell Smart's signature catchphrase in earnest: "Missed it by that much!"

The Lincoln Navigator eluded capture for several more minutes, but Beverly Hills officers were able to form an impassable blockade at Brighton Way and Crescent Drive near the historic Art Deco hideaway the Crescent Hotel, aborting any chance of a getaway. Pulling their quarries from the SUV, the officers were taken aback by what they discovered: the "flesh" of both men's ill-fitting faces had been ripped and shredded in a frantic attempt to tear it off. Ragged strips of Caucasian-colored latex epidermis still clung to their heads. Underneath, the truth was apparent: both fugitives—brothers Brian and Anthony Crite—were Black.

A decade earlier, Brian Crite wore the badge and uniform of law enforcement himself as a sworn officer with the Detroit Police Department. The trouble began when the rookie cop, just twenty years old, also donned that very same uniform while he brazenly committed a string of startling shakedowns.

While off duty and still under probation, on August 16, 1988, Crite and his accomplice—also in police uniform, although actually a seventeen-year-old ninth grader hoping for extra cash to buy new clothes—embarked on a crime spree in a police scout car across Detroit's east side, including five armed robberies over three hours. In each case, the victims had pulled over believing they'd committed a routine traffic violation, only to be threatened with arrest if they didn't hand over their valuables—money, jewelry, and, in one case, drugs. In a particularly egregious encounter, after pulling over a man and a woman at 1:15 a.m. and insisting they exit so he could search their car, Crite grabbed the woman's purse, announcing, "You have two choices—give us your jewelry or go to jail." The woman refused, so Crite stranded her with the car but no ignition key. He drove the man several blocks away, stripped him of his gold rings, watch, and bracelet, and abandoned him on the street.

Despite a city-wide alert, Crite and the teenager evaded detection until days later when a victim coincidentally arrived at Crite's assigned precinct on another matter and recognized him, confronting him outside and demanding the return of his property. Crite consented, but the victim informed Crite's superiors regardless, resulting in the rookie's arrest. Identified by multiple victims and charged with four counts each of armed robbery and felony firearm possession as well as kidnapping, both Crite and the teenager pled guilty to two of the armed robbery charges and were each sentenced to twelve to forty years in state prison—all for a haul that barely exceeded $1,000.

After serving nine years in various penal facilities around Michigan, Brian Crite was incarcerated at Camp Koehler, a low-security prison camp in remote Kinross Charter Township, fifteen miles south of Sault Ste. Marie in the state's Upper Peninsula and over 330 miles from Detroit. Thirty years old, over the course of his prison stint, he'd accrued twenty-one misconduct violations and tested positive for drugs.

And then, on December 28, 1997, he vanished.

Not uncoincidentally, over a month later on February 2, a man stylishly dressed in a navy business suit, a black beret, and a beige trench coat walked into a Comerica bank branch on West East Mile in Detroit. The man told the bank manager he was looking to secure sponsorship for the Police Athletic League sports program before flashing a handgun and revealing a crude, homemade-looking device he'd hidden under the trench coat: a makeshift bomb. After threatening to detonate the explosive, the man escaped with $115,000. On May 15, the same man walked into another Comerica branch on Northwestern Highway in the Detroit suburb of Southfield and, using the same gambit with the bomb, walked off with a cool $238,000. By then, federal investigators had a sneaking suspicion that the notorious Brian Crite, his crime game considerably elevated, had returned home to the Motor City.

But he wouldn't remain there for long. The ex-cop from Motown had gone Hollywood.

Shortly after May 15, flush with cash and confidence after amassing over $350,000 in just two bank jobs, Crite traveled to a potentially more lucrative playing field: Southern California, accompanied by a new partner in crime, his twenty-three-year-old brother Anthony. His crimes to date had been driven by gimmicks—the power of a police badge's authority or the destructive promise of a homemade explosive—and he had a fresh innovation in mind that suited his new environs to a tee.

If Brian Crite was going to go Hollywood, he was going to go big.

On June 10, the Crite brothers took a meeting at the Make-up Designory in Burbank, an educational institute dedicated to the highly specialized arts of advanced makeup design, everything from high-fashion cosmetics to the otherworldly special effects prosthetics frequently employed in cutting-edge Hollywood productions. They met with one of the school's principals, Karl Zundel, who'd previously worked on the NBC sci-fi miniseries *Invasion* and Nickelodeon's teen sketch comedy series *All That*. Under the alias Derrick Miles, Brian offered to hire Zundel, using his technical artistry to craft a challenging effect for an exciting project the brothers had in play: transforming two Black men into two white men. A deal was struck, and the Crite brothers returned the following day with the makeup wizard's payment.

After spending several days at the Ramada hotel across the street from Wells Fargo, on June 19 the brothers underwent their metamorphosis at the makeup school. Despite their surplus of cash, they'd cut considerable corners when budgeting such a costly scheme: instead of appearing convincingly Caucasian, the effect was even more unconvincing than the famously jarring look of the Wayans Brothers in their race-swapping, cross-dressing film comedy *White Chicks* six years later. Encased in rubbery-looking latex that had a translucent striping effect, they might have been better off attempting to pass as aliens from another planet. But by then, the seed money had been spent, along with additional investments in handheld police scanners—tuned to the Beverly Hills police's frequencies—plus pistols, holsters, and a second set of quick-change clothing for each in case they needed to swap out their disguises, capped off by that brand-new Lincoln Navigator.

At the very least, they'd been rendered unrecognizable. The job was on.

Along with shredded remnants of latex, scanners, holsters, and getaway outfits, police found evidence that led them to a nondescript motel in Torrance, the beachy South Bay community forty-five minutes away from Beverly Hills. A contingent of Beverly Hills detectives led by two of its most revered investigators—Tom Edmonds, the tough yet soft-spoken veteran who'd served under every chief since Clinton Anderson and was highly regarded for his cool-headed demeanor, shrewd instincts, and ability to coax a confession out of just about any suspect; and Les Zoeller, another facile deductive intellect known for unraveling a slew of knotty cases, including the Menendez murders—descended on a room rented by the brothers, only to discover that Brian Crite still had one more weird curveball at the ready: the detectives found themselves face to face with what looked very convincingly like a homemade bomb.

"A couple of guys with me thought it was real and were scared," Edmonds told me—but he had both a reliable gut and ice water in his veins (when we spoke in 2023, he was still regularly racing motorcycles in his late eighties). "I just took a chance and said, 'No, it's a fake,' and we went about doing what we do. And it didn't blow up."

Along with the ersatz explosive and a wealth of evidence suggesting that the Crite brothers were professional criminals preparing to embark on a significant crime spree, police also found a telling clue: a newspaper clipping recounting the February 2 robbery—and the role of the phony bomb—in Detroit.

Federal investigators showed three Comerica employees an array of mug shots; each identified Brian Crite—wearing his own face at the time— as the man with the bomb. Even the brothers' parents agreed it was Brian in security camera footage from the local bank jobs. Facing an assortment of charges in Beverly Hills as well as Brian's recent felonies in Michigan and outstanding conviction record, the brothers pled guilty to second-degree robbery and assault with a semiautomatic firearm, with Brian also admitting to conspiracy to commit a robbery.

Anthony Crite received six years in prison; Brian Crite thirty-five years to life, which proved a life sentence: by 2001, he was dead at thirty-four.

That was the end of his story, in stark black and in white.

THE SKETCHY CHAUFFER

When it came to the original Picasso art that he was angling to sell, Tony Hargain sounded like knew his stuff. *Faune*, a rendered ink-on-paper sketch depicting a mythological half-man/half-deer, had been created in 1937 during artist Pablo Picasso's peak period, and its prestigious pedigree ensured its potential value to discerning collectors. Hargain knew this and much more, speaking with erudition about the surrealist sketch's various attributes.

Outwardly, the well-dressed, handsome, athletic, and charismatic thirty-five-year-old Black man—who said he was a professional football player by way of explaining his means to possess a $100,000 sketch—presented an air of legitimacy in the reception area of the famed auction house Christie's sleek, minimalist gallery space on Camden Drive, discussing the finer points of Picasso's sketch on May 3, 2001. But as Nathalie, Christie's contemporary art specialist, listened closely to the details, somethng didn't sit right with her. Although he described the sketch precisely, Hargain hadn't brought the artwork in with him, claiming he was concerned the auction house might underhandedly photograph the sketch to create their own prints to sell. That struck Nathalie as oddly paranoid reasoning, and the more he talked, the more it seemed he only possessed superficial knowledge of the art and its provenance. At one point, he'd even denigrated the sketch as "really ugly"—not exactly the savviest selling pitch—suggesting he wasn't quite the connoisseur he claimed to be. And there was his initial offer to accept a check for $60,000 with no strings attached; Christie's could keep any profit it made at a sale—a red flag that he was looking to unload the sketch as quickly as possible.

Nodding and smiling all the while, Nathalie politely excused herself to conduct a little more research on the sketch; instead, she vigilantly entered its specifics into a stolen art database. As she suspected, the sketch was hot, recently boosted from the home of a private collector.

Nathalie alerted Christie's security chief, who immediately contacted Det. Don Hyrcyk, the Los Angeles Police Department's art theft specialist, who'd been investigating the missing sketch. "It was a delicate situation," Hyrcyk told me at the time, fearing the Beverly Hills police might "come in like gangbusters" and apprehend Hargain too soon, leaving no evidence to definitively link him to the theft or recover the stolen Picasso—all that would be remain was a strong suspicion he was the culprit.

Hyrcyk directed the Christie's staffer to continue to calmly negotiate with Hargain, and in doing so, to try to get a good description of his vehicle and its license plate number. If he had, in fact, brought the sketch with him, secreted in his car, and the staff could entice him to bring it inside for appraisal, even better. But as they were formulating a plan, the auction house's general manager Linda entered the reception area hoping to stall the would-be seller, only to discover that Tony Hargain had gotten antsy and walked out of the building.

But the man that the Christie's staff had encountered was never actually Tony Hargain to begin with. The *real* Tony Hargain had been that man's college football teammate, a fellow wide receiver at the University of Oregon who'd gone on to play several seasons in the NFL—including stints with the Los Angeles Rams and San Francisco 49ers—and, later, to own a line of specialty sports apparel designed for billiards players. The "Tony Hargain" in Beverly Hills had appropriated both the Picasso and his ex-teammate's identity.

For someone who'd grown up in the California Central Valley city of Stockton within a family of "no-good-niks," as a police investigator once opined—practically every member of his immediate kin, including each of his seven brothers and sisters, served jail time—Sammie Archer III demonstrated an admirable ability to beat any odds against him. Tall, lean, powerfully built, and possessing innate athletic prowess, Archer bettered himself through sports, earning a spot on the Oregon Ducks football team in 1986. But despite his gridiron skills, Archer was unable to realize his dream of being drafted into the NFL. Instead, he landed in the World League of American Football as a wide receiver for the Sacramento Surge; in the organization's brief two-season existence, Archer's roster became the only American team to win the league's World Bowl. But he again faced disappointment when the WLAF folded in 1992 and he failed to receive any subsequent NFL offers.

Still, Sammie Archer had built quite a life for himself, transcending his early, troubled origins: A churchgoing man who didn't drink, smoke, or carouse, he was by all accounts deeply devoted to his wife and their growing brood of children; through his church, he taught Bible classes and counseled married couples. His football career concluded, he reinvented himself in even more glamorous and exciting environs, moving to Los Angeles and serving as the chauffeur for superstar comedian Chevy Chase and his family. Driving for Chase offered Archer a vicarious, tantalizing taste of what living the Good Life felt like, which only stoked Archer's belief that he was destined to achieve significant success. That promise glimmered ever brighter when Archer left Chase's employ to work for an even more powerful, more influential, and far wealthier Hollywood player: uber-producer Peter Guber.

After a successful run as an independent film producer, including a decade working in tandem with his producing partner Jon Peters—the former Rodeo Drive hairdresser and Barbra Streisand beau—resulting in blockbuster hits like *Batman* and prestige fare like *Rain Man*, Guber and Peters ascended. Their company was acquired for $200 million, positioning them at the forefront of Sony Pictures Entertainment, the new studio formed by the Japanese electronic colossus' $4.7 billion purchase of venerable Columbia Pictures, recently beefed up with its own string of acquisitions and further bolstered by a new home, the Culver City lot that had once housed fabled MGM Studios. The duo would shepherd the revitalized studio for several years, creating an enviable, record-breaking string of box office successes and awards-winning critical darlings, though corporate balance sheets and executive shuffles were chaotic. Guber took a platinum parachute in 1995, forming the multimedia Mandalay Entertainment Group and taking ownership stakes in the Los Angeles Dodgers and the Golden State Warriors. Along the way, he'd amassed untold millions and lived, with his wife Tara and their family, in one of the largest private estates in West Los Angeles, a jaw-dropping Mediterranean Revival mansion atop ten rambling hillside acres in Bel-Air previously owned by network executive Grant Tinker and his then-wife Mary Tyler Moore. It was a property tastefully packed with an abundance of décor and to-die-for objects *d'art*, each more extravagant than the last—Alexander Caulder mobiles, Eileen Gray tables, Christian Liaigre furniture, Hervé Van der Straeten lamps, an Isamu Noguchi sculpture, a Robert Rauschenberg print, Jim Dine mixed-media canvases, Picasso plates, and an Henri Matisse original on the dining room mantelpiece merely scratched the surface of the Gubers' assorted finery.

For Archer, the cumulative effect of such opulence was overwhelming. A switch seemed to flip inside him when he entered Guber's orbit, sparking a crisis of character. Very quickly, his marriage crumbled as he began partying and carousing until all hours of the night. Bizarrely, Archer adopted an alter ego for the new persona he'd slipped on, assuming the name of former teammate Tony Hargain and bifurcating his identity as if living out the fantasy life of the NFL player he once dreamed he might be. He was roleplaying his way into the Good Life: during his torrid affair with a beautiful model, she not only had no clue the flashy fleet of exotic automobiles he squired her around in belonged not to Archer but to his employer, she legitimately believed her boyfriend's name was Tony Hargain.

"He was surrounded by opulence, and he wanted that opulence for himself," investigator Don Hyrcyk came to understand. "He was no longer satisfied being a bit plater." But there was only so much of that rarefied world he could claim as a driver—the props he borrowed from Guber weren't enough. He needed cash of his own to fund his increasingly ambitious lifestyle, and he needed it right away.

It was time for Sammy Archer—or in this case, "Tony Hargain"—to make a big play.

The Guber family spent the December 2000 holidays away from their estate; when they returned, Peter was dismayed to discover that a break-in had occurred. The property manager had surveyed the house daily in their absence and one morning discovered a pile of broken glass at a rear entrance. A laminated window at the home was kicked in and a small portion of Guber's prized art collection had gone missing: a classic Tiffany lamp that had been appraised at $75,000; a bronze sculpture of an African elephant; several Picasso plates; and a sketch by the same artist, *Faune*, which Guber had purchased from the Pace-Wildenstein Gallery in New York, which in turn had acquired it directly from Picasso's daughter Paloma—the drawing was estimated to be worth $100,000. The culprit had escaped with a haul totaling more than $200,000. Maybe more. As it would turn out, maybe a lot more.

Here, Don Hyrcyk entered the picture. As an eight-year veteran of LAPD's Art Theft Detail—often the *only* investigator dedicated to the division—the fifty-year-old detective had learned to be resourceful, relying on the expertise of a well-cultivated network of curators, experts, and academics and a deep well of patience; some cases would take years, sometimes even decades, to crack, crimes involving every kind of precious collectible, Chagalls, Picassos, Rothkos, Lichtensteins, Stradivariuses, even a set of comics books featuring pristine editions of *Action Comics* #1 and *Detective Comics* #27—the first appearances, respectively, of Superman and Batman—owned by actor Nicolas Cage. He recovered property in the millions, including heirlooms holding priceless value to their owners.

Experience told Hyrcyk that cases like Guber's were frequently inside jobs—a theory swiftly confirmed when he examined the break-in entry point and spotted an amateurish detail: the position of the shattered shards of glass, still loosely held together by plastic lamination, indicated the window had been kicked in from *within* the home, rather than from the outside. There was no actual indication of forced entry into the mansion. There was, however, a telltale trail of muddy boot tracks, still visibly stamped in the carpeting, leading instead from a side door through the billiard room— likely caused by the grounds-dampening sprinkler system which activated at 4 a.m. A closer inspection of the tread patterns revealed the prints were made by rather distinctive size-twelve Timberlands. Objects of greater value had been left behind, and while Hyrcyk encountered a share of cases where genuine aficionados stole precious artwork out of sheer, obsessive covetousness, this one showed all evidence of a rush job with no particular care in the choosing or handling of the purloined bounty.

This was most certainly an inside job.

Consulting with Guber, less concerned about the missing art than for the safety of his family, Hyrcyk asked the studio executive if there was anyone among his twenty-nine-member staff he had reason to suspect. The chauffer's name came up—Sammie Archer, who had unfettered access to the estate during the family's vacation, was slated to be laid off in the next month due to household cost-cutting following a downturn in film production. During his subsequent interview with Archer, Hyrcyk took note of the driver's affable charm as he denied any involvement—as well as the fact that the ex-athlete later failed to show up for a scheduled polygraph test.

Running a routine background check on Sammie Archer III, Hyrcyk was surprised to discover a lengthy rap sheet full of priors, including several stints in prison. He wondered how such a habitual criminal could come into the employ of someone like Peter Guber—until he took a closer look at the mug shots attached to the records he was examining: there was a resemblance, but this felon was definitely *not* the same Sammie Archer III he'd recently interviewed.

Hyrcyk was at an impasse. Archer's record was clean, and there was no direct evidence linking him to the crime. Yet.

Five months later, Linda, the general manager of Christie's Beverly Hills, stepped outside the auction house to see Tony Hargain behind the wheel of a BMW, about to pull away from the curb. She intercepted him before he could drive off, gradually enticing him to return to the auction house. The company's Picasso expert was on the way over, she told him, and they were very interested in hammering out an equitable deal.

Jangled nerves effectively soothed, Tony returned to the reception area and awaited the arrival of the expert. Growing more relaxed, he offered that he might also possess a set of Picasso plates he was interested in selling— perhaps the specialist would like to appraise those, too?

Meanwhile, Hyrcyk alerted the Beverly Hills police department. A contingent of patrol officers silently converged on Christie's: one motor-cycle officer stealthily slid in the back door and took a position in the security room, monitoring Tony on the closed-circuit security cameras. More officers covertly covered each exit and, from a distance, kept an eye on Tony's BMW. Told the Picasso expert had just arrived, Tony finally let down his guard and admitted he had the sketch with him all along. He retrieved an object wrapped in a man's shirt from the trunk of his car and presented it to Linda and Nathalie, unwrapping it carefully as they watched in anticipation.

And there it was: Picasso's *Faune*.

Moments later, Hyrcyk entered the auction house to discover Sammie Archer III in handcuffs. "When I walked in, he kind of smiled," Hyrcyk told me of the chagrinned look he saw on Archer's face. "He recognized me, and I recognized him."

Archer had been busy in the months since Hyrcyk last encountered him. After leaving Guber's employ, he'd swiftly disposed of most of the loot through an unsuspecting Beverly Hills antiques dealer and subsequently tore through the ill-gotten windfall on what he admitted were frivolous purchases—including a hedonistic vacation in Las Vegas and, emulating the real Tony Hargain, a Harley-Davidson. He'd fared particularly well when unloading the vintage Tiffany lamp after approaching Christie's apparently more lax New York office, which purchased it without determining if it had been stolen. From there, the lamp became an in-demand commodity among collectors, passing through no less than five owners in a four-month period and rapidly escalating in value from $75,000 to $275,000. Along with demonstrating just how fast and far stolen art could travel in a short period, Archer had unknowingly doubled the tally of the losses he was responsible for, hiking the total up to $400,000.

He'd shown greater restraint when it came to *Faune*. When arrested, he had in his pocket a handwritten list of ten additional high-end art galleries, antique dealers, and auction houses in and around Beverly Hills he'd methodically visited over months, feeling out the sketch's potential value and educating himself about its provenance and characteristics, learning a bit more with each stop. By the time he walked into Christie's he looked to maximize his profits to finance the next leg in his self-indulgent journey.

Serving a search warrant on Archer's luxe new apartment in Marina del Rey, Hyrcyk retrieved a pair of size-twelve Timberland boots with treads matching the prints left behind in Bel-Air. An unexpected discovery: Tony Hargain wasn't the only identity that Archer had appropriated—he'd also taken out multiple credit cards in Peter Guber's name and sky-high credit rating—with the bills sent to a post office box, where he'd extend their usefulness by paying minimum balances. By the time his scam was discovered, Archer racked up more than $40,000 in debt in his ex-employer's name.

Archer was charged with first-degree burglary, grand theft, receiving stolen property, and embezzlement, with an enhancement for theft of property over $150,000. His bail was set at a whopping $480,000—roughly the same amount he'd pilfered from Guber. After pleading guilty to the first three charges, he was sentenced to a year in county jail and five years' probation, along with a $5,000 fine.

Hyrcyk was admittedly baffled by Archer's near-total descent, from a promising young man who'd continually defied the odds to a greedy, hedonistic hustler. "What's sad about this thing is that he looked on the surface like a real success story," the detective told me prior to Archer's conviction. "You'd think if he was going to raise hell and steal things, he would've done it long ago."

There was one final, karmically appropriate turn to the tale: while in custody at the Wayside jail in Castaic awaiting his court appearance, Sammie Archer III came face to face with a fellow inmate wearing a wristband bearing a familiar name: *Sammie Archer III*. The same Sammie Archer

III with the extensive rap sheet who'd puzzlingly surfaced during Hyrcyk's background check. It was also one of Sammie Archer's brothers, who for years had assumed his sibling's identity whenever he ran afoul of the law.

Even Picasso would agree that it was all very, very surreal.

THE BANK BALANCE BUTTON MAN

In late August 1999, Sheila Holden Hamilton was a pretty, petite forty-two-year-old with an enviable position as a personal banker at City National Bank in Beverly Hills—among the city's most prestigious financial institutions since its founding there in 1954. Her office was in the thirteen-story building at its original berth at 400 Roxbury Drive, where Hamilton was accustomed to handling the enormous sums of money routinely channeled through her client's accounts. But at some point, the temptation to add to her own bank balance became too powerful to resist.

While having repair work done on her vehicle at Ravi's Body Shop on Pico Boulevard, Hamilton met the auto shop's owner, Ravinder Chawla, and subsequently convinced him to open a $40,000 savings account at City National Bank, and she would help grow the funds. Over the course of two years, however, the account dwindled by more than $34,000—Hamilton was quietly embezzling her client's cash, but not so quietly that Chawla didn't eventually discover how much had been drained away. The banker knew it was only a matter of time before her client went to her management, or worse, the authorities, and was desperately searching for a way out.

She confided her woes to her neighbor in West Los Angeles's Beverlywood area, Cynthia Lockhart; the two met a little over a year earlier when their teenage children were dating, and they remained friendly. During an otherwise innocuous phone call, Hamilton suddenly revealed her quandary: she was the target of an extortion plot, she confided to Lockhart, and someone was demanding money from her. Then she asked the $34,000 Question: did Lockhart know anyone who could make the problem "go away?"

"What do you mean 'go away?'" an incredulous Lockhart asked.

"I mean go away—permanently," Hamilton replied.

"Like, dead?"

"Yes, dead."

Surprisingly, Cindy Lockhart said she *might* know someone who could make such a problem go away.

Hamilton soon received a phone call from a mysterious figure who gave his name as Lorenzo Wright, responding to Lockhart's referral. The two negotiated a contract—a murder-for-hire contract in which Wright would eliminate her client Chawla for an agreed-upon, surprisingly reasonable, fee of $7,500. Hamilton sent full payment via Express Mail to a Long Beach post office box, along with the name, address, and description of the intended victim. That same day, Lockhart stopped by Hamilton's apartment accompanied by her tall, handsome boyfriend of six months, forty-three-year-old Kenneth Maurice Scott. Meeting Scott for the first time, Hamilton understood him to be either her friend's fiancé or imminently about to be. As a thank you to Lockhart for connecting her to the solution to her worries, Hamilton offered to help her unemployed friend craft a professional resume on her computer—but wanted to do more: she offered Lockhart a "finder's fee," but Lockhart demurred; she didn't feel comfortable accepting payment, even admitting she was ill at ease with the entire arrangement she'd helped broker. Nevertheless, when Lockhart returned home, she opened the envelope containing copies of her new resume and discovered a $500 bonus stashed within by her grateful neighbor.

This was turning out to be a most convivial contract killing.

That was, until Hamilton got a jarring phone call from Cynthia Lockhart's beau Scott, a former Los Angeles Unified School District Police Officer who, for the last three-and-a-half years, had been on duty with the Santa Monica Police Department, headquartered by the beach eight miles to the west of Beverly Hills. A well-liked patrol officer specializing in DUI investigations who played on the department's basketball team, Scott told Hamilton he'd gotten wind of the scheme to murder Ravinder Chawla and confronted Lorenzo White, warning the hitman not to go through with the plot. Because of Hamilton's friendship with Lockhart, Scott didn't plan to inform his law enforcement brethren but warned her that if she tried to follow through or go to authorities herself for any reason, he would make certain "everyone" involved in the sordid mess would end up behind bars.

Now not only was Hamilton out a total of $8,000, but she also faced the very daunting possibility that Chawla might still expose her embezzlement to the police himself. More panicked and desperate than ever, she worked up to courage to approach Chawla and come clean, offering him $25,000 in repayment. To her great relief, the auto shop owner accepted and agreed that the matter would end there.

It did not end there.

By October, Cindy Lockhart and Kenneth Scott's relationship was rapidly deteriorating. Whatever Scott had done to cool their ardor, Lockhart felt like a woman scorned. Looking for retribution, she walked into Santa Monica police headquarters with a juicy story to tell. Without asking for preferential treatment, she told the force's Internal Criminal Division officer something her about-to-be-ex's employers hadn't known about their brother-in-blue:

Kenneth Scott *was* Lorenzo Wright.

Powerfully built and six-foot-four, Scott certainly looked imposing enough to be a professional assassin. But his alter ego had merely been a devious ruse crafted to take advantage of Sheila Hamilton's plot after Lockhart revealed it to him. Never intending to carry out the contract, Scott instead pocketed the eight grand and split it evenly with Lockhart, a seemingly perfect scam after warning Hamilton not to pursue the matter any further. Over time, Lockhart had grown increasingly remorseful about her role in the scheme, finally spurred to action after her falling out with Scott.

Santa Monica investigators turned the matter over to Beverly Hills police detectives, holding jurisdictional precedent given Hamilton's initial crimes had originated there. From Lockhart's memory of the P.O. box number—remarkably, she was only one number off—Det. Marcelo Rodriguez and Det. Tom Linehan tracked it to a Long Beach mail drop, discovering that Scott was running a clever con indeed: earlier in the year, in anticipation of receipt of the hit fee, he'd changed his account, removing his personal information and even replacing his address with a phony locale, telling the clerk he was an undercover cop on a dangerous investigation and cautioning her never to reveal his identity to anyone. Scott had made such a strong, imperative impression on the clerk that she initially resisted giving his info until the detectives persuaded her that their investigation was legitimate.

The investigation had taken five months. Finally, on February 24, 2000, Linehan and Rodriguez walked into Santa Monica police headquarters. When they left, in a humiliating gesture, Officer Kenneth Maurice Scott was perp-walked out in handcuffs.

I got my first look at Kenneth Scott at Beverly Hills Superior Court, where he was arraigned on charges of conspiracy to cheat or defraud, grand theft, and receiving stolen property. I marveled at his towering height and was impressed by the caliber of his criminal defense attorney, the respected Errol H. Stambler, who'd previously represented Los Angeles police officers tried in relation to the Rampart Division corruption scandal as well as the occasional celebrity like Guns 'N' Roses guitarist Slash. Stambler's presence was quite a coup after two public defender's offices declined to take Scott's case. Despite Stambler presenting his client as a well-adjusted man who still had considerable support among the Santa Monica ranks, Judge Elden S. Fox—who later presided over actress Winona Ryder's shoplifting trial—ordered Scott to stand trial. With no indication that Scott had ever planned to actually commit the contracted murder, Fox set his bail at $50,000—reduced from $250,000—but required him to wear an electronic ankle monitor at all times.

Within days of Scott's arrest, Sheila Hamilton and Cindy Lockhart were taken into custody, Hamilton once again in considerably dire straits. Not only was she charged with solicitation of murder and embezzlement, but detectives took an even closer look at Hamilton's accounts at City National Bank: the $8,000 comprising Scott's hit payoff and Lockhart's bonus finder's fee was culled from $9,000 drained from the Arthur and Sally Moore Trust—indeed, Sally Moore had noticed the discrepancy and recently filed a complaint with the Beverly Hills police. Over $12,000 had gone missing from an account belonging to Stonehouse Investments, a Beverly Hills–based firm where, perhaps not uncoincidentally, Sheila Hamilton was once employed as a secretary.

It wouldn't be a Beverly Hills case without celebrity connections: an additional $9,400 had been drained from the account of Melissa Bochco, the daughter of prolific actress Barbara Bosson and the revered television producer Steven Bochco, known for *Hill Street Blues*, *Doogie Howser, M.D.*, and *NYPD Blue*, while $25,000 had been curiously paid out in a City National Bank check issued to auto shop owner Ravinder Chawla, strongly hinting that Sheila Hamilton had embezzled from one account to pay back her embezzlement from another—an account belonging to Richard Penniman, better known to generations of rock and roll fans as Little Richard.

One can only imagine the decibel level of the "Wooooooo!" when he found out.

Sheila Holden Hamilton pled guilty to a single count of embezzlement, accepted on the condition that she pay a total of $87,839.03 in restitution to City National Bank; she was sentenced to twenty-eight months in state prison. Lockhart was represented by attorney Christopher Darden, who'd left the L.A. District Attorney's office after the disillusioning acquittal of O.J. Simpson, joining the faculty of the Southwestern University School of Law and opening his own legal firm specializing in criminal defense and civil litigation. Unlike the Simpson trial, there was no courtroom theatrics for Darden to contend with: in exchange for her cooperation in exposing the scheme, Lockhart was allowed to plead guilty to a misdemeanor charge for receiving stolen property. She agreed to cooperate in any further prosecution of Hamilton and Scott, and be responsible for $4,000 in restitution to City National Bank should Hamilton fail in her own repayment. She was sentenced to three years' probation.

Pressure was intensified on Kenneth Scott when he was hit with additional felony charges of computer access and fraud: during a search of the tarnished officer's home in Carson, detectives Rodriguez and Linehan found evidence that Scott had conducted unauthorized DMV and criminal history searches on Cindy Lockhart from his home computer, utilizing California Department of Justice databases restricted solely for law enforcement investigations. "It's not appropriate to use them to check up on your girlfriend," prosecutor Elizabeth Munisoglu told me at the time. After much wrangling, just ten days before his case was set to go to trial, Scott pled no contest to one felony privacy invasion charge and a misdemeanor charge of receiving stolen property. He was given three years' probation and six days in jail, for which he was credited for having been incarcerated for that length while his bail was raised. At the end of his sentencing appearance, Scott walked out of the Airport Courthouse a free man.

The D.A.'s office was satisfied with the outcome "Any civilian who had the same charges would probably get the same deal," said Munisoglu. "All he did was steal, and he stole from a thief."

And along with his legal fees, all it cost Scott was his badge.

THE COOL BREEZE BURGLAR

Shortly after noon two days before Christmas—Monday, December 23, 1996—Officer Russell Sharp was on patrol, guiding his motorcycle unit along Wilshire Boulevard at the city's eastern border, a few blocks past Robertson Boulevard. As he neared the office building at the corner of Hamel Drive at 8693 Wilshire, he spied a man frantically flagging him down. Sharp pulled over to the curb to investigate, and the man dashed toward him with an urgent plea.

"Officer, please stop that man!"

He pointed to a sizable, portly figure in work coveralls trotting, as fast as he could, down the street in the opposite direction. The heavyset man seemed to be discarding objects as he sought cover.

The assistant building manager of the office building explained that the fleeing figure had just looted several valuables from the various offices inside. "It's him, from the paper," the manager said matter-of-factly. "It's the Cool Breeze Burglar."

Who? Sharp thought.

I was at my desk at the *Beverly Hills Courier* during the first full week of November when the receptionist transferred a call from Lt. Jimmy Smith, the white-maned veteran of the detective division who also occasionally filled in as the force's press liaison. Smith had a request: Beverly Hills was experiencing a rash of commercial burglaries throughout the city, marked by an unusually specific *modus operandi*, and he asked if I could put word out in the newspaper to place the community on guard—particularly the legions of office workers that ballooned the local population during business hours. The burglar was growing increasingly bold, striking at least three times in the past two months—and twice in the last week.

Smith detailed the burglar's signature ploy: he would typically arrive at small local offices during regular hours, wearing a blue, slightly dirty coverall-style work uniform—minus any distinguishing logo—and a heavy toolbelt laden with equipment, a large flashlight in his hand. Despite a scruffy appearance, he was genial and charming as he explained building management sent him to inspect or service the air conditioning system. He'd frequently time his visits immediately after heavy rainfall, telling the occupants he was there "to check for leaks."

Once allowed inside and left to his own devices, he poked around temperature controls and eyeballed air vents, fading into the background as the office workers returned to their duties. But for the duration of his visit, the workman covertly prowled well-stocked hunting grounds, surreptitiously lifting cash, wallets and other valuables out of desktops, drawers, and unattended purses—sometimes taking entire handbags. On occasion, he'd even make off with office equipment, computers, and other high-tech hardware, though the detectives were baffled as to exactly how he slipped the devices out unnoticed.

The burglar's stealthy knack for evading detection was belied by his outward appearance. As Smith described, you franklycouldn't miss him: a white male in his thirties, between six-foot-three and six-foot-six, weighing about 300 pounds or more. He was sometimes bearded, sometimes not, with a gap between his front teeth. His hands, witnesses noted, were dotted with small cuts and scabs.

This was the grungy 1990s' heir apparent to Beverly Hills's suave, polished master cat burglar Gerard Graham Dennis?

Given the suspect's imposing bulk, Smith cautioned anyone encountering him to avoid confrontation—affability might merely be part of his masquerade. Instead, the detective advised employees encountering surprise inspections or otherwise unscheduled air conditioning maintenance visits to ask for identification and contact the building management for confirmation. And take the usual sensible precautions: keep the stuff you don't want to be swiped out of sight or locked away.

I was happy to oblige Smith—himself a walking iteration of "affable"—and wrote an item for publication. But as was my self-amusing custom, I just needed to concoct a catchy nickname for this latest local criminal mastermind. I'd coined snarky sobriquets for a rogues gallery of local lawbreakers who committed crimes with a certain flair—the Big Spender Bandit, the Ersatz Record Exec, the Silver-Haired Devil, and more—and the readership seemed to enjoy them. For this similarly noteworthy malefactor, I mulled over the air conditioning angle and his version of Gerry Dennis's vanishing act. Like an ill wind…he blows in and blows back out…

The Cool Breeze Burglar. You're welcome, Beverly Hills.

After the story ran, the Cool Breeze Burglar resurfaced in the city a few weeks later, playing out his familiar charade on Wednesday, November 27, perhaps assuming, in people's preoccupation with Thanksgiving plans the following day, they'd be especially likely to overlook his light-fingered touch. Around 11 a.m., clad in workman-style blue jeans and red flannel shirt, he entered a fourth-floor dentist's office in an office building on Wilshire Boulevard and amiably delivered his "inspection" spiel. But the dentist's receptionist was dubious: the office had recently undergone a major remodel, and an array of legitimate inspectors swept in and out over the past several weeks. Something about this new arrival read wrong to her.

Still, she allowed him to survey the air conditioning system while keeping a close eye on him. He spent about five minutes going through the motions, inspecting ducts and vents with his flashlight, assessing distances with a tape measure, and moving from room to room before finally informing her he was stepping out and would be right back.

And then he was gone with the wind, never to return.

After talking to the receptionist, the dentist, too, sensed something hinky had gone down. Assured by building management there were no inspections scheduled for the day, the dentist scoured his office and discovered that his wallet—left unattended during Cool Breeze's tour—had been relieved of missing the cash and credit cards it had contained. The con artist had still managed to score a brisk windfall to kick off his holiday shopping season.

"'Cool Breeze Burglar' Blows Back into Beverly Hills," proclaimed the headline in the *Courier*.

Just short of a month later, Officer Russell Sharp ran down the tall, corpulent fugitive on the street, wrestling him to the ground as he tried in vain to scale a wall and escape, all while tossing away various items on his person—items that later revealed to be the personal property of employees at the office building he'd just swept through. Soon enough, Sharp had his suspect handcuffed and in custody.

Sharp also got clarity as to what, exactly, a "Cool Breeze Burglar" was. The vigilant manager had read my *Courier* stories about Beverly Hills's latest number one public enemy, and when a man so distinctively matching the newspaper's description showed up for a "surprise inspection," he discreetly kept tabs on the suspicious workman exploring the office of a CPA tenant and, when Cool Breeze finally exited, tailed him outside, flagging down the first police officer he saw.

"BHPD Sticks 'Cool Breeze' In Deep Freeze," read the final *Courier* headline.

Detectives suspected the burglar was responsible for at least twenty commercial burglaries across Los Angeles's Westside. Ultimately, thirty-nine-year-old Robert Drew Greenwood was charged with six individual crimes occurring between February and December, including raids on a Beverly Hills physician and a local investment management company, a Westwood entertainment law firm, and the Century City office of the Swiss private banking firm Bank Julius Baer; he also faced a charge of receiving stolen property, a swiped Discover Card. Greenwood pled guilty to one count of second-degree burglary and was sentenced to three years in prison.

There was, in the end, an "only-in-Beverly Hills" twist to the otherwise routine tale: the detectives informed me that Cool Breeze was employed as a prop master at the legendary 20th Century Fox Studios, a quick drive down Pico Boulevard from Beverly Hills, overseeing the acquisition, use, fabrication, and placement of the various items during the production of films and television shows. As it was explained to me, outfitting himself with items gathered from the props department like the flashlight and tool belt gear to make his ruse more convincing, Greenwood would slip away from the studio lot during lunch hours and lengthy production breaks, drive to Beverly Hills and other nearby neighborhoods with concentrations of office buildings ripe for the plucking, then nonchalantly return to work after the day's plundering—a literal side hustle.

The only thing more surprising to me was the unexpected revelation that, due to the role of my reporting in his capture, the police department had decided to credit *me* with the arrest of the Cool Breeze Burglar (informally, I assumed—especially since the lion's share of credit belonged with the brave, quick-acting assistant building manager, whose name was never made public).

Ultimately, BHPD got the prop man, and I got the props.

Beverly Hills was my professional home base for some time, and even as my career path shifted toward the more nebulous geography of Hollywood—the industry, not the neighborhood—I still spend many hours working within 90210, usually interviewing movie and TV actors and creators in luxury hotel suites and only occasionally visiting courtrooms. But as I reflect on my experiences there, the instincts of my three-decades-ago self were pretty accurate right from the start.

Interesting? Always.

Hilarious? Frequently.

Bonkers? Endlessly.

Yet, every day is just another day in Beverly Hills.

GIRL, INTERRUPTED

"It wasn't like the crime of the century!"

—Winona Ryder

I'd previously sat in Judge Elden S. Fox's courtroom at the Beverly Hills Superior Court on a handful of occasions, covering various legal proceedings for the *Beverly Hills Courier* newspaper during the years that I'd worked there, and the most memorable thing about it—and the courthouse overall—was that, unlike just about every other building and business within the city limits, there was no lacquered sheen or filigreed flourishes that distinguished it as "Beverly Hills." It looked as unremarkable as any other courtroom in any other courthouse in any other jurisdiction in America.

But with a quick scan of the room on October 28, 2002, I could see that this would be a trial markedly different from anything I'd ever reported on before.

It was the opening day of legal arguments following two brisk days of jury selection, my first day covering the trial since preliminary hearings that summer. On the bench was Judge Fox, who was no stranger to headlines. As a former deputy district attorney, he'd practically specialized in high-profile felonies involving notorious defendants, including Steven Livaditis, the holdup man whose day-long standoff at Van Cleef & Arpels left three hostages dead, and Cathy Smith, the Canadian backup singer/part-time drug dealer convicted of administering the lethal narcotic cocktail that ended the life of comic superstar John Belushi, as well as celebrity-centric cases featuring Zsa Zsa Gabor, Harry Nilsson and Axl Rose. As a judge, he typically struck a genial tone but drew firm lines when his patience was tried, often presiding over legal skirmishes involving late-night mayhem committed by young stars *Beverly Hills 90210* actress Shannen Doherty and Motley Crüe drummer Tommy Lee clubbing around West Hollywood. Even so, Fox was still the *least* unusual presence in the court.

Seated in the back row of the jury box was Peter Guber, the movie producer-turned-studio executive who I knew of – along with his towering reputation in Hollywood as a pop hitmaker who could also craft compelling Oscar bait – from his involvement as the crime victim of his ex-chauffer who'd tried to pass off the rare Picasso sketch purloined from the movie mogul. Guber's presence weighing the fate of the particular defendant on trial defined it, by Hollywood standards, as a jury of one's peers.

Seated a few chairs away from me in the courtroom gallery was former Assistant District Attorney Marcia Clark, of the ubiquitously televised, relentlessly scrutinized, and ultimately unsuccessful prosecution of O.J. Simpson, tried for the murder of his wife Nicole Brown Simpson and restaurant server Ronald Goldman. Clark was simply a media spectator at this trial: seven years earlier, she'd resigned from the D.A.'s office, was highly compensated for writing her bestselling memoir *Without a Doubt*, and had embarked on a second act as a television commentator/correspondent specializing in celebrity crime. Covering this trial for *Entertainment Tonight*, Clark would frequently sit alongside the Associated Press's veteran criminal trial reporter Linda Deutsch, who'd covered a plethora of historic court proceedings, including the trials of Simpson, cult leader Charles Manson, Robert F. Kennedy's assassin Sirhan Sirhan, heiress-turned-hostage-turned-domestic terrorist Patty Hearst, serial killer Richard Ramirez and the parricidal Beverly Hills brothers Lyle and Eric Menendez.

At the head of the defense table sat another face familiar to ardent TV trial-watchers (the Simpson case had, along with a 24/7 cable news cycle, ushered in an era of ratings-grabbing live trial coverage): the tall, brush-mustached, power-suited criminal defense attorney Mark Geragos. The L.A. born-and-bred Loyola Law School graduate was the son of Paul Geragos, a legendarily hard-driving homicide prosecutor in the D.A.'s office—the younger Geragos felt that from a young age, "it was as if I was programmed to be a lawyer." But he found himself temperamentally unsuited to pursuing convictions, drawn instead to defending those he deemed "underdogs" facing overwhelming odds, their guilt or innocence irrelevant to vigorous advocacy, a quality he attributed to his Armenian heritage (indeed, cases involving survivors of the Armenian Genocide became a specialty). He'd entered the modern pantheon of celebrity legal counsel, renowned for skillfully navigating the treacherous tides of public scandal both in and out of the courtroom. His prominence rose from his role in one of the most intensely dissected legal dramas of the 1990s, the "Whitewater" trail of

President Bill Clinton's former business partner Susan McDougal. While McDougal achieved various acquittals, she was convicted of fraud but ultimately pardoned by Clinton, due in no small part to Geragos's efforts. He also prevailed in McDougal's subsequent trial for allegedly embezzling from her former employer, actress Nancy Kovack Mehta, wife of conductor Zubin Mehta.

As a result, forty-five-year-old Geragos—the principal of the L.A.-based law firm Geragos & Geragos, initially founded by his father—developed a highly visible sideline as a prolific legal expert/talking head on TV—most visibly, CNN's *The Larry King Show* where he regularly bantered with the host while offering perspectives on the nation's courtroom preoccupations of the moment. Thanks to those telegenic sound bites and his comfort around artistic personalities cultivated when, as a law school sideline, he booked ascending bands like the B-52s, X, and Oingo Boingo in a Pasadena music venue, he'd graduate to defending rich and famous clients in court, including earning a wrist-slapping sentence for West Coast rapper Nathaniel "Nate Dogg" Hale on gun charges.

Finally, there was the person in the room who inextricably drew every eye to her: Geragos's client, the world-famous, two-time Academy Award–nominated actress, and Gen X icon Winona Ryder. With her stylishly short hair pulled back in a broad black headband, thick silver bangles circling her wrist, and clad in a chic short-sleeved, knee-length black designer dress with bright pink flowers elaborately embroidered on Peter Pan collar wings, she looked more ready for a high-fashion photo shoot than her reckoning in court. At five foot three inches and just five days shy of her thirty-first birthday, she was famously petite and delicately pixyish, yet simultaneously larger than life.

It'd been over five years since I left my staff position at the *Beverly Hills Courier* newspaper, where it wasn't unusual to encounter famous faces who lived, shopped, and dined locally on a regular basis. I'd been covering the entertainment industry full time for over a year, both on staff at Hollywood.com—one of the earliest websites to gain regular access to A-list talent (within just a few days on the job, I found myself interviewing top stars like Tom Cruise, Michael Douglas, and Halle Berry) and as a freelancer for national magazines and regional publications. I'd encountered more than my share of celebrities.

But Winona Ryder was something unique indeed: a star roughly the same age as me who I'd seen grow up on screen while I did in real time, maturing with a signature blend of winsome charm, world-weary cynicism, and porcelain-white-on-obsidian-black beauty. She swiftly evolved from an ingenue who popped off the screen in early films like *Beetlejuice* and *Heathers* to an appealing, box office-generating poster girl for our shared demographic in *Edward Scissorhands, Bram Stoker's Dracula*, and *Reality Bites* to full-blown superstardom as an accomplished, twice-Oscar-nominated actress following turns in challenging fare like *Little Women, The Age of Innocence*, and *Girl, Interrupted.* All the while every twist and turn of her romantic life with real, reported, and rumored paramours—most notably, Johnny Depp—would be chronicled breathlessly in the pages of then red-hot celebrity-centric magazines like *Us Weekly* and my soon-to-be freelance client, *People Magazine*.

Though her meteoric career had cooled by a degree or two, she'd remained firmly at the apex of Hollywood for a remarkable fifteen years and counting, commanding as much as $5 million per film, up to the very incident that had led her to court. That, too, marked Ryder as unique in my experience: I'd never personally witnessed a star occupying such a great height on the brink of such a potentially calamitous fall.

Taking in the courtroom room and its assembly of occupants, all firmly at the crossroads of the entertainment industry and the criminal justice system, I was reminded of a thought I'd had often over the years: *all the glitz and glamour aside, Beverly Hills wat one* damn *small town.*

When Winona Ryder walked into Beverly Hills's Saks Fifth Avenue department store a year earlier, around 4 p.m. on December 12, 2001, she did not cut quite the same fashionable figure she would in court, though she toted an armload of bags from high-end retailers that implied her discerning taste for luxurious couture.

The Saks Fifth Avenue located at 9600 Wilshire Boulevard, just a couple of blocks west of Rodeo Drive, had been a shopping institution in Beverly Hills ever since the ritzy New York City retailer opened its West Coast flagship operation there in 1938. Saks would be joined there throughout the years by various neighbors, including I. Magnin, Neiman-Marcus and Barney's New York, firmly establishing the corridor on Wilshire as "Department Store Row." The elegant exterior was rendered in sleek, stately Streamline Moderne lines and curves by father-and-son architects Jon and Donald Parkinson, its glamorously grand interiors conceived to reflect a private estate aesthetic by the visionary Black architect Paul Revere

Williams, who gracefully curated each department's color, shape and style to reflect the mood of the merchandise on display within.

Through a significant expansion in 1940, various subtler modernizations and makeovers, and the 1995 acquisition of the adjacent I. Magnin building to serve as a freestanding menswear store—Saks would play host to countless celebrity customers, none more famously than Marilyn Monroe. Monroe, who also modeled for Saks early in her career, was a regular habitue with a particular penchant for the bright, playful designs made exclusively for the store by Emilio Pucci (she was even buried in a Pucci dress)—today her signed Saks sales receipts sell at auction for thousands. Over the decades, as department store fortunes rose and fell, the Beverly Hills berth consistently ranked among the chain's top three highest-performing outlets.

That day, with mussed hair a shade lighter than usual and minimal makeup, Ryder appeared effortlessly beautiful, though her outfit, while pricey, decidedly downplayed her allure. Dressed in a bulky three-quarter-length cashmere coat, a thick white sweater over a dark top, and a long black skirt with its hem dangling just above her chunky-heeled shoes, she struggled with an overload of constantly shifting baggage—a long, heavy garment bag, a large Neiman-Marcus shopping bag, an oversized Oilily tote that doubled as a purse, and—after the purchase of a pair of $275 Gucci shoes within the department store—a red Saks shopping bag.

As she wandered a circuitous route through Saks's first floor, something about the way the diminutive shopper constantly wrestled and fidgeted with her armload of bags as she inspected item after item appeared *off*— enough to catch the attention of the store's in-house security team; enough that her movements were soon being tracked by the department store's closed circuit security cameras. When loss prevention manager Kenneth Evans was called to monitor Ryder's movements at around 4:17 p.m., the never-especially-starstruck employee didn't recognize the glammed-down actress—indeed, he first thought she was a disheveled homeless woman who'd wandered in off the street—but he did recognize a pattern of behavior he'd become familiar with during a career in retail security. The woman, Evans suspected, was prowling for a five-finger discount.

Ryder had violated a cardinal rule of her profession: always know when a camera is on you. For about eighty minutes, security kept a close electronic eye on her, toggling between forty surveillance cameras and zooming in to better scrutinize her actions. She tried on several hats, finally perching a black fedora with an upturned brim on her head, price tag dangling down. After casually applying lipstick, she cruised the Donna Karan section to consider a selection of socks, which disappeared amid her ever-shifting bundle of bags. In the Gucci section, she admired an elegant white slip dress with a fringed hem before removing it from its hanger and draping it over her arm atop the garment bag—the dress, too, would soon vanish.

That prompted Evans to summon another security officer to observe any further penchant for prestidigitation up close. As Ryder ventured into a spacious second-floor fitting room—conveniently absent of any video surveillance, guaranteeing customer privacy and propriety—she was subtly shadowed by twenty-eight-year-old Colleen Rainey, the store's lead asset protection agent for the past year following an internship with the Bureau of Alcohol, Tobacco, and Firearms. Though she, too, initially suspected that her target might be a transient due to her disheveled appearance, Rainey quickly had an inkling that the pint-sized woman she was surveilling just might be *Winona Ryder, movie star.*

Peering through the wooden slats on the door of the fitting room and shrewdly using the mirror hanging within to observe the woman from more obscured angles, Rainey watched Ryder kneel on the floor and arrange a staggering array of merchandise secreted within her bags and about her person before of her. Using a pair of orange-handled scissors stashed in her Oilily tote, Ryder cut away the Sensormatic security tags—which sound alerts exiting the store unless removed by salesclerks—from a pair of designer handbags, then struggled in vain to free more tags from a white Calvin Klein clutch and an aqua Marc Jacobs bag. Suddenly, the actress was bleeding—it appeared she'd accidentally sliced her finger with the scissors, staining the clutch with her blood. Abandoning both purses and a pink Donna Karan blouse, Ryder instead wrapped an assortment of socks and a selection of pricey hair accessories in tissue paper produced from the deep Neiman-Marcus bag, crafting the illusion each had been packaged with the same care and attention as a purchased item, all the while sucking her finger to staunch the blood flow.

Ryder emerged into the designer sportswear section—back on camera—wrangling her precarious jumble of bags, the black hat she donned now no longer visible. Approaching sales associate Shirley Warren, she revealed her wounded digit and asked—nervously, Warren noted—for an adhesive bandage to stanch the blood flow. Band-Aids were something Saks

Fifth Avenue didn't mind giving away for free to its clientele, nor were complimentary Coca-Colas, and Warren delivered both to the actress.

After more meandering through the store, Ryder asked sales associate Sophie Seyranian to escort her to a specific dressing room on the third floor, larger and more private than the one she'd just occupied—then sent the clerk off to fetch another Coke. After several minutes, the actress emerged to offer her credit card to Seyranian, purchasing a brown leather Dolce & Gabbana bomber jacket and two Yves St. Laurent blouses.

Asset protection manager Evans had continually resisted the urge to order his personnel to interrupt the petite woman's apparent spree, preferring to offer latitude for a sudden crisis of conscience that would prompt her to pay for the hidden horde before crossing a line of no return. But just after 5:30 p.m. as Ryder returned to the first floor, still shuffling and reshuffling now-bulkier bags, she walked directly past three cash registers and strode confidently through the double doors of the store's south entrance into the parking lot. But before making it back to her getaway car—a 1999 Mercedes Benz S Series—she was intercepted by Rainey and two beefy security guards, who blocked her escape and confronted her about the merchandise she'd stashed away. Ryder was cooperative and pleasant—friendly, even—but dismayed. "Didn't my assistant pay for it?" she asked, appearing perplexed and apologetic. Having observed her for the better part of an hour and a half, security knew she'd entered the store alone, no personal assistant anywhere to be seen. It was one of the few instances in which Winona Ryder had failed to give a convincing performance.

It was time to improvise.

"I was told that I should shoplift," a penitent Ryder offered, after shaking Ken Evans's hand while she was being detained in Saks Fifth Avenue's security room, he'd recall. Her foray into light-fingered larceny was, she explained, committed in pursuit of a role as a kleptomaniac in the film *Shopgirl*, based on the seriocomic novella published by actor-comedian Steve Martin a year earlier and set at the Neiman-Marcus outpost a block and a half away. It was an exercise to attain real-world experience, to better delve into the part's psychology. "The director said I should try it out. I should have notified the store I was going to shoplift, and I'm sorry."

She only wanted to steal *scenes*.

If her claim were true, the actress had gone fully Method in pursuit of authenticity. The security team retrieved a staggering array of top-dollar merchandise from Ryder's omnipresent bags: a $760 Marc Jacobs waffle knit cashmere thermal top; a $540 Natori handbag; two $55 black beaded Pierre Ubach purses; a $525 black leather Dolce & Gabbana handbag; a $795 white Calvin Klein clutch (now stained with her blood); a $225 hat and a $350 beret, both by Eric Javitz; a $750 Yves St. Laurent blouse; a $140 black velvet hairband, a $120 black rhinestone ponytail holder and a $220 matching black rhinestone bow and hair clip combo, all from hair designer Frederick Fekkai; an $80 pair of Donna Karan cashmere blended socks; an additional $20 pair of brown Donna Karan socks, two pairs of $38 cream Saks socks; and three pairs of Calvin Klein socks, two in gray, one in purple, at $16.50 each.

And security had yet to include the $1,595 white Gucci slip dress, stashed away in Ryder's garment bag, because they initially believed it belonged to her: she told them she'd previously purchased it at the Maxwell boutique, despite a lack of receipt—only later did a review of the tape reveal the slip dress had been removed from a Saks display. While she'd paid roughly $3,700 for four items—the Gucci shoes, two blouses, and the bomber jacket—more than twenty others were discovered stashed away. Three of the recovered items—the Marc Jacobs thermal, the YSL blouse, and the Gucci clutch—were now in unsaleable condition, the former two damaged when the actress scissored off the sensor tags, the latter stained with Ryder's blood. The pilfered merchandise totaled $5,560.

This latest, only mildly plausible, yet still illegal, explanation instantly invalidated the initial suggestion that the actress's non-present personal assistant had been tasked with paying for the items, as well as any notion that Ryder availed herself of the Saks' Fifth Avenue Club's personal shopping services available to its elite clientele for an annual fee, which would've allowed her to take merchandise from the store without paying for it upfront as long as she signed a "borrow book" accepting responsibility. What her claim of shoplifting-as-research was, however—paired with the fact that she'd put a portion of the couture on her credit card while secretly in possession of additional items—was an admission of culpability.

During the roughly ninety minutes that Ryder was detained in the security room, the loss prevention team had to make a critical decision: whether to summon the police to arrest her. Once Ryder's very public-facing identity became apparent, the incident was fraught with concerns regarding the publicity that might ensue; Evans contacted Saks's corporate office to weigh in. It wouldn't be the first time a Beverly Hills business had let a notable offender off the hook with little more than a warning and possibly a ban from the premises. But there was the additional matter of what Saks security had *also* discovered within the actress's purse: a bottle of liquid Demoral, a potent, potentially addictive opioid typically used to manage acute short-term pain; a bottle of liquid Diazepam, another potentially habit-forming medication used to treat severe anxiety and control neurological disorders; and a syringe. Neither bottle held a prescription label, something Ryder explained away, saying she'd intentionally disposed of anything featuring her famous name and personal information, lest they fall into unwanted hands.

Ryder was presented with a pair of civil demand notices listing an inventory of the stolen merchandise and a line stating "I, Winona Ryder, agree that I have stolen these items," which witnesses later affirmed Ryder signed without protest.

With the corporate green light—company policy in California dictated that police be called if the property loss exceeded $950, marking the theft as a felony, rather than misdemeanor shoplifting—Evans alerted the Beverly Hills Police Department. Before officers arrived, the store's asset protection team snapped Polaroids of their detainee, as was procedure whenever a shoplifter was apprehended on the premises. Still putting on a cooperative face even as the magnitude of her situation grew ever more apparent, Ryder offered a slight smile.

It was around 7 p.m. when police arrived at Saks Fifth Avenue. Patrol officer Mark Parker was a twenty-year veteran of the force who, earlier in the year had made an unplanned cameo appearance on the MTV docuseries *The Osbournes*, albeit with his features digitally pixilated. As a watch officer, he responded when Ozzy and Sharon Osbourne and their frequently-bleeped brood feuded with their noisy neighbors on posh Doheny Road, launching various items—including a cooked ham—into the next-door mansion's yard; Parker and his partner defused the situation and no charges were filed by either party, even as prime reality TV was made.

Detective George Elwell, the son of a retired veteran Los Angeles County Sheriff's Department deputy and husband to one of BHPD's dispatchers, had joined the department a dozen years earlier and previously served on the undercover crime suppression unit, patrolling the city in an unmarked car seeking to interrupt crimes and traffic offenses in progress.

I had first met Elwell in the mid-'90s when I accompanied the detail's sergeant on a lengthy ride-along, convening with the entire team in the field at one point. The second time I encountered Elwell, a few months later, was more memorable—at least for me: I was walking back to the parking lot of the *Beverly Hills Courier*'s Olympic Boulevard offices after a late dinner across the street with my editor Mia Kaczinski Dunn following a long night closing the next day's edition. Suddenly a car raced into to the alleyway between Clark and Swall Drives and screeched to a stop in front of us. The car window was unrolled and a stern-looking face with a chevron mustache looked back at me, asking, *"You're that reporter, aren't you?"* As I attempted to shield Mia by stepping in front of her—in vain, as she'd already bolted away to a less vulnerable space—I had a split-second to wonder who I might have pissed off with something I wrote and exactly how serious the consequences were about to be. But the driver—who I hadn't immediately recognized as Elwell, dressed down in plainclothes—explained who he was; he was looking for a suspect who'd just mugged someone in the vicinity. Had I seen anybody run by? I hadn't, and he sped away in search of his quarry, leaving me and my freshly spiked heart rate behind.

Upon Elwell and Parker's arrival and after a pat-down by Rainey, Ryder kept up her accommodating demeanor but grew visibly more nervous as the investigation accelerated. No one found reason to suspect she was under the influence of drugs or alcohol. While Parker reviewed the store's paperwork to determine if the circumstances merited Ryder's arrest, he heard her reiterating that she'd only shoplifted at the behest of a director, this time for a film adaptation of author James Ellroy's searing *White Jazz*, the capstone in his acclaimed "L.A. Quartet" series of crime noir novels including *L.A. Confidential*, made into an Academy Award–nominated film four years prior. Both *Shopgirl* and *White Jazz* were indeed in active development and considered hot properties, but the actress didn't offer further details that would allow the detectives to verify her claim. Neither book features shoplifting as a critical element of their storylines, certainly not by any character potentially portrayed by a star of Ryder's stature.

Parker was told Ryder had offered to pay the hefty balance for the swag; she said she understood that in the months immediately following the terrorist attacks of September 11, 2001, "the economy was in such bad shape." She was placed under arrest—given that she'd conceded, verbally and in writing, that she'd taken the items, a reading of her Miranda rights was not legally required—and the detectives took possession of the evidence, medication, and closed-circuit videotapes. Parker asked Ryder if she was carrying any concealed weapons, and she told him about the scissors in her pocket, which were confiscated. She permitted the detectives to search her Mercedes, which revealed no additional stolen items, and she was allowed to retain everything determined to be her personal property: her purchases and the garment bag (still containing the white Gucci dress, which had not yet been recognized as having been stolen).

Ryder was taken into custody and ferried to police headquarters, where—after a strip search by a female officer—she was guided through the booking process. Along with the controlled medications already discovered, a search of her purse at the station produced equally curious results: a small bottle of Aleve, the over-the-counter painkiller which Ryder said had been given to her by her physician. But when the detectives examined the bottle, they found forty white tablets stamped "VP," later identified as the opioid Vicoprofen; two white caplets marked "Watson 187," recognized as Vicodin; a small yellow caplet marked as "Kadian," a morphine sulfate used to manage severe, sustained pain; and a single yellow tablet labeled "Endo 610," or Percodan, also used for relief of severe pain. Ryder's purse also contained a yellow plastic pill box filled with six blue tablets of Valium, a brand name for Diazepam, and two white tablets identified as Endocet, a generic brand of Percoset, another opioid-based pain reliever. There was no apparent documentation that any of the drugs had been prescribed to her.

Already facing second-degree burglary, grand theft, and vandalism charges, the latest discovery further compounded Ryder's legal jeopardy by adding possession of a controlled substance—if convicted on all charges, she was looking at as many as three years and eight months in prison.

After she spent nearly four hours kept in an interrogation room rather than one of the jail cells, Ryder's attorney Geragos arrived and posted the $20,000 bail at 11:40 p.m., spiriting her back to the Los Angeles area residence she'd purchased from songwriter Bernie Taupin in 1998 for $2.6 million. The secluded Spanish villa, built in 1936, occupied a third of an acre, hidden behind a thick hedge of ficus trees and canopies of bougainvillea and wisteria, its interiors appointed with tastefully romantic décor selected by her close friend and frequent premiere escort Kevin Haley, an actor and interior designer whose aesthetic sense mirrored her own. Nestled north of the Sunset Strip at 1320 Doheny Drive, her property stood about five miles from the Beverly Hills police station, just outside of the city limits.

A year after purchasing the home, Ryder produced and starred in the 1999 film *Girl, Interrupted*, based on author Susanna Kaysen's bestselling memoir chronicling the aftermath of her emotional breakdown and suicide attempt at age eighteen. Emotionally raw and fragile, Kaysen was institutionalized against her will in a 1960s-era psychiatric hospital for borderline personality disorder. The movie adaptation offered career-boosting showcases for rising stars Angelina Jolie and Brittany Murphy—Jolie won the coveted trifecta of Hollywood trophies, an Academy Award, a Golden Globe, and a Screen Actors Guild Award, in the Supporting Actress Category for her turn—while Ryder, who after acquiring the rights championed the film version through a lengthy development hell, calling it "a child of my heart," garnered much acclaim for her authentic portrayal of Kaysen. Indeed, the actress held a profound identification with the sardonic but sensitive Susanna, who struggled with her very real demons and would "hurt yourself on the outside to try to kill the thing on the inside," but questioned if she was truly mentally ill.

"Have you ever confused a dream with life? Or stolen something when you have the cash? Have you ever been blue? Or thought your train was moving while sitting still?" Ryder, as Susanna, mused in a voiceover narration. "Maybe I was just crazy. Maybe it was the '60s. Or maybe I was just a girl…interrupted."

As the rest of the world would discover in a few short hours, Winona Ryder was about to experience her own moment of interruption.

As news of Ryder's arrest spread around the globe like wildfire the following day—as it inevitably would, particularly in the celebrity-crime-obsessed culture that prevailed in the wake of the O.J. Simpson murder trial—one question was commonplace: how did she go from her perch at the absolute pinnacle of Hollywood stardom to a police holding room in Beverly Hills?

Ryder had first revealed her shoplifting bona fides during a 1997 interview with *Buzz* magazine: as a tween freshly relocated with her family to the quiet, picturesque, and, in her view, somewhat staid town of Petaluma in Northern California's Sonoma County in the early 1980s, Winona Laura Horowitz swiped a comic book from a local retailer in an act of youthful rebellion. Her pilfering skills were not sufficiently advanced that the crime went unnoticed. Immediately detained, placed under citizen's arrest and handcuffed, she was delivered in the back seat of a police car to her parents, whom she'd suspected had their own colorful history with cops given their long involvement in protest movements. The anecdote's kicker: "The police brought me home, and my parents tried to beat them up."

While the story may be embellished, it reveals a hearty distrust for authority baked in Ryder's very DNA, with intellectual, artsy beatnik parents who were *deeply* embedded in the counterculture of their era: mother Cynthia Palmer, a writer, video producer and *avant-garde* video artist, and father Michael D. Horowitz, an author, editor, publisher and antiquarian bookseller. Michael also worked as an archivist for Harvard psychologist and trippy icon Timothy Leary, notoriously deemed "the most dangerous man in America" by no less an establishment figurehead than Richard M. Nixon for Leary's tireless and showy advocation of the mind-expanding potential of the psychedelic drug LSD, and coiner of the famous term "tune in, turn on and drop out." Leary was so dear to the couple that he was named godfather to their first child together, Winona, and was a constant, much-admired presence in her life. Throughout her life, she'd frequently return to another oft-quoted motto of Leary's: "Question authority."

The Horowitz-Palmer clan was unconventional in all respects, creative, and free-spirited. Michael had Russian-Romanian-Jewish heritage but was predominately atheist in practice, while Cindy was a Buddhist. Their family, which included Cindy's son Jubal and daughter Sunyata from a prior marriage, led an informal, vagabond existence, regularly uprooting and pursuing an adventurous, alternative existence. Neither was overly concerned with formalizing their union until Winona, their first child together, was born on October 29, 1971, during a stint living on a farm in Winona, Minnesota. In a bit of kismet, the town served as her namesake—"Winona" meant "first-born daughter in the language of the native Dakota tribe—and her middle name was chosen in tribute to their friend, writer, and lecturer Laura Huxley, the wife of author/philosopher Aldous Huxley, another towering bohemian idol. Even the very birth of Winona—"Noni," affectionately, to her family—was unorthodox: as an adult, she'd laughingly call herself "a shoelace baby," arriving in such a remote location, far from medical facilities, that her panicked father sterilized a shoelace in boiling water to tie off the umbilical cord.

The family—expanded again by the addition of Winona's younger brother Uri—gained prominence in fringe culture and antiestablishment circles. Exposure to artistic accomplishment and radical characters was routine: along with Leary and the Huxleys, their circle included high-minded mavericks like Beat poets Allen Ginsberg and Lawrence Ferlinghetti and sci-fi author and Scientology founder Philip K. Dick. In 1978, after a quasi-mysterious stint living with revolutionaries in Chile, they settled in tiny

Elk in California's Mendocino County for three years, sharing an isolated, redwood-dotted 300-acre property with several other families in the commune Rainbow, with next to no electricity, running water, heat or other common amenities. The environment, Ryder later insisted, was far more co-op than cult. "It wasn't as hippie-do as it sounds. It was more like a weird suburb, with a bunch of houses on a chunk of land," she explained. Years later, though, she would concede to *LIFE*, "Everyone grew their own everything. If you know what I mean," and reflected on witnessing adults experiencing "terrifying" bad acid trips as a child.

Literature formed voracious young reader Winona's foundational window into a world she lived largely apart from; her mother, a university projectionist, would also screen classic and art films for friends and family on a sheet hanging in an old barn. What books and films couldn't quite satisfy, her rich imagination would, turning outdoor playtime into performances that transfixed the other children—and, frequently, the adults, suggesting to her parents that their daughter would one day make a tremendous "teller of tales."

But by the time of the family's move to Petaluma—where Michael and Cindy would establish Flashback Books in 1985, dealing in rare, limited, and out-of-print editions centered on the history and culture of psychoactive drugs and other psychedelia—Winona longed for a more conventional existence, with stricter rules and firmly imposed structure, and the tight-knit, picturesque community seemed tailor-made to provide one. Expressing her own distinct rebellious style, she dyed her naturally blonde-brown hair jet-black, sheared boyishly short, and embraced Salvation Army-chic with military jackets and motorcycle boots, an early adopter of the era's emerging punk rock aesthetic, complete with her own skateboarding crew. She returned again and again to the pages of her favorite book, *The Catcher in the Rye*, J.D. Salinger's ode to alienation, which she proclaimed, "my personal bible," finding a kindred spirit in Holden Caulfield and his disdain for superficiality and phoniness; her obsessive reading habits were a mark of her own growing adolescent alienation. "The way I dealt with loneliness was finding books," she'd recall. "They became my friends."

Her avid pop cultural and artistic passions were all-consuming, veering between the vintage and the cutting edge—a seeming incongruity that would eventually define her. She devoured an eclectic menu of literature, music, theater, fashion, and film: in service of her abiding love for the latter, she draped her bedroom windows in black so she could single-mindedly absorb—practically breathe in—movies on TV in her own private screening room, developing an encyclopedic appreciation for actors and filmmakers across the decades. "I used to have this fantasy—there was this old movie theater in Petaluma, where I saw *The Man Who Fell to Earth*, and I used to dream I could live in it," she'd recall. "Just take the seats out, put my bed there, and a bathtub and a bicycle and a refrigerator and my books. And I'd just live there. Actually, it still sounds like an amazing fantasy."

Amid it all, she maintained a perfect grade point, the high standard of academic achievement her parents insisted on and one of the few areas they were unyieldingly strict about. Ironically, where her parents and their contemporaries wholeheartedly evangelized mood-enhancing, mind-expanding substances, she became steadfastly opposed to taking them herself, outside of some expected youthful experimentation.

Petaluma seemed idyllic for providing the normalness she craved—initially. "It was what I wanted, but I had no idea it was going to be horrible," she'd recall. The hippie-dippy family tooling about in the psychedelically painted van they named "Veronica" was viewed with thinly veiled disdain by their conventional new community. Ryder began to suffer first from deep fear and mistrust of her neighbors, then near-crippling bouts of anxiety expressed in an overwhelming terror of being abducted or murdered—not entirely unrealistic, as Northern California was rife with news reports of missing and kidnapped children, as well as unsettling accounts of the Green River Killer, a relentless serial murderer and sex offender targeting girls and women the Pacific Northwest; she fretted that she would become his next victim (Gary Ridgeway, believed responsible for over seventy murders, would not be caught until 2001, just a month before Ryder's own arrest).

At school, her anxieties were compounded by very real torments from fellow students, reflecting their parents' scorn for her family's otherness by targeting her for bullying. She would famously recount one incident in seventh grade in which a swarm of classmates confronted her in the hallway—mistaking her for a diminutive gay boy due to her androgynous appearance—punched her in the stomach, slammed her head into a locker, and "kicked the shit out of me," an assault that fractured her ribs and required six stitches to her head. She'd later claim *she* was asked to leave the school for causing "a distraction."

She proved such a startlingly quick learner during months of homeschooling that, in a bid to stave off her reclusiveness, her parents enrolled their imaginative daughter in youth acting classes at San Francisco's admired

American Conservatory Theater, where she thrived and caught the attention of a Hollywood talent scout, who screen-tested her opposite young River Phoenix. She didn't land that movie role, but an agency signed her at age twelve without even meeting her, even despite her lack of professional credits. Later Ryder would credit her bullies for setting her on her career path, but also reveled in noting how, after her success, a female former classmate—one of the seventh graders who assaulted her—asked her for an autograph in a coffee shop. She reminded the woman of the traumatizing incident: "That kid was me. Go fuck yourself!"

Rechristening herself with the surname Ryder—a hat-tip to rocker Mitch Ryder of the Detroit Wheels, a music favorite—with just a handful of scenes in her 1986 film debut *Lucas* she made a powerful impression, demonstrating a doe-eyed blend of innocence, vulnerability, and wisdom beyond her years—and an undeniable screen magnetism. The off-kilter 1988 supernatural comedy *Beetlejuice* proved a defining experience: not only did the film establish her early persona as a seeming dreary, dearth-obsessed proto-Goth Girl with relatable reservoirs of joy underneath that would resonate with audiences, but it also cemented her creative and personal bond with filmmaker Tim Burton; they would long collaborate on his creepy-quirky post-modern fairytales. The pitch-black 1989 comedy *Heathers*, darkly upending the conventions of teen films, marked Ryder as a real-deal actress with deep range: she ditched her early "ugly duckling" mold to play a pretty, popular high schooler who breaks from a domineering clique of mean girls after falling for edgy outsider Christian Bale; the disruption to the established social pecking order spirals into a quagmire of blackmail, bullying and murder.

Having found three vehicles—an indie darling, a pop blockbuster, and a pitch-black cult comedy—that ideally reflected her own inner multitudes, Winona Ryder forged an onscreen connection with a legion of moviegoers who on one level felt the same way, and on another wished they could be her. By age eighteen, she'd announced herself as a full-fledged movie star, with all the necessary off-screen ingredients as well: the colorful family backstory, enchanting a receptive press with quotable anecdotes from her eccentric upbringing; side-gigs offering an abundance of cool-celeb cachet, like cameoing in and directing MTV music videos and performing a voice role on *The Simpsons*. And she boasted an increasingly admired and emulated personal style: her love of vintage clothing and thrift store finds helped fuel an enduring surge of popularity for second-hand fashion—she'd occasionally wear ten-dollar finds to major red carpets—while her discerning taste in contemporary couture, usually with throwback twists, routinely landed her on best-dressed lists and boosted the fortunes of designers she favored, putting rising couturiers like Badgley Mischka on the map.

Her lively string of romances with a procession of famous actors and rockers reached a crescendo when she fell for Johnny Depp—nine years her senior, similarly great-looking, talented, and, despite a worshipful teen magazine following, possessing grungy, alt/emo edges. They met in June 1989 at the New York premiere of her film *Great Balls of Fire!* at the Ziegfeld Theatre; two months later, they embarked on a whirlwind romance; five months after that, they were engaged—and also headlining Burton's charmingly peculiar and poignant *Edward Scissorhands*. Publicly, they were the ultimate Gen X "It" Couple, complete with a trendy totem, the "Winona Forever" tattoo on Depp's right arm. "He was my first everything. My first real kiss. My first real boyfriend. My first fiancé. The first guy I had sex with. So he'll always be in my heart. Forever... Kind of funny, that word," she'd recall later. They were together four years, until, plagued by relentless drama and location-shoot distance, the relationship collapsed in 1993; Depp notoriously altered his ink to read "Wino Forever" and embarked on another, more tempestuous relationship with supermodel Kate Moss. The entirety of the Depp-Ryder entanglement was heady fuel for breathless headlines documenting every twist and turn, the type of ubiquity that makes already-shining stars explode into blindingly bright superstars.

At the same time, eager to expand her range beyond teen angst and geek dream girl roles, Ryder was elevated into the upper echelons of Hollywood when she earned an Academy Award nomination for Best Supporting Actress following her turn in her as innocent but iron-willed May Welland in filmmaker Martin Scorsese's prestigious Gilded Age romance *The Age of Innocence*, a lavishly detailed, precisely mannered adaptation of Edith Wharton's novel—which Ryder admired, having written a high school book report on it. Another even younger, prodigy-like actress, eleven-year-old Anna Paquin, claimed the Oscar for *The Piano*, though Ryder garnered other trophies, including a Golden Globe. The following year she received a second Oscar nomination in the Best Lead Actress category for her portrayal of Jo March in the film adaptation of Louisa May Alcott's cherished novel *Little Women*, another book precious to Ryder in her youth.

Somehow, Winona Ryder's dreams of living inside the books and movies she loved had become a reality.

As a counterbalance to her increasingly glossy sheen, she demonstrated a heartfelt sense of public spiritedness and philanthropy to causes she felt personally invested in. After the 1993 abduction of twelve-year-old Polly Klaas from her home in Petaluma—a horrific real-world incident mirroring the actress's worst childhood fears—sparked a massive police and volunteer search and an outpouring of compassion across the country, Ryder, deeply empathetic and desperate to help, returned to Petaluma, connected investigators with psychologists and law enforcement specialists who'd recently helped her navigate a disturbing stalker scenario, comforted and supported the terrified family, manned call-in lines, joined search parties, put forth a $200,000 reward for the girl's safe return, and in all respects amplified the case in a way few others could.

Tragically, two months later, the body of the missing girl—who'd dreamed of one day meeting the famous movie star from her hometown—was discovered in a makeshift grave, murdered at the hands of her abductor, Richard Allen Davis. Ryder grieved alongside the Klaas family, turned the premiere of her slacker-culture comedy *Reality Bites* into a benefit for the Polly Klaas Foundation, and would dedicate *Little Women*—based on the book as beloved by Polly as it was by Winona—to her memory.

Despite that heartbreaking conclusion, Ryder continued upward on a seemingly charmed trajectory. She had, essentially, her choice of movie projects and—occasionally, to her representatives' chagrin—even more determinedly picked only those that spoke to her. She found love again with Soul Asylum's Dave Pirner, reveling in the relative normalcy of laying low in his native Minneapolis, away from the Hollywood machinery. She also found refuge at her other homes—an apartment on Park Avenue in New York overlooking Gramercy Park; a splendidly preserved 1902 Victorian house in San Francisco's coveted Cow Hollow neighborhood; and with her family in Petaluma—escapes that grew more necessary, she felt, as she began to sense her omnipresent celebrity was provoking a backlash in the media and, subsequently, the public. "I remember thinking, 'I just can't win,'" she later revealed. "'Maybe if I just don't work, they'll like me?'" She was increasingly distressed by fallen-child-star narratives. "I get really angry when I hear people making fun of those young actors who turn to drugs or crime," she told *Vogue*. "I don't think it's a joke. I think that sometimes the industry can be a form of child abuse."

For Ryder, someone who'd deeply identified with Holden Caulfield, her success within the inherent artifice of Hollywood created a cognitive dissonance that clashed with her self-perception: she struggled to allow permission to truly enjoy the fruits of her success. Anxiety attacks, paranoic spells, phobias, depression, insomnia—all the persistent, nagging issues from her childhood encroached and took deeper, paralyzing root, amplified by the seductive yet often punishing Tinseltown culture. "You can't look to the industry to validate you as a person because that can just lead to incredible disappointment," she'd tell *TIME* years after. "I will admit I was guilty of that when I was younger because you get caught up in it, surrounded by people that are telling you that it's the most important thing, and you're young and you believe it."

She became dependent on sleeping pills, until Michelle Pfeiffer convinced her "to flush them down the toilet." She spent two weeks on location "trying to be an alcoholic," mixing screwdrivers alone in her hotel room after shooting, smoking cigarettes and repeatedly listening to Tom Waitts's melancholy *Nighthawks at the Diner*, until one night she fell asleep with a lit cigarette and, despite no blaze igniting, was scared sober by the experience. Diving headlong into a peak creative period, her workaholism fueled self-neglect, which led to an epiphany while shooting a torture scene for the film *The House of the Spirits*.

"I would look at these fake bruises and cuts on my face, and I would struggle to see myself as this little girl. 'Would you be treating this girl like you're treating yourself?'" she'd recount to *Harper's Bazaar* in 2022. "I remember looking at myself and saying, 'This is what I'm doing to myself inside.' Because I just wasn't taking care of myself."

Her breakup with Pirner after four years and a string of much-hoped-for but unrealized film projects only compounded her melancholy. Making *Girl, Interrupted*, which she'd deeply identified with when she read the book galleys, was a form of therapy through art; she hoped sharing some of her ennui and anguish openly and bluntly while promoting the film would, at the least, help de-stigmatize mental health issues for others suffering as she was, especially young women. She told *20/20*'s Diane Sawyer how sleepless nights prompted solitary, aimless drives around Los Angeles, "wishing so badly that I had someone to talk to, a friend, *someone*." On one excursion, she came upon a newsstand displaying the latest issue of *Rolling*

Stone, herself on the cover proclaimed, "The Luckiest Girl in the World." "It broke my heart, because there I was in so much pain and feeling so confused, feeling so lost in my life. I wasn't allowed to complain, because I was so lucky, so blessed, I made a lot of money, and my problems weren't 'real' problems," she would say. "I'm as nauseated as the next person when actors complain about their lives…but the stuff that I was going through *was* difficult."

Feeling not exactly suicidal but increasingly desperate for some way out of her predicament, she revealed she'd even checked into a psychiatric ward for five days before seeking private therapy on her own. "I didn't want anyone to think that I was crazy, and I felt like I was going crazy," she admitted. "The worst part of it was not being able to describe it—the overwhelming horror of the anxiety attacks—even to my own family, to the people closest to me."

Ryder was also routinely plagued by lifelong health maladies—flu and chronic insomnia, sometimes the result of her workaholic tendencies, which would, ironically, force her to drop out of projects. In 1990, shortly after arriving on the set of *The Godfather Part III* in Rome, she famously exited the production when the set doctor diagnosed her with "nervous exhaustion," prompting director Francis Ford Coppola to recast the role of Michael Corleone's daughter Mary with his daughter Sophia (despite a critical drubbing, the younger Coppola would rebound as an acclaimed filmmaker in her own right). She would suffer a herniated disk in her back while rehearsing for 1997's *Alien: Resurrection*. And in early 2001, while shooting a scene for the film *Mr. Deeds*—a contemporary retelling of the Frank Capra classic *Mr. Deeds Goes to Town* playing, with no small irony, a dirt-digging TV tabloid show reporter—where Ryder and leading man Adam Sandler rode a bicycle down a long flight of stairs in Central Park, the heel of her shoe got caught in the pedal, and the duo took a tumble. She soldiered through the rest of the scene, but the next morning, discovered she'd broken her arm in three places—joint breaks that didn't require a cast, which enabled her to complete the film though the persistent pain required further treatment. A few months later, she withdrew from the lead role in the British indie *Lily and the Secret Planting* after just two days on the London set, hospitalized with a stomach bug for two days. Such physical setbacks—and the rumors and media blowback she now recognized they inevitably provoked—only further aggravated her still-raw psyche.

"One of my worst fears is being a self-indulgent person, and I really was very self-indulgent, and I was wallowing," she told Sawyer in 1999, noting that she'd leaned hard into her belief that the greatest actors were tortured artists—as she viewed herself—and admitting she remained prone to bouts of depression. "And I got really sick of it. I got sick of myself. Really sick of myself."

Throughout 2001, the public retained an insatiable appetite for Ryder, still a highly visible Hollywood figure even in a rare year in which she didn't have any films of her own to promote. Her oft-chronicled love life had cooled again: a year prior, she'd ended her engagement to her most recent celebrity paramour, actor Matt Damon, after a two-year romance.

She made appearances at the Academy Awards as a presenter and visited the elite *Vanity Fair* afterparty at Morton's restaurant; in New York, she attended *Interview Magazine*'s gala dinner at Fifth Avenue's Hugo Boss Store with her grungy-glam rocker pal Courtney Love—lead singer of the boundary-pushing band Hole, widow of Nirvana singer Kurt Cobain, recovering addict and a recently minted fellow Oscar-nominated actress. After Ryder introduced the singer at a cabaret-style benefit at the Russian Tea Room, between torch songs, Love—a Beverly Hills police arrestee after a 1994 overdose incident at the city's Peninsula Hotel—proclaimed of her friend, "We're the two most fucked-up Jewish intellectual cunts on the planet!"

The *Sun-Herald* reported that Ryder and Love were involved in a violent scuffle with two men during Bono and Gwen Stefani's encore duet on *What's Going On* attending a U2 concert at Los Angeles's Staples Center. She inadvertently created a paparazzi furor when she ventured to the upscale resale shop Decades to deliver a selection of designer wear culled from her enviable closet to auction off for charity, including items she'd worn to the Academy Awards, the Cannes Film Festival, and other high profile events, as well as clothing and accessories once belonging to Claudette Colbert, Katharine Hepburn, Audrey Hepburn, Joan Crawford, and Mae West; she had to be disguised behind shopping bags and hustled out the store's back entrance. She remained an ever-zeitgeist-y presence, cameoing as herself in Ben Stiller's film comedy *Zoolander* and guest-starring on the phenomenally popular sitcom *Friends*.

And then, the day following her arrest at Saks, she was suddenly headline fodder on every media outlet imaginable, from the trusted and reputable to the sleazy and salacious.

On December 13—which happened to be my birthday—the Beverly Hills Police Department held a press conference outside police headquarters led by press spokesman Lt. Gary Gilmond—a forty-five-year-old BHPD veteran with over two decades in a variety of divisions before being elevated into the communications position. I'd accompanied Gilmond on a couple of evening ride-alongs in his black-and-white patrol cruiser when he was still on uniform duty, and knew him to be affable, easygoing, and—even while we were pulling over possible suspects in the just-committed armed robbery of a restaurant—decidedly coolheaded. Gilmond told the assembled reporters Saks's security team witnessed Ryder removing Sensormatic tags from merchandise "both visually and by video" before stashing them within her bags—an only partially accurate statement that Ryder's attorney Mark Geragos, on hand to follow up with statements on her behalf, took note of Gilmond chuckled when a reporter asked if he knew the brand names of the stolen items—he didn't, nor did he disclose the pharmaceuticals recovered during the arrest—then noted that during her arrest officers had found the actress "very friendly, very polite, very cooperative and she comported herself to be a very nice lady."

Such a glowing description of an arrestee, famous or otherwise, was unique in my experience, given the department's typically terse, on-the-record recounting of events. Only once before had I heard such a warm account of an arrest suspect—when Chevy Chase was booked in 1995 for driving under the influence and had the arresting officers and department staff practically doubled over in laughter with non-stop, jokingly penitent riffing,

Never one to miss an opportunity to spin a case in front of the cameras, Geragos stepped before the cluster of microphones. "I'm telling you right now, it's a misunderstanding on the part of the store," he enthused, explaining that Ryder would produce both receipts for the clothing and valid prescriptions for the medication in her possession—the latter of which he said he was carrying on him at that moment. "When the facts come out, it will be clear that there was no theft involved," the attorney said, chalking it up to a lack of communication between store clerks. "The left hand didn't know what the right hand was doing. My client never had any intent to deprive anybody of any property. She did buy items yesterday. We anticipate that all the counts, all the charges that she was arrested on will be dismissed once I give them the full story." The District Attorney's office would have roughly a month to make that determination.

Geragos elaborated to *Newsweek*, adamant that Ryder, who he'd warmed to right away, was "far from troubled," and not acting under the influence of drugs. "Everybody who talked to her the evening of the incident said she was fine. The police said she was extremely cooperative. I spent hours with her yesterday and there was nothing untoward that I saw. She was delightful. She's obviously concerned, as anyone would be. She's a little bit traumatized, but she's all there."

What was yet to play out was how the public would react to one of Hollywood's most prominent big-screen sweethearts embroiled in a scandal as tawdry as shoplifting, especially when she had the means to buy out half the store, and most especially when the various excuses for the incident—she was researching a role; her assistant had paid for it; it was all a big misunderstanding—were starting to multiply.

Hers wasn't the first incident of a celebrity caught in the act of shoplifting, but the closest parallel to Ryder's tale concerned Hedy Lamarr, the glamorous Viennese actress of Hollywood's Golden Age, billed as "the most beautiful girl in the world." Her smoldering sex appeal was rivaled by a keen intellect: an amateur inventor with no formal training, during World War II, she and a friend patented a technology to protect radio-guided torpedoes from being tracked or jammed, which became foundational for later innovations, including wi-fi, Bluetooth, and GPS.

Lamarr was arrested in 1966—after her screen heyday and six marriages but, at fifty-one, on the verge of her first new film in years—for allegedly slipping two dozen items—including a knit suit, a pair of bikini underwear, a string of beads, eight greeting cards and a fifty-cent makeup brush—into her shopping bag after purchasing a pair of shoes and a coat from the May Co. department store at Wilshire and Fairfax boulevards (today the home of the prestigious Academy Museum of Motion Pictures). The haul totaled a mere $86, even as Lamarr was carrying in her handbag two crumpled, uncashed checks—for a memoir advance and a cosmetics endorsement—totaling $14,000. Released on $550 bail, Lamarr held a press conference at the popular Beverly Hills restaurant The Bistro, where she and her attorney insisted there had simply been a misunderstanding. "I'm still mystified and surprised. It's hardly possible," she told reporters. "It happened quite suddenly. I'm quite in a shock."

Despite having to be hospitalized for exhaustion a few days later, Lamarr was flabbergasted when the May Co. refused her offer to pay for the items and pressed charges, prompting her to plead not guilty. In court, a series of witnesses, including psychiatrists and her own children, testified that Lamarr—revealed to have a checkered history of shoplifting incidents—suffered under crushing emotional and financial strain due to a litany of reasons, including the collapse of her sixth marriage, the threat of eviction from her Coldwater Canyon home, a painful infected tooth, anxiety about her return to the screen and a growing despondence over her gradually fading beauty. Lamarr took the stand to reluctantly affirm all the mounting stressors, adding that during her excursion at the May Co., she was also in a heartsick tailspin after watching the film *The Pawnbroker* two weeks earlier, its storyline about a refugee from Nazi Germany triggering traumatic memories of her own perilous flight from Hitler's forces in 1937.

Defense attorney Jordan Wank argued that the admittedly forgetful and distracted Lamarr simply shopped "differently" than most people due to her long history of privilege and hadn't intentionally stolen. The actress, he claimed, was treated with "Gestapo tactics" while detained, denied water, bathroom breaks, or legal representation for hours. Fresh out of law school, prosecutor Ira Reiner countered that the film star didn't merit special consideration simply because she was Hedy Lamarr.

It took jurors five hours of deliberation to acquit the screen siren, prompting applause from admirers packing the courtroom gallery. Joyous, Lamarr thanked and shook the hands of every juror, lingering in the courtroom to sign autographs. Years later, Reiner—who, as Los Angeles County District Attorney, would oversee trials including the serial killer "Night Stalker" Richard Ramirez and the arrest and beating of Rodney King during the 1992 riots—would not treat the beguiling movie star too deferentially. He admitted that several jurors confided to him that they believed she was guilty, but it seemed clear to them the prosecutor didn't want them to convict her. "That was the last time I was Mr. Nice Guy in the courtroom," he admitted.

Lamarr's defense proved an excellent playbook for earning an acquittal for a fallen but still adored star. And Mark Geragos was a savvy enough attorney to learn from its lessons.

By February 1, 2002, the District Attorney's office announced it would prosecute Winona Ryder on four felony counts: second-degree commercial burglary, grand theft of personal property, vandalism with more than $400 damage, and possession of a controlled substance, Oxycodone. Where some court-watchers were surprised, others suspected that D.A. Steve Cooley was eager to use the case to refute the nagging perception that his office had historically been soft on celebrity crime, especially given the outcome of the O.J. Simpson trial—Cooley's campaign slogan had literally been "Money Talks, Celebrities Walk"—and in that vein recommended that her bail be increased to $30,000. Similarly, eyebrows were raised when Ryder's defense was still posturing, refusing to enter a no-contest plea or strike a deal, especially given the potentially ruinous damage a public trial could do to her standing in Hollywood.

Geragos, who supplied enough legitimate prescription information to get the drug charges whittled down, was performatively apoplectic in the press, calling the D.A.'s decision "mind-boggling...I believe that this is overcharged for the conduct they alleged," he declared. "I don't know why the necessity was felt to make this a media circus."

By March, the eighty-minute Saks surveillance video, edited from six hours to feature only the Ryder segments, was screened by the *Los Angeles Times*, *Extra*, and a handful of other media outlets. The newspaper revealed, as if reviewing one of Ryder's films, that the footage failed to live up to the advance hype: it didn't include any imagery of the actress cutting away the security tags as suggested in the police press conference. Any truly incriminating evidence, the newspaper suggested, had to come from the eyewitness accounts of staffers. "Contrary to public perception, this tape exonerates her," crowed Geragos, tweaking the many snarky headlines Ryder's arrest had inspired over the past few months, "I'd say this is prosecution, interrupted." Investigators at the D.A.'s office and BHPD hadn't made the tape public, and not so subtly suggested that Geragos did, fretting that any public airing of the tape could potentially impact the local L.A.-based jury pool by creating a favorable image of the actress. "I'm sure that's something *we'd* be accused of [if we released evidence]," a Beverly Hills officer told me anonymously at the time.

As expected, Ryder's name became one of the buzziest topics of conversation in Hollywood, across the country, and all over the increasingly pervasive internet, appearing everywhere from national news broadcasts, widely circulated publications, late-night talk show monologues, and non-sequitur name-drops for cheap chuckles in articles on any manner of topics. She'd been dissected, mocked, criticized, parodied, and/or condemned on a near-daily basis for three straight months. When asked by reporters how his client was faring during the overwhelming onslaught of press attention while facing real jail time, Geragos was blunt but sanguine: "She's had better days. But she is as tough as they come."

Meanwhile, an unexpected phenomenon emerged, fittingly for a star famous as a fashion muse. A month following Ryder's arrest, a fifteen-dollar tee silk-screened with the retro-graphic face of a woman resembling Ryder taken from a vintage wig ad and emblazoned with the words "Free Winona!" become one of the hottest commodities in L.A.'s hipster style scene. The brainchild of Billy "Billy T" Tsangares, owner and operator of the kitschy novelty shop Y-Que (Spanish translation: "So what?"), the Warholian parody shirt he designed when he was unable to persuade Beverly Hills police to release Ryder's mug shot became a must-have for irony-adoring Gen Xers eager for an edgy pop topic to have fun with in the grim wake of September 11. "This type of humor is a way to be political without necessarily taking a stand that's going to offend somebody," Tsangares told *Vogue*. "This gives people an expression that is radical and at the same time meaningless."

Yet the briskly purchased shirts, the store's all-time best-seller, also signaled that amid all the media scrutiny, there was an unexpected groundswell of public affection for the actress amid her legal travails—a sympathetic bent Winona Ryder and her team recognized might be turned to her advantage.

She'd conspicuously stayed out of the public eye after the arrest, sitting out habitual appearances at the Academy Awards and the *Vanity Fair* party (though she did quietly swing by the annual super-exclusive private party at the home of her powerful ICM agent Ed Limato). But she gradually emerged from her estate, not only for a few fleeting court appearances as the timing of her trial date was hammered out: soon enough, paparazzi caught her strolling around Los Angeles, once accompanied by her *Girl, Interrupted* co-star Brittany Murphy, and popping up at parties on both coasts. And in early May, she winsomely graced the cover of *W Magazine*'s June 2002 issue, clad in stylishly ripped jeans and, provocatively, a "Free Winona" tee.

Ostensibly consenting to the interview to promote the June 28 release of *Mr. Deeds* but demurring, on the advice of her lawyer, to discuss her legal situation, she was otherwise garrulous on a number of topics. She dutifully detailed her motivation to make the film and her admiration of Adam Sandler, playfully debunked her supposedly prolific dating life, effusively broke down her lifelong music-geek bona fides, and revealed her thwarted intentions to purchase her literary idol J.D. Salinger's love letters at auction to offer them back to the notoriously private author or, alternatively, burn them. The last anecdote allowed her to offer a not-so-subtle message. "I know a little bit what that's like," she explained. "I love being an actress, but I never, ever thought that meant anybody had the right to know anything about my personal life. I still stand by the idea that acting does not mean you have to give up your personal privacy."

The self-aware *W* interview and photoshoot were so roundly applauded as a coy-but-canny P.R. move that Ryder was emboldened to continue making strategic stops on the *Mr. Deeds* promotion circuit, including sticking to plans to host the May 18, 2002, season finale of *Saturday Night Live*, which elevated poking fun at her arrest to a new level, beginning with teaser ads proclaiming "Winona Ryder: she'll steal your heart, she'll steal everything."

Her monologue quickly cut to the topic foremost in the audience's mind: Ryder commiserated with cast member Tracy Morgan: "People have been acting a little strange around me," she explained, perplexed. "There's been a lot of locking of doors and shifty eyes, and a lot of frisking…To my face everyone's so sweet and nice, but I always feel like someone's looking over my shoulder." Morgan pointed out that the show installed closed circuit cameras that very week, to Ryder's dismay, but he assures her it wasn't because of her. He rolls footage culled from the cameras spotlighting a series of amusing backstage dramas among the cast to demonstrate that she wasn't the target, culminating with a clip from the night before: after giving Ryder, grateful for the opportunity to host, a supportive hug in her dressing room, executive producer Lorne Michaels thoroughly pats himself down to ensure the actress hasn't picked his pockets. A second sketch even more brazenly plays off her notoriety: shopping in Barney's New York, Ryder, Chris Kattan, and musical guest Moby have forgotten their wallets, and it's suggested that they shoplift. Ryder wryly declares, *"Stealing is wrong!"*

Her stint on *SNL* alternately praised for its self-parody and pilloried for making light of her alleged felony, Ryder ventured out more that spring, keeping a low profile among the celebrity guests attending *The Pussycat Dolls Live* burlesque show—the cabaret-style incarnation that preceded the pop group—at the Roxy Theater on the Sunset Strip, and attending a Jean-Michael Basquiat exhibit party at the Gagosian Gallery in Beverly Hills. During the MTV Movie Awards at the Shrine Auditorium on June 1, 2002, I watched Ryder take the stage with Adam Sandler for one last

Mr. Deeds plug. "I don't want to put you on the spot, I don't want to be a jerk, but there's a lot of people out there, they want to know the truth, so I'm gonna ask you," said Sandler, prompting Ryder to brace herself for a bombshell before offering a switcheroo. "Are your boobs real?"

"No, they're actually made of Jell-O Pudding," she replied. The faux-Q&A bit continued in a more labored fashion for a few more minutes, culminating awkwardly with Sandler requesting to touch one of her breasts, doing so gingerly with her encouragement. It was not quite the shrewdly amusing slam-dunk *SNL* had been, but the bit served its purpose, continuing to pre-rehab her image and bolster *Mr. Deeds*'s box office potential. It would be the final round of public playfulness for Ryder—she wouldn't participate in the press tour or appear in the movie posters—as she was due in court for a preliminary hearing in two days, and things were about to take a serious—and surprisingly painful—turn.

While Ryder courted public opinion with self-spoofing, the investigation quietly progressed. A few days after Ryder's arrest, loss prevention chief Ken Evans conveyed Saks's intent to press charges and be compensated for its losses. Reviewing surveillance video, he spotted telltale moves that prompted him to examine clothing displays on the sales floor. He'd noticed Ryder slipping her hand into the pocket of a coat in the Gucci department, but when he went to inspect it, the coat was no longer in the store. His next search proved more fruitful: he discovered a clandestine stash of four discarded Sensormatic tags in the left breast pocket of a Chanel overcoat—three of them still contained small swatches of material, which he matched to the Fekkai hairbow and the Natori and Dolce & Gabbana handbags found in Ryder's possession.

Neglecting to formally record the sensor tags in the store's log, Evans instead placed them in an evidence locker for police detectives to collect, though he wouldn't actually turn the tags over for nearly three months. Det. Elwell would subsequently lock them in his desk drawer alongside the case file, eventually entering them into evidence as the case progressed. Later, when Saks security discovered another pair of sensor tags stuffed underneath the cushion of a chair in the same dressing room where Ryder was observed cutting tags from merchandise, Evans simply placed those tags back into circulation.

Elwell had continued to investigate the many pharmaceuticals found in Ryder's possession following chemical evaluation by the Los Angeles

County Sheriff's Department Scientific Services Bureau's laboratory to determine the nature of each medication. A week after the Saks incident, Elwell was contacted by a representative of the California Medical Board and informed that eight days prior to Ryder's arrest, the board had issued a search warrant for the home and office of Dr. Jules Lusman, a physician treating a patient named Emily Thompson. Her file contained personal information and documents—including a photocopy of a California driver's license—indicating that "Emily Thompson" was, in fact, Winona Ryder. Lusman had dispensed a variety of Schedule II drug prescriptions to Ryder in both her own name and the Thompson alias, though neither identity had prescriptions on record for oxycodone or hydrocodone—CMB's investigation suggested Lusman had acted illegally and unethically while treating a variety of patients, earning an underground reputation for making house/hotel calls for privileged patients, including several celebrities, as a "Dr. Feelgood."

During an interview to determine her eligibility for probation, Ryder offered details about her history with substances, explaining that she'd been "terrified" of illegal drugs since childhood and had avoided them her whole life, though she'd certainly been exposed to them. "If I wanted to take a drug because I was in school and everybody was doing it, I could go to my parents and say, 'I really want to try this.' And they'd say, 'If you do this, okay, but this is what can happen to you…' They'd say 'Don't get it in the streets, because it could be really bad and make you freak out. Don't take it in a crowded place, because you'll panic'…They would tell me the effect of the drug, and I'd end up not wanting to do it."

At nineteen, after a messy breakup with Depp, she'd been prescribed the sleep aid and anti-anxiety drug Klonopin, which she discontinued because she felt its effects were "too much," replacing it with Xanax. It wasn't until she fractured her arm while shooting *Mr. Deeds* that she was prescribed a succession of painkillers. She revealed that she'd reinjured her arm on December 8, four days before her arrest, spraining it during a skateboarding mishap when a friend grabbed her while preventing her from taking a fall. She was prescribed Vicoprofin, which she used to manage her pain until mid-February.

The CMB rep shared her suspicions with Elwell: because Ryder not only held prescriptions in her own name and as the Emily Thompson alias but a half-dozen additional aliases as well, it seemed likely she was "doctor shopping," consulting several physicians at once to amass a greater supply and faster flow of opiate-derived prescriptions. An investigation by the federal Drug Enforcement Administration subsequently revealed that, between the calendar years 1996 and 1998, the actress had received thirty-seven different prescriptions written by twenty different doctors.

If Ryder's pharmacological backstory wasn't eyebrow-raising enough, Elwell and his colleagues also fielded a deluge of telephone calls after her arrest made headlines, each volunteering information about past five-fingered shopping forays. Much of what the callers conveyed was hearsay, but the detective had to give serious scrutiny to some of the more compellingly detailed claims, including allegations of a history of shoplifting well after the comic book in Petaluma. The investigation unearthed claims that Ryder had been observed on not one, not two, but *three* prior occasions—including two captured on surveillance video—appearing to exit high-end department stores with merchandise she hadn't paid for. The first allegedly occurred at the legendary Barney's New York's Madison Avenue flagship in Manhattan on May 14, 2000, followed by a second episode there over a year later, on October 10, 2001; the third reported incident was said to take place at Neiman-Marcus in Beverly Hills on November 29, 2001, two blocks west of Saks Fifth Avenue and just thirteen days before her arrest. Although neither blow-by-blow accountings nor video were ever made public, a closed-door session of the trial proceedings revealed that in one instance, Ryder was allegedly observed casually placing a hat on her head before strolling out of the store, similar to behavior caught on camera at Saks. In another, the actress was reportedly asked to pay for a sweater found concealed under her overcoat; in yet another, she allegedly escaped detention because no female security officer was on duty to conduct a body search. Ryder was never arrested or charged in any of the purported instances, though potential witnesses were lined up by the D.A. to bolster the reports.

The sum total of the revelations was concerning to Elwell, who suspected Ryder had been addicted to prescription painkillers for some time. A theory even began to form that the actress had perhaps taken to shoplifting to either sell merch for quick cash or eliminate any paper trail of her spending habits, because some concerned individual in her own camp was monitoring her finances, on alert for telltale signs of drug dependency. Elwell favored probation and some form of intervention program for Ryder—in his view, help would be the best thing for her, and the probation report concurred.

Early on June 3, it had been less than forty-eight hours since I'd last seen Winona Ryder at the MTV Movie Awards, playful and charming on stage with Adam Sandler in a tummy-exposing white wifebeater and designer jeans, but she'd yet to make her entrance in Judge Fox's third-floor courtroom for her preliminary hearing. As I sat alongside Marcia Clark, the journalists passed the time watching the judge preside over a steady procession of other cases: an Iranian man in need of a translator irked Fox with his alleged inability to produce simple proof of his attendance at Alcohol Anonymous meetings conducted in Farsi; a stunningly beautiful young model/actress-y blonde under house arrest was missing meetings with her parole officer; another man—also a client of Mark Geragos—arrested allegedly carrying five separate driver's licenses with matching social security cards, none of which reportedly belonged to him; and a case with a lower-profile Hollywood pedigree, a man accused of burglarizing the production company office of director Tom Shadyac, the filmmaker behind comedies like *Ace Ventura: Pet Detective* and *Liar, Liar*. An otherwise typical day in the Beverly Hills courthouse.

Det. Elwell arrived carrying several shopping bags and women's blouses—the evidence—followed by deputy District Attorney Julie Jurek, and finally Geragos himself, who earlier in the morning had introduced the latest of many motions seeking yet another delay in his client's proceedings—the fifth, to date. He promised Ryder was no more than fifteen minutes away (her home was about a ten-minute drive from the courthouse). The judge, however, was annoyed that the actress had yet to arrive and ordered her attorney to summon her to court ASAP. As the judge heard other cases and motions, forty-five more minutes passed before Ryder finally arrived in the courtroom, looking decidedly different from the relaxed, casual, even saucy star I'd seen two days earlier. Her short, blonde-streaked hair pulled back with a stylish white headband, she was elegantly, even glamorously outfitted in a chic ecru jacket and white top with a W-shaped black collar. She appeared pale, her eyes wary and nervous after dodging the paparazzi and camera crews on the way in.

Geragos animatedly argued his last-minute motion for delay, accusing the prosecution of staging a "dog and pony show," but Judge Fox ordered the preliminary hearing to commence immediately. Momentarily stymied, Geragos offered a surprise countermove: he had placed the D.A.'s veteran Public Information Officer Sandi Gibbons, chief liaison to the media, on the defense's witness list; thus, she was required to exit the courtroom, which she did with no small hint of exasperation. It was the first major signal that Geragos had come ready to brawl.

Security chief Ken Evans took the stand first, using a diagram of Saks's three retail floors and digital stills from the closed-circuit footage to illustrate the surveillance of Ryder in minute detail. As Jurek frequently called for him to identify, one by one as they appeared in his narrative, the designer items Ryder was accused of stealing, the prosecutor retrieved them from the evidence cachet and hung them on a clothing rack, on showy display for the everyone in the courtroom. Jurek, too, had come with gloves off.

The D.A.'s office was rankled by Ryder's media appearances, making light of the serious charges against her and making its displeasure public. "From just a human being's perspective, I don't shop at Saks," Gibbons later told the Associated Press. "I'm more inclined to shop at Target, as are most people. I don't know what kind of jury she's going to have; but if they're people like me, then perhaps they won't be laughing either."

Around 12:30 p.m., Judge Fox called for an hour-long lunch recess: I couldn't stay to observe the petite defendant's procession through the cadre of photographers and video crews awaiting outside the courthouse—I had to rush to my car and drive a few blocks east to the Four Seasons Hotel to attend a press conference for Tom Cruise, who was promoting *Minority Report*, his first film with director Steven Spielberg. As I dashed past the courthouse parking exit to where I'd parked my car at the neighboring for a cleaner getaway, I narrowly avoided being clipped by Judge Fox's SUV as he drove off for lunch.

By the time I returned from my audience with Cruise, which, like virtually every Hollywood press event, ran late, Ryder and her legal team were again nowhere to be found. My journalist colleagues revealed that I'd missed a dramatic action sequence that would've played well on the big screen: as Geragos and Ryder had returned to the courthouse around 1:30 p.m., the media swarm outside grew increasingly frenzied, encircling the pair as they made their way into the building and pushing in as cameras were shoved mere inches from Ryder's face. A sheriff's deputy was attempting to clear a path when the actress bumped into one local news videographer, causing a chain reaction: the cameraman stumbled, and his video rig knocked into another deputy's head, prompting a pushback. In the resultant melee, something struck Ryder's right arm—the same one she'd fractured on *Mr. Deeds* and reinjured while skateboarding—causing her to wince sharply and cry out in pain. Gergaos ushered her safely inside to Judge Fox's courtroom, where he explained that Ryder, her injured limb wrapped in a makeshift bandage, needed to be excused to seek medical treatment.

I really had missed all the excitement.

The judge excused the attorney and his client (as well as the injured bailiff), but not without sternly chiding the media for its aggressive pursuit of photographs, ordering the press to stay seated as Ryder left the court-house and not to get within ten feet of the actress as she entered and exited the courthouse over the course of the hearing. Two hours later, Judge Fox was about to move on to other cases when Geragos's call finally came in: after a hushed telephone conference and a quick sidebar with prosecutors, the judge informed the courtroom that Ryder's case would "not be proceed-ing today."

When I called the District Attorney's office after 5 p.m. to inquire about Ryder's condition, Sandi Gibbons told me that while she could divulge Ryder's newly rescheduled court date three days hence, she was unable to communicate any other information regarding the actress or her case since being placed on Geragos's witness list. The attorney's legal strategy had now effectively blocked the D.A.'s primary press spokesperson from…speaking to the press. At about 7 p.m., Ryder's personal publicist Mara Buxbaum called me to report that Ryder had X-rays taken and reviewed by a trio of radiologists, revealing that her client had, once again, re-fractured her right elbow. But she was otherwise willing and able to attend the next trial date.

"It appears that it's a clean fracture, so it looks like it'll heal," Geragos would tell Larry King on CNN, which was quickly becoming his unofficial media megaphone. "She's quite a trouper. She wanted to stay there and continue with the preliminary hearing…I'm looking at the arm and telling her, 'I'm not going to sit here as your arm's blowing up.' The deputy's telling her she's not going to allow her to do it. We're both telling her that, and she's saying, 'No, I want to get through this, I want to deal with it.'"

First day. First unexpected twist. I suspected I might just be in for a potboiler.

Winona Ryder did indeed show for her next court appearance, chauf-feured by her attorney in his BMW and bypassing an even larger phalanx of reporters outside with the aid of increased bailiff and police protection. With her right arm wrapped in an elastic bandage and held in a pale blue sling, the actress was dressed in a knee-length black skirt with her hair stylishly mussed. Geragos, attentive and solicitous, smoothed her hair and brushed lint from her clothes. Informed that Ryder was not taking pain medication for her injury, Judge Fox asked her to inform him if she needed to take a break due to any discomfort.

Drama-free outside the courtroom, the proceedings inside started out lively enough when the judge announced Geragos withdrew Sandi Gibbons as a defense witness, allowing her to resume her duties as usual. Jurek asked Ken Evans three final questions: Does Saks sell scissors? Did the store have an arrangement that allowed Ryder to take items as she pleased and arrange to pay for them later? And had any receipts for the twenty-one items ever been located? Evans answered no to each inquiry. On the cross, Geragos attempted to punch holes in Evans's testimony by introducing a controversial new claim, positing that, contrary to Evans's assertion that he hadn't recognized the actress, security had *specifically targeted* Ryder in hopes of arresting a celebrity shoplifter just prior to the holiday shopping season as a publicity device. "You always knew it was Winona Ryder and you wanted to bust her for shoplifting," proclaimed Geragos, further insinuating that Evans might have sold his story to the tabloids for profit.

"Have you seen my car?" chuckled Evans. "No."

Saks security guard Colleen Rainey recounted her brief initial impression that she was tailing a homeless woman. Ryder took the characterization without reaction, staying poker-faced through most of the testimony—it was only when her father Michael entered the court late into the proceedings that she smiled and gave him a small wave. Further offering a glimpse of his defense strategy, Geragos insinuated that Rainey had been captured on tape acting "excited" and "giddy" when she came out of the fitting room, as if thrilled to have caught a movie star shoplifting. After additional testimony from law enforcement, Geragos demanded the dismissal of all charges, but Judge Fox ruled that the D.A.'s office had met its burden of proof. "There is sufficient cause to believe that Ms. Winona Ryder is guilty," the judge declared, ordering her to stand trial and scheduling her formal arraignment and plea for June 14—just two weeks before *Mr. Deeds* was set to bow in theaters.

Outside, a defiant Geragos advanced his conspiracy narrative to the press by labeling the Saks employees' testimonies "close to full-blown perjury." He asserted, "Those witnesses lied through their teeth. I believe that Saks targeted her as a celebrity. We have a lot of other evidence we did not produce."

In a surprise appearance before the media, Marc Klaas, Polly's father, offered his firsthand experience with Ryder to bolster her credibility as a decent, caring human being. "I can certainly speak to the character of Winona Ryder," Klaas told the Associated Press. "I think it's terrible what they're doing to her. She understands the seriousness of crime in our society."

Within two weeks, Ryder briefly returned to court to formally enter a plea of not guilty. Then, on June 28, despite savage critical reviews, *Mr. Deeds* opened nationwide, earning over $37 million in its first weekend, leading to a global box office gross of over $171.2 million—suggesting, even factoring in the phenomenally popular Sandler's fervently devoted audience, that the moviegoing public just might not have soured on Winona Ryder.

And the plot continued to thicken.

Though Ryder would keep a low profile over the summer months—skipping the New York premiere of *Mr. Deeds* in June and the L.A. premiere of *S1m0ne*, the Al Pacino-led sci-fi film that featured the actress in a supporting role, in August—there was no shortage of legal drama. Geragos argued the prosecution had an agenda to humiliate Ryder, particularly through the public statements of press spokesperson Gibbons, and lobbied for Judge Fox to disqualify the D.A.'s office from trying the case, instead turning it over to the California Attorney General's office, though the A.G. indicated it saw no reason for stepping in. Judge Fox rejected Geragos's motions, which offered no compelling motivation for any prejudice beyond the case's high profile. Then, despite Geragos's confident claims that charges would ultimately be dismissed, there was suddenly buzz of a plea bargain in the works. "I don't know that anyone welcomes going through a trial," he tune-changed. But less than a month after negotiations began, talks fell apart; court scuttlebutt suggested the deal would've had Ryder plead guilty to a single felony grand theft charge in exchange for community service, probation, and no jail time, but the actress was resistant to adding "convicted felon" to her hyphenates. The D.A. withdrew the offer, and the trial would proceed. "Everyone keeps asking me why doesn't this settle out. But there is this meddlesome little problem of her being not guilty!" Geragos spun.

Julie Jurek had already demonstrated ample spine; the new lead prosecutor was now Ann Rundle, the poised and steely thirty-four-year-old deputy D.A. with a facile mind and occasionally sharp tongue who'd previously negotiated a plea bargain with filmmaker Oliver Stone on drug possession and DUI charges, and settled a body armor violation charge with Wu-Tang Clan member Russell T. Jones, a.k.a. Ol' Dirty Bastard.

At least eight lawyers and paralegals had been devoted full time to the case, despite one deputy D.A. anonymously grousing to the *Los Angeles Times*, "Most of the lawyers here think this is just a spectacle—and an utterly ridiculous waste of resources for such a petty case." There were signs the public agreed: that fall, Geragos's firm would commission a poll that indicated 67 percent of Los Angelenos felt Ryder's prosecution was a frivolous use of tax dollars; another 58 percent suspected she was being treated unfairly. In September, *Celebrity Justice*—a syndicated television series produced by journalist, former attorney, and legal analyst Harvey Levin (later founder of the gossip outlet TMZ) devoted to covering the legal dramas of the rich and famous—dedicated a segment of its debut episode to an analysis of cases similar to Ryder's. The show reported that among defendants in 16 Beverly Hills shoplifting cases from the prior year involving merchandise valued at $1,000 or more taken from high-end retailers, none of the accused faced as many charges as Ryder: none had a grand theft charge paired with both burglary and vandalism charges, as Ryder did. The same was true of about two dozen other Beverly Hills shoplifting cases that involved merchandise worth between $1,000 and $4,000, the minimal amount for felony grand theft.

"None of them had the book thrown at them like Winona," Ross McLaughlin, the reporter who conducted the *Celebrity Justice* investigation told Reuters. "I honestly thought I wouldn't find anything like this, and I was surprised by it." The D.A.'s spokesperson Gibbons countered, "The charges filed against Ms. Ryder are the same charges that we would file against Jane Doe if we had evidence that she committed a similar crime."

Ryder appeared to have both hard data and a softhearted portion of the public in her corner; she also had the unflagging support of her parents, Michael and Cindy, leaning into their fight-the-power ethos. "She's been living in a Kafka novel...or like a character in 'The Crucible,'" Michael reportedly told *Us Weekly*, alluding to his daughter's role in the 1996 film adaptation of Arthur Miller's play using the Salem Witch Trials as a parable for anti-Communist inquisitions of the 1950s. "Not the [role] she played, but the victims of a witch hunt!" Michael made little attempt to disguise his indignation. "The DA turned a minor allegation to a major crime spree... four felonies? You have to wonder what's behind this." Cindy's belief in her daughter, too, remained steadfast: "She's tough and true and her humor and feistiness have gotten her through this."

In mid-October, as the trial date loomed just days away, Ryder could allow herself one significant pre-trial sigh of relief when the felony drug charges were dropped. The D.A.'s office determined that since Ryder had been prescribed the painkillers by a physician, she "lacked criminal knowledge" regarding any misuse of her medications. Dr. Lusman would bear the burden of responsibility for his alleged ethical and legal lapses soon enough, Rundle hinted.

Finally, as the trial started in earnest on October 25, even jury selection sparked a kerfuffle. As with many high-profile cases, potential jurors were all instructed not to read news articles about the case, follow television or radio coverage, or converse about it with family and friends; further, they were admonished not to watch any films or TV shows featuring the defendant and asked to provide answers to a two-page questionnaire determining sympathy or antipathy for the actress's public persona. They would not be sequestered but escorted by sheriff's deputies to and from court each day. When asked if anyone had *never* heard of Winona Ryder, not a single hand was raised; every prospective juror conceded they were aware of the shoplifting charges against the actress. Dozens of the pool members revealed professional or personal ties to the entertainment industry, prompting Judge Fox to deadpan, "I think we have all the studios represented." As Ryder took copious notes on a yellow legal pad and occasionally offered smiles to the interviewees, the attorneys winnowed down the jury pool: among their many questions, Geragos asked if the fact his client was "rich and pretty" might prejudice their judgment; Rundle inquired if any of the industry professionals harbored hopes of one day working with the defendant. Both received unanimously negative responses.

The resulting six-woman, six-man panel included a television programming development executive, a legal secretary at Sony Studios, and the husband of an executive at the Walt Disney Company, as well as a teacher, a UCLA graduate student, a fast-food worker, an aerospace engineer, an employee of a mortgage company, and an obstetrician-gynecologist that the judge knew from their shared membership in the Beverly Hills Rotary Club. If that wasn't evidence enough of Beverly Hills's small-town nature, there was also the case of juror Peter Guber, the sixty-year-old former studio head and now president of his own production company, Mandalay Entertainment, responsible for films like *Donnie Brasco* and *Wild Things*.

"I have about as much chance of getting on this jury as the man in the moon," Guber was overheard musing out loud on the packed elevator during its always-slow trek to the third-floor courtroom on the first day of jury selection. "I only made three pictures with the lady." Indeed, Guber explained he had reason to expect to be excused during *voir dire*: "I was the chairman of Sony when one of the companies under our control, she made a picture for them." It was either a modest or indirect way of saying that while Guber served as the co-chairman of Sony Pictures Entertainment from 1989 to 1994—one of the most powerful positions in the entertainment industry—the studio's film division Columbia Pictures made 1992's *Bram Stoker's Dracula*, 1993's *The Age of Innocence*, and 1994's *Little Women*, each starring (and one produced by) Ryder at the height of her Hollywood career. As the top executive, Guber was, in fact, Ryder's ultimate employer; he greenlit all three films, the company made tens of millions of dollars, and the actress made millions and garnered both of her future payday-boosting Oscar nominations. Yet despite the shared history, Guber insisted he could be objective.

"You're not afraid of not working in this town again if you get on this case, are you?" Geragos quipped to Guber, prompting laughter from the gallery before the film executive answered no. With no preemptory strikes exercised by either counsel, Guber joined the jury—prompting a far more feverish debate within the Hollywood grapevine as the executive's impartiality was dissected. Some felt he couldn't help but be biased toward a fellow Hollywood luminary; others suggested that his just-published book with Peter Bart, *Shoot Out: Surviving Fame and (Mis)Fortune in Hollywood*, revealed a subtle disdain for actors which might work against her. "Talk about absurdity," an anonymous studio chief sniped to the *New York Times*. "Talk about confirming everyone's impression that Southern California is the capital of wacko."

Picking up on the appearance of a conflict of interest, several reporters asked Gibbons about the seeming incongruity. She shared their inquiries with Judge Fox, who, on the first day of trial, called a closed-door meeting in his chambers with the producer. But after twenty minutes of deliberation, the judge, the defense, and the prosecution remained satisfied with Guber's ability to remain impartial, and he took his seat in the back row of the panel.

There was one last unique requirement for the jurors: Judge Fox instructed them not to shop at Saks Fifth Avenue for the duration of the trial. "I'm sure they won't appreciate that, but I think you can get along for five to seven days," he added.

Small town, indeed.

Here, my narrative arrives back to October 28, 2002, the day of opening arguments, where the bizarre convergence of celebrity and the law would imbed in my memory. "You will find that all this case amounts to is a simple case of theft—nothing more, nothing less," went Rundle's opening salvo in strict, no-nonsense terms. The deputy D.A. explained that by bringing scissors, an obfuscating armload of shopping bags, and hidden tissue paper into the store, Ryder signaled her premeditated intention to shoplift; Rundle teased a pending introduction of the complete surveillance footage, promising jurors a curious sight when they monitored the red Saks bag the actress was toting following her purchase of the Gucci shoes: "You will begin to watch that shopping bag grow and grow." Despite cash and credit cards in her purse, "Ms. Ryder had in mind a little two-for-one bonus program. For everything she purchased, she helped herself to a little something extra," Rundle explained. "She paid for four items, and she had twenty-something extra items concealed in her bag or under her coat."

Geragos, too, was breathing fire from the outset, insisting all the video revealed was a famous movie star shopping in a store she regularly frequented, one he claimed retained her credit card on file and was expected to charge her for any items taken from the store, whether she stopped to have a salesclerk ring them up or not. He claimed the D.A.'s office, failing to find any blatantly visible evidence of Ryder's shoplifting, had "panicked" and conspired to invent an alternate scenario, the one that had Colleen Rainey supposedly observing cutting off sensor tags and concealing merchandise. He told jurors any testimony from Saks staff was "bald-faced lies," insisting his client had been framed. "Various people had a motive to set up Winona," he intoned, foreshadowing his defense strategy. "This is a case about a woman who has been wronged and wronged terribly. This is a case about some security guards who got out of control."

Over the ensuing days, the proceedings intensified as the damaging store video was shown to the rapt, note-taking the jurors, who studiously inspected the sensor tags still bearing ragged swatches of snipped-off material. Much of the damning pretrial testimony was reiterated—this time with key corrections and clarifications from earlier witness recollections, intended to block Geragos's already-telegraphed intent to poke holes in inconsistencies, even as the defense attorney concocted new curveballs to hurl.

He came hard at Evans, taking a cue from Hedy Lamarr's playbook by accusing the security manager of Gestapo tactics, demanding that Ryder, supposedly braless under two layers of clothing, lift her shirt to reveal if merchandise was hidden underneath, even as she "screamed" for the guards to stop; Evans countered that the defendant had, unprompted when first detained, exposed an inch or two of her midriff to indicate nothing was secreted under her clothes. Evans was asked about a lunch with a former co-worker following Ryder's arrest, who alleged that Evans exclaimed, "I'm gonna nail her!" and "I'm gonna get her one way or another!" The lunch happened, Evans testified; the melodramatic proclamations had not. Geragos repeatedly accused him of lying; when Judge Fox warned Geragos that he was trying the court's patience, the lawyer barked back, "The witness is trying *my* patience!"

The defense attorney proved even more relentless while attempting to impugn the testimony of Colleen Rainey, the prosecution's key eyewitness, in a ninety-minute-long grilling, accusing Rainey of giddily wallowing in Ryder's celebrity cachet immediately after she was detained. "Didn't you go through her Filofax and say, 'That's Bono's number, that's so-and-so's number?'" he asked. "Didn't you say, 'Oh, my God, I love Keanu Reeves,' and take his number?" He demanded to know if Rainey had called his client "a bitch." At each provocation, Rainey offered firm, unequivocal denials. Geragos then presented financial documents he'd subpoenaed: since leaving the department store's employ to pursue an MBA, Rainey and her husband, a fledgling screenwriter, launched a writing and business services company two weeks after the D.A. filed charges against Ryder; they'd subsequently deposited amounts totaling $50,000 into their business's account, and her husband had purchased a new Ford Expedition. Geragos showily posited that the infusion of cash was the result of the couple selling Rainey's account of the arrest to TV shows—the very kind Geragos appeared on regularly—or tabloids, all part of a conspicuous for-profit scheme to tar his client.

Rainey explained that those profits were generated solely from her husband's work as a financial consultant and insisted she'd never given any interviews to the press. Lacking palpable evidence of such a transaction, Geragos intimated that Rainey should study the handwriting on her financial information carefully, saying, "I don't want you to commit a further act of perjury"—earning the attorney a sharp contempt of court warning from Judge Fox.

As relentlessly as Geragos hammered away at Evans and Rainey—and to a lesser extent, newly minted Det. Mark Parker, whose memory of who retrieved the scissors from Ryder was admittedly hazy—there were glimmers that the defense's theatrical display wasn't having its desired effect, at least on the gallery. Witness accounts, mounting evidence, and Ryder's multiple, oft-contradictory excuses—particularly repeated testimony affirming her admission that she'd shoplifted at the direction of a filmmaker to prepare for a movie role, though even her publicist Mara Buxbaum told the press such a notion was "utterly ridiculous"—accumulated. When Saks sales associates Shirley Warren and Sophie Seyranian testified Ryder did not leave her credit card imprint with them or instruct them to keep her account open, each added a small but potentially telling detail: they'd both been dispatched to fetch Cokes for the actress, leaving Ryder unattended with her accumulated merchandise in the respective dressing rooms. Low gasps could be heard from the court-watchers in the gallery as they recognized the convenient strategic potential of the winsome star's requests.

As the prosecution methodically aligned its case in the face of Geragos's apparently baseless theorizing, two key questions increasingly loomed large: would Winona Ryder take the witness stand? And if so, would she be able to convey her version of events as compellingly as she did fictional narratives on screen? "I can't tell you now," offered Geragos, keeping the press in suspense.

The actress spent her thirty-first birthday in court, three days into the proceedings. The only evidence that the day carried any celebratory meaning was that she'd arrived even more dressed to impress than usual, her eye-catching couture having shifted into a higher gear since her trial began. That day, she elevated her consistent ladylike-but-glam factor by a few degrees in a figure-conscious, long-sleeve, knee-length black Marc Jacobs sweater dress featuring thin black piping and lacy detailing at the hem and cuffs, with a pale pink trompe l'oeil contrasting collar with matching midriff and cuff detailing. If wearing a designer whose label appeared on one of the items she was accused of stealing was intended to send a message, Ryder kept it to herself.

As ever, Ryder's style choices had not gone unnoticed by fashion columnists, sparking considerable conversation about what sort of sartorial statements she was making. "Throughout her trial, Ryder looked splendid," opined the *Washington Post*'s style writer Robin Givhan. "For all of her courtroom appearances she was outfitted in a perfectly chic, refined and demure ensemble. She may be a shoplifter, but she has impeccable taste." But in her analysis of the actress' conservatively impeccable wardrobe and the not-too-trendy, not-too-classic array of unpaid-for items in her shopping bags, Givhan wondered if some of Ryder's hyper-feminine fashion flourishes—chaste flowing fits, delicate detailing like lace and embroidery, demure Mary Janes—weren't slyly manipulative in their overt imagery of innocence. "With her style so self-assured, with her clothes so obviously of-the-moment, with her public presentation so clearly of the pampered-princess ilk, could it be that even for a Beverly Hills jury Ryder was just a tad too well put together?"

Meanwhile, Slate's court chronicler Dahlia Lithwick snarked at the obsessive dissection of Ryder's courtroom couture. "As a rule, for every paragraph the media have devoted to the legal developments in the trial, two were devoted to what she was wearing and how she wore her hair," Lithwick wrote. "This wasn't a person on trial, it was Felony Barbie."

The actress had remained largely inscrutable, sitting typically alone at the defense table as Geragos parried at witnesses, sometimes dutifully taking notes, sometimes gazing out in the gallery, unfocused on any fixed point. Once, though, her eyes welled with tears when Ken Evans recounted asking Beverly Hills police if there was any way to file charges on a different day to spare her the humiliation of being publicly taken into custody at the store. Occasionally, frustration and annoyance would flicker across her face during testimony—even feeling compelled to roll her eyes, shake her head, and take deep, calming breaths. Other times, she would smile, wave, and blow kisses to her tight-knit circle of supporters in the gallery, including her parents, her publicist, and several friends—a respectable turnout that nevertheless took up far less real estate in the courtroom than the many members of the press. During a break on her birthday, Winona walked over to where her father was sitting and embraced him. They clung to each other for several minutes.

I'd also occasionally recognize other familiar faces among the interested parties. I spied Billy "Billy T" Tsangares, of those trendy "Free Winona" tees, whose presence made a certain self-promoting sense. More puzzling was the prolific character actor Tracey Walter, a specialist in creepy-kooky roles who was among the regular acting ensemble employed by director Jonathan Demme in movies like *Silence of the Lambs* and most famously played Bob the Goon, henchman to Jack Nicholson's Joker, in *Batman*, which was produced by Peter Guber and directed by Ryder's frequent collaborator Tim Burton. Other than those tenuous connections, I *still* have no idea what might have drawn Walter to the Beverly Hills courthouse; all I can offer is that he appeared fascinated—and frequently amused—by the goings-on.

Ryder would continue to stay silent before the crowds of reporters lining the plaza coming to and from court, but after the prosecution rested she did take a moment to sign autographs for two teenage fans, writing to one of them, "Lots and lots of love and peace." At this juncture in the trial, she certainly recognized the value of both.

In his zealous defense of his client, Geragos had one more significant bomb to drop: the attorney called his chosen witnesses, including Beverly Hills police press officer Gary Gilmond and D.A. spokesperson Sandi Gibbons, who both explained that their early public statements about Ryder being visually caught on tape stealing merchandise was the result of a chain reaction of misunderstanding. Next, Geragos introduced the jury to Michael Shoar, a former employee of Saks Fifth Avenue in Costa Mesa who, in sworn testimony, claimed to have had two conversations with Ken Evans, first by phone and again over lunch in Beverly Hills shortly after Ryder's arrest, in which Evans revealed his intent to "bring [Ryder] down—one way or another."

"I asked [Evans] how he was doing," Shoar offered, recalling the lunch chat. "He said he had a very important case now and basically he would 'nail that rich Beverly Hills bitch' on shoplifting charges," Shoar said that later Evans, stressed over the high-profile case, vindictively pledged to manufacture enough evidence to ensure Ryder's conviction.

The explosive charge was barely still hanging in the air when deputy D.A. Rundle set to defusing it, getting Shoar to admit that he had an axe to grind against the department store chain since being barred from any Saks Fifth Avenue property after his job was ended over the summer. Rundle revealed that Shoar and his wife had allegedly threatened to sue the company over purported sexual harassment his wife experienced by another Saks employee, and that if the store refused to fire the man he claimed was responsible, Shoar'd vowed to take his case to—*surprise*—Mark Geragos. Which Shoar did, but Geragos had demurred, citing a potential conflict of interest, and referred the ex-employee to another attorney. Rundle came with an audio recording of Shoar's threats to a Saks executive and got Shoar to concede he hadn't come forward with his story about Evans until *after* he'd broken with the company and his wife pursued a civil lawsuit. Finally, Rundle had Evans tell the jury how, just a month before Ryder's trial began, Shoar had staged a protest outside Saks Fifth Avenue Beverly Hills, an example of the disruptive behavior that earned him the company's property-wide ban. Rundle created such an effective portrait of Shoar as a disgruntled ex-employee that when he denied being "very angry" at Saks Fifth Avenue on the stand, it was laughter, rather than gasps, that rippled through the gallery.

The next day, Geragos told the media that, though Ryder wanted to testify "in the worst way," he felt he'd created ample reasonable doubt in the jurors' minds.

The jury would not be privy to everything that either the prosecution or the defense hoped to put in front of them. In a closed-door session, the D.A.'s office argued to admit witness testimony and video evidence pertaining to the three shoplifting incidents that allegedly occurred prior to her arrest to illustrate that Ryder had an M.O. and debunk arguments that she'd paid for items she'd taken. But Judge Fox ruled that since Ryder wasn't detained, arrested, or convicted in any of the incidents, admitting the information, "far more prejudicial than probative," could unnecessarily jeopardize her chance for a fair trial. Geragos opposed the admission of the confession Ryder had signed at the store by insisting she'd signed it under duress, but Rundle argued that Geragos's conspiracy theory opened the door: it was voluntary, signed without coercion. Geragos claimed Ryder had refused to sign the confession, but mistakenly did so when it was lumped in with paperwork she signed agreeing to never return to the store. Judge Fox ruled to exclude it but did allow the jury to see an itemized list of the merchandise found on Ryder that she had acknowledged with her signature.

For his part, Geragos was denied the opportunity to call a last-minute witness, a former roommate of Colleen Rainey's who claimed she'd been involved in a scheme to defraud a Neiman-Marcus store in which one would purchase merchandise at an employee discount and then the other would return the items for full retail value. But even if true, the judge deemed it to have occurred so long ago as to be irrelevant to the case at hand.

As closing arguments commenced on November 4, I'd been covering the case—sometimes strange, sometimes surreal, always surprising—for nearly eleven months since Ryder's arrest, with never a shortage of twists, turns, and bombshells along the way. Heading into the climax, I expected at least a few more firework displays; I wouldn't be disappointed, but I was caught off guard when no-nonsense prosecutor Ann Rundle revealed her own keen sense of showmanship.

Rundle began her closing in typically direct style, methodically yet briskly laying out how the actress had walked into the department store carrying burglary tools—the scissors, the excess bags, the tissue paper—demonstrating her intent, and walked out of the store with over $5,000 in unpaid merchandise, all illustrated on the surveillance video. "Would you think this was a glamorous celebrity or someone preparing to shoplift?" she asked. "Is there anyone else in the store lugging around this much stuff?" Rundle directed attention to salient video clips, such as Ryder subtly slipping the antitheft sensor tags into the pocket of the Chanel jacket and sending the salesclerks to fetch Cokes, buying herself more time unobserved. At various points in her narrative, Rundle displayed the stolen items discovered on Ryder when she was detained.

Then, Rundle's argument took a turn for the theatrical as she pivoted to a poster placed on an easel that read—reminiscent of comedian David Letterman's long-running routine on his late-night talk shows—"Top Ten Things the Law Doesn't Say." The poster offered a checklist of items which Rundle ran down point by point, explaining in increasingly blunt, even brutal terms how each applied to the case:

1. *Only poor people steal.* "It must have occurred to some of you, 'Why would Winona Ryder steal?'" Rundle asked. "Nowhere does it say people steal because they have to. People steal out of greed, envy, spite, because it's there or for the thrill." The prosecutor invoked the portentous, life-imitating-art dialogue Ryder delivered in *Girl, Interrupted.* "*Have you ever confused a dream with life? Or stolen something when you have the cash?*" Rundle wasn't going to offer the jury any detailed motivation—Ryder's actions, in her view, spoke to her guilt clearly enough—but she did take a beat to speculate.

"She may have been stealing for the sheer thrill of seeing if she could get away with it."

2. *If there's no video, there's no crime.* Though the surveillance video did not capture Ryder cutting sensor tags off merchandise, Rundle urged jurors to believe the eyewitness, Colleen Rainey, who saw the actress snip away.

3. *Crime is OK if your "director" tells you to do* it. "Even if you are researching a role, it is wrongful to cut off security tags and destroy the property," Rundle reminded jurors, adding, "And there is no evidence a director told her to do it."

4. *It's not stealing if you paid for some items.* Purchasing four items from Saks, Rundle pointed out, didn't give Ryder the right to steal twenty more.

5. *The D.A. must call every person working at Saks that day.* Rundle explained she didn't need to call every possible witness, only employees who witnessed Ryder stealing.

6. *Only defense attorneys or celebrities can buy a nice car.* In a not-so-subtle dig at Porsche-driving Geragos, Rundle said Rainey shouldn't be discounted because her husband recently bought a new vehicle.

7. *If it is not in the first report, it didn't happen.* Here, Rundle addressed various omissions in original reports by the Saks security team, which they testified were unintentionally left out due to the rush to complete them and which they detailed on the witness stand.

8. *If you sell $200 hair bows, you deserve to get ripped off.* Even if Saks's merchandise seems outrageously overpriced, Rundle said that didn't give Ryder free rein to commit a felony.

9. *Two wrongs make a right.* Rundle addressed the mistaken wording of the press statements by Beverly Hills police and District Attorney's spokespeople, noting that neither had seen the videotape at that point, and they publicly amended their errors later, which shouldn't offer Ryder any wiggle room for her own actions.

10. *There is a higher standard of proof for celebrities.* "The law is the law, no matter who you are," Rundle told the jury matter-of-factly. "The law treats everybody the same."

She offered another graphic as well, revealing a poster-sized photo of Ryder festooned with several cartoon word balloons coming from the actress's mouth, each offering one of the myriad defense excuses floated in the wake of her arrest: she had an open account; her assistant should have paid for it; she was getting into character for a role; she was researching for *Shopgirl*; she was researching for *White Jazz*, and so on.

"They want you to give her the celebrity discount," Rundle continued, adding that the actress *still* hadn't returned the missing Gucci dress she'd mistakenly been allowed to take home after her arrest. "Even after she's caught...she has the nerve to walk out the door with a $1,590 dress," Rundle marveled. "I am asking you to hold Ms. Ryder responsible for her conduct on December 12. It's a simple case of theft...She came, she stole, she left. End of story."

If the deputy district attorney's dynamic, potentially devastating dismantling of the defense's arguments was designed to be intentionally bracing, it had the desired effect. The impact of her words lingered for long moments.

In his own bid to sway the jurors, Geragos was as fast on his feet as ever, again suggested a plot against his client, one that had the Saks security team fabricating testimony and planting evidence—including the orange-handled scissors—fueled by devious intentions. He claimed Rainey had profited from selling her story; Evans had appeased his corporate bosses and basked in an intended "fifteen minutes of fame," while the department score—which he insisted scored a "coup" by busting a celebrity, a warning to would-be shoplifters on the brink of the holiday season—sought to insulate the company from civil liability, since by Geragos's reckoning the actress had simply left her account open to be charged for the items later. "They've all got the best reasons in the world to fabricate evidence," he proclaimed. The defense attorney presented a web of would-bes and could-bes to bolster his conspiracy scenario, questioning if Saks Fifth Avenue actually *did* have surveillance video cameras in its dressing rooms but held back footage that might exonerate his client and pointing out at Saks attorneys had attended the entirety of the trial. "I invite you to speculate," he told jurors.

Then Geragos attacked the evidence itself, waving one of white Yves St. Laurent blouses marred by holes where the sensor tags had been and scoffing at the notion his client—an internationally admired style icon "known for her fashion sense"—would be caught dead in damaged clothing. "Would she really start a new fashion in 'Winona Wear' by cutting holes in this blouse?" he asked, prompting Ryder, among others in the gallery, to laugh out loud. Holding the blouse before "this glamorous actress," Geragos insisted she'd never wear such tacky styles; grinning sheepishly, Ryder began to rise as if to better juxtapose herself against his display, but an unamused Judge Fox sharply instructed Geragos to move on. All his arguments, Geragos summarized, added up to a logical conclusion of reasonable doubt. "There is no shame in coming back with a not guilty verdict for Winona," he assured jurors.

As a prosecutor, Rundle would have the last word in court. During rebuttal, she, too, provoked an unexpected reaction out of the long-stoic defendant, if less mirthful. When Rundle described the scissors as having been handed over to Saks security with Beverly Hills police present, Ryder indignantly blurted aloud, "That's not true!" several times in apparent frustration, admonished by the judge. Pressing forward, Rundle dismissed Gergaos' campaign of "insinuation, accusation and speculation," saying focusing the defense narrative on the Saks employees was a means to draw attention away from Ryder's more blatant crimes. And Rundle had one more visual aid up her sleeve, a poster board obscured with four sheets of paper, each representing a pillar of the defense's argument—"discrepancies," "overzealous security," "conspiracy," and "woman wronged"—which the prosecutor removed, piece by piece, with each counterargument, until the words on the poster were exposed, which read "NOTHING BEHIND DEFENSE."

"We've presented the truth," she told the jury. "They've presented a story that could only have been written in Hollywood." But Hollywood—the business in which many of the jurors toiled and thrived—could be capable of believing many things. The result of the jury's deliberations would reveal if and how they might suspend their disbelief.

Until then, Rundle had one last offer to extend to the defendant. She and Ryder had an otherwise convivial relationship throughout the trial, but the poster graphics affected Ryder, who asked an inaudible question about them. "After it's over, you can have it," Rundle told her.

Put off, Ryder rolled her eyes and responded with unfiltered sarcasm, "Oh, *thank you.*"

It had been an even more fiery buildup than I'd expected. It was a shame, then, that I had to miss the climax, for the most ironic of reasons: I'd been called for jury duty.

Two days after closing arguments, on November 7, I'd gotten the heads-up that a verdict was imminent, and I'd want to be at the Beverly Hills Courthouse by 11:15 a.m. My problem was that by 9 a.m. I had already reported to the Stanley Mosk Courthouse in downtown Los Angeles, reluctantly performing my civic duty by waiting to be, I hoped, swiftly dismissed from the jury pool due to my occupation as a journalist who'd reported on crime and legal proceedings—either the prosecution or the defense would likely strike me. I was indeed dismissed—it turned out I'd not only recently done business multiple times with one of the victims of fraud, proving L.A. is, in its way, a small town, too—but didn't realize there was no "swiftly" about it. By the time I was released, the world had learned Winona Ryder's legal fate without my help. The CNN-operated media pool cameras inside the courtroom—the first time filming had been allowed during the trial—broadcast the verdict live.

At 11:40 a.m., the clerk revealed the jury's conclusions after five-and-a-half hours of deliberation. On the second-degree commercial burglary count: *not guilty*. On the vandalism charge: *guilty*. And on the felony grand theft count: *guilty*.

Judge Fox thanked and excused the jurors, commended them for conducting themselves "in an exemplary manner under some very difficult circumstances," and reminded them that they couldn't accept payment for writing or being interviewed about the case for 90 days—"Essentially, Jerry Springer and Oprah Winfrey are off limits for three months," the judge quipped.

Rundle told reporters that given Ryder's lack of prior criminal history, she wouldn't be seeking a jail sentence, preferring probation. "This was never about her character, only her conduct," she said. Her boss, D.A. Steve Cooley, released a statement consistent with his campaign messaging: "The jury trial verdicts indicate that in Los Angeles County justice is blind regardless of the status of the accused." Uncharacteristically tight-lipped, Geragos said he planned to file a motion for a new trial, before motoring away in his black Porsche.

Juror Peter Guber issued a statement that afternoon, saying, "I have fulfilled my obligation to the court as a private citizen and will have no further comment on the matter." A day after the verdict, juror Walter Fox, the seventy-four-year-old obstetrician and Rotarian colleague of the similarly surnamed judge, told the *Los Angeles Times* that the jurors were never starstruck by the celebrity defendant, but they were definitely entertained when she watched herself on the surveillance video. "She made wonderfully dramatic faces," Fox said. "She looked shocked. She sees herself walking out the door with all this junk and she's shocked? Gimme a break." He reported the jurors, who got along well and quickly arrived at unanimity on the grand theft and vandalism charges, were too sophisticated to be distracted by Geragos's attacks on the witnesses. But given the provision that proof of intent was necessary in the burglary count, the jurors broke for the day, slept on it, and returned to a consensus for acquittal the next morning. "We could not peer into her mind to know what her intent was when she entered the store," said Fox.

Leaving the courthouse on Geragos's arm, Ryder—mostly impassive after the verdicts were revealed, beyond offering a dejected smile to friends and family—politely declined to open any window into her mind. "I'm sorry," she softly offered the press. "Thanks for asking. I just can't talk right now."

By the time she returned for sentencing a month later on December 6, Ryder's mood had appreciably lightened as she warmly greeted bailiff Pat Scales with a hug and a kiss—the two women had formed a downright adorable bond during the time that Scales had been assigned to escort Ryder in and out of the courtroom. Sources inside Ryder's camp informed me that the actress had been laying low at home in relatively good spirits, receiving support from family, friends, and the Hollywood community. She'd felt optimistic, given the prosecution's ultra-rare promise not to seek jail time, and was already receiving "numerous" offers of work again, though holding out until after her sentencing was complete. An appeal, I was told, was in no way a certainty. But despite her upbeat entry into the courtroom, her brow furrowed with concern as she listened to lawyers debating the consequences of her conviction.

Ken Metzner, an attorney for Saks Fifth Avenue, told Judge Fox that Geragos's strategy had unfairly vilified the store's employees and, worse, subjected them to "intense and malicious scrutiny" by the defense's private investigators "merely because they had the misfortune of apprehending a movie star." Saks, too, suffered a tremendous, unfair blow to its image, Metzner explained, due to Ryder's notorious media appearances mocking the trial: the company received e-mails and phone calls from customers complaining that it was the store, and not the legal system, that was trying to take the actress down. Saks favored a strict and thorough punishment.

Calling the store's position "outrageous," Geragos tried to shift the focus onto Ryder's many philanthropic and humanitarian efforts, particularly her involvement with Polly Klaas—indeed, Polly's father Marc had been expected in court to speak to Ryder's character but was delayed when a driver was late picking him up at the airport. In the first instance of anything resembling an acknowledgment of his client's culpability, Geragos contended that the "ten years...of good" Ryder had accomplished outweighed "the one day of bad."

That statement, and the frequency with which Geragos had peppered his remarks with mentions of Polly Klaas, didn't sit well with Ann Rundle. "What's offensive to me is to trot out the body of a dead child and in some way say because she supported the family—" the prosecutor huffed, before being interrupted by Geragos. And in that moment, something finally snapped inside Winona Ryder: she glared at Rundle with her mouth agape and slowly rose from her seat, a look of astonished outrage on her face. It was the rawest emotion the actress had publicly revealed since her legal travails began, and even as she sunk back into her chair, simmering, she refused to unfix her gaze on Rundle as the judge admonished the prosecutor.

By this point, the concerning extent of the prescription medications found in Ryder's possession had been made public, and the attorneys also wrangled over how to best address her obvious narcotics issues. "She had more medication in her purse than would be given to a person with a terminal disease," Rundle said. Geragos conceded that Ryder "had a pain-management problem—she's still working on it," but argued suggesting debating the matter would just cause her more public embarrassment. "She should be allowed to go forward with some degree if dignity and privacy."

Although he explained he had no intention of making an example out of the actress, Judge Fox sternly delivered his sentencing decree. "You have disappointed many people who have been entertained and inspired by your talent and your acts of humanity," he told Ryder, recounting how his own sixteen-year-old son had asked why someone as wealthy and successful as Winona Ryder would steal. "You're probably the only person that is going to be able to answer my son's question." Her sentence would include 36 months of probation, almost $6,400 in restitution to Saks for the stolen and damaged merchandise and an additional $3,700 to the courts in restitution and penal fines; 480 hours of community service, split among the City of Hope medical center in Duarte, the Junior Blind Foundation and Caring for Babies with AIDS; and psychiatric and drug counseling. Fox noted that the actress may also have her driver's license revoked due to the vandalism conviction, though he would allow her to travel for acting work.

"You have refused to accept personal responsibility," he said, warning that she stood at a pivotal crossroads where her next actions could define "your reputation and image and possibly your future freedom." He urged her to confront the personal issues that landed her in his courtroom.

"If you steal again, you will go to jail. Understand that?" he asked.

After a pause, she replied solemnly, "Yes, Your Honor, I do."

Outside the courthouse, late-arriving Marc Klass passionately defended his friend while accepting her new reality. "Winona Ryder may be a double-felon, but she's a double-felon with a very big heart and a very generous spirit, and nobody should ever forget that," he said.

Reactions—or were they reviews?—to the outcome were fueled by discussion of how Ryder's Hollywood celebrity had dominated at every turn. "As a legal proceeding, the Winona Ryder shoplifting trial was a waste of time. But as a window on the folkways of Hollywood, it set a new standard," opined the *New York Times*. "Anywhere else, this petty crime by a first-time offender would have quickly ended with a plea bargain. The prosecutors, of course, made high-minded statements about the need to prove no one is above the law. But the truth is that in the great Hollywood tradition, this clunky script was green-lighted simply because a big star's name was attached. Ms. Ryder gamely stoked the publicity machine, dressing for trial in chic outfits and posing for a fashion magazine's cover in a 'Free Winona' T-shirt."

Slate's Dahlia Lithwick believed even Ryder's own defense team was dazzled by the patina of fame and glamour enveloping the case. "Geragos, so blinded by Ryder's celebrity, never managed to make this trial about anything other than Ryder's celebrity. She was either too famous to have done this, or she was being framed for being famous. Either way, her only defense was her celebrity." Lithwick countered that "simply walking into a courtroom, she'd already proved that she was life-size to the only people who really counted: the jury."

Those who knew the actress remained in her corner. "Last time I talked to her, she seemed relieved more than anything else," Marc Klaas told

People. "This has held up her life and career. She wants to do other things than contemplate a public humiliation."

"The way they dragged her through the…I would say mud, but in fact it was broken glass," Johnny Depp told *20/20*'s Elizabeth Vargas six months after Ryder's conviction. "She's a good kid and she's also a very strong spirit. She'll make her way through."

"When she was being pilloried in the press, to me it was like, 'This too shall pass'—that somehow her true colors would come out and she would get past it because she's a great woman," Matt Damon told *Playboy*. "That part sucks, seeing somebody you care about being treated poorly in public."

"Noni's one of those people who soaks in every experience and learns from it," Brittany Murphy, who'd grown close with Ryder and viewed her as her "ultimate mentor," told *People.* "She should have won an Oscar for never cracking and never having a picture taken of her looking anything but fabulous. We'll always remember her image during that time."

Only ever-outspoken Courtney Love would address the more troubling issues the trial exposed. "She's got a problem," the actress-rocker told *People.* "It's not a physical addiction. It's a compulsion. It's the same madness as any other shopaholic." Since Ryder's arrest, Love had sustained a cameo role in her friend's unfolding dramas. She was about to have her turn in the spotlight.

Hollywood loves a franchise, and the trial of Winona Ryder immediately served up not a sequel but a sort of spinoff: on the day of her sentencing, the Medical Board of California revoked the license of Dr. Jules Lusman for his "cash-and-carry" prescription services, providing highly addictive narcotics to elite clients. The forty-nine-year-old South African physician, whose stated specialty was tattoo- and hair-removal laser surgery, built a lucrative sideline charging exorbitant "retainer fees" in the thousands of dollars to satiate the controlled-substance appetites of wealthy, often famous patients who'd have otherwise had to turn to riskier street-level sources.

The medical board likened the scheme to "the sub-plot of a Raymond Chandler novel." One of the eight identified patients had been issued around 360 different prescriptions over a five-year period; for others, Lusman wrote multiple prescriptions in the same week, sometimes even the same day; well-to-do patients would spy Lusman sporting valuable belongings like Rolex watches and could only take his word—and sketchy bills of sale—that he'd purchased the items from them while they were clouded in a narcotic haze. Lusman borrowed $164,000 from one patient; took $20,000 to invest from another, as well as a Japanese art print for appraisal and had to be sued for the return of both the funds and the art. He asked another to co-sign his mortgage while injecting her with Demerol. Already disciplined in his native country for improperly prescribing medications before relocating his practice first to New York and then, in 1990, to Santa Monica, the predatory physician targeted his deep-pocketed patients—who often had histories of mental illness, emotional instability, and drug addiction—by marketing himself in the Yellow Pages and through flyers distributed to concierges at high-end hotels. The board report called Lusman "a drug pusher with a medical license."

Patients were referred to in the report only by their initials. Twenty-nine-year-old "E.T.," a "well-known entertainer," was treated by Lusman for "anxious pain," insomnia, scoliosis, and an injured wrist, along with cosmetic laser surgery, amassing prescriptions for an array of drugs including a staggering volume of Vicoprofin pills, despite no evidence of any actual medical procedures being performed. The patient's initials, of course, corresponded with "Emily Thompson," the alias Ryder had adopted for many of her prescriptions; "E.T.'s" age and medical complaints also aligned with the actress.

Another patient, "C.L.," was a "fairly well-known musician" who "at one time had been married to 'Mr. C,' who had passed away." Treated during the summer of 2001, "C.L." was one of several Lusman patients issued liquid Demerol and syringes for injection, as well as Xanax and Ambien. The press quickly outed "C.L." as Courtney Love, widow of Nirvana's Kurt Cobain, now one of Ryder's fellow headliners in the emerging medical melodrama. Famously litigious, Love had her attorney send the website The Smoking Gun, then one of the internet's foremost sources for celebrity courtroom scoop, a fiery four-page letter threatening legal action if the site didn't remove excerpts from the board's report. If her demand didn't already strongly suggest she was the patient in question, The Smoking Gun's point-by-point examination of the evidence—plus the rocker's own well-known, publicly acknowledged history of narcotics abuse—sealed it, attracting even further media attention to Love's connection to the disgraced doctor. When the *Los Angeles Times* confirmed her identity, any legal showdown became moot.

Reportedly referred by Love, Ryder came to Lusman in 2001 for treatment of back pain and her fractured elbow. Prescribing Vicoprofen, then

Endocet, Valium, and a growing pharmacy of painkillers and anti-anxiety meds, he'd soon become a frequent visitor to her Doheny Drive home, even attending her thirtieth birthday party a month and a half before her arrest at Saks Fifth Avenue, posing for photos alongside Ben Stiller, Benicio Del Toro, and Adam Sandler. During the shoplifting investigation, Ryder's identification as a Lusman patient led to a partial revocation of his license and a $75,000 fine. Yet as late as April 2002, Ryder offered support for the physician, signing a declaration proclaiming Lusman—who'd formally copped to providing her with the oxycodone-based Endocet pills—"to be professional and beyond reproach. He has never harmed me and never constituted a threat to me or the community or public health and safety." By November, though the felony drug charges against Ryder were dropped, Lusman was neck-deep in hot water with the medical board.

"I can hardly be compared to Elvis Presley's doctor," he huffed to the *Sydney Morning Herald*, but his license was fully, permanently revoked in December 2002. Seven months later, Lusman was charged with four felony and four misdemeanor counts related to practicing medicine illegally, performing cosmetic medical procedures on two women at his Brentwood condo, offering a discount when one of them balked at receiving injections—including Perlane, a facial filler not approved by the FDA. Even as Lusman complained he was the victim of an overzealous attempt to police his industry and called Hollywood "the home of narcissism," he also sought out an agent to peddle his life rights and sold his story—including a claim that Ryder had stolen a prescription pad from him—to tabloids like the *National Enquirer*. Despite vows to fight the charges, he ultimately entered a no-contest plea and was sentenced to five years' probation. Lusman returned to his native Cape Town, where, against all odds, he was eventually practicing medicine once again.

A few months after her conviction, Winona Ryder's legal team floated an idea: since the various merchandise that had been taken from Saks Fifth Avenue were just gathering dust in some evidence storage space somewhere, and the department store indicated it would prefer that the clothing and accessories be destroyed once their legal utility was over, what if the actress were to auction them off for charity?

"It seems to me to be silly to take thousands of dollars' worth of merchandise and burn it in a bonfire," Mark Geragos suggested at Ryder's first probation progress report as he and the client returned to Judge Fox's courtroom on April 7, 2003. Using the high-dollar items to help a worthy cause—Geragos speculated that he could raise as much as $100,000 from the goods—seemed a magnanimous gesture; that it could bolster any mounting campaign to rehabilitate Ryder's public reputation was the part that went unsaid.

But Ann Rundle took serious issue with the stunt. "While it has been reported that the defendant intends to auction the items off 'for charity,' the defendant would nevertheless maintain a tax deduction benefit, as well as a publicity advantage," the deputy D.A. responded in court papers. "Once again, this would not serve the purpose of deterring her future criminal conduct—as well as sending the message to the community that 'Crime DOES Pay.'"

Judge Fox—otherwise duly impressed with Ryder's progress since her sentencing, having completed her community service hours, paid all her fines and fees, and received glowing reports from her probation officer, therapist, and other counselors—was inclined to agree with Rundle's argument, but decided to give the notion further consideration.

Saks Fifth Avenue made its position even clearer when, within a week of Ryder's progress hearing, the company donated $6,355.40—the exact sum of the actress' court-ordered restitution—to the City of Hope, the children's charity where Ryder served the bulk of her community service. "We believe that auctioning the merchandise would glamorize the crime, thereby sending the wrong message to children," a spokesperson for the store added.

No charity auction of the lifted loot would ever come to pass. But that didn't mean crime wouldn't pay.

The ink on her sentencing documents had barely dried when fashion designer Marc Jacobs—he who crafted the thermal top snared in Ryder's sticky-fingered shopping spree, as well as the glamorously coquettish sweater dress she wore to court on her birthday—chose Ryder as the face of the label's Spring 2003 campaign. Jacobs had become even more besotted with the actress—a devotee (paying or otherwise) who'd also walked the catwalk for Jacobs at a fall 2000 fashion show—and perhaps especially all the free publicity she'd generated for his brand over the past year. "I asked Winona to do the campaign because I thought she looked so beautiful in all these pictures that we've seen recently, regardless of whether they were from the trial," the designer told *Women's Wear Daily*. "She's always loved the clothes, she's always been a good customer, she's always worn the clothes."

"Of course it'll be controversial, but it won't be in a negative way. She's been wearing Marc Jacobs for years," company president Robert Duffy agreed, poo-pooing rumors the photo shoot would take place in a court-room or department store. "It's an ad for Marc Jacobs, not *The Enquirer*." Instead, photographer Juergen Teller snapped a heroin-chic-styled Ryder in caught-off-guard poses within a Chateau Marmont hotel suite in West Hollywood, where one shot featured the actress rifling through a pile of clothes, with a pair of orange-handled scissors strategically visible atop a nearby desk.

"Winona sent me the nicest note with beautiful flowers," Jacobs revealed. "She wrote, 'I'm thrilled that you asked me—I've always loved wearing the clothes, and it's a great honor for me.'" The collaboration would mark the beginning of a long and fruitful professional and personal relationship for both designer and model: he would later describe her as "a brilliant mind, talent, and physical beauty like no other," his "ultimate muse." Over the course of two decades, Ryder would serve as the center-piece of several different campaigns for Jacobs' various ready-to-wear, acces-sory, and beauty lines.

It couldn't have worked out better if she *had* paid upfront for that $760 cashmere top.

Despite accusations of staging a "show trial," Los Angeles County District Attorney Steve Cooley, having demonstrated to his constituents that he wouldn't be soft on celebrity crime, was re-elected in 2004 and again in 2008—the first three-time D.A. since Buron Fitts in the '30s and '40s. Cooley's office would further wrangle with the rich and infamous, success-fully prosecuting record producer Phil Spector for murder, and Michael Jackson's physician Dr. Conrad Murray for involuntary manslaughter; less successful were bids to convict actor Robert Blake for the murder of his ex-wife, and attempts to extradite fugitive filmmaker Roman Polanski to answer for outstanding statutory rape charges that prompted him to flee to Europe in 1978. Cooley even impressed Mark Geragos. "He's the gold standard for handling high-profile cases," the defense attorney would later say. "I deal with prosecutors all over the country, and in my mind his office is at the top of their game in these types of cases." Cooley's deputy on Ryder's case, Ann Rundle, would remain with the D.A.'s office until 2009, seeing over 100 felony trials to verdict without a single acquittal.

Despite Ryder's case landing in his loss column, Geragos effectively demonstrated the lengths he was willing to go to when mounting vigorous defenses for "underdog" clients, as well as an increasing mastery of using the media to his advantage. His position among talking-head legal commentators on the broadcast and cable news channel circuit was enshrined for the next several decades as he took on cases of even more import and even greater headline-generating potential: he initially mounted music icon Michael Jackson's highly visible defense against molestation charges, though he was discharged as counsel before Jackson's acquittal; was unable to prevent the conviction of Scott Peterson for the murder of his pregnant wife Laci and their unborn child; and negotiated a plea deal for R&B singer Chris Brown, charged with brutally assaulting his then-girlfriend, bestselling music artist Rihanna. A short-lived ABC legal drama, *Notorious*, was loosely based on the symbiotic relationship between Geragos and *Larry King Live* producer Wendy Walker. In 2022, Geragos took his fruitful romance with the media a step further, co-purchasing venerable *Los Angeles*, the region's longest-running city magazine.

In his 2013 book *Mistrial: An Inside Look at How the Criminal Justice System Works…and Sometimes Doesn't*, co-written with legal colleague Pat Harris, Geragos fondly recalled Ryder as a model client. "No one was kinder and more down to earth than Winona Ryder, despite the fact that she was being destroyed in the media on a daily basis during her shoplifting trial," he wrote. "She knew the charges were going to harm her career, yet she never complained or second-guessed anything. She must have been very sad during the whole process, but she never let it show—she was the one always asking how everyone else was doing…She was probably the least self-absorbed of any movie stars we have ever met."

Judge Elden S. Fox would see further troubled former teen stars pass through his courtroom: Lindsay Lohan—in 2010, Fox would spare her six months behind bars, instead sending her to rehab at Rancho Mirage's Betty Ford Center following Lohan's previous jail sentence, missed court appearances, probation violations and failed drug tests in the wake of multiple incidents of intoxication behind the wheel; and Amanda Bynes—the judge handled aspects of the first of the Nickelodeon actress' string of bizarre DUI arrests, a precursor to the public revelation of Bynes's struggles with bipolar disorder and substance abuse.

Indeed, Ryder's trial had set the stage for a succession of beautiful, hard-partying young starlets, pop idols and reality TV personalities in legal jeopardy with seemingly reckless abandon throughout the 2000s—Lohan, Britney Spears, Tara Reid, Mischa Barton, Paris Hilton, and Nicole Richie among them, though none with quite the same prestige as Ryder—perfectly timed to serve as fodder for an emerging, click-driven 24/7 digital news cycle further supercharged by a new breed of media—snark-driven, scandal-craving, often vicious gossip blogs and websites like Gizmodo, Gawker, Perez Hilton, Just Jared, and TMZ—and the increased reach of juicy gossip items shared exponentially across another novel new format, social media.

The effect of her trial's legacy did not go unnoticed by the actress herself. "It's so interesting when you look at the early aughts," she told *Harper's Bazaar* in 2022, expressing empathy for those who followed in her intensely scrutinized footsteps. "It was a kind of cruel time. There was a lot of meanness out there."

While a film adaptation of James Ellroy's novel *White Jazz* never came to fruition, Steve Martin's novella *Shopgirl* would be translated to the big screen, albeit without Winona Ryder. Claire Danes, Jason Schwartzman, and Martin himself would instead headline the poignant story of a young, disenchanted would-be artist (Danes) going through the motions of her drab job as a sales clerk at a department store glove counter, "selling things that nobody buys anymore" as she navigates two markedly different suitors, a wealthy, suave older customer (Martin) and an awkward, aimless graphic designer her own age (Schwartzman).

Joining the actors in a surprise supporting role in *Shopgirl* was Saks Fifth Avenue.

The novella had been set at Neiman-Marcus, the department store chain's Beverly Hills neighbor since 1979 and near-century-long corporate rival, which Martin portrayed as a cold and shallow backdrop for his melancholic romance. But, perhaps spurred on by the spate of unpleasant publicity that had connected the retailer with the Ryder case, Saks eagerly lobbied to fill its competitor's berth in the storyline. Through the company's representative, the Beverly Hills-based William Morris Endeavors Agency, Saks submitted a proposal that subtly but distinctively shifted the mood and tone of the story's environs into a warmer, more inviting and sun-dappled locale awash with elegance and aspiration as a counterpoint to the characters' existential ennui. The filmmakers were impressed, especially when the store offered unfettered access and synergistic marketing tie-ins across the vast retail chain upon release, including its coveted display windows in New York and Beverly Hills, so each could benefit from the other's unique cachet. Over six days of filming inside and outside the Wilshire Boulevard store, Saks Fifth Avenue was lavishly, gorgeously photographed, emerging, the producers told the retailers, as "the hero of the story."

Released in late 2005, the film was glowingly received by most critics and performed modestly at the box office. It may not have been a zeitgeist bonanza, but it ably reflected the chic and tasteful elegance of the retailer's image. And it demonstrated, once and for all, that *Shopgirl* was decidedly *not* about a shoplifter. The only thing stolen in the film were the scenes in which the glamorous store appeared.

Hollywood quickly signaled in the wake of Ryder's conviction that she would not be considered a pariah. Publicists, agents, producers, crisis managers, and even heads of major studios opined in print that her transgressions would be forgiven and forgotten, and she would be welcomed back to work. "I certainly would hire her again in a minute," 20th Century Fox's chairman Tom Rothman, whose studio made two films with Ryder under his leadership, told the *Los Angeles Times*. "She's reliable, committed, disciplined." In fact, some suggested, her newfound infamy might mark her as an even-more in-demand commodity than she'd been before she walked into Saks Fifth Avenue on December 12. "When something from your personal life is a big part of the public's perception of you, you have to deal with it," offered *Saturday Night Live* creator Lorne Michaels, who'd recognized that maxim when he welcomed her to host the show during her troubles. "You have to be topical."

But even as a steady flow of offers resumed, insurance necessary to secure completion bonds for filming proved difficult to obtain, an obstacle that forced filmmaker Woody Allen to nix his intention to hire both Ryder and the then-similarly legally challenged Robert Downey, Jr., as the leads of his comedy *Melinda & Melinda*. Her potential comeback momentum impeded, Ryder remained largely absent from the big screen in the years immediately following her run-in with the law, creating an impression that her industry had abandoned her; she busied herself in what she felt was a healthier, more productive manner. "A lot of people had the perception that I just disappeared in the 2000s," she would reflect to Net-a-Porter. "And I did, but only from that [Hollywood] world. I appeared elsewhere, I promise you. I was transformed into doing stuff I really wanted to do—it was a great awakening. It just wasn't in the public eye."

As she had before, she found refuge at what would always be home, journeying back to the comforting envelope of San Francisco, where she sought to discover what new things life had to offer and interest her out-side of a career that had consumed such a substantial portion of her youth. "I definitely retreated," Ryder explained to *Harper's Bazaar* years later. "I was in San Francisco. But I also wasn't getting offers. I think it was a very mutual break."

Ryder would rarely directly—often only elliptically—address exactly the chain of events that led to her conviction. But in 2007, she'd open up to *Vogue*, offering her take on how her prescription drug addiction had escalated, and its role in her behavior. "Two months prior to [the shoplift-ing arrest], I broke my arm in two places, and the doctor, a sort of quack doctor, was giving me a lot of stuff and I was taking it at first to get through the pain," she explained. "And then there was this weird point when you don't know if you are in pain but you're taking it. That's, I guess, the really scary point, because that's when people get hooked. In a way [that inci-dent] happening at that time, in a very weird way, was a blessing, because I couldn't do that [painkillers] anymore."

"Have you ever done painkillers? It isn't a reckless [state], like you're out of your head," she continued. "It's just confusion. I wonder if I hadn't had that going on if I wouldn't have done things differently. I can't or won't ever know. But I remember being really confused."

But she stopped short of detailing how and why she'd shoplifted; indeed, she still seemed to believe her courtroom defense, insisting that it was all some big misunderstanding, or worse, a conspiracy. "When you are in the public eye, you are treated differently at these places. And you're used to shopping with someone who is like…you feel like things are being sort of…everything is taken care of," she offered. "I mean, there had been times when I had come home and there were things I didn't know that I had got or when I was charged for things that I didn't get. That can be a big scam in L.A."

Despite venturing into victim-blaming, she revealed that she was nat-urally no longer a habitual department store shopper. "To this day, I don't go into those stores, because when I do, there have been many times that I felt like they're watching me, and I don't blame them."

Among her family, she said, "No one ever got angry with me. Concerned, yes, but not concerned with a drug problem or anything like that. Because after that night I pretty much didn't ever…If you are ever arrested, you can't ever do that again. I was very honest with them about that. So [for them] it was protecting me, and being angry at things people were saying. Being angry at the court itself. Being angry at the charges. Being angry at the statements."

After her conviction, her commitment to the terms of her probation satisfied the court: in June 2004, Judge Fox reduced her felony sentences to misdemeanors and placed her on unsupervised probation through 2005 due to her good behavior. But if anyone was expecting florid public apologies or *mea culpas*, she told *Vogue* she wasn't particularly penitent. "I didn't have a tremendous sense of guilt, because I hadn't hurt someone," she said. "Had I hurt someone in any way, had I rear-ended…had I done anything, even in the past, that I felt this was some kind of retribution for, had I physically harmed someone or caused harm to a human being, I think it would've been an entirely different experience. I could never wrap my head around what I was supposed to be feeling and the perception of what I was going through. I just sat there. I never said a word. I didn't release a statement. I just waited for it to be over."

To Ryder, everything was part of a confluence of events that, at that moment in her life, seemed inevitable, almost necessary. "Psychologically, I must have been at a place where I just wanted to stop," she told *Interview* in 2013. "I won't get into what happened, but it wasn't what people think. And it wasn't like the crime of the century! But it allowed me time that I really needed, where I went back to San Francisco and got back into things that…I just had other interests, frankly."

She was drawn to seemingly esoteric subjects like constitutional law, linguistics, and etymology that, years earlier, she might have only sampled if a film role required it. "As terrible as this sounds, when you're making movies, you think that those other things are not as important—the most important thing is that you do a good job in the movie and that you're prepared. So just getting that kind of perspective on life really helped me," she told *Harper's Bazaar*.

And that, she explained, was how she got through the experience of going from one of the most famous movie stars in the world to "that girl who stole from Saks Fifth Avenue."

"You just do," she said. "In the scheme of things, there are much bigger problems to worry about."

I would eventually reencounter Winona Ryder. During her self-imposed hiatus, the actress had come to a revelation: she really did want to continue to pursue her passion for acting, if not stardom, and gradually began to resurface on screen in primarily independent films as she toe-dipped her way back while simultaneously demonstrating to the completion bond companies she remained professionally reliable.

My path into entertainment journalism widened, focusing on film and television coverage and personality profiles over criminal justice, writing for an array of print and online clients including *People, InStyle, Variety, The Hollywood Reporter*, and more. So I'd eventually find myself face to face with Ryder, first while covering her 2006 film *A Scanner Darkly*, where she offered up an amusing throwaway moment on the red carpet at the premiere. Amid a scrum of reporters, I asked her how it felt being back in the glitzy Hollywood whirl once again, and she exaggeratedly looked around at the plethora of cameras pointed at her, put on an exaggerated smile, and exclaimed with faux-enthusiasm and not-so-couched irony "Delightful! I *love* it!" And with personal questions declared verboten by her handlers before the premiere started, that was about as revealing an exchange as would be allowed.

I would continue to encounter Ryder as her projects grew in profile and prestige, at premieres like the 2009 reboot of *Star Trek*, playing Spock's mother Amanda in the franchise dear to her sci-fi-fan heart; at an American Film Institute screening of *Black Swan*, her most darkly dynamic role in ages, however brief; the press conference for a happy, long-awaited reunion with Tim Burton in *Frankenweenie*; and in a sit-down chat for the crime thriller *The Iceman*. As one of the legions of press faces fleetingly paraded past her over the years, I harbored no illusion that she retained any memory of our infrequent encounters from project to project, let alone from her trial—such is often the nature of my profession.

But it was especially intriguing in July 2016 when I ventured over to the fabled Mack Sennett Studios, where a century earlier silent films helped invent what would become the entertainment industry, to cover the premiere of the then-upstart streaming network Netflix's early entry into original programming, the soon-to-be-smash hit *Stranger Things*, which Ryder attended on the arm of her beau of several years, fashion designer Scott

McKinley Hahn of the sustainable label Loomstate. Then, still so under the radar that I was one of only about a dozen or so reporters to cover the premiere, *Stranger Things* offered a fresh yet fitting vehicle for Ryder, with its spookily atmospheric, supernatural/science fiction bent and ideally retro-'80s vibes; the charming kid-centric cast featuring, akin to Ryder, a preternaturally talented young breakout actress in Millie Bobbie Brown; and nostalgia-drenched soundtrack ("That was stuff that I listened to—and still do," Ryder told me. "It was like, 'Oh, do you have my tape on?' I still listen to mix tapes"). Even Ryder's character Joyce Byers, who spends much of the initial season in an agonizing search for her missing son, offered a callback to her own efforts to help locate and rescue Polly Klaas.

Ryder revealed to me how impressed she was with her young co-stars, who she found deeply enjoyed the acting process, unlike some other teen actors she'd worked opposite who appeared forced into the profession by overambitious stage parents. "They just genuinely really, really loved it—which I did too at that age," she said of the bonds she'd formed. At forty-four, she was also reveling in the opportunity to sink her teeth into the kind of age-appropriate, anti-glam adult role she'd been waiting for practically her entire career. "It was nice to be able to play my age for a change, because I went through a whole period where I was too young or too old, or they didn't know, so it was kind of liberating in that sense. I grew up on movies like 'Alice Doesn't Live Here Anymore' and the Marsha Mason movies about single mothers who are not perfect and very human and flawed and just trying to make ends meet." This project, which would drop her directly back into the cultural zeitgeist as it mushroomed into a full-fledged phenomenon, renewing and redefining her iconic status, afforded her an opportunity to plumb some genuinely harrowing emotional depths—"I was sort of a wreck for a few months every day"—and she relished the opportunity. A new generation of fans embraced her, and for longtime admirers, bygones were bygones.

In this new era, I had to reassess Winona Ryder as well, and—especially after sharing so many long hours in the courtroom in what was certainly one of her lowest moments—reconcile the young woman of wealth and privilege I'd observed then, resisting responsibility for something that by all reliable accounts and evidence she appeared to have clearly and deliberately done, with the woman I would encounter nearly two decades later: still visibly delicate, effortlessly stylish, practically an emotional tuning fork as a performer, but also more relaxed, more mature, wiser. How was *this* woman now *that* woman then]?

When I reflected on it, I found myself inwardly reworking that bit of dialogue from one of her films, the one that also echoed back at her trial, to reflect the circumstances:

Had she just been given too much, too soon, except the tools to handle it all? Was she acting out to numb her emotional and physical pain, maybe even hoping to get caught? Or did that anti-establishment streak simply run strong in her family? Maybe she never really cared. Maybe it was the aughts.

Or maybe she was just a girl…interrupted.

ACKNOWLEDGMENTS

My most sincere thanks and appreciation go out to the many people who helped make this long-dreamed-of book a reality, beginning with my former *People* colleague and accomplished true crime journalist Elaine Aradillas, who introduced me to her agent, Frank Weimann of Folio Literary Management, who in turn became *my* agent and brought the book to Post Hill Press, which became my publisher. I'm endlessly grateful to you all.

To Patrick Lee and Amanda Champagne Meadows for research assists, constructive feedback, and enthusiastic support; to Dr. Mark Huston, Paul Thompson, Carita Rizzo, Scott Johnson, Andrea Simpson, John Halecky, Jasmin Rosemberg, and Matthew Reynolds for boundless encouragement and bent ears; to Heather Newgen, Maria Virobik Lee and Jim Vejvoda for cheerleading these stories over Zoom and cocktails during the pandemic; to Melody Chiu and the staff of *People*, and all my other freelance clients for their support, assistance, and patience through the writing of the book.

To Tara Dennis Gatto, for helping me crack open the mystery of her father, the gentleman jewel thief Gerard Graham Dennis, who was my gateway into this ceaseless obsession three decades ago; to Anne Dennis Altman for filling in the blanks; to retired Captain Frank Salcido of the Beverly Hills Police Department, my first press liaison there, for his professionalism, patience, wisdom and good humor; to the entire Beverly Hills police force and support staff throughout the organization's remarkable history; and to the one-of-a-kind community of Beverly Hills, still unparalleled in its mix of cosmopolitan opulence and small-town splendors.

Lastly, my eternal gratitude goes out to the truly countless number of journalists, editors, columnists, authors, bloggers, historians, memoirists, librarians, archivists, law enforcement agents, investigators, prosecutors, defense attorneys, judges, courthouse staff, witnesses, crime victims and everyone else whose contributions put the details of these cases on the record. For chronicling the epic history of the region and the entertainment industry that's long powered it, and for informing my understanding of a century-plus of crime, sin and scandal in 90210, you are, as far as I'm concerned, the heroes of all these stories.

ABOUT THE AUTHOR

Photo credit: Lindsey Foard

*a*uthor Scott Huver has covered the inner workings of Beverly Hills, the entertainment industry, and the Los Angeles-area elite for three decades. Huver began as a police and crime reporter for a local Beverly Hills newspaper. He then co-authored the book *Inside Rodeo Drive: The Stores, the Stars, the Story*. Today he's one of the most prolific entertainment journalists working in Hollywood, having written and reported for prominent outlets including *People*, CNN, *InStyle*, *TV Guide*, Vulture, *Variety*, and *The Hollywood Reporter*. His insight on Hollywood true crime has been featured on outlets such as E! Entertainment and projects including the hit podcast *Fatal Voyage: The Mysterious Death of Natalie Wood*.